Mme (Jeanne-Louise-Henriette) Campan

Memoirs of the Court of Marie Antoinette

Mme (Jeanne-Louise-Henriette) Campan

Memoirs of the Court of Marie Antoinette

ISBN/EAN: 9783743310599

Manufactured in Europe, USA, Canada, Australia, Japa

Cover: Foto ©ninafisch / pixelio.de

Manufactured and distributed by brebook publishing software (www.brebook.com)

Mme (Jeanne-Louise-Henriette) Campan

Memoirs of the Court of Marie Antoinette

MEMOIRS

OF THE

COURT OF

MARIE ANTOINETTE

BY MADAME CAMPAN
FIRST LADY OF THE BEDCHAMBER TO THE QUEEN

WITH A

BIOGRAPHICAL INTRODUCTION FROM "THE HEROIC
WOMEN OF THE FRENCH REVOLUTION"

IN TWO VOLUMES—VOLUME II

LONDON
H. S. NICHOLS & CO.
3 SOHO SQUARE AND 62A PICCADILLY W.
MDCCCXCV

CONTENTS TO VOL. II

CHAPTER I

The diamond necklace—Account of Bœhmer the jeweller—His interview with Madame Campan—The Cardinal de Rohan interrogated in the King's Cabinet—Particulars relative to Madame de Lamotte and her family—Steps taken by the Cardinal's relations—The prosecution—The clergy remonstrate—Decree of the Parliament—The Queen's grief—Remark of Louis XVI. 1

CHAPTER II

The Archbishop of Sens is appointed to the Ministry—The Abbé de Vermond's joy on the occasion—The Queen is obliged to take a part in public business—Money sent to Vienna contrary to her inclination—Anecdotes—The Queen supports the Archbishop of Sens in office—Public rejoicings on his dismissal—Opening of the States-General—Cries of "Vive le Duc d'Orleans!"—Their effect upon the Queen—Mirabeau—He requests an embassy—The Queen's misfortunes induce her to yield to superstitious fears—Anecdotes—Prejudices of the provincial deputies of the Tiers-Etat—Causes of these prejudices—Death of the first Dauphin—Anecdotes . 22

CHAPTER III

Oath of the tennis court—Insurrection of the 14th of July—The King goes to the National Assembly—Anecdotes—Spectacle presented by the courtyard of the Castle of Versailles—Report that the National Assembly is threatened—The King's speech rebutting these odious suspicions—Anecdotes—Disposition of the troops—Departure of the Count d'Artois, the Prince de Condé and the Duke and Duchess de Polignac—The latter is recognised by a postilion, who saves her—The King goes to Paris—Alarm at Versailles—The Queen determines to go to the National Assembly—Affecting speech prepared by her—The King's return—Bailly's speech—Assassination of MM. Foulon and Berthier—Plans presented by M. Foulon to the King for arresting the progress of the Revolution—Horrid remark by Barnave—His repentance . . . 37

CHAPTER IV

Creation of the National Guard—Departure of the Abbé de Vermond—The French guards quit Versailles—Entertainment given by the body-guards to the regiment of Flanders—The King, the Queen and the Dauphin are present at it—Proceedings of the 5th and 6th of October—Detestable threats against the Queen—Devotedness of one of the body-guard—The life of Marie Antoinette in danger—The Royal Family repair to Paris—Residence at the Tuileries—Change of feeling—The Queen applauded with enthusiasm by the women of the populace—Private life—Ingenuous observations of the Dauphin—Affecting anecdote—It is proposed to the Queen to quit her family and France—Her noble refusal—She devotes her attention to the education of her children—Picture of the Court—Anecdote respecting Luckner—Exasperating state of feeling 53

CHAPTER V

Affair of Favras—His prosecution and death—His children are imprudently presented to the Queen—Plan laid for carrying off the Royal Family—Singular letter from the Empress Catherine to Louis XVI.—The Queen is unwilling to owe the re-establishment of the throne to the *emigrés*—Death of the Emperor Joseph II.—First negotiation between the Court and Mirabeau—Louis XVI. and his family inhabit St. Cloud—New plans for escaping 83

CHAPTER VI

First federation—Attempts to assassinate the Queen—Remarkable observations of that Princess—Affecting scene—Account of the affair of Nancy, written by Madame Campan at night in the Council Chamber, by the King's dictation—Madame Campan calumniated—Marks of confidence bestowed upon her by the Queen—Interview between that Princess and Mirabeau in the gardens of St. Cloud—He treats with the Court—Scoffs at the revolutionary party—Plan formed by the Princess for re-entering France through Lyons—Imprudence of persons attached to the Queen—Anecdote relative to M. de la Fayette—Departure of the King's aunts—Death of Mirabeau 98

CHAPTER VII

Preparations for the journey to Varennes—The Queen watched and betrayed—Madame Campan's departure for Auvergne precedes that of the Royal Family for Versailles—Madame Campan hears of the King's arrest—

Note written to her by the Queen immediately upon her return to Paris—Anecdotes—Measures taken for keeping the King at the Tuileries—The Queen's hair turns white from grief—Barnave gains the esteem and confidence of Marie Antoinette during the return from Versailles—His honourable and respectful conduct: she contrasts it with that of Pétion—Anecdote honourable to Barnave—His advice to the Queen—Particulars respecting the Varennes journey 115

CHAPTER VIII

Acceptance of the Constitution—Opinion of Barnave and his friends approved of by the Court of Vienna—Secret policy of the Court—The Legislative Assembly deliberates upon the ceremony to be observed on receiving the King—Offensive motion—Louis XVI. is received by the Assembly with transport—He gives way to profound grief when with his family—Public *fêtes* and rejoicings—M. de Montmorin's conversation with Madame Campan upon the continued indiscretions of the people about the Court—The Royal Family go to the Théâtre Francais—Play changed—Personal conflicts in the pit of the Italiens—Double correspondence of the Court with foreign Powers—Maison Civile—Method adopted by the Queen respecting her secret correspondence—Madame Campan's conduct when attacked by both parties—Particulars respecting the conduct of M. Genet, her brother, *chargé d'affaires* from France to Russia—Written testimony of the Queen in favour of Madame Campan's zeal and fidelity—The King comes to see her and confirms these marks of confidence and satisfaction—Projected interview between Louis XVI. and Barnave—Attempts to poison Louis XVI.—Precautions taken—The Queen consults Pitt about the Revolution—His reply—The *émigrés* oppose all alliance with the Constitutionals—Letter from Barnave to the Queen 134

CHAPTER IX

Fresh libel by Madame de Lamotte—The Queen refuses to purchase the manuscript—The King buys it—The Queen performs her Easter devotions secretly in 1792—She dares not confide in General Dumouriez—Barnave's last advice—Gross insult offered to the Queen by one of the mob—The King's dejection—The 20th of June—The King's kindness to Madame Campan—Iron closet—Louis XVI. entrusts a portfolio to Madame Campan—Importance of the documents it contained—Procedure of M. de la Fayette; why it is unsuccessful—An assassin conceals himself in the Queen's apartments . . . 165

CHAPTER X

Madame Campan's communications with M. Bertrand de Molleville for the King's service—Hope of a speedy deliverance—The Queen's reflections upon the character of Louis XVI.—Insults—Enquiry set on foot by the Princess de Lamballe respecting the persons of the Queen's household—The Tenth of August—Curious particulars—Battle—Scenes of carnage—The Royal Family at the Feuillans, ... 192

CHAPTER XI

Pétion refuses Madame Campan permission to be confined in the Temple with the Queen—She excites the suspicions of Robespierre—Domiciliary visits—Madame Campan opens the portfolio she had received from the King—Papers in it, with the Seals of State—Mirabeau's secret correspondence with the Court—It is destroyed, as well as the other papers—The only document preserved—It is delivered to M. de Malesherbes, upon the trial of the unfortunate Louis XVI.—End of the Memoirs. . . . 222

CHAPTER XII

From the Committal to the Temple to the Death of Louis XVI.

Committal of the Royal Family to the Temple—Removal of the Princess de Lamballe—Description of the Temple—Apartments occupied—Attendance—Expenses—Extract from Cléry's Journal—Habits of the Royal Family—Studies—Massacres in the prisons of Paris—Murder of the Princess de Lamballe—Brutality of the mob—Sufferings of the Royal Family—Abolition of Royalty—Trial of Louis XVI.—Separation from his family—His execution—Destruction of his remains 233

CHAPTER XIII.

From the Death of Louis XVI. to the Release of Madame Royale.

Increased sufferings of the Royal Family after the execution of Louis XVI.; from Thiers' History—The Dauphin committed to the care of Simon, the shoemaker—Separation of the Family—Marie Antoinette committed to the Conciergerie—Her privations—She is brought before the revolutionary tribunal—Accusations against her—Her conviction—Execution—Joy of the Jacobins—Execution of Madame Elizabeth—Extract from the Memoirs of the Duchess d'Angoulême; from Alison—Death of the Dauphin—Release of his sister—Successors of Louis XVI. 263

Recollections, Sketches and Anecdotes, by Madame Campan   279
Historical Illustrations by Madame Campan   336
Historical Illustrations and Official Documents   368

MEMOIRS
OF
MARIE ANTOINETTE

CHAPTER I

The diamond necklace—Account of Bœhmer the jeweller—His interview with Madame Campan—The Cardinal de Rohan interrogated in the King's Cabinet—Particulars relative to Madame de Lamotte and her family—Steps taken by the Cardinal's relations—The prosecution—The clergy remonstrate—Decree of the Parliament—The Queen's grief—Remark of Louis XVI.

SHORTLY after the public mind had been highly excited by the performance of the *Marriage of Figaro*, an obscure plot, contrived by swindlers and matured in the haunts of dark depravity, implicated the Queen's character in a vital point, and directly assailed the majesty and honour of the throne.

I mean the celebrated affair of the bracelet, purchased, as it was said, for the Queen by the Cardinal de Rohan. I will relate every circumstance that came to my knowledge respecting this business; the most minute particulars will prove how little reason the Queen had to apprehend the blow with which she was threatened, and which must be attributed to a fatality that human prudence could not have foreseen, though prudence might have been more successfully exerted to extricate Her Majesty from the consequences of this unfortunate affair.[1]

I have already said that in 1774 the Queen purchased jewels of Bœhmer to the value of 360,000 francs, that she paid for them out of her own private funds, and that it required several years to enable her to complete the payment. The King afterwards presented her with a set of rubies and diamonds of a fine water, and subsequently with a pair of bracelets worth 200,000 francs. The Queen after having her diamonds reset in new patterns, told Bœhmer that she found her jewel-case rich enough and was not desirous of making any addition to it; still the jeweller busied himself for some years in forming a collection of the very first diamonds circulating in

---

[1] In order to comprehend the account about to be given by the authoress of the Memoirs, and to appreciate her historical testimony on this subject, the reader should be in possession of the leading facts. There are many remarkable circumstances which, though connected with Madame Campan's narrative, do not form part of it, because she speaks only of what she herself well knew. A great number of persons acted base or culpable parts in this shameful drama; it is necessary to be acquainted with them. No one knew the whole affair better than the Abbé Georgel, but at the same time no one was more devoted to the Cardinal de Rohan, or showed more ingenuity in discovering means of defending him, or greater skill in throwing with artfully affected delicacy a false light upon the irreproachable conduct of a Princess exposed to the most shocking suspicions, either through the blind credulity or the depravity of a Prince of the Church. The Abbé shows in this part of his Memoirs a respectful hatred (if we may be allowed the expression) of Marie Antoinette. He supposes the Queen to have been aware of the transaction at a time when she was still wrapt in all the security of a woman whose imagination could not even conceive the idea of such a masterpiece of intrigue. In the *Historical Illustrations* (A), we give a copious extract from Georgel's Memoirs. The reader who is desirous of information and of forming a judgment upon this subject is recommended to glance over this extract first, in order to observe in what points the assertions it contains are rendered doubtful, and how far they are utterly confuted by Madame Campan's testimony.—NOTE BY THE EDITOR.

commerce, in order to compose a necklace of several rows which he hoped to induce Her Majesty to purchase. He brought it to M. Campan, requesting him to mention it to the Queen, that she might ask to see it and thus be excited to wish to possess it. This M. Campan refused to do, telling him that he should be overstepping the line of his duty were he to propose to the Queen an expense of 1,600,000 francs, and that he believed that neither the lady of honour nor the tire-woman would take upon herself to execute such a commission. Bœhmer persuaded the King's first gentleman for the year to show this superb necklace to His Majesty, who admired it so much that he himself wished to see the Queen adorned with it, and sent the case to her; but she assured him she should much regret the incurring of so great an expense for such an article; that she had already very beautiful diamonds; that jewels of that description were not now worn at that Court more than four or five times a year; that the necklace must be returned, and that the money would be much better employed in building a man-of-war.[1] Bœhmer, in deep tribulation at finding his expectations delusive, endeavoured, as it is said, for some time to dispose of his necklace among the various Courts of Europe, but without meeting

---

[1] "Messrs. Bœhmer and Bassange, jewellers to the Crown, were proprietors of a superb diamond necklace, which had, as it was said, been intended for the Countess du Barry. Being under the necessity of selling it, they offered it, during the last war, to the King and Queen; but Their Majesties gave the jewellers the following prudent answer: '*We have more need of ships than of diamonds.*'" ("Secret Correspondence of the Court of Louis XVI.").—NOTE BY THE EDITOR.

with any person willing to become the purchaser of an article of such value. A year after his fruitless attempts Bœhmer again caused his diamond necklace to be offered for sale to the King, proposing that it should be paid for partly by instalments, and partly in life annuities. This proposal was represented as highly advantageous, and the King mentioned the matter once more to the Queen; this was in my presence. I remember the Queen told him that, if the purchase was really not inconvenient, he might make it, and keep the necklace until the marriage of one of his children; but that, for her part, she would never wear it, being unwilling that the world should have to reproach her with having coveted so expensive an article. The King replied that their children were too young to justify such an expense, which would be greatly increased by the number of years the diamonds would remain useless, and that he would finally decline the offer. Bœhmer complained to everybody of his misfortune, and all reasonable people blamed him for having collected diamonds to so considerable an amount without any positive order for them. This man had purchased the office of jeweller to the Crown, which gave him the right of entry at Court. After several months spent in ineffectual attempts to carry his point, and in idle complaints, he obtained an audience of the Queen, who had with her the youngest Princess, her daughter. Her Majesty did not know for what purpose Bœhmer sought this audience, and had not the slightest idea that it was to speak to her again about an article twice refused by herself and the King.

Bœhmer threw himself on his knees, clasped his hands, burst into tears, and exclaimed, "Madam, I am ruined and disgraced if you do not purchase my necklace. I cannot outlive my misfortunes. When I go hence I shall throw myself into the river." "Rise, Bœhmer," said the Queen, in a tone sufficiently severe to call him to himself; "I do not like these rhapsodies; honest men have no occasion to fall on their knees to make their requests. If you were to destroy yourself I should regret you as a madman in whom I had taken an interest, but I should not be responsible for that misfortune. I not only never ordered the article which causes your present despair, but whenever you have talked to me about fine collections of jewels, I have told you that I should not add four diamonds to those which I already possessed. I told you myself that I declined taking the necklace; the King wished to give it to me, but I refused him also: then never mention it to me again. Divide it, and endeavour to sell it piecemeal, and do not drown yourself. I am very angry with you for acting this scene of despair in my presence, and before this child. Let me never see you behave thus again. Go!" Bœhmer withdrew, overwhelmed with confusion, and nothing further was then heard of him.

When Madame Sophie was born, the Queen informed me that M. de Saint-James[1] had apprised her that Bœhmer was still intent upon the sale of his necklace, and that Her Majesty ought, for her own satisfaction, to endeavour to learn what the man had

---

[1] A rich financier.—NOTE BY MADAME CAMPAN.

done with it. She desired me not to forget, the first time I should meet him, to speak to him about it, as if from the interest I took in his welfare. I spoke to him about his necklace, and he told me he had been very fortunate, having sold it at Constantinople for the favourite Sultana. I communicated this answer to the Queen, who was delighted with it, but could not comprehend how the Grand Seignior came to purchase his diamonds at Paris.

The Queen for a long time avoided seeing Bœhmer, being fearful of his rash character; and her *valet de chambre*, who had the care of her jewels, did the necessary repairs to her ornaments unassisted. On the baptism of the Duke d'Angoulême, the King made him a present of a diamond epaulette and buckles, and directed Bœhmer to deliver them to the Queen. Bœhmer presented them to Her Majesty upon her return from Mass, and at the same time gave into her hands a letter in the form of a petition. In this paper he told the Queen that he was happy to see her "in possession of the finest diamonds known in Europe, and entreated her not to forget him." The Queen read Bœhmer's address to her aloud, and saw nothing in it but a proof of mental aberration, being unable otherwise to account for his complimenting her upon the beauty of her diamonds, and begging her not to forget him. She lighted the note at a wax taper standing near her, as she had some letters to seal, saying, "It is not worth keeping." She afterwards much regretted the loss of this enigmatical memorial.[1] After having burnt the paper, Her Majesty

---

[1] The reader will compare the clear and simple particulars with

said to me, "That man is born to be my torment; he has always some mad scheme in his head. Remember, the first time you see him, to tell him that I do not like diamonds now, and that I will buy no more as long as I live; that if I had any money to spare, I would rather add to my property at St. Cloud by the purchase of the land surrounding it. Now, mind you enter into all these particulars, and impress them well upon him." I asked her whether she wished me to send for him. She replied in the negative, adding that it would be sufficient to avail myself of the first opportunity afforded by meeting with him, and that the slightest advance towards such a man would be injudicious.

On the 1st of August I left Versailles for my country house; on the 3rd came Bœhmer, extremely uneasy at not having received any answer from the Queen, to ask me whether I had any commission from her to him. I replied that she had entrusted me with none; that she had no commands for him; and I faithfully repeated all she had desired me to say to him. "But," said Bœhmer, "the answer to the letter I presented to her—to whom must I apply for that?" "To nobody," answered I. "Her Majesty burnt your memorial without even comprehending its meaning." "Ah! madam," exclaimed he, "that is impossible; the Queen knows she has money to pay

---

that part of the Abbé Georgel's Memoirs in which he supposes the Queen to have been long aware of the purchase of the necklace. Was it, then, in Bœhmer's obscure expressions that she could fathom an intrigue so complicated, so scandalous and so foreign to her imagination, deeply affecting as it did her dignity and her person?—NOTE BY THE EDITOR.

me!" "Money, M. Bœhmer? Your last accounts against the Queen were discharged long ago." "How, madam? are you not in the secret? A man who is ruined for want of payment of 1,500,000 francs can hardly be said to be satisfied." "Have you lost your senses?" said I; "for what can the Queen owe you so extravagant a sum?" "For the necklace, madam," replied Bœhmer, coolly. "How?" returned I; "that necklace, again, about which you have teased the Queen so many years! Did you not tell me you had sold it at Constantinople?" "The Queen desired me to give that answer to all who should speak to me on the subject," said the wretched dupe. He then told me that the Queen had determined to have the necklace, and had had it purchased for her by the Cardinal de Rohan. "You are deceived!" I exclaimed; "the Queen has not once spoken to the Cardinal since his return from Vienna; there is not a man at her Court less favourably looked upon." "You are deceived yourself, madam," said Bœhmer; "she must see him in private, for it was to His Eminence that she gave 30,000 francs, which were paid me on account. She took them, in his presence, out of the little *secrétaire* of Sèvres porcelain next the fireplace in her boudoir." "And the Cardinal told you all this?" "Yes, madam, himself." "What a detestable plot!" cried I. "Indeed, to say the truth, madam, I begin to be much alarmed, for His Eminence assured me that the Queen would wear the necklace on Whit-Sunday; but I did not see it upon her, and it was that which induced me to write to Her Majesty." He then asked me what he ought to do. I advised him to go on to Versailles, instead of returning to Paris, from whence he had just arrived; to obtain an immediate audience from the Baron de Breteuil, who, as the head of the King's household, was the minister of the department to which Bœhmer belonged, and to be circumspect; and I added that he appeared to me extremely culpable, not as a diamond merchant, but because, being a sworn officer, he had acted without the direct orders of the King, the Queen or the minister. He answered that he had not acted without direct orders; that he had in his possession all the notes signed by the Queen, and that he had even been obliged to show them to several bankers in order to induce them to extend the time for his payments. I hastened his departure for Versailles, and he assured me that he would go thither immediately. Instead of following my advice, he went to the Cardinal; and it was of this visit of Bœhmer's that His Eminence made a memorandum, found in a drawer overlooked by the Abbé Georgel when he burnt, by order of His Eminence, all the papers which the latter had at Paris. The memorandum was thus worded: "On this day, 3rd of August, Bœhmer went to Madame Campan's country house, and she told him that the Queen had never had his necklace, and that he had been cheated."

When Bœhmer was gone I was anxious to follow him and go to the Queen at Trianon. My father-in-law prevented me, and ordered me to leave the minister to elucidate an affair of such importance, observing that it was an infernal plot, that I had advised Bœhmer very properly, and had nothing more to do with the business.

After seeing the Cardinal, Bœhmer did not go to the Baron de Breteuil, but went to Trianon, and sent a message to the Queen purporting that I had advised him to come back and speak to her. His very words were repeated to Her Majesty, who said, "He is mad; I have nothing to say to him, and will not see him." Two or three days afterwards she sent for me to Trianon. I found her alone in her boudoir. She talked to me of various trifles, but all the while I was answering her I was thinking of the necklace and seeking for an opportunity of telling her what had been said to me about it, till at length she said, "Do you know that that idiot, Bœhmer, has been here asking to speak to me, and saying that you advised him to do so? I refused to receive him," continued the Queen. "What does he want—have you any idea?" I then communicated what the man had said to me, which I thought it my duty not to withhold, whatever pain it might give me to mention such infamous affairs to her. She made me relate several times the whole of my conversation with Bœhmer, and complained bitterly of the vexation she felt for the circulation of forged notes signed with her name, but she could not conceive how the Cardinal could be involved in the affair; this was a labyrinth to her, and her mind was lost in it. She immediately sent for the Abbé de Vermond and the Baron de Breteuil. Bœhmer had never said one word to me about the woman De Lamotte, and her name was mentioned for the first time by the Cardinal in his answers to the interrogatories put to him before the King.

For several days the Queen, in concert with

the Baron and the Abbé, consulted what was proper to be done on the occasion. Unfortunately, an inveterate and implacable hatred for the Cardinal rendered these two counsellors the men of all others the most likely to lead Her Majesty out of the line of conduct she ought to have pursued. They only contemplated the utter ruin of their enemy at Court, and his disgrace in the eyes of all Europe; and never considered how circumspectly such a delicate affair required to be managed. If the Queen had called in the Count de Vergennes to advise, his experience of men and things would have induced him at once to pronounce that a swindling transaction, in which the august name of Marie Antoinette might be compromised, ought to be hushed up.

On the 15th of August the Cardinal, who was already dressed in his pontifical garments, was sent for at noon into the King's closet, where the Queen then was. The King said to him, "You have purchased diamonds of Bœhmer?" "Yes, Sire." "What have you done with them?" "I thought they had been delivered to the Queen." "Who commissioned you?" "A lady, called the Countess de Lamotte-Valois, who handed me a letter from the Queen, and I thought I was gratifying Her Majesty by taking this business on myself." The Queen here interrupted him, and said: "How, sir, could you believe that I should select you, to whom I have not spoken these eight years, to negotiate anything for me; and especially through the mediation of such a woman?" "I see plainly," said the Cardinal, "that I have been duped;

I will pay for the necklace. My desire to be of service to Your Majesty blinded me; I suspected no trick in the affair, and I am sorry for it." He then took out of his pocket-book a letter from the Queen to Madame de Lamotte, entrusting her with the commission. The King took it and, holding it towards the Cardinal, said, "This is neither written nor signed by the Queen. How could a Prince of the House of Rohan, and a Grand Almoner of France, ever think that the Queen would sign 'Marie Antoinette de France?' Everybody knows that Queens sign only by their baptismal names.¹ But, sir," pursued the King, handing him a copy of his letter to Bœhmer, "did you ever write such a letter as this?" Having glanced over it, the Cardinal said, "I do not remember having written it." "But what if the original, signed by yourself, were shown to you?" "If the letter be signed by myself it is genuine." "Then explain to me," resumed the King, "the whole of this enigma. I do not wish to find you guilty; I had rather you would justify yourself. Account for all the manœuvres

---

¹ The following passage occurs in the "Secret Correspondence":—"The Cardinal ought, it was said, to have detected the forgery of the approbations and signature to the instructions. His place of Grand Almoner gave him ample opportunity of knowing both Her Majesty's writing and her manner of signing her name. To this important objection it was answered that it was long since M. de Rohan had seen her writing; that he did not recollect it; that, besides having no suspicions, he had no inducement to endeavour to verify it; and that the Crown jewellers, to whom he showed the instrument, did not, any more than himself, detect the imposition."

With submission to the authors of the "Secret Correspondence," this answer is nugatory; for merchants are better acquainted with commercial signatures than those of Courts, and they might very possibly be ignorant of customs which ought to be familiar to the Cardinal; and the Abbé Georgel himself admits as much.—NOTE BY THE EDITOR.

with Bœhmer, these securities and these notes." The Cardinal then, turning pale, and leaning against the table, said, "Sire, I am too much confused to answer Your Majesty in a way——" "Compose yourself, Cardinal, and go into my cabinet. You will there find paper, pens and ink; write what you have to say to me." The Cardinal went into the King's cabinet, and returned a quarter of an hour afterwards with a document as confused as his verbal answers had been. The King then said, "Withdraw, sir." The Cardinal then left the King's chamber with the Baron de Breteuil, who gave him in custody to an ensign of the body-guard, with orders to take him to his apartment. M. d'Agoult, adjutant of the body-guard, afterwards took charge of him and conducted him to his hotel, and from thence to the Bastille. But while the Cardinal had with him only the young ensign of the body-guard, who was himself much embarrassed at having such an order to execute, His Eminence met his *heyduke* at the door of the Saloon of Hercules; he spoke to him in German, and then asked the ensign if he could lend him a pencil; the officer gave him that which he carried about him, and the Cardinal wrote to the Abbé Georgel, his grand vicar and friend, instantly to burn all Madame de Lamotte's correspondence, and all his letters in general.[1] This commission was executed before

---

[1] The "Secret Correspondence," in relating these circumstances, thus explains the officer's conduct and confusion:

"The ensign, being reprimanded for suffering the Cardinal to write, replied that his orders did not forbid it, and that besides he had been so much disconcerted by the unusual address of the

M. de Crosne, lieutenant of police, had received an order from the Baron de Breteuil to put seals upon the Cardinal's papers. The destruction of all His Eminence's correspondence, and particularly that with Madame de Lamotte, threw an impenetrable cloud over the whole of this affair. Madame the King's step-sister was the sole protectress of that woman; and her patronage was confined to allowing her a slender pension of twelve or fifteen hundred francs. Her brother was in the navy, but the Marquis de Chabert, to whom he had been recommended, could never make a good officer of him.

Baron de Breteuil, 'In the King's name, sir, follow me,' that he had not recovered himself and did not perfectly know what he was about. This excuse is not very satisfactory, though it is true that this officer, who was very irregular in his conduct, was much in debt, and at first apprehended that the order intimated to him by the Baron concerned himself personally."

The Abbé Georgel relates the circumstances of the note in a very different manner:

"The Cardinal, at that dreadful moment, which might have been expected to deprive him of his senses, gave an astonishing proof of his presence of mind: notwithstanding the escort which surrounded him, favoured by the attendant crowd, he stopped, and stooping down with his face towards the wall, as if to fasten his buckle or his garter, snatched out his pencil, and hastily wrote a few words upon a scrap of paper placed under his hand in his square red cap. He rose again and proceeded. On entering his house, his people formed a lane; he slipped this paper unperceived into the hand of a confidential *valet de chambre*, who waited for him at the door of his apartment." This little tale is scarcely credible: it is not at the moment of a prisoner's arrest, when an inquisitive crowd surrounds and watches him, that he can stop and write unperceived. However, the *valet de chambre* posts off to Paris. He arrives at the palace of the Cardinal between twelve and one o'clock, and his horse falls dead in the stable. "I was in my apartment," says the Abbé Georgel; "the *valet de chambre* entered wildly, with a deadly paleness on his countenance, and exclaimed, 'All is lost; the Prince is arrested!' He instantly fainted and fell, dropping the paper of which he was the bearer." The portfolio enclosing the papers which might compromise the Cardinal was immediately placed beyond the reach of all search.—NOTE BY THE EDITOR.

The Queen in vain endeavoured to call to mind the features of this person, whom she had often heard spoken of as an intriguing woman who came frequently on Sundays to the gallery at Versailles; and at the time when all France was taken up with the prosecution against the Cardinal, the portrait of the Countess de Lamotte-Valois was publicly sold. Her Majesty desired me one day, when I was going to Paris, to buy her the engraving, which was said to be a tolerable likeness, that she might ascertain whether she could recollect in it any person whom she had seen in the gallery.[1]

The woman De Lamotte's father was a peasant at Auteuil, though he called himself Valois. Madame de Boulainvilliers once saw from her terrace two pretty little peasant girls, each labouring under a heavy bundle of sticks; the priest of the village, who was walking with her, told her that the children possessed some curious papers, and that he had no doubt they were descendants of a Valois, an illegitimate son of one of the Princes of that name.

The family of Valois had long ceased to appear in the world. Hereditary vices had gradually plunged them into the deepest misery.

I have heard that the last Valois occupied the estate called Gros Bois; that as he seldom came to Court, Louis XIII. asked him what he was about that he remained so constantly in the country, and that this M. de Valois merely answered: "Sire, I am

---

[1] The public, as the reader knows, with the exception of persons dressed in the style of the lowest of the people, were admitted into the gallery and larger apartments of Versailles as they were into the park.—NOTE BY MADAME CAMPAN.

doing nothing but what I ought to do."[1] It was shortly afterwards discovered that he was engaged in *coining*.

As soon as the news of the Grand Almoner's arrest spread through Paris, the Prince de Condé, who had married a Princess of the House of Rohan, the Maréchal de Soubise, and the Princess de Marsan, exclaimed indignantly against the arrest of a Prince of their family. The clergy, from the cardinals down to the youths in the seminaries, gave vent to their affliction at the disgraceful apprehension of a Prince of the Church, and an infinite number of persons were eagerly desirous to see the Court humbled for so harsh a proceeding.

I must interrupt my narrative of the famous necklace plot to say something about this woman De Lamotte. Neither the Queen herself nor any lady about her ever had the slightest connection with that swindler; and during her prosecution, she could point out but one of the Queen's servants, a man named Desclos, a valet of the Queen's bed-chamber, to whom she pretended she had delivered Bœhmer's necklace. This Desclos was a very honest man; upon being confronted with the woman De Lamotte, it was proved that she had never seen him but once, which was at the house of the wife of a surgeon-accoucheur at Versailles, the only person she visited at Court; and that she had not given him the necklace. Madame de Lamotte married a private in Monsieur's body-guard; she lodged at Versailles at the Belle Image, a very inferior furnished hotel; and it is inconceivable

[1] *Je ne fais que ce que je dois:* which also means, "I only make what I owe;" and in that sense was a true answer.

how so obscure a person could succeed in making herself believed to be a friend of the Queen, who, though so extremely affable, very seldom granted audiences, and only to titled persons.

The trial of the Cardinal is so generally known that it is unnecessary for me to repeat the circumstances of it here.[1] The point most embarrassing to him was the interview he had in February, 1785, with M. de Saint-James, to whom he confided the particulars of the Queen's pretended commission, and showed the contract approved and signed "Marie Antoinette de France." The memorandum, found in a drawer of the Cardinal's bureau, in which he had himself written what Bœhmer told him after having seen me at my country house, was likewise an unfortunate document for His Eminence.

---

[1] The letters patent, which gave the Parliament cognisance of the process, were couched in these terms:

"Louis, &c. Having been informed that the Sieurs Bœhmer and Bassange sold the Cardinal de Rohan a necklace of brilliants; that the said Cardinal de Rohan, without the knowledge of the Queen our beloved spouse and consort, told them he was authorised by her to purchase it at the price of 1,600,000 livres, payable by instalments, and showed them false instructions to that effect, which he exhibited as approved by the Queen; that the said necklace having been delivered by the said Bœhmer and Bassange to the said Cardinal, and the first payment agreed on between them not having been made good, they had recourse to the Queen; we could not without just indignation see an august name, dear to us on so many accounts, thus daringly abused, and the respect due to Royal Majesty violated with such unheard-of temerity; we therefore deemed it incumbent on our justice to cite before us the said Cardinal, and upon his declaration to us that he had been deceived by a woman named Lamotte, called De Valois, we judged it indispensable to secure his person and that of the said Lamotte called De Valois, and to take those steps suggested to us by our wisdom for the discovery of the authors or accomplices of such an attack; and we have thought fit to make you acquainted with these matters, that the process may be instituted and decided by you, the great chamber and criminal court assembled." — NOTE BY THE EDITOR.

I offered to the King to go and declare that Bœhmer had told me and maintained that the Cardinal assured him he had received from the Queen's own hand the 30,000 francs given as earnest upon the bargain being concluded, and that His Eminence had seen Her Majesty take that sum in bills from the porcelain *secrétaire* in her boudoir. The King declined my offer and said, "Were you alone when Bœhmer told you this?" I answered that I was alone with him in my garden. "Well," resumed he, "the man would deny the fact; he is now sure of being paid his 1,600,000 francs, which the Cardinal's family will find it necessary to make good to him.¹ We cannot rely upon his sincerity; it would look as if you were sent by the Queen, and that would not be proper."

The Attorney-General's information was severe on the Cardinal. The House of Condé, that of Rohan, the majority of the nobility and the whole of the clergy, saw nothing in this affair but an attack upon the Prince's rank and the privileges of a cardinal. The clergy required that the unfortunate business of the Prince Cardinal de Rohan should be sent to the ecclesiastical jurisdiction, and the Archbishop of Nar-

---

1 The King's good sense had fathomed this intrigue; a fact related in the "Secret Correspondence" proves it: "The guilty woman no sooner knew that all was about to be discovered than she sent for the jewellers, and told them that the Cardinal had perceived that the agreement which he believed to have been signed by the Queen was a false and forged document. 'However,' added she, 'the Cardinal possesses a considerable fortune, *and he can very well pay you.*' These words reveal the whole secret. The Countess had taken the necklace to herself, and flattered herself that M. de Rohan, seeing himself deceived and cruelly imposed upon, would determine to pay and make the best terms he could, rather than suffer a matter of this nature to become public. And that was, in fact, the best thing he could do."—NOTE BY THE EDITOR.

bonne, then President of the Convocation, made representations upon the subject to the King;[1] the bishops wrote to His Majesty to remind him that a private ecclesiastic implicated in the affair then pending would have a right to claim his constitutional judges, and that this right was refused to a cardinal, his superior in the hierarchical order.[2] In short, the clergy and the greater part of the nobility were at that time outrageous against authority, and chiefly against the Queen.

The Attorney-General's conclusions, and those of a part of the heads of the magistracy, were as severe towards the Cardinal as the information had been, yet he was *fully acquitted* by a majority of three voices; the woman De Lamotte was condemned to be whipped, branded and imprisoned, and her husband, for contumacy, was condemned to the galleys for life.

The Queen's grief was extreme. As soon as I

---

[1] *Vide*, in the *Historical Illustrations* (B), fragments of the speech delivered by the Archbishop of Narbonne in presence of the clergy then assembled.—NOTE BY THE EDITOR.

[2] "While the process was pending," says a paper of the time, "there appeared a brief from the Pope, addressed to the Cardinal, in which the Pope informs him that, having held a consistory respecting him, they had unanimously resolved that he had essentially sinned against his dignity as a member of the Sacred College, by recognising a foreign and secular tribunal; that he was consequently suspended for six months; and that if he persisted in so irregular a line of conduct, he would be struck off the list of cardinals."

All this was but an empty threat; for the Abbé Lemoine, a doctor of the Sorbonne, having appeared for Prince Louis de Rohan, proved that His Eminence could not avoid submitting to a tribunal appointed for him by the King, his master; and that, with regard to the preservation of the prerogatives of his dignity, he had made the customary protests. The Sovereign Pontiff was so satisfied that, after all the requisite formalities, he declared the Cardinal de Rohan reinstated in all the rights and honours of the Roman purple.—NOTE BY THE EDITOR.

learned the substance of the decision, I went to her, and found her alone in her closet; she was weeping. "Come," said Her Majesty to me, "come and lament for your Queen, insulted and sacrificed by cabal and injustice. But rather let me pity you as a Frenchwoman. If I have not met with equitable judges in a matter which affected my reputation, what could you hope for in a suit in which your fortune and character were at stake?"[1] The King came in at this moment, and said to me, "You find the Queen much afflicted; she has great reason to be so. They were determined throughout this affair to see only an ecclesiastical Prince—a Prince de Rohan; while he is in fact a needy fellow." (I use His Majesty's own expression). "And all this was but a scheme to put money into his pockets, in endeavouring to do which he found himself the party cheated instead of the cheat. Nothing is easier to see through; and it is not necessary to be an Alexander to cut this Gordian knot."

The opinion sanctioned by time is that the Cardinal was completely duped by the woman De Lamotte and Cagliostro. The King may have been in error in thinking him an accomplice in this miserable and

---

[1] "Will it be believed," says the Abbé Georgel, "that it was necessary to use caution in announcing the Cardinal's triumph to the Queen?" Will it be believed, we ask in our turn, that the Abbé Georgel felt any surprise on the occasion? Was not the *triumph* of a prelate who had compromised the name of his Queen in France and Europe by his scandalous connections, by an imbecile credulity, and perhaps even by criminal hopes, a sad and sufficient cause for affliction to Marie Antoinette? Perhaps the Abbé Soulavie, whose animosity against Marie Antoinette at least equals the Abbé Georgel's hatred (they were both Jesuits), less clearly betrayed his feelings by his calumnies than the Cardinal de Rohan's friend did his by his insolent exclamation. What should a woman, a wife and a Queen, hold more dear than her honour and the majesty of the throne?—NOTE BY THE EDITOR.

criminal scheme; but I have faithfully given His Majesty's judgment concerning it.

However, the generally received opinion, that the Baron de Breteuil's hatred for the Cardinal was the cause of the scandal and result of this unfortunate affair, contributed to the disgrace of the former still more than his refusal to give his grand-daughter in marriage to the son of the Duke de Polignac.

The Abbé de Vermond threw the whole blame of the imprudence and impolicy of the affair of the Cardinal de Rohan upon the minister, and ceased to be the friend and supporter of the Baron de Breteuil with the Queen.[1]

---

[1] Madame Campan was aware of the importance of her testimony in the affair of the necklace. Among her manuscripts are two accounts of that unfortunate business. One is that which we have just read; in the other, the ground-work of which is the same, a few circumstances are presented in a different light, and several new particulars give it considerable interest. The second interview of the Queen with Bœhmer, in which she learns the meaning of the fatal enigma, for instance, is a curious fact. The style of the latter narrative is more free and more animated than that of the former. The *dramatis personæ* disclose their emotions, passions and dispositions more clearly. It especially shows the application of the vague manner in which the Queen, in the above account, calls in question the *equity of the judges*. We see by what sort of spirit the Parliament was animated. It is certain that a part of the magistracy, then performing a prelude to the resistance it soon afterwards made to the Royal authority, was less intent on securing a *triumph* for the Cardinal than a mortification for the Court. The Abbé Georgel himself admits it. He points out the magistrates who favoured the Cardinal, not with that moderate and scrupulous interest which an equitable judge feels for the accused, but with all the ardour of party spirit.

Madame Campan's second version throws a still purer and brighter light than the first upon the Queen's conduct, her grief and her generous indignation at this crisis. We give this second narrative in her *Historical Illustrations* (Note No. 1), under a persuasion that the reader will readily overlook a few repetitions in consideration of new particulars.—NOTE BY THE EDITOR.

CHAPTER II

The Archbishop of Sens is appointed to the Ministry—The Abbé de Vermond's joy on the occasion—The Queen is obliged to take a part in public business—Money sent to Vienna contrary to her inclination—Anecdotes—The Queen supports the Archbishop of Sens in office—Public rejoicings on his dismissal—Opening of the States-General—Cries of "Vive le Duc d'Orleans!"—Their effect upon the Queen—Mirabeau—He requests an embassy—The Queen's misfortunes induce her to yield to superstitious fears—Anecdotes—Prejudices of the provincial deputies of the Tiers-Etat—Causes of these prejudices—Death of the first Dauphin—Anecdotes.

THE Abbé de Vermond could not suppress his exultation when he succeeded in getting the Archbishop of Sens appointed President of the Council of Finance. I have often heard him say that seventeen years of patience were not too great a price for success at Court; that he spent all that time in gaining the end he had in view; but that at length the Archbishop was where he ought to be, for the good of the State. The Abbé from this time no longer concealed his credit and influence in the Queen's private circle; nothing could equal the confidence with which he displayed the extent of his ambition. He requested the Queen to order that the apartments appropriated to him should be enlarged, telling her that, being obliged to give audiences to bishops, cardinals and ministers, he required a residence suitable to his present circumstances. The Queen continued to treat him in general as she did before the Archbishop's arrival at Court; but the household observed a variation which indicated increased consideration: the word *Monsieur* preceded that of Abbé; and, such is the influence of favour, that, from that moment, not only the livery servants, but also the people of the ante-chambers, rose when *Monsieur l'Abbé* was passing, though there never was, to my knowledge, any order given to that effect.

The Queen was obliged, on account of the King's disposition, and the very limited confidence he placed in the Archbishop of Sens, to take a part in public affairs. While M. de Maurepas lived she kept out of that danger, as may be seen by the censure which the Baron de Besenval passes on her in his Memoirs for not availing herself of the conciliation he had promoted between the Queen and that minister, who counteracted the ascendency which she and her intimate friends might otherwise have gained over the King's mind.

The Queen has often assured me that she never interfered respecting the interests of Austria but once, and that was only to claim the execution of the treaty of alliance at the time when Joseph II. was at war with Prussia and Turkey; that she then demanded that an army of 24,000 men should be sent to him, instead of 15,000,000 livres—an alternative which had been left to option in the treaty, in case the Emperor should have a just war to maintain; that she could not obtain her object, and M. de Vergennes, in an interview which she had with him upon the subject, put an end to her importunities by observing that he was answering the mother of the Dauphin, and not the sister of the Emperor.[1] The 15,000,000 livres were sent. There was no want of money at Vienna, and the value of a French army was fully appreciated. "But how," said the Queen, "could they be so wicked as to send off those fifteen millions from the general post-office, diligently publishing, even to the street porters, that they were loading the carriages with money that I was sending to my brother—whereas it is certain that the money would equally have been sent if I had belonged to another House; and, besides, it was sent contrary to my inclination."

The Queen never disguised her dislike to the American War; she could not conceive how anybody could advise a Sovereign to aim at the humiliation of England, through an attack on the Sovereign authority, and by assisting a people to organise a Republican Constitution. She often laughed at the enthusiasm with which Franklin inspired the French; and, upon the peace of 1783, she treated the English nobility and the ambassador from England with marked distinction.

When the Count de Moustier set out on his mission to the United States, after having had his public audience of leave, he came and asked me to procure him a private one. I could not succeed, even with the strongest solicitations: the Queen desired me to wish him a good voyage, but added,

---

[1] *Vide* **Historical Illustrations** (C), a passage respecting the delicate situation in which M. de Vergennes was placed in the midst of the parties which divided the Court.—NOTE BY THE EDITOR.

that none but ministers could have anything to say to him in private, since he was going to a country where the names of *King* and *Queen* must be detested.

Marie Antoinette had, then, no direct influence over State affairs until after the deaths of M. de Maurepas and M. de Vergennes and the retirement of M. de Calonne. She frequently regretted her new situation, and looked upon it as a misfortune which she could not avoid. One day, while I was assisting her to tie up a number of memorials and reports which some of the ministers had handed to her to be given to the King, "Ah!" said she, sighing, "there is an end of all happiness for me, since they have made an intriguer of me." I censured the word. "Yes," resumed the Queen; "that is the right term; every woman who meddles with affairs above her understanding or out of her line of duty is an intriguer and nothing else; you will remember, however, that it is not my own fault, and that it is with regret I give myself the title. The Queens of France are happy only so long as they meddle with nothing, and merely preserve influence sufficient to advance their friends and reward a few zealous servants. Do you know," added that excellent Princess—thus reluctantly forced to act in opposition to her principles—"do you know what happened to me lately? One day, since I began to attend private committees at the King's, while crossing the 'bull's eye,' I heard one of the musicians of the chapel say, so loudly that I lost not a single word, 'A Queen who does her duty will remain in her apartment to knit.' I said within myself, 'Poor creature, thou art right; but thou knowest not my situation. I yield to necessity and my unfortunate destiny.'" This situation was the more painful to the Queen inasmuch as Louis XVI. had long accustomed himself to say nothing to her respecting State affairs; and when, towards the close of his reign, she was obliged to interfere in the most important matters, the same closeness in the King frequently kept from her particulars which it was proper she should know. Obtaining, therefore, only partial information, and guided by persons more ambitious than skilful, the Queen could not be useful in the grand march of affairs; yet, at the same time, her ostensible interference drew upon her from all parties and all classes of society an unpopularity, the rapid progress of which alarmed all those who were sincerely attached to her.

Led away by the brilliant language of the Archbishop of Sens, and encouraged in the confidence she placed in that minister by the incessant eulogies of the Abbé de Vermond on his abilities, the Queen unfortunately followed up her first mistake — that of bringing him into office — by the equally unfortunate error of supporting him at the time of his disgrace, which was conceded to the despair of a whole nation. She thought it was due to her dignity to give him some marked proof of her regard. Misguided by her feelings, she sent him her portrait enriched with jewellery, and a patent for a situation of lady of the palace for Madame de Canisy, his niece, observing that it was necessary to indemnify a minister sacrificed to Court intrigues and the factious spirit of the nation; that otherwise none would be found willing to devote themselves to the interests of the Sovereign. However, on the day of the Archbishop's departure, the public joy was universal both at Court and among the people of Paris. There were bonfires; the attorneys' clerks burnt the Archbishop in effigy, and on the very evening of his disgrace more than a hundred couriers were sent out from Versailles to spread the happy tidings among the country seats round Paris and Versailles.[1] I have since seen the Queen shed bitter tears at the recollection of the errors she committed at this period, when subsequently, a short time before her death, the Archbishop had the audacity to say, in a speech which was printed, that the sole object of one part of his operations, during his administration, was to promote the salutary crisis which the Revolution had produced.[2]

When the fruitless measure of the Assembly of the Notables[3] and the rebellious spirit of the Parlia-

---

[1] The *Illustrations* (D) give some curious particulars respecting the circumstances which accompanied and followed the Archbishop's dismission.—NOTE BY THE EDITOR.

[2] We will here mention a caricature of the time, which shows the nature of the attacks which then began to be made against the throne and the most august personages. It represented the King at table with his consort; he had a glass in his hand; the Queen was raising a morsel to her lips; the people were crowding round the table with their mouths open. Below was written, "The King drinks; the Queen eats; the people cry out." ("Anecdotes of the Reign of Louis XVI." vol. i.)—NOTE BY THE EDITOR.

[3] The Assembly of the Notables, as may be seen in Weber's Memoirs, vol. i., overthrew the plans and caused the downfall of M. de Calonne. A Prince of the Blood presided over each of the *bureaux* of that Assembly. Monsieur, afterwards Louis XVIII., presided over the first. "Monsieur," says a paper of the time, "gained great reputation at the Assembly of the Notables in 1787. He did not miss attending his *bureau* a single day, and he displayed truly patriotic virtues. His care in discussing the weighty matters

ments had created the necessity for summoning the States-General, it was long discussed in Council whether they should be assembled at Versailles or at forty or fifty leagues from the capital. The Queen was for the latter course, and insisted to the King that they ought to be far away from the immense population of Paris. She began to fear that the people would influence the deliberations of the deputies. Several memorials were presented to the King upon that important question; but M. Necker's opinion prevailed, and Versailles was the place fixed upon, which affords room for the supposition that M. Necker, in his schemes—not supposing that the popular commotions, which he undoubtedly hoped to be able to regulate, would extend to the annihilation of the monarchy—calculated that they would be useful to him.

Politicians were occupied with the double representation granted to the Tiers-Etat; it was the sole topic of conversation; some foresaw all the inconveniences of the measure, while others overrated its advantages.

The Queen adopted the plan to which the King had agreed. She thought the hope of obtaining ecclesiastical favours would secure the clergy of the second Order, and that M. Necker felt assured that he

---

of administration, in throwing light upon them, and in defending the interests and the cause of the people, was such as even to inspire the King with some degree of jealousy. Monsieur always thought, and constantly said, openly, 'That a respectful resistance to the orders of the monarch was not blamable, and that authority might be met by argument, and forced to receive information, without any offence whatever.'"—NOTE BY THE EDITOR.

possessed the same degree of influence over the lawyers, and other people of that class, who formed the Third Estate. The Count d'Artois, holding the contrary opinion, presented a memorial in the names of himself and several Princes of the Blood to the King against the double representation granted to the Tiers-Etat. The Queen was displeased with him for this; her confidential advisers infused into her apprehensions that the Prince was made the tool of a party; but his conduct was approved of by Madame de Polignac's circle, which the Queen thenceforward frequented, merely to avoid the appearance of a change in her habits. She almost always returned unhappy. She was treated with the profound respect due to a Queen; but all the touching graces of friendship had vanished to make way for the duties of etiquette, which wounded her deeply. The existing coolness between her and the Count d'Artois was also very painful to her, for she had loved him as tenderly as if he had been her own brother.

The opening of the States-General took place on the 4th of May. The Queen on that occasion appeared, for the last time in her life, in regal magnificence.

I will not pass over unnoticed a well-known fact which proves that before this period a faction had begun its operations against this Princess. During the procession on the opening of the States-General some low women, on seeing the Queen pass, cried out, "Vive le Duc d'Orleans!" in so threatening a manner that she nearly fainted. She was obliged to be supported, and those about her were afraid it would be necessary to stop the procession. The Queen, however, recovered herself, and much regretted that she had not been able to command more presence of mind.

The first sitting of the States took place on the following day. The King delivered his speech with firmness and dignity; the Queen told me that he had taken great pains about it, and repeated it frequently, that he might perfectly adapt it to the intonations of his voice.

His Majesty gave public marks of attachment and respect for the Queen, who was applauded; but it was easy to see that these applauses were in fact a homage rendered to the King alone.

It was evident during the first sittings that Mirabeau would be very dangerous to the Government. It is affirmed that at this period he communicated to the King, and still more fully to the Queen, a part of his scheme and his proposals for renouncing them. He had brandished the weapons afforded him by his eloquence and audacity, in order to treat with the party he meant to attack. This man played a game of revolution in order to make his fortune. The Queen told me that he asked for an embassy, and if my memory does not deceive me, it was that of Constantinople. He was refused with well-deserved contempt, though policy would doubtless have concealed it, could the future have been foreseen.

The general enthusiasm prevailing at the opening of this Assembly, and the debates between the Tiers-Etat, the Nobility, and even the Clergy, daily increased the alarm of Their Majesties, and all who were attached to the cause of monarchy; but this era of our history is too well known, and has been already too ably described, to require that I should go into any further details than those which are peculiarly within my province.

The Queen went to bed late, or I should rather say that this unfortunate Princess began to lose the enjoyment of rest. One evening, about the latter end of May, she was sitting in the middle of her room, relating several remarkable occurrences of the day; four wax candles were placed upon her toilette; the first went out of itself, and I relighted it; shortly afterwards the second, and then the third, went out also; upon which the Queen, squeezing my hand with an emotion of terror, said to me, "Misfortune has power to make us superstitious; if the fourth taper should go out like the rest, nothing can prevent my looking upon it as a fatal omen." The fourth taper went out.

It was remarked to the Queen that the four tapers had probably been run in the same mould, and that a defect in the wick had naturally occurred at the same point in each, since the candles had all gone out in the order in which they had been lighted.

The deputies of the Tiers-Etat arrived at Versailles full of the strongest prejudices against the Court. The falsehoods of the metropolis never failing to spread themselves into the surrounding provinces, they believed that the King indulged in the pleasures of the table to a shameful excess; that the Queen was draining the Treasury of the State in order to satisfy the most unreasonable luxury: they almost all determined to see Little Trianon. The extreme plainness of the retreat in question not answering the ideas they had formed, some of them insisted upon seeing the very smallest closets, saying that the richly furnished apartments were concealed from them. In short, they spoke of one which, according to them, was wholly ornamented with diamonds, and with wreathed columns studded with sapphires and rubies. The Queen could not get these foolish ideas out of her mind, and spoke to the King on the subject. From the description given of this room by the deputies to the keepers of Trianon, the King concluded that they were looking for the scene enriched with paste ornaments, made in the reign of Louis XV. for the theatre of Fontainebleau.

The King supposed that his body-guards, upon their return into the country, after having performed their quarterly duty at Court, related what they had seen, and that their exaggerated accounts being repeated became at last totally perverted. This first idea of the King, upon the search after the diamond chamber, suggested to the Queen that the mistake about the King's supposed propensity to drinking also sprang from the guards who accompanied his carriage when he hunted at Rambouillet. The King, who disliked sleeping out of his usual bed, was accustomed to leave that hunting-seat after supper. He generally slept soundly in his carriage, and awoke only on his arrival at the courtyard of his palace. He used to get down from his carriage in the midst of his body-guards staggering, as a man half awake will do, which was mistaken for a state of intoxication.¹

The majority of the deputies, who came imbued with prejudices produced by error or malevolence, went to lodge with the most humble private individuals of Versailles, whose inconsiderate conversation contributed not a little to the nourishment of such mistaken notions. Everything, in short, tended to render the deputies subservient to the schemes of the leaders of the rebellion.

Shortly after the opening of the States-General the first Dauphin died. That young Prince fell, in a few months, from a florid state of health into the rickets, which curved his spine, lengthened his face, and rendered his legs so weak that he could not walk without being supported like a decayed old man.²

---

1 It is curious to compare the following anecdote with the unjust censure thrown upon Louis XVI., the cause of which Madame Campan explains so naturally.

"Boursault's play of *Æsop at Court* contains a scene in which the Prince permits the courtiers to tell him his failings. They all join chorus in praising him beyond measure, with the exception of one, who reproaches him with loving wine and getting intoxicated, a dangerous vice in anyone, but especially in a King. Louis XV., in whom that disgusting propensity had almost grown into a habit, in the year 1739 found fault with Boursault's piece and forbade its performance at Court. After the death of that King, the time of mourning being expired, Louis XVI. commanded *Æsop at Court* for performance, found the play full of good sense, and proper for the instruction of Royalty, and directed that it should be often performed before him."—NOTE BY THE EDITOR.

2 Louis, Dauphin of France, who died at Versailles on the 4th of June, 1789, gave promise of intellectual precocity. The following particulars, which convey some idea of his disposition and of the assiduous care bestowed upon him by the Duchess de Polignac, will be found in a work of that time.

"At two years old the Dauphin was very pretty; he articulated well, and answered questions put to him intelligently. While he was at La Muette everybody was at liberty to see him. Having received, in the presence of the visitors, a box of sweetmeats sent

How many maternal tears did his languishing condition, the certain forerunner of death, draw from the Queen, already overwhelmed with apprehensions respecting the state of the kingdom! Her grief was enhanced by petty intrigues, which, when frequently renewed, became intolerable. An open quarrel between the families and friends of the Duke d'Harcourt, the Dauphin's governor, and those of the Duchess de Polignac, his governess, added greatly to the Queen's affliction. The young Prince showed a strong dislike to the Duchess de Polignac, who attributed it either to the Duke or the Duchess d'Harcourt, and came to make her complaints respecting it to the Queen. It is true that the Dauphin twice sent her out of the room, saying to her, with that maturity of manner which languishing sickness always gives to children, "Go

---

him by the Queen with her portrait upon it, he said: 'Ah! that's mamma's picture.'

"The Dauphin was always dressed very plainly, like a sailor; there was nothing to distinguish him from other children in point of external appearance but the cross of Saint-Louis, the blue ribbon, and the Order of the Fleece, decorations particularly belonging to his birth.

"The Duchess Jules de Polignac, his governess, scarcely ever left him for a single instant; she gave up all the Court excursions and amusements in order to devote her whole attention to her precious charge.

"A truly affecting trait is related of the young Dauphin, whom death snatched from us. The Prince always manifested a great regard for M. de Bourset, his *valet de chambre*. After falling into a state of weakness, from the sickness of which he died, he one day asked for a pair of scissors; that gentleman reminded him that they were forbidden. The child insisted mildly, and they were obliged to yield to him. Having got the scissors, he cut off a lock of his hair, which he wrapped in a sheet of paper: 'There, sir,' said he to his *valet de chambre*; 'there is the only present I can make you, having nothing at my command; but when I am dead you will present this pledge to my papa and mamma, and while they remember me I hope they will not forget you.'"—NOTE BY THE EDITOR.

out, Duchess; you are so fond of using perfumes, and they always make me ill"—and yet she never used any. The Queen perceived also that his prejudices against her friend extended to herself; her son would no longer speak in her presence. She had observed that he was fond of sugared sweetmeats, and offered him some marshmallow and jujube lozenges. The under-governors and the first *valet de chambre* requested her not to give the Dauphin anything, as he was to receive no food of any kind without the consent of the faculty. I forbear describing the wound this prohibition inflicted upon the Queen; she felt it the more deeply because she was aware it was unjustly believed she gave a decided preference to the Duke of Normandy, whose ruddy health and loveliness did, in truth, form a striking contrast to the languid look and melancholy disposition of his elder brother. At least she could not doubt that a project to deprive her of the affection of a child whom she loved as a good and tender mother ought, and whose sufferings made him an object of increased interest to her, had for some time existed. Previous to the audience granted by the King on the 10th of August, 1788, to the envoy of the Sultan Tippoo Saib, she had begged the Duke d'Harcourt to divert the Dauphin—whose deformity was already apparent—from his intention to be present at that ceremony, being unwilling to expose him in his then decrepit state to the gaze of the crowd of inquisitive Parisians who would be in the gallery. Notwithstanding this injunction, the Dauphin was suffered to write to his mother, requesting her permission to be present at the audience. The Queen was obliged to refuse him, and warmly reproached the governor, who merely answered that he could not oppose the wishes of a sick child. A year before the death of the Dauphin, the Queen lost the Princess Sophie, who was not weaned. This first misfortune was, as the Queen said, the beginning of all that followed from that moment.[1]

---

[1] The article dedicated to the memory of Louis XVI. in the "Biographie Universelle" makes no mention of the Princess Sophie. "This Prince," says the work in question, "had three children: Louis the Dauphin, who died in 1789, Louis XVII. and Marie Theresa Charlotte, now the Duchess d'Angoulême." The error, or rather the omission, is of little importance, but we are surprised, when the family of Louis XVI. is spoken of, to meet with this mistake in an article signed "Bonald."—NOTE BY THE EDITOR.

CHAPTER III

Oath of the tennis court—Insurrection of the 14th of July—The King goes to the National Assembly—Anecdotes—Spectacle presented by the courtyard of the Castle of Versailles—Report that the National Assembly is threatened—The King's speech rebutting these odious suspicions—Anecdotes—Disposition of the troops—Departure of the Count d'Artois, the Prince de Condé and the Duke and Duchess de Polignac—The latter is recognised by a postilion, who saves her—The King goes to Paris—Alarm at Versailles—The Queen determines to go to the National Assembly—Affecting speech prepared by her—The King's return—Bailly's speech--Assassination of MM. Foulon and Berthier—Plans presented by M. Foulon to the King for arresting the progress of the Revolution—Horrid remark by Barnave—His repentance.

THE ever-memorable oath of the States-General, taken at the tennis court of Versailles, was followed by the Royal sitting of the 23rd of June. The Queen looked upon M. Necker's not accompanying the King as treachery or criminal cowardice. She said that he had converted a salutary remedy into poison; that, being in full popularity, his audacity had emboldened the factions and led away the whole Assembly, and that he was the more culpable inasmuch as he had, the evening before, given her his word to accompany the King to this sitting. In vain did M. Necker endeavour to excuse himself by saying that his advice had not been attended to.

Soon afterwards, the insurrections of the 11th, 12th

and 14th of July opened the disastrous drama with which France was threatened. The massacre of M. de Flesselles and M. de Launay drew bitter tears from the Queen, and the idea that the King had lost such devoted subjects wounded her to the heart.

The character of the insurrection was not merely that of a popular tumult; the cries of "Vive la nation!" "Vive le Roi!" "Vive la liberté!" threw the strongest light upon the extended plan of the reformers. Still the people spoke of the King with affection, and appeared to think his character favourable to the desire of the nation for the reform of what were called abuses; but they imagined that he was restrained by the opinions and influence of the Count d'Artois and the Queen; and those two august personages were therefore objects of hatred to the malcontents. The dangers incurred by the Count d'Artois determined the King's first step with the National Assembly. He attended there on the morning of the 15th of July with his brothers, without pomp or escort. He spoke standing and uncovered, and pronounced these memorable words: "Upon you I throw myself. It is my wish that I and the nation should be one, and, in full reliance on the affection and fidelity of my subjects, I have given orders to the troops to remove from Paris and Versailles." The King returned from the chamber of the National Assembly to his palace on foot; the deputies crowded after him and formed his escort, and that of the Princes who accompanied him. The rage of the populace was pointed against the Count d'Artois, whose unfavourable opinion of the double representation was an odious crime in their eyes. They repeatedly cried out, "The King for ever, in spite of you and your opinions, Monseigneur." One woman had the impudence to come up to the King and ask him whether what he had been doing was done sincerely, and whether he would not be forced to retract it.

The courtyards of the castle were thronged with an immense concourse of people. They demanded that the King and Queen should make their appearance in the balcony with their children. The Queen gave me the key of the inner doors, which led to the Dauphin's apartments, and desired me to go to the Duchess de Polignac, to tell her that she wanted her son, and had directed me to bring him myself into her room, where she waited for him to show him to the people. The Duchess said this order indicated that she was not to accompany the Prince. I did not answer; she squeezed my hand, saying, "Ah! Madame Campan, what a blow for me!" She embraced the child with tears, and bestowed a similar mark of attachment upon myself. She knew how much I loved and valued the goodness and the noble frankness of her disposition. I endeavoured to compose her by saying that I should bring back the Prince to her; but she persisted, and said she understood the order and knew what it meant. She then retired into her private room, holding her handkerchief to her eyes. One of the sub-governesses asked me whether she might go with the Dauphin. I told her the Queen had given no order to the contrary, and we hastened to Her Majesty, who was waiting for the Prince, to show him from the balcony.

Having executed this painful commission, I went down into the courtyard, where I mingled with the crowd. I heard a thousand vociferations. It was easy to see, by the difference between the language and the dress of some persons among the mob, that they were in disguise. A woman, whose face was covered with a black lace veil, seized me by the arm with some degree of violence and said, calling me by my name, "I know you very well. Tell your Queen not to meddle with government any longer. Let her leave her husband and our good States-General to effect the happiness of the people." At the same moment a man, dressed much in the style of a market man, with his hat pulled down over his eyes, seized me by the other arm and said, "Yes, yes; tell her over and over again that it will not be with these States as with the others, which produced no good to the people; that the nation is too enlightened in 1789 not to make something more of them, and that there will not now be seen a deputy of the Tiers-Etat making a speech with one knee on the ground. Tell her this, do you hear?" I was struck with dread. The Queen then appeared in the balcony. "Ah!" said the woman in the veil, "the Duchess is not with her." "No," replied the man; "but she is still at Versailles. She is working underground, mole-like; but we shall know how to dig her out." The detestable pair moved away from me, and I re-entered the palace, scarcely able to support myself. I thought it my duty to relate the dialogue of these two strangers to the Queen. She made me repeat the particulars to the King.

About four in the afternoon I went across the terrace to Madame Victoire's apartments; three men had stopped under the windows of the throne-chamber. "Here is that throne," said one of them aloud, "the vestiges of which will soon be sought for in vain." He added a thousand invectives against Their Majesties. I went in to the Princess, who was at work alone in her closet, behind a canvas blind, which prevented her from being seen by those without. The three men were still walking upon the terrace; I showed them to her, and told her what they had said. She rose to take a nearer view of them, and informed me that one of them was named Saint-Huruge; that he was a creature of the Duke d'Orleans, and was furious against government because he had been confined once under a *lettre-de-cachet* as a bad character.

The King was not ignorant of all these popular threats; he also knew the days on which money was scattered about Paris, and once or twice the Queen prevented my going there, saying there would certainly be a riot the next day, because she knew that a quantity of crown pieces had been distributed in the faubourgs.[1]

On the evening of the 14th of July the King came to the Queen's apartments, where I was with Her Majesty alone. He conversed with her respecting the horrid report disseminated by the factious, that he had

---

[1] I have seen a six-franc crown piece, which certainly served to pay some wretch on the night of the 12th of July; the words "*Midnight, 12th of July, three pistols*," were rather deeply engraven on it. They no doubt communicated a signal for the first insurrection.—NOTE BY MADAME CAMPAN.

had the chamber of the National Assembly undermined in order to blow it up; but, he added, that it became him to treat such silly assertions with contempt, as usual. I ventured to tell him that I had, the evening before, supped with M. Begouen, one of the deputies, who said that there were very respectable persons who thought that this horrible contrivance had been proposed without the King's knowledge. "Then," said His Majesty, "as the idea of such an atrocity did not seem absurd to so worthy a man as M. Begouen, I will order the chamber to be examined early to-morrow morning." In fact, it will be seen by the King's speech to the National Assembly on the 15th of July that the suspicions excited deserved his attention. "I know," says he in the speech in question, "that unworthy insinuations have been spread about; I know there are those who have dared to assert that your persons are not safe. Can it be necessary to give you assurances upon the subject of reports so culpable, which a knowledge of my disposition ought to have refuted in their origin?"

The proceedings of the 15th of July produced no mitigation of the disturbances. Successive deputations of *poissardes* came to request the King to visit Paris, where his presence alone would put an end to the insurrection.

On the 16th a committee was held in the King's apartments, at which a most important question was discussed—whether His Majesty should quit Versailles and set off with the troops, whom he had recently ordered to withdraw, or go to Paris to tranquillise the minds of the people. The Queen was for the departure.

On the evening of the 15th she made me take all her jewels out of their cases, to collect them in one small box, which she might carry off in her own carriage. With my assistance she burnt a large quantity of papers, for Versailles was then threatened with an early visit of armed men from Paris.

The Queen, on the morning of the 16th, before attending another committee at the King's, having got her jewels ready and looked over all her papers, gave me one folded up but not sealed, and desired me not to read it until she should give me an order to do so from the King, and that then I was to execute its contents. But she returned herself about ten in the morning; the affair was decided; the army was to go away without the King; all those who were in imminent danger were to go at the same time. "The King will go to the Hôtel de Ville to-morrow," said the Queen to me. "He did not choose this course for himself; there were long debates on the question; at last the King put an end to them, by rising and saying, '*Well, gentlemen, we must decide; am I to go or to stay? I am ready to do either.*' The majority were for the King's stay; the time will show whether the right choice has been made." I returned the Queen the paper she had given me, which was now useless. She read it to me; it contained her orders for the departure. I was to go with her, as well on account of my office about her person as to serve as a governess to Madam. The Queen tore the paper and said, with tears in her eyes, "When I wrote this, I thought it would be useful; but fate has ordered otherwise, to the misfortune of us all, as I much fear."

After the departure of the troops, the new Administration received thanks; M. Necker was recalled. The artillery soldiers were undoubtedly corrupted. "Wherefore all these guns?" exclaimed the crowds of women who filled the streets. "Will you kill your mothers, your wives, your children?" "Don't be afraid," answered the soldiers; "these guns shall sooner be levelled against the tyrant's palace than against you."

The Count d'Artois, the Prince de Condé and their children set off at the same time with the troops.[1] The Duke and Duchess de Polignac, their daughter the Duchess de Guiche, the Countess Diana de Polignac, the Duke's sister and the Abbé de Balivière, also emigrated on the same night. Nothing could be more affecting than the parting of the Queen and her friend: the extremes of misfortune had banished from their minds the recollection of differences, to which

---

[1] A few particulars, honourable to the bravery of the Prince de Condé and relative to the birth of the Duke d'Enghien, which latter appear the more remarkable and affecting, when compared with his tragical end, will not be read without interest.

The Prince de Condé acquired reputation in his youth. Instances were related of his courageous behaviour at the battle of Artenback, in the Seven Years' War. It was said that on being requested to remove ten paces to the left in order to avoid the fire of a battery which was making horrid slaughter by his side, he replied to M. de Touraille, "I find none of these precautions in the history of the Great Condé."

He afterwards distinguished himself at the battle of Minden, in 1759, charging the enemy at the head of his reserve, over a piece of meadow strewed with the bodies of officers of the *gendarmerie* and carbineers. His talents displayed themselves to still greater advantage when he had a separate body of troops under his command, with which he gained several advantages over the Prince of Brunswick. Louis XV., by way of reward, gave him the enemy's cannon; and the Prince of Brunswick, afterwards visiting him at Chantilly and not finding the guns there, the Prince de Condé having had them removed out of sight, said, "You were determined to conquer me twice—in war by your arms, and by

political opinions alone had given rise. The Queen several times wished to go and embrace her once more after their sorrowful adieu, but her motions were too closely watched, and she was compelled to forego this last consolation. She, however, desired M. Campan to be present at the departure of the Duchess, and gave him a purse of 500 louis, requesting him to insist upon her allowing the Queen to lend her that sum, to defray her expenses on the road. The Queen added that she knew her situation, that she had often calculated her income, and the expenses occasioned by her place at Court; that both husband and wife, having no other fortune than their official salaries, could not possibly have saved anything, however differently people might think at Paris. M. Campan remained till midnight with the Duchess to see her get into her carriage. She was disguised

---

your forbearance in peace." The battle of Johannisberg carried his reputation to its height, for with an inferior reserve, he gained a complete victory over Prince Ferdinand. He held his council of war in the midst of a fire of musketry and remained master of the field of battle.

The Duke de Bourbon, the son of the Prince de Condé, when scarcely past childhood, became enamoured of Mademoiselle d'Orléans and showed so much attachment that he was married to that Princess at the age of fourteen, though she was more than six years older than himself.* But it was determined that he should travel a year or two before he should be suffered to cohabit with his wife; he eluded the vigilance of those appointed to watch him and carried her off from the convent in which she was placed. The Duchess de Bourbon was brought to bed of the Duke d'Enghien, in 1771, after having suffered pains which women alone can conceive for forty-eight hours. The child was born perfectly black and motionless. He was wrapped in linen, steeped in spirit of wine; but this experiment had nearly proved fatal to him, for by some means the linen took fire. The accident was, however, prevented from becoming fatal by the care of the accoucheur and physician.—NOTE BY THE EDITOR.

* It was on occasion of this marriage that Laujon composed his pretty piece, called *The Lover of Fifteen*.

as a *femme de chambre*, and got up in front of the berlin. She requested M. Campan to speak of her frequently to the Queen, and then quitted for ever that palace, that favour and that influence which had raised her up such cruel enemies. On their arrival at Sens the travellers found the people in a state of insurrection; they asked all those who came from Paris whether the Polignacs were still with the Queen. A group of inquisitive persons put that question to the Abbé de Balivière, who answered them in the firmest tone, and with the most cavalier air, that they were far enough from Versailles, and that we had got rid of all such bad people. At the following stage the postilion got upon the door-step and said to the Duchess, "Madam, there are some good people left in the world; I recognised you all at Sens." They gave the worthy fellow a handful of gold.

On the breaking out of these disturbances an old man, above seventy years of age, gave the Queen an extraordinary proof of attachment and fidelity. M. Peraque, a rich inhabitant of the colonies, father of M. d'Oudenarde, was coming from Brussels to Paris; while changing horses he was met by a young man who was leaving France, and who recommended him if he brought any letters from foreign countries to burn them immediately, especially if he had any for the Queen. M. Peraque had one from the Archduchess, the Governante of the Low Countries, for Her Majesty. He thanked the stranger, and carefully concealed his packet; but as he approached Paris the insurrection appeared to him so general and so violent that he thought no means could be relied on for securing this letter from seizure. He took upon him to unseal it, and learned it by heart, which was a wonderful effort for a man at his time of life, as it contained four pages of writing. On his arrival at Paris he wrote it down, and then presented it to the Queen, telling her that the feelings of an old and faithful subject had given him courage to form and execute such a resolution. The Queen received M. Peraque in her closet and expressed her gratitude in an affecting manner, most honourable to the respectable old man. Her Majesty thought the young stranger who had apprised him of the state of Paris was Prince George, of Hesse-Darmstadt, who was much attached to her, and who left Paris at that very time.

The Marchioness de Tourzel succeeded the Duchess de Polignac. She was selected by the Queen as being the mother of a family and a woman of irreproachable conduct, and who had superintended the education of her own daughters with the greatest success.

The King went to Paris on the 17th of July, accompanied by the Marshal de Beauvau, the Duke de Villeroy, and the Duke de Villequier; he also took the Count d'Estaing[1] and the Marquis de Nesle, who were then very popular, with him in his carriage. Twelve body-guards and the town-guard of Versailles escorted him to the Pont-du-Jour, near Sèvres, where the Parisian guard was waiting for him. His depar-

---

[1] The Count used to go and dine with the butchers at Versailles, and flattered the people by the meanest condescensions.—NOTE BY MADAME CAMPAN.

ture caused equal grief and alarm to his friends, notwithstanding the calmness he evinced. The Queen restrained her tears and shut herself up in her private rooms with her family. She sent for several persons belonging to her Court. Their doors were locked; terror had driven them away. A deadly silence reigned throughout the palace; fear was at its height; the King was hardly expected to return.[1] The Queen had a robe prepared for her, and sent orders to her stables to have all her equipages ready. She wrote an address of a few lines for the Assembly, determining to go thither with her family, the officers of her palace and her servants, if the King should be detained prisoner at Paris. She got this address by heart. I remember it began with these words: "Gentlemen, I come to place in your hands the wife and family of your Sovereign; do not suffer those who have been united in heaven to be put asunder on earth." While she was repeating this address her voice was often interrupted by her tears, and by the sorrowful exclamation, "They will never let him return!"

It was past four when the King, who had left Versailles at ten in the morning, entered the Hôtel de Ville. At length, at six in the evening, M. de Lastours, the King's first page, arrived; he was not half an hour in coming from the Barriere de la Conférence to Versailles. Everybody knows that the moment of calm at Paris was that in which the Sovereign received the tricoloured cockade from M. Bailly, and placed

---

[1] For the particulars of this journey, see Ferrière's Memoirs, where they are related with equal feeling and sincerity.—NOTE BY THE EDITOR.

it in his hat. A shout of "Vive le Roi!" arose on all sides; it had not been once uttered before. The King breathed again at that moment, and, with tears in his eyes, exclaimed that his heart stood in need of such shouts from the people. One of his equerries (M. de Cubières) told him the people loved him, and that he ought never to have doubted it. The King replied in accents of profound sensibility: "Cubières, the French loved Henry IV., and what King ever better deserved to be beloved?"[1]

His return to Versailles filled his family with inexpressible joy. In the arms of the Queen, his sister, and his children, he congratulated himself that no accident had happened, and it was then that he repeated several times, "Happily, no blood has been shed, and I swear that never shall a drop of French blood be shed by my order"—a determination full of humanity, but too openly avowed in such factious times!

---

[1] Louis XVI. cherished the memory of Henry IV. He at that moment thought of his deplorable end; but he long before regarded him as a model for himself. This is what Soulavie says on the subject:

"A tablet, with the inscription *Resurrexit*, placed upon the pedestal of the statue of Henry IV. on the accession of Louis XVI. flattered him exceedingly. '*What a fine compliment would that be,*' said he, '*were it but true. Tacitus himself never wrote anything so concise or so happy.*'

"Louis XVI. wished to take the reign of that Prince for a model. In the following year the party that raised a commotion among the people on account of the dearness of corn removed the tablet inscribed *Resurrexit* from the statue of Henry IV. and placed it under that of Louis XV., whose memory was then detested. Louis XVI., who was informed of it, withdrew into his private apartments, where he was found in a fever shedding tears; and during the whole of that day he could not be prevailed upon either to dine, walk out, or sup. From this circumstance we may judge what he endured at the commencement of the Revolution, when he was accused of not loving the French people."—NOTE BY THE EDITOR.

The King's last measure raised a hope in many that general tranquillity would soon enable the Assembly to resume its labours and bring its session to a close. The Queen never flattered herself with so favourable a result. M. Bailly's speech to the King equally wounded her pride and hurt her feelings: "Henry IV. conquered his people, and here are the people conquering their King." The word *conquest* offended her; she never forgave M. Bailly for his fine academical antithesis.

Five days after the King's visit to Paris, the departure of the troops, and the removal of the Princes and some of the nobility, whose influence seemed to alarm the people, a horrible deed, committed by hired assassins, proved that the King had descended from his throne without having effected a reconciliation with his people.

M. Foulon, who was added to the administration while M. de Broglie was commanding the army assembled at Versailles, had concealed himself at Viry. He was there recognised, and the peasants seized him and dragged him to the Hôtel de Ville. The cry for death was heard in the Assembly. The electors, the members of the committee, and M. de la Fayette, at that time the idol of Paris, in vain endeavoured to save the unfortunate man. After tormenting him in a manner the particulars of which make humanity shudder, his body was dragged about the streets and to the Palais Royal, and his heart was carried—shall I tell it?—by women —in the midst of a bunch of white carnations.[1]

---

[1] This horrible circumstance is related nowhere else. No historian, no record of the time, makes any mention of it. It is

M. Berthier, M. Foulon's son-in-law, intendant of Paris, was seized at Compiègne at the same time that his father-in-law was seized at Viry, and treated with still more relentless cruelty.

The Queen was always persuaded that this horrible deed was occasioned by some piece of indiscretion; and she imparted to me that M. Foulon had drawn up two memorials for the direction of the King's conduct at the time of his being called to Court on the removal of M. Necker; and that these memorials contained two schemes, of totally different nature, for extricating the King from the dreadful situation in which he was placed. In the first of these projects, M. Foulon expressed himself without reserve respecting the criminal views of the Duke d'Orleans; said that he ought to be put under arrest, and that no time should be lost in commencing a prosecution against him while the criminal tribunals were still in existence. He likewise pointed out such deputies as should be apprehended at the same time, and advised the King not to part with his army until order was restored.

His other plan was that the King ought to make himself master of the Revolution before its complete explosion. He advised His Majesty to go to the Assembly, and there, in person, to demand the minute books and papers, and to make the greatest sacrifices to satisfy the legitimate wishes of the people, and not to give the factious time to enlist them in aid of their criminal designs. Madame Adelaide had

---

probable the fact never took place—at least, for the honour of humanity, we ought to believe so.—NOTE BY THE EDITOR.

M. Foulon's two memorials read to her in the presence of four or five persons. One of them[1] was very intimate with Madame de Staël, and that intimacy gave the Queen reason to believe that the opposite party had gained information of M. Foulon's schemes.

It is known that young Barnave, during a lamentable aberration of mind, since expiated by sincere repentance, and even by death, uttered these atrocious words, "Is then the blood now flowing so pure?" when M. Berthier's son came to the Assembly to invoke the eloquence and filial piety of M. de Lally to entreat that body to save his father's life. I have since been informed that a son of M. Foulon, having returned to France after these first ebullitions of the Revolution, saw Barnave, and gave him one of those memorials, in which M. Foulon advised Louis XVI. to prevent the revolutionary explosion by voluntarily granting all that the Assembly required before the 14th of July. "Read this memorial," said he; "I have brought it to increase your remorse; it is the only revenge I wish to inflict on you." Barnave burst into tears, and said all that the profoundest grief could dictate.

---

[1] Count Louis de Narbonne.—NOTE BY MADAME CAMPAN.

CHAPTER IV

Creation of the National Guard—Departure of the Abbé de Vermond—The French guards quit Versailles—Entertainment given by the body-guards to the regiment of Flanders—The King, the Queen and the Dauphin are present at it—Proceedings of the 5th and 6th of October—Detestable threats against the Queen—Devotedness of one of the body-guard—The life of Marie Antoinette in danger—The Royal Family repair to Paris—Residence at the Tuileries—Change of feeling—The Queen applauded with enthusiasm by the women of the populace—Private life—Ingenuous observations of the Dauphin—Affecting anecdote—It is proposed to the Queen to quit her family and France—Her noble refusal—She devotes her attention to the education of her children—Picture of the Court—Anecdote respecting Luckner—Exasperating state of feeling.

AFTER the 14th of July, by a manœuvre for which the most skilful factions of any age might have envied the Assembly, the whole population of France was armed and organised into a National Guard. A report was spread throughout France on the same day, and almost at the same hour, that four thousand brigands were marching towards such towns or villages as it was wished to induce to take up arms. Never was any plan better laid; terror instantly spread all over the kingdom, and found its way into the most retired districts. In 1791 a peasant showed me a steep rock in the mountains of the Mont d'Or on which his wife concealed herself on the day when the four thousand brigands were to attack their village, and told me they had been obliged to make use of ropes to let her down from the place which fear alone had enabled her to climb.

Versailles was certainly the place where the national military uniform appeared most offensive. All the King's valets, even of the lowest class, were metamorphosed into lieutenants or captains; all the musicians of the chapel ventured one day to make their appearance at the King's Mass in a military costume; and an *Italian soprano* sang a motet in the garb of a grenadier captain. The King was very much offended at this conduct, and forbade his servants to appear in his presence in so unbecoming a dress.

The departure of the Duchess de Polignac naturally left the Abbé de Vermond exposed to all the dangers of favouritism. He was already talked of as an adviser dangerous to the nation. The Queen was alarmed at it, and recommended him to remove to Valenciennes, where Count Esterhazy was in command. He was obliged to leave that place in a few days and set off for Vienna, where he remained ever after.

On the night of the 17th of July the Queen, being unable to sleep, made me watch by her until three in the morning. I was extremely surprised to hear her say that it would be a very long time before the Abbé de Vermond would make his appearance at Court again, even if the existing ferment should subside, because he would not readily be forgiven for his attachment to the Archbishop of Sens, and that she had lost in him a very devoted servant. Then, on a sudden, she remarked to me that, although he was not much prejudiced against me, I could not have much regard for him, because he could not bear my father-in-law to hold the place of secretary of the closet. She went on to say that I must have studied the Abbé's character, and, as I had sometimes drawn her portraits of living characters, in imitation of those which were fashionable in the time of Louis XIV., she desired me to sketch that of the Abbé, as its features struck me, without any reserve. My astonishment was extreme; the Queen spoke of the man who, the day before, had been in the greatest intimacy with her with the utmost coolness, and as a person whom, perhaps, she might never see again! I remained petrified; the Queen persisted, and told me that he had been the enemy of my family for more than twelve years, without having been able to injure it in her opinion; so that I had no occasion to dread his return, however severely I might depict him. I promptly collected my ideas about the favourite; but I only remember that the portrait was drawn with sincerity, except that everything which could denote hatred was kept out of it. I shall quote but one extract from it: I said that he had been born talkative and indiscreet, and had assumed a character of singularity and bluntness in order to conceal those two failings. The Queen interrupted me by saying, "Ah! how true that is!" I have since that time had an opportunity of discovering that, notwithstanding the high favour which the Abbé de Vermond enjoyed, the Queen took precautions to guard herself against an ascendency the consequences of which she could not calculate.

On the death of my father-in-law his executors placed in my hands a box containing a few jewels, deposited by the Queen with M. Campan upon the departure from Versailles of the 6th of October, and two sealed packets, each inscribed, "Campan will take care of these papers for me." I took the two packets to Her Majesty, who kept the jewels and the larger packet, and, returning me the smaller, said, "Take care of that for me as your father-in-law did."

After the fatal 10th of August, 1792, at the moment when my house was about to be surrounded, I determined to burn the most interesting papers of which I was the depositary; I thought it, however, my duty to open this packet, which it might perhaps be necessary for me to preserve at all hazards. I saw that it contained a letter from the Abbé de Vermond to the Queen. I have already related that in the earlier days of Madame de Polignac's favour he determined to remove from Versailles, and that the Queen had recalled him by means of the Count de Mercy. This letter contained nothing but certain conditions for his return. It was the most whimsical of treaties; I confess I greatly regretted being under the necessity of destroying it. He reproached the Queen with her infatuation for the Countess Jules, her family and associates, and told her several truths about the possible unfortunate consequences of a friendship which ranked that young lady among the favourites of Queens of France, a title always disliked by the nation. He complained that his advice was neglected, and then came to the conditions of his return to Versailles. After strong assurances that he would never in all his life aim at the higher Church dignities, he said that he delighted in an unbounded confidence, and that he asked but two things of Her Majesty as essential: the first was, not to give him her orders through any third person, but to write to him herself; he complained much that he had had no letter in her own hand since he had left Vienna; then he demanded of her an income of 80,000 livres, in ecclesiastical benefices; and concluded by saying that if she condescended to assure him herself that she would set about procuring him what he wished, her letter would be sufficient in itself to show him that Her Majesty had accepted the two conditions he ventured to make respecting his return. No doubt the letter was written; at least it is very certain that the benefices were granted, and that his absence from Versailles lasted only a single week.

In the course of July, 1789, the regiment of French guards, which had been in a state of insurrection from the latter end of June, abandoned its colours. One single company of grenadiers remained faithful to its post at Versailles. The Baron de Leval commanded this company. He came every evening to request me to give the Queen an account of the disposition of his soldiers; but M. de la Fayette having sent them a note, they also deserted during the night and joined their comrades, who were enrolled in the Paris guard; so that Louis XVI. on rising saw no guard whatever at the various posts.

The mad decrees of the 4th of August, by which all privileges were abolished, are well known.[1] The

---

[1] "It was during the night of the 4th of August," says Rivarol,

King sanctioned all that tended to the diminution of his own personal gratifications; but refused his consent to the other decrees of that tumultuous night. This refusal was one of the chief causes of the ferments of the month of October.

In the early part of September meetings were held at the Palais Royal, and propositions made to go to Versailles. It was said to be necessary to separate the King from his evil counsellors, and keep him, as well as the Dauphin, at the Louvre. The proclamations by the municipal officers of the district for the restoration of tranquillity were ineffectual; but M. de la Fayette succeeded this time in dispersing the populace. The Assembly declared itself permanent; and during the whole of September, in which no doubt the preparations were made for the great insurrections of the following month, the Court was not disturbed.

"that the demagogues of the Nobility, wearied with a protracted discussion upon the rights of man, and burning to signalise their zeal, rose all at once, and with loud exclamations called for the last sighs of the feudal system. This demand electrified the Assembly.

"All heads were frenzied. The younger sons of good families, having nothing, were delighted to sacrifice their too fortunate elders upon the altar of the country; a few country curates felt no less pleasure in renouncing the benefices of others; but what posterity will hardly believe is that the same enthusiasm infected the whole Nobility; zeal walked hand in hand with malevolence; they made sacrifice upon sacrifice. And as in Japan the point of honour lies in a man's killing himself in the presence of a person who has offended him, so did the deputies of the Nobility vie in striking at themselves and their constituents. The people who were present at this noble conflict increased the intoxication of their new allies by their shouts; and the deputies of the Commons, seeing that this memorable night would only afford them profit without honour, consoled their vanity by wondering at what Nobility, grafted upon the Third Estate, could do. They named that night 'The night of dupes'; the Nobles called it 'The night of sacrifices.'"
—NOTE BY THE EDITOR.

The King had the Flanders regiment removed to Versailles; unfortunately the idea of the officers of that regiment fraternising with the body-guards was conceived, and the latter invited the former to a dinner, which was given in the great theatre of Versailles, and not in the Saloon of Hercules, as some chroniclers say. Boxes were appropriated to various persons who wished to be present at this entertainment. The Queen told me she had been advised to make her appearance on this occasion; but that, under existing circumstances, she thought such a step might do more harm than good; and that, moreover, neither she nor the King ought directly to have anything to do with such a festival. She ordered me to go, and desired me to observe everything closely in order to give a faithful account of the whole affair.

The tables were set out upon the stage; around them were placed one of the body-guard and an officer of the Flanders regiment alternately. There was a numerous orchestra in the room, and the boxes were filled with spectators. The air, "O Richard! O mon Roi!" was played, and shouts of "Vive le Roi!" shook the roof for several minutes. I had with me one of my nieces and a young person brought up with Madame by Her Majesty. They were crying "Vive le Roi!" with all their might when a deputy of the Third Estate, who was in the next box to mine, and whom I had never seen, called to them and reproached them for their exclamations; it hurt him, he said, to see young and handsome Frenchwomen brought up in such servile habits, screaming so outrageously for the life of one man, and with true fanaticism exalting him in their hearts above even their dearest relations. He told them what contempt worthy American women would feel on seeing Frenchwomen thus corrupted from their earliest infancy. My niece replied with tolerable spirit; and I requested the deputy to put an end to the subject, which could by no means produce him any satisfaction, inasmuch as the young persons who were with me lived, as well as myself, for the sole purpose of serving and loving the King. While I was thus checking the conversation, what was my astonishment at seeing the King, the Queen and the Dauphin enter the theatre! It was M. de Luxembourg who had effected this change of determination in the Queen.

A general enthusiasm prevailed. The moment Their Majesties arrived, the orchestra renewed the air I have just mentioned, and afterwards played a song in *The Deserter*, "Can we grieve those whom we love?" which also made a powerful impression upon those present. On all sides were heard praises of Their Majesties, exclamations of affection, expressions of regret for what they had suffered, clapping of hands, and shouts of "Vive le Roi!" "Vive la Reine!" "Vive le Dauphin!" It has been said that white cockades were worn on this occasion. That was not the case; the fact is, that a few young men belonging to the National Guard of Versailles, who were invited to the entertainment, turned the white lining of their national cockades outwards. All the military men quitted the theatre and reconducted the King and his family to their apartments. There was a mixture of intoxication with all these ebullitions of joy: a thousand extravagances were committed by the military, and many of them danced under the King's windows; a soldier belonging to the Flanders regiment climbed up to the balcony of the King's chamber in order to shout "Vive le Roi!" nearer His Majesty. This very soldier, as I have been told by several officers of the corps, was one of the first and most dangerous of the insurgents in the riots of the 5th and 6th of October. On the same evening another soldier of that regiment killed himself with a sword. One of my relations, chaplain to the Queen, who supped with me, saw him stretched out in a corner of the Place d'Armes; he went to him to give him spiritual assistance, and received his confession and his last sighs. He destroyed himself from regret at having suffered himself to be corrupted by the enemies of his King, and said that since he had seen him, and the Queen and Dauphin, remorse had turned his brain.

I returned home delighted with all that I had seen. I found a great many people there. M. de Beaumetz, deputy for Arras, listened to my description with a chilling air, and when I had finished, told me that all that had passed was terrific; that he knew the disposition of the Assembly, and that the greatest misfortunes would follow close upon the drama of that night, and he begged my leave to withdraw that he might take time for deliberate reflection whether he should on the very next day emigrate, or pass over to the left side of the Assembly.

He adopted the latter course, and never appeared again among my associates.

On the 2nd of October the military entertainment was followed up by a breakfast given at the hotel of the body-guards. It is said that a discussion took place whether they should not march against the Assembly; but I am utterly ignorant of what passed at that breakfast. From that moment Paris was constantly in commotion; there were continual mobs, and the most virulent proposals were heard in all public places; the conversation was invariably about proceeding to Versailles. The King and Queen did not seem apprehensive of such a measure, and took no precaution against it. Even when the army had actually left Paris, on the evening of the 5th of October, the King was shooting at Meudon, and the Queen was entirely alone in her gardens at Trianon, which she then beheld for the last time in her life. She was sitting in her grotto, absorbed in painful reflection, when she received a note from the Count de Saint-Priest, entreating her to return to Versailles. M. de Cubières at the same time went off to request that the King would leave his sport and return to his palace; the King did so on horseback, and very leisurely. A few minutes afterwards he was informed that a numerous body of women, which preceded the Parisian army, was at Chaville, at the entrance of the avenue from Paris.

The scarcity of bread and the entertainment of the body-guards were the pretexts for the insurrection of the 5th and 6th of October; but it is clear to demonstration that this new movement of the people was a part of the original plan of the factious, insomuch as, ever since the beginning of September, a report had been industriously circulated that the King intended to withdraw, with his family and ministers, to some stronghold; and at all the popular assemblies there had been always much said about going to Versailles to seize the King.

At first only women showed themselves; the grated doors of the castle were closed, and the body-guard and Flanders regiment were drawn up in the Place d'Armes. As the details of that dreadful day are given with precision in several works, I will only observe that consternation and disorder reigned throughout the interior of the castle.

I was not in attendance on the Queen at this time. M. Campan remained with her till two in the morning. As he was leaving her, she condescendingly, and with infinite kindness, desired him to make me easy as to the dangers of the moment, and to repeat to me M. de la Fayette's own words, which he had just used on soliciting the Royal Family to retire to bed, undertaking to answer for his army.

The Queen was far from relying upon M. de la Fayette's loyalty; but she has often told me that she believed on that day that La Fayette, having affirmed to the King, in the presence of a crowd of witnesses, that he would answer for the army of Paris, would not risk his honour as a commander, and was sure of being able to redeem his pledge. She also thought the Parisian army was wholly devoted to him, and that all he said about his being forced to march upon Versailles was mere pretence.

On the first intimation of the march of the Parisians, the Count de Saint-Priest prepared Rambouillet for the reception of the King, his family and suite, and the carriages were even drawn out; but a few cries of "Vive le Roi!" when the women reported His Majesty's favourable answer, occasioned the intention of going away to be given up, and orders were given to the troops to withdraw.[1] The body-guards were, however, assailed with stones and musketry while they were passing from the Place d'Armes to their hotel. Alarm revived; again it was thought necessary that the Royal Family should go away; some carriages still remained ready for travelling; they were called for; they were stopped by a wretched player belonging to the theatre of the town, seconded by the mob: the opportunity for flight had been missed.

The insurrection was directed against the Queen in particular. I shudder even now at the recollection of the *poissardes*, or rather furies, who wore white aprons, which, they screamed out, were intended to receive the bowels of Marie Antoinette, and that they would make

---

[1] We shall not urge the necessity of comparing this account with the particulars given in the Memoirs of Ferrières, Weber and Bailly; all those readers who desire information will feel the utility of this research. But a still more important testimony exists respecting these events, which had so unfortunate an influence; it is the testimony of a person who was at the time one of the King's ministers: it is, in short, the testimony of the very Count de Saint-Priest, who is mentioned in this passage of Madame Campan's Memoirs. M. de Saint-Priest, whose rank at Court, whose place in the council, and whose attachment for the King, enabled him to see and know all that was passing, has left a valuable account of events which his advice might have prevented, or at least delayed, if it had been followed. We owe this account to the kindness of M. de Saint-Priest, the Minister's son. It will be found among the *Historical Illustrations* (No. 2).—NOTE BY THE EDITOR.

cockades of them; mixing the most obscene expressions with these horrible threats. Such are the atrocious sentiments with which the ignorance and cruelty, to be found in the mass of every populace, can inspire them in times of disturbance! So necessary is it that a vigorous and parental authority should, while it defends good citizens against their own failings, also guard them against all the calamities brought on by factions.

The Queen went to bed at two in the morning and went to sleep, being tired out with the events of so distressing a day. She had ordered her two women to go to bed, imagining there was nothing to dread, at least, for that night; but the unfortunate Princess was indebted for her life to that feeling of attachment which prevented their obeying her. My sister, who was one of the two ladies in question, informed me the next day of all that I am about to relate.

On leaving the Queen's bed-chamber these ladies called their *femmes de chambre*, and all the four remained sitting together against Her Majesty's bedroom door. About half-past four in the morning they heard horrible yells and discharges of firearms. One ran in to the Queen to awaken her and get her out of bed; my sister flew to the place from which the tumult seemed to proceed. She opened the door of the ante-chamber which leads to the great guard-room, and beheld one of the body-guard holding his musket across the door, and attacked by a mob who were striking at him. His face was covered with blood. He turned round and exclaimed, " Save the Queen, madam! they are come to assassinate her." She hastily shut the door upon the unfortunate victim of duty, fastened it with the great bolt, and took the same precaution on leaving the next room. On reaching the Queen's chamber, she cried out to her, "Get up, madam! don't stay to dress yourself! fly to the King's apartment." The terrified Queen threw herself out of bed; they put a petticoat upon her without tying it, and the two ladies conducted her to the "bull's-eye." A door which led from the Queen's toilette-closet to that apartment had never before been fastened but on her side; it was found to be secured on the other side. What a dreadful moment! They knocked repeatedly with all their strength; a servant of one of the King's *valets de chambre* came and opened the door; the Queen entered the King's chamber, but he was not there. Alarmed for the Queen's life, he had gone down the staircase and through the corridors under the "bull's-eye," by means of which he was accustomed to go to the Queen's apartment without being under the necessity of crossing that room. He entered Her Majesty's room and found no one there but some body-guards who had taken refuge in it. The King, unwilling to expose their lives, told them to wait a few minutes, and afterwards sent to desire them to go to the "bull's-eye." Madame de Tourzel, at that time governess of the children of France, had just taken Madame and the Dauphin to the King's apartments. The Queen saw her children again. The reader must imagine this scene of tenderness and despair.[1]

---

[1] It is in the middle of this very scene of *tenderness and despair* that certain Memoirs, recently published in England, have en-

It is true that the assassins penetrated to the Queen's chamber, and pierced the bed with their swords. The fugitive body-guards were the only persons who entered it, and if the crowd had reached so far they would have been massacred. Besides, when the rebels had forced the doors of the ante-chamber, the footmen and officers on duty, knowing that the Queen was no longer in her apartments, told them so with that air of truth which always carries conviction. The abandoned horde instantly rushed towards the "bull's-eye," hoping, no doubt, to intercept her on her way.

Many have asserted that they recognised the Duke of Orleans at half-past four in the morning, in a great-coat and slouched hat, at the top of the marble staircase pointing out with his hand the guard-room which preceded the Queen's apartments. This fact was deposed to at the Châtelet by several individuals in the course of the enquiry instituted respecting the transactions of the 5th and 6th of October.[1]

---

deavoured to inflict the most cruel blow that could possibly be aimed at the Queen. Madame Campan cannot have read, without a sentiment of equal indignation and grief, what they have attempted to pass under the authority of her name. We shall not explain ourselves further, and we shall be commended for our reserve. We will merely add, that if they were desirous of putting an accusation against Marie Antoinette into the mouth of Madame Campan, they chose their time very ill in fixing precisely on the moment wherein she has represented that Princess in the most affecting and exalted point of view.—NOTE BY THE EDITOR.

[1] Justice and impartiality require us to direct the reader to the extract from the proceedings which accompany Weber's Memoirs. It will be well to consult with the *Historical Illustrations* (Note 2) we have before collected on that subject, those which are added under letter (E).—NOTE BY THE EDITOR.

The prudence and honourable feelings of several officers of the Parisian guards, and the judicious conduct of M. de Vaudreuil, lieutenant-general of marine, and of M. de Chevanne, one of the King's guards, brought about an understanding between the grandees of the National Guard of Paris and the King's guard. The doors of the "bull's-eye" were closed, and the ante-chamber, which precedes that room, was filled with grenadiers who wanted to get in to massacre the guards. M. de Chevanne offered himself as a victim, if they wished for one, and demanded of them what they would have. A report had been spread through the ranks that the body-guards set them at defiance, and that they all wore black cockades. M. de Chevanne showed them that he wore, as did the corps, the cockade of their uniform; and promised that the guards should exchange it for that of the nation. This was done; they even went so far as to change the grenadiers' caps for the hats of the body-guards; those who were on guard took off their shoulder-belts; embracings and the transports of fraternisation instantly succeeded to the savage eagerness to murder the band which had showed so much fidelity to its Sovereign. The cry was now, "Vivent le Roi, la Nation et les Gardes-du-corps!"

The army occupied the *Place d'Armes*, all the court-yards of the château, and the entrance to the avenue. They called for the Queen to appear in the balcony; she came forward with Madame and the Dauphin. There was a cry of "No children." Was this with a view to deprive her of the interest she inspired, accompanied as she was by her young family, or did the leaders of the democrats hope that some madman would venture to aim a mortal blow at her person? The unfortunate Princess certainly was impressed with the latter idea, for she sent away her children, and, with her hands and eyes raised towards heaven, advanced upon the balcony like a self-devoted victim.

A few voices shouted, "To Paris!" The exclamation soon became general. Before he agreed to this removal the King wished to consult the National Assembly, and caused that body to be invited to sit at the castle. Mirabeau opposed this measure. While these discussions were going forward it became more and more difficult to restrain the immense disorderly multitude. The King, without consulting anyone, now said to the people: "You wish, my children, that I should accompany you to Paris. I consent, but on condition that I shall not be separated from my wife and family." The King added that he required safety also for his guards. He was answered by shouts of "Vive le Roi, vivent les Gardes-du-corps!" The guards, with their hats in the air turned so as to exhibit the cockade, shouted "Vive le Roi, vive la Nation!" Shortly afterwards a general discharge of all the muskets took place in token of joy. The King and Queen set off from Versailles at one o'clock—the Dauphin, Madame the King's daughter, Monsieur, Madame, Madame Elizabeth and Madame de Tourzel were in the carriage; the Princess de Chimay, the ladies of the bed-chamber for the week, and the King's suite and servants followed in Court carriages; a hundred deputies in carriages and the bulk of the

Parisian army closed the procession. Great God! what a procession!

The *poissardes* went before and around the carriage of Their Majesties crying, "We shall no longer want bread—we have the baker, the baker's wife and the baker's boy with us." In the midst of this troop of cannibals the heads of two murdered body-guards were carried on poles. The monsters who made trophies of them conceived the horrid idea of forcing a hairdresser of Sèvres to dress them up and powder their bloody locks. The unfortunate man who was forced to perform this dreadful work died in consequence of the shock it gave him.[1]

The progress of the procession was so slow that it was near six in the evening when this august family, made prisoners by their own people, arrived at the Hotel de Ville. Bailly received them there; they were placed upon a throne just when that of their ancestors had been overthrown. The King spoke in a firm yet condescending manner. He said that *he always came with pleasure and confidence among the inhabitants of his good city of Paris.* M. Bailly repeated this observation to the representatives of the Commune, who came to address the King; but he forgot the word *confidence*. The Queen, instantly and loudly, reminded him of the omission. The King and Queen, their children and

---

[1] Nothing can be more destitute of proof than the atrocity here spoken of by Madame Campan, and which is mentioned also in the Memoirs of Bertrand de Molleville; it appears much better authenticated that the remains of the unfortunate bodyguards who so nobly fell victims to their duty and fidelity were not borne, as was at first said, under the eyes of Marie Antoinette and the King. As Bertrand de Molleville has described this sad procession, we think it right to extract his description from his Memoirs. See Note (F).—NOTE BY THE EDITOR.

Madame Elizabeth retired to the Tuileries. Nothing was ready for their reception there. All the lodging-rooms had been long given up to persons belonging to the Court; they hastily quitted them on that very day, leaving their furniture, which was purchased by the Court. The Countess de la Marck, sister to the Marshals de Noailles and de Mouchy, was the occupier of the apartments which were now appropriated to the Queen. Monsieur and Madame retired to the Luxembourg.

The Queen had sent for me on the morning of the 6th of October to leave me and my father-in-law in charge of her most valuable property. She took away only her casket of diamonds. Count Gouvernet de la Tour-du-Pin, to whom the military government of Versailles was entrusted *pro tempore*, came and gave orders to the National Guard, which had taken possession of the apartments, to allow us to remove everything that we should deem necessary for the Queen's accommodation.

I saw Her Majesty alone in her private apartments a moment before her departure for Paris. She could hardly speak; tears bedewed her face, to which all the blood in her body seemed to have rushed. She condescended to embrace me, gave her hand to M. Campan[1] to kiss, and said to us, "Come immediately and settle at Paris. I will lodge you at the Tuileries. Come! and do not leave me henceforward. Faithful servants at moments like these become useful

---

[1] Let me here pay a well-merited tribute to the memory of my father-in-law. In the course of that one night he declined from the highest pitch of health into a languishing condition, which brought him to the grave in September, 1791.

friends. We are lost—dragged away, perhaps, to death! When Kings become prisoners they have not long to live."

I had frequent opportunities, during the course of our misfortunes, of observing that the people never obey factions with steadiness, but easily escape their control when reflection or some other cause reminds them of their duty. As soon as the most violent Jacobins had an opportunity of seeing the Queen more near at hand, of speaking to her and of hearing her voice, they became her most zealous partisans; and, even when she was in the prison of the Temple, several of those who had contributed to place her there perished for having attempted to get her out again.

On the morning of the 7th of October the same women who had the day before surrounded the carriage of the august prisoners, riding on cannons and uttering the most abusive language, assembled under the Queen's windows, upon the terrace of the castle, and desired to see her. Her Majesty appeared. Among mobs of this description there are always orators —that is to say, beings of more assurance than the rest. A woman of this description, setting up for counsellor, told her that she must now remove far from her all such courtiers as ruin Kings, and that she must love the inhabitants of her good city. The Queen answered that she had loved them at Versailles and would likewise love them at Paris. "*Yes, yes,*" said another; "*but on the 14th of July you wanted to besiege the city and have it bombarded; and on the 6th of October you wanted to fly to the frontiers.*" The Queen replied affably that they had been told so and had believed it; that there lay the cause of the unhappiness of the people and of the best of Kings. A third addressed a few words to her in German. The Queen told her she did not understand, that she had become so entirely French as even to have forgotten her mother tongue. This declaration was answered with bravos and clapping of hands. They then desired her to make a compact with them. "Ah!" said she, "how can I make a compact with you since you have no faith in that which my duty points out to me, and which for my own happiness I ought to respect?" They asked her for the ribbons and flowers out of her hat. Her Majesty unfastened them herself and divided them among the party, which for above half an hour cried out without ceasing, "Marie Antoinette for ever! Our good Queen for ever!"

Two days after the King's arrival at Paris the city and the National Guard sent to request the Queen to appear at the theatre and prove, by her presence and the King's, that it was with pleasure they resided in their capital. I introduced the deputation which came to make this request. Her Majesty replied that she should have infinite pleasure in acceding to the invitation of the city of Paris, but that time must be allowed her to soften the recollection of the distressing events which had just occurred, and from which she had suffered too much. She added that having come into Paris, preceded by the heads of the faithful guards who had perished before the door of their Sovereign, she could not think that such an entry into the capital ought to be followed by rejoicings;

but that the happiness she had always felt in appearing in the midst of the inhabitants of Paris was not effaced from her memory, and that she should enjoy it again, as heretofore, as soon as she should find herself able to do so.

Their Majesties found some consolations in their private life.[1] From Madame's gentleness of manners, and her tender attachment to the august authors of her days; from the accomplishments and vivacity of the little Dauphin, and the attention and tenderness of the pious Princess Elizabeth, they still derived moments of happiness. The young Prince gave daily proofs of sensibility and penetration. He was not yet beyond female care; but a private tutor[2] gave him all the instruction suitable to his age. His memory was highly cultivated, and he recited verses with much grace and feeling.

The day after the arrival of the Court at Paris, terrified at hearing some noise in the gardens of the Tuileries, he threw himself into the arms of the Queen, crying out, "*Good God, mamma! is to-day yesterday again?*" A few days after this affecting exclamation he went up to the King, and looked at him with a

[1] "On the 19th of October, that is to say, thirteen days after he had taken up his abode at Paris, the King went, almost alone and on foot, to review some detachments of the National Guard. After the review, Louis XVI. met with a child sweeping the street, who asked him for money. The child called the King *M. le Chevalier*. His Majesty gave him six francs. The little sweeper, surprised at receiving so large a sum, cried out, 'Oh! I have no change; you will give me money another time.' A person who accompanied the monarch said to the child, 'Keep it all, my friend. The gentleman is not *chevalier;* he is the eldest of the family.'"—NOTE BY THE EDITOR.

[2] The Abbé Davout, whose talents were proved by the astonishing progress of the young Prince.—NOTE BY MADAME CAMPAN.

pensive air. The King asked him what he wanted. He answered, that he had something very serious to say to him. The King having prevailed on him to explain himself, the young Prince requested to know why his people, who formerly loved him so well, were all at once angry with him, and what he had done to irritate them so much. His father took him upon his knees, and spoke to him nearly as follows: "I wished, child, to render the people still happier than they were; I wanted money to pay the expenses occasioned by wars. I asked my people for money, as my predecessors have always done. Magistrates composing the Parliament opposed it, and said that my people alone had a right to consent to it. I assembled the principal inhabitants of every town, whether distinguished by birth, fortune or talents, at Versailles; that is what is called the States-General. When they were assembled they required concessions of me which I could not make, either with due respect for myself or with justice to you, who will be my successor. Wicked men, inducing the people to rise, have occasioned the excesses of the last few days; the people must not be blamed for them."

The Queen made the young Prince clearly comprehend that he ought to treat the commanders of battalions, the officers of the National Guard, and all the Parisians who were about him, with affability. The child took great pains to please all these people; and when he had had an opportunity of replying obligingly to the Mayor or members of the Commune he came and whispered in his mother's ear, "Was that right?"

He requested M. Bailly to show him the shield of Scipio, which is in the Royal library; and M. Bailly asking him which he preferred, Scipio or Hannibal, the young Prince replied, without hesitation, that he preferred him who had defended his own country. He gave frequent proofs of ready wit. One day, while the Queen was hearing Madame repeat her exercises in ancient history, the young Princess could not at the moment recollect the name of the Queen of Carthage. The Dauphin was hurt at his sister's want of memory, and though he never spoke to her in the second person singular, he bethought himself of the expedient of saying to her, "But *dis donc* the name of the Queen to mamma; *dis donc* what her name was."[1]

Shortly after the arrival of the King and his family at Paris, the Duchess de Luynes came, in pursuance of the advice of a committee of Constitutionals, to propose to the Queen a temporary retirement from France, in order to leave the Constitution to perfect itself, so that the patriots should not accuse her of influencing the King to oppose it. The Duchess knew how far the schemes of the factions extended, and her attachment to the Queen was the principal cause of the advice she gave her. The Queen perfectly comprehended the Duchess de Luynes's motive, but replied that she would never leave either the King or her son; that if she thought herself alone obnoxious to public hatred, she would instantly offer her life as a sacrifice; but that it was the throne

---

[1] The words *dis donc* (tell *thou* then) in French have the same sound with *Didon* (Dido).—TRANS.

which was aimed at, and that, in abandoning the King, she should be merely committing an act of cowardice, since she saw no other advantage in it than that of saving her own life.

One evening in the month of November, 1790, I returned home rather late. I there found the Prince de Poix. He told me he came to request me to assist him in regaining his peace of mind; that at the commencement of the sittings of the National Assembly, he had suffered himself to be seduced into the hope of a better order of things; that he blushed for his error, and that he abhorred plans which had already produced such fatal results; that he broke off with the reformers for the rest of his life; that he had just given in his resignation as a deputy of the National Assembly; and, finally, that he was anxious that the Queen should not sleep in ignorance of his sentiments. I undertook his commission, and acquitted myself of it in the best way I could; but I was totally unsuccessful. The Prince de Poix remained at Court; he there suffered many mortifications, never ceasing to serve the King in the most dangerous commissions with that zeal for which his house has always been distinguished.

When the King, the Queen and their children were suitably established at the Tuileries, as well as Madame Elizabeth and the Princess de Lamballe, the Queen resumed her usual habits. She employed her mornings in superintending the education of Madame, who received all her lessons in her presence, and she herself began to work large pieces of tapestry. Her mind was too much occupied with passing events and surrounding dangers to admit of her applying herself to reading; the needle was the only employment which would divert her mind.[1] She received the Court twice a week before going to Mass, and on those days dined in public with the King. She spent the rest of the time with her family and children. She had no concert, and did not go to the play until 1791, after the acceptation of the Constitution.[2] The Princess de Lamballe, however, had some evening parties in her apartments at the Tuileries, which were tolerably brilliant in consequence of the great number of persons who attended them. The Queen was present at a few of these assemblies, but being soon convinced that her present situation forbade her appearing in large circles, she remained at home, and conversed as she sat at work.[3] The sole topic of her

---

[1] There is still at Paris, at the house of Mademoiselle Dubuquois, tapestry worker, a carpet worked by the Queen and Madame Elizabeth for the large room of Her Majesty's ground-floor apartments at the Tuileries. The Empress Josephine saw and admired this carpet, and desired it might be preserved in hope of one day sending it to Madame.—NOTE BY MADAME CAMPAN.

[2] A judgment may be formed of the situation in which the Queen found herself placed during the earlier part of her residence at Paris from the following letter written by her to the Duchess de Polignac:

"I shed tears of affection on reading your letters. You talk of my courage, it required much less to go through that dreadful crisis which I had to suffer than is daily necessary to endure our situation, our own griefs, those of our friends and those of the persons who surround us. This is a heavy weight to sustain, and but for the strong ties by which my heart is bound to my husband, my children and my friends, I should wish to sink under it. But you bear me up; I ought to sacrifice such feelings to your friendship. But it is I who bring misfortune on you all, and your troubles are on my account." ("History of Marie Antoinette," by Montjoie.)—NOTE BY THE EDITOR.

[3] The Queen returned one evening from one of these assemblies very much affected; an English nobleman, who was playing at the same table with Her Majesty, ostentatiously displayed an enormous ring, in which was a lock of Oliver Cromwell's hair.—NOTE BY MADAME CAMPAN.

discourse was, as may well be supposed, the Revolution. She sought to discover the real opinions of the Parisians respecting her, and how she could have so completely lost the affections of the people, and even of many persons in the higher ranks. She well knew that she ought to impute the whole to the spirit of party, to the hatred of the Duke d'Orleans, and the folly of the French, who desired to have a total change in the Constitution; but she was not the less desirous of ascertaining the private feelings of all the people in power.[1]

---

[1] The Count d'Escherny, in the extract we are about to give, shrewdly describes the blind fury of those who overthrew the ancient edifice of monarchy, and the folly of such as, at this time, attempt to reinstate it upon the old basis.

"I picture France before the year 1789 to myself as a great theatre, where magnificent operas were represented. The places were badly distributed; the pit paid all the expenses of the performance; the people in that part of the house were left standing, squeezed together and uncomfortable, while the little band of the favourites of intrigue and fortune reclined luxuriously in gilded niches and elegant recesses. But the crowd below drank in pleasure at all their senses, while the others were yawning above them. The wearisomeness of the boxes balanced the inconveniences of the pit. The latter, except so far as vanity (which is but a poor set-off against *ennui*) was concerned, was not the worst off, so that all were nearly satisfied.

"Certain men came and undertook to undeceive the pit as to their enjoyments, and to persuade them that their pleasures, being mixed with vexations, were no pleasures at all. The stage revolved on a large pivot. They gave it a revolutionary movement, making it turn round on its own centre. They brought to sight what was before concealed by the scenes and curtains. They pushed back what was in front, and brought forward what was behind. They afterwards made holes in the scenes, undid the framework and pulleys, cut the cords, unhung the clouds, and presented to the astonished spectator all the oily, black and smoky ruins. 'Infatuated admirers!' cried they, 'behold the objects of your fascination! These are your gods, your ancestors, your Kings, your heroes! And now prostrate yourselves again!'

"He who, to help the French legislators out of their difficulties, should at this day hold this language to them, 'Gentlemen, you see you are struggling in vain! You are drowning; anarchy is gaining upon you; you have but one course to pursue, that is to reinstate

From the very commencement of the Revolution General Luckner indulged in violent sallies against her. Her Majesty, knowing that I was acquainted with a lady who had been long connected with the General, desired me to discover through that channel what was the private motive on which Luckner's hatred against her was founded. On being questioned upon this point, he answered that Marshal de Segur had assured him he had proposed him for the command of a camp of observation, but that the Queen had made a dash against his name, and that the *tash*, as he called it in his German accent, he could not forget. The Queen ordered me to repeat this reply to the King myself, and said to him, " See, Sire, whether I was not right in telling you that your ministers, in order to give themselves full scope in the distribution of favours, persuaded the French that I interfered in everything. There was not even a license given out in the country for the sale of salt and tobacco but the people believed it was given to one of my favourites." " That is very true," replied the King; " but I find it very difficult to believe that Marshal de Segur ever said any such thing to Luckner; he knew too well that you never interfered in the distribution of favours. That Luckner is a good-for-nothing fellow, and Segur is a brave and honourable man, who never uttered such

---

the theatre.' A person who could say so would certainly be little better than an idiot. To him I should reply, ' My friend, the mischief is done, the illusion is destroyed, and that for some time to come. It will be long ere the raging sea will be anything more than so many pieces of pasteboard, or the enchanted palaces other than daubs upon rough cloth lighted by mutton-fat.' " ("The Philosophy of Politics," vol. ii., pp. 202-204.)—NOTE BY THE EDITOR.

a falsehood. However, you are right; and because you provided for a few dependents, you are most unjustly reported to have disposed of all offices, civil and military.

All the Nobility who had not left Paris made a point of presenting themselves assiduously to the King, and there was a considerable influx to the Palace of the Tuileries. Marks of attachment were exhibited even in external symbols; the women wore enormous bouquets of lilies in their bosoms and upon their heads, and sometimes even bunches of white ribbon.

At the play there were often disputes between the pit and the boxes about removing these ornaments, which the people thought dangerous emblems. National cockades were sold in every corner of Paris; the sentinels stopped all who did not wear them. The young men piqued themselves upon breaking through this regulation, which was in some degree sanctioned by the acquiescence of the hapless Louis XVI. Frays took place, which were to be regretted, because they excited a spirit of rebellion. The King adopted conciliatory measures with the Assembly, in order to promote tranquillity; the Revolutionists were but little disposed to think him sincere. Unfortunately the Royalists encouraged this incredulity by incessantly repeating that the King was not free, and that all he did was completely null and in no way bound him for the time to come. Such was the heat and violence of party spirit that persons the most sincerely attached to the King were not even permitted to use the language of reason, and recommend greater reserve in conversation. People would talk and argue at table without considering that all the servants belonged to the hostile army; and it may truly be said that there was as much imprudence and levity in the party assailed as there was cunning, boldness and perseverance in that which made the attack.

CHAPTER V

Affair of Favras—His prosecution and death—His children are imprudently presented to the Queen—Plan laid for carrying off the Royal Family—Singular letter from the Empress Catherine to Louis XVI.—The Queen is unwilling to owe the re-establishment of the throne to the *Emigrés*—Death of the Emperor Joseph II.—First negotiation between the Court and Mirabeau—Louis XVI. and his family inhabit St. Cloud—New plans for escaping.

IN February, 1790, the affair of the unfortunate Favras gave the Court much uneasiness. This individual had conceived the scheme of carrying off the King and effecting what was then called a counter-revolution.[1] Monsieur, probably out of mere benevolence, gave him some money, and thence arose a report that he thereby wished to favour the execution of the enterprise. The step taken by Monsieur in going to the Hôtel de Ville to explain himself upon this affair was unknown to the Queen; it is more than probable that the King was acquainted with it. When judgment was pronounced upon M. de Favras, the Queen did not conceal from me her fears about the confessions of the unfortunate man in his last moments.

I sent a confidential person to the Hôtel de Ville.

---

[1] *Vide*, in the *Illustrations* (G), the particulars given by Bertrand de Molleville of this tragic episode of the Revolution.—NOTE BY THE EDITOR.

She came to inform the Queen that the condemned had demanded to be taken from Notre Dame to the Hôtel de Ville to make a final declaration and give some particulars verifying it. These particulars compromised nobody. Favras corrected his last will after writing it over, and went to the scaffold with heroic courage and coolness. The judge who read his condemnation to him told him that his life was a sacrifice which he owed to public tranquillity. It was asserted at the time that Favras was given up as a victim in order to satisfy the people and save the Baron de Besenval, who was a prisoner in the Abbaye.[1]

---

[1] The "Biographie Universelle" (vol. xiv., p. 221) gives the following particulars of the designs, prosecution and death of this unfortunate man:

"Favras (Thomas Mahy, Marquis of), born at Blois in 1745, entered the service first in the corps of *mousquetaires*, and made the campaign of 1761 with them. He was afterwards captain and adjutant in Belsunce's regiment, and subsequently lieutenant of the Swiss guard of Monsieur the King's brother, and resigned that commission in 1775 to go to Vienna, where his wife was acknowledged the only and legitimate daughter of the Prince d'Anhalt-Schauenbourg. He commanded a legion in Holland on the insurrection against the Stadtholder, in 1787. Possessing a warm imagination and a head fertile in expedients, Favras always had something to propose in all cases and upon every point. He presented a great number of plans on the subject of finance; and at the breaking out of the Revolution he tendered some upon political measures, which rendered him an object of suspicion to the revolutionary party. It is well known that in the highly excited state of the minds of the people, if the leaders of factions pointed out a victim, it was impossible for him to escape from popular fury. Favras was accused in the month of December, 1789, of having conspired against the Revolution and planned the introduction of armed men into Paris during the night, in order to make away with the three principal members of the Administration, to attack the King's guard, to carry off the Great Seal, and even to remove the King and his family to Péronne. Having been arrested by order of the committee of enquiry of the National Assembly, he was transferred to the Châtelet, where he defended himself with much coolness and presence of mind, repelling the accusations brought against

On the morning of the Sunday following this execution, M. de la Villeurnoy[1] came to my house to tell me that he was going on that very day to the public dinner of the King and Queen to present the widow Favras and her son, both of them in mourning for the brave Frenchman who fell a sacrifice for his King, and that all the Royalists expected to see the Queen load the unfortunate family with favours. I did all that lay in my power to prevent this proceeding. I foresaw the effect it would have upon the Queen's feeling heart, and the painful constraint she

---

him by Morel, Turcati and Marquie with considerable force. These witnesses declared he had imparted his plan to them. It was to be carried into execution by 12,000 Swiss and 12,000 Germans, who were to be assembled at Montargis, thence to march upon Paris, carry off the King and assassinate Bailly, La Fayette and Necker. The greater number of these charges he denied, and declared that the rest related only to the levy of a troop intended to favour the revolution preparing in Brabant. The judge having refused to disclose who had denounced him, he complained to the Assembly, which passed to the order of the day. His death was obviously inevitable. During the whole time of the proceedings the populace never ceased threatening the judges and shouting 'A la lanterne!' It was even necessary to keep numerous troops and artillery, constantly ready to act, in the courtyard of the Châtelet. The judges, who had just acquitted M. de Besenval in an affair nearly similar, doubtless dreaded the effects of this fury. When they refused to hear Favras's witnesses in exculpation, he compared them to the tribunal of the Inquisition. The principal charge against him was founded on a letter from one M. de Foucault asking him, 'Where are your troops? In which direction will they enter Paris? I should like to be employed among them.' Favras was condemned to make the *amende honorable* in front of the cathedral and to be hanged at the Place de Grève. He heard this sentence with wonderful calmness, and said to the judges, 'I pity you much if the testimony of two men is sufficient to induce you to condemn.' The judge having said to him, 'I have no other consolation to hold out to you than that which religion affords,' he replied nobly, 'My greatest consolation is that which I derive from my innocence.'"—NOTE BY THE EDITOR.

1 M. de la Villeurnoy, Master of the Requests, was deported to Sinamary on the 18th Fructidor, by the Executive Directory, and there died.—NOTE BY MADAME CAMPAN.

would experience, having the horrible Santerre, the commandant of a battalion of the Parisian guard, behind her chair during dinner-time. I could not make M. de la Villeurnoy comprehend my argument. The Queen had gone to Mass, surrounded by her whole Court, and I had not even the means of apprising her of this intention.

When dinner was over I heard a knocking at the door of my apartment, which opened into the corridor next that of the Queen; it was herself. She asked me whether there was anybody with me. I was alone. She threw herself into an arm-chair, and told me she came to weep with me, entirely at her ease, over the foolish conduct of the ultras of the King's party. "We must fall," said she, "attacked as we are by men who possess extraordinary talent and shrink from no crime, while we are defended only by those who are no doubt very estimable, but have no adequate idea of our situation. They have exposed me to the animosity of both parties by presenting the widow and son of Favras to me. Were I free to act as I wish, I should take the child of the man who has just sacrificed himself for us and place him at table between the King and myself; but, surrounded by the assassins who have destroyed his father, I did not dare even to cast my eyes upon him. The Royalists will blame me for not having appeared interested in this poor child; the Revolutionists will be enraged at the idea that his presentation should have been thought agreeable to me." However, the Queen added that she knew Madame Favras's situation; that she was aware she was in want; and that she desired me to send her the next day, through a person who could be relied on, a few rouleaus of fifty louis, and to direct that she should be assured Her Majesty would always watch over her fortune and that of her son.

The Queen wished to send some man devoted to the King's cause with letters to the Princes then at Turin. She cast her eyes upon an officer, a chevalier of St. Louis, intimately connected with M. Campan's family, and of whom she had frequently heard me speak in terms of commendation. I did not hesitate a moment between the pleasure of seeing one of my friends entrusted with a commission which would do him honour and the danger of entrusting that charge to a man whom I had the misfortune to see carried away by the fatal opinions of the times.[1] This I told the Queen, and entreated her to make another selection. Her Majesty was gratified by my sincerity. The commission was given to M. de J——, who from that time invariably evinced the greatest discretion, the most undoubted sagacity and a zeal that never for a moment slackened.

In the month of March following I had an opportunity of ascertaining the King's real sentiments respecting the schemes which were continually proposed

---

[1] In 1791 this man was chosen a member of the Legislative Assembly. So long as I had only his opinions to combat I did not cease to receive him. When, however, I had his actions to dread, I requested him, from the very day of his installation in the Assembly, to visit me no more. He became afterwards a conventional——. But I was indebted to my principles and prudence for the satisfaction of having long ceased all communication with a man who ranked himself among the enemies of my Sovereigns, and subsequently was one of their murderers. — NOTE BY MADAME CAMPAN.

to him for making his escape. One night, about ten o'clock, the Count d'Inisdal, who was deputed by the Nobility, came to request I would hear him in private, as he had an important matter to communicate to me. He told me that on that very night the King would be carried off; that the section of the National Guard which was that day commanded by M. d'Aumont[1] was gained over, and that sets of horses, furnished by some good Royalists, were placed in relays at suitable distances; that he had just left a party of Nobles assembled for the execution of this scheme, and that he had been sent to me that I might, through the medium of the Queen, obtain the King's positive consent to it before midnight; that the King was aware of their plan, but that His Majesty never would speak decidedly, and that at the moment of action it was necessary he should consent to the undertaking. I remember that I greatly displeased the Count d'Inisdal by expressing my astonishment that the Nobility, at the moment of the execution of so important a project, should send to me, the Queen's first woman, to obtain a consent which ought to have been the basis of any well-concerted scheme. I told him also that it would be impossible for me to go at that time down into the Queen's apartments without exciting the attention of the people in the ante-chambers; that the King was at cards with the Queen and his family, and that I never broke in

---

[1] A brother of the Duke de Villequier, who had joined the revolutionary party; a man of no weight or respectability, who desired he might be called James Aumont. A far different man from his brave brother, who always proved himself entirely devoted to the cause of his King.—NOTE BY MADAME CAMPAN.

upon their privacy unless I was called for. I added, however, that M. Campan could enter without being called, and that if he chose to give him his confidence he might rely upon him. My father-in-law, to whom the Count d'Inisdal repeated what he had said to me, undertook the commission, and went to the Queen's apartments. The King was playing at whist with the Queen, Monsieur and Madame; Madame Elizabeth was kneeling upon a stool near the table. M. Campan informed the Queen of what had been communicated to me. Nobody uttered a word. The Queen broke silence, and said to the King, " Do you hear, Sire, what Campan says to us ? " " Yes, I hear," said the King, and continued his game. Monsieur, who was in the habit of introducing passages from plays into his conversation, said to my father-in-law, " M. Campan, *that pretty little couplet again*, if you please "; and pressed the King to reply. At length the Queen said, " But something must be said to Campan." The King then spoke to my father-in-law in these words: " Tell M. d'Inisdal that I cannot consent to be carried off! " The Queen enjoined M. Campan to take care and report this answer faithfully. " You understand," added she, " *the King cannot consent to be carried off.*" The Count d'Inisdal was very much dissatisfied with the King's answer, and went out, saying, " I understand; he wishes to throw all the blame beforehand upon those who are to devote themselves for him." He went away, and I thought the enterprise would be abandoned. However, the Queen remained alone with me till midnight, preparing her cases of valuables, and ordered me not to go to bed. She imagined the King's answer would be understood as a tacit consent, and merely a refusal to participate in the design. I do not know what passed in the King's apartments during the night, but I occasionally looked at his windows. I saw the garden clear; I heard no noise in the palace, and day at length confirmed my opinion that the project had been given up. "We must, however, fly," said the Queen to me shortly afterwards. "Who knows how far the factious may go? The danger increases every day."[1] This Princess received advice and memorials from all quarters. Rivarol addressed several to her, which I read to her. They were full of ingenious observations, but the Queen did not find that they contained anything of essential service under the circumstances in which the Royal Family were

---

[1] If the following anecdote be not true, it is, after what we have just read, at least very probable.
"The disturbances of the 13th of April, 1790, occasioned by the warmth of the discussions upon Don Gerle's imprudent motion in the National Assembly, having afforded room for apprehension that the enemies of the country would endeavour to carry off the King from the capital, M. de la Fayette promised to keep a good look out, and told Louis XVI. that if he saw any alarming movements among the disaffected, he would give him notice of it by the discharge of a cannon from Henry IV.'s battery upon the Pont Neuf. On the same night a few casual discharges of musketry were heard from the terrace of the Tuileries. The King, deceived by the noise, flew to the Queen's apartments. He did not find her in her room; he ran to the Dauphin's room, where he found the Queen holding her son in her arms. 'Madam,' said the King to her, 'I have been seeking you; I was uneasy about you.' The Queen showing her son, said to him, 'I was at my station.' This answer was perfectly worthy of the Queen's maternal feelings." ("Anecdotes of the Reign of Louis XVI.")—NOTE BY THE EDITOR.

placed. The Count de Moustier also sent memorials and plans of conduct. I remember that in one of his writings he said to the King, "Read *Telemachus* again, Sire. In that book, which delighted Your Majesty in infancy, you will find the first seeds of those principles which, erroneously followed up by men of ardent imaginations, are bringing on the explosion we expect every moment." I read so many of these memorials that I could hardly give a faithful account of them, and I am determined to note in this work no other events than such as I witnessed—no other words than such as (notwithstanding the lapse of time) still, in some measure, vibrate in my ears.

The Count de Ségur, on his return from Russia, was employed some time by the Queen, and had a certain degree of influence over her; but that did not last long. Count Augustus de la Marck likewise endeavoured to negotiate for the King's advantage with the leaders of the factious. M. de Fontanges, Archbishop of Toulouse, possessed also the Queen's confidence; but none of the endeavours which were made at home produced any beneficial result. The Empress Catherine II. also conveyed her opinion upon the situation of Louis XVI. to the Queen, and Her Majesty made me read a few lines in the Empress's own handwriting, which concluded with these words: "Kings ought to proceed in their career undisturbed by the cries of the people, as the moon pursues her course unimpeded by the howling of dogs." I shall certainly not enter into any discussion on this maxim of the despotic Sovereign of Russia;

but it was very inapplicable to the situation of a captive King.

All this private advice, whether given from abroad or at home, led to no decision of which the Court could avail itself. Meanwhile the revolutionary party followed up its audacious enterprise in a determined manner, without meeting any opposition. The advice from without, as well from Coblentz as from Vienna, made various impressions upon the members of the Royal Family, and those Cabinets were not in accordance with each other. I often had reason to infer from what the Queen said to me that she thought the King, by leaving all the honour of restoring order to the Coblentz party, would, on the return of the emigrants, be put under a kind of guardianship which would increase his own misfortunes. She frequently said to me, "If the emigrants succeed, they will give the law for a long time; it will be impossible to refuse them anything. To owe the crown to them would be contracting too great an obligation." It always appeared to me that she wished her own family to counterbalance the claims of the emigrants by disinterested services. She was fearful of M. de Calonne, and with good reason. She had proof that this minister was now her bitterest enemy, and that he made use of the basest and most criminal means in order to blacken her reputation. I can *testify* that I have seen in the hands of the Queen a manuscript copy of the infamous Memoirs of the woman De Lamotte, which had been brought to her from London, and in which all those passages where a total ignorance of the customs of Courts had occasioned that wretched woman to make blunders which would have been too palpable were corrected in M. de Calonne's own handwriting.

The King's two guards who were wounded at Her Majesty's door on the 6th of October were M. du Repaire and M. de Miomandre de Sainte-Marie. On the dreadful night of the 6th of October the latter took the post of the former the moment he became incapable of maintaining it.

M. de Miomandre was at Paris, living on terms of friendship with another of the guards who, on the same day, received a gunshot wound from the brigands in another part of the castle. These two officers, who were attended and cured together at the infirmary of Versailles,[1] were almost constant companions; they were recognised at the Palais Royal and insulted. The Queen thought it advisable for them to quit Paris. She desired me to write to M. de Miomandre de Sainte-Marie to ask him to come to me at eight o'clock in the evening, and then to communicate to him her wish to hear of his being in safety; and ordered me, when he had made up his mind to go, to open her chest and tell him

---

[1] A considerable number of the body-guards who were wounded on the 6th of October betook themselves to the infirmary at Versailles. The presence of mind of M. Voisin, head surgeon of that infirmary, saved their lives. The brigands wanted to make their way into the infirmary in order to massacre them. M. Voisin ran to the entrance-hall, invited the assailants to refresh themselves, ordered some wine to be brought, and found means to direct the superior to remove the guards into a ward appropriated to the poor and to dress them in the caps and great-coats furnished by the institution. The good sisters executed this order with so much promptitude that the guards were removed, dressed as paupers, and their beds fresh made while the assassins were loitering to drink. They searched all the wards, and fancied they saw no persons there but the sick poor; thus the guards were saved.—NOTE BY MADAME CAMPAN.

in her name that gold could not repay such a service as he had rendered; that she hoped some day to be in sufficiently happy circumstances to recompense him as she ought; but that for the present her offer of money was only that of a sister to a brother situated as he then was, and that she requested he would take whatever might be necessary to discharge his debts at Paris and defray the expenses of his journey. She told me also to desire he would bring his friend Bertrand with him, and to make him the same offer as I was to make to M. de Miomandre.

The two guards came at the appointed hour, and each accepted, I think, one or two hundred louis. A moment afterwards the Queen opened my door. She was accompanied by the King and Madame Elizabeth. The King stood with his back against the fireplace; the Queen sat down upon a sofa, and Madame Elizabeth sat near her. I placed myself behind the Queen, and the two guards stood facing the King. The Queen told them that the King wished to see, before they went away, two of the brave men who had afforded him the strongest proofs of courage and attachment. Miomandre spoke, and said all that the Queen's affecting and flattering observations were calculated to inspire. Madame Elizabeth spoke of the King's sensibility; the Queen resumed the subject of their speedy departure, urging the necessity of it; the King was silent, but his emotion was evident, and his eyes were suffused with the tears of sensibility. The Queen rose, the King went out, and Madame Elizabeth followed him. The Queen stopped and said to me, in the recess of a window, "I am sorry I brought the King here! I am sure Elizabeth thinks with me. If the King had but given utterance to a fourth part of what he thinks of those brave men they would have been in ecstasies; but he cannot overcome his diffidence."

The Emperor Joseph died about this time. The Queen's grief was not excessive. That brother, of whom she had been so proud, and whom she had loved so tenderly, had probably suffered greatly in her affections. She reproached him sometimes, though with great moderation, for having adopted several of the principles of the new philosophy, and perhaps she knew that he looked upon our troubles with the eye of the Sovereign of Germany rather than that of the brother of the Queen of France.[1]

Mirabeau never entirely gave up the hope of becoming the last resource of the oppressed Court, and I remember that at this time some communications passed between the Queen and him. The question was about an office to be conferred upon him. This transpired, and it must have been about this period that the Assembly decreed that no deputy could hold an office as a minister of the King until the expiration of two years after the cessation of his legislative functions. I know that the Queen was much hurt at this decision, and considered that the Court had lost a promising opening.

---

[1] The Emperor Joseph sent the Queen an engraving which represented unfrocked nuns and monks. The first were trying on fashionable dresses; the latter were getting their hair dressed. This engraving was always left in a closet, and never hung up. The Queen told me to have it taken away; for she was hurt to see how much influence the philosophers had over her brother's mind and actions.—NOTE BY MADAME CAMPAN.

The Palace of the Tuileries was a very disagreeable residence during the summer, which made the Queen wish to go to St. Cloud. The removal was decided on without any opposition. The National Guard of Paris followed the Court thither. At this period new plans of escape were presented; nothing would have been more easy at that time than to execute them. The King had obtained leave to go out without guards, and to be accompanied only by an aide-de-camp of M. de la Fayette. The Queen also had one on duty with her, and so had the Dauphin. The King and Queen often went out at four in the afternoon, and did not return until eight or nine.

This is one of the plans of emigration which the Queen communicated to me, the execution of which seemed infallible. The Royal Family were to meet in a wood four leagues from St. Cloud. Some persons who could be fully relied on were to accompany the King, who was always followed by his equerries and pages. The Queen was to join him with her daughter and Madame Elizabeth. These Princesses, as well as the Queen, had equerries and pages, of whose fidelity no doubt could be entertained. The Dauphin, likewise, was to have been at the place of rendezvous with Madame Tourzel: a large berlin and a chaise for the attendants were sufficient for the whole family. The aides-de-camp were to have been gained over or mastered. The King was to leave a letter for the National Assembly upon his bureau at St. Cloud. The people in the service of the King and Queen would have waited until nine in the evening without anxiety, because the family sometimes did not return until that hour. The letter could not be forwarded to Paris until ten o'clock at the earliest. The Assembly would not be sitting at that hour; and as the President must have been sought for at his own house or elsewhere, it would have been midnight before the Assembly could have been summoned, and couriers could have been sent off to have the Royal Family stopped; but the latter would have been six or seven hours beforehand, as they would have started at six leagues' distance from Paris, and at this period travelling was not as yet impeded in France. The Queen approved of this plan, but I did not venture to interrogate her, and I even thought if it was put in execution she would leave me in ignorance of it. One evening, in the month of June, the people at the Castle, finding the King did not return by nine o'clock, were walking about the courtyards in a state of great anxiety. I thought the family was gone, and I could scarcely breathe amidst the confusion of my good wishes when I heard the sound of the carriages. I confessed to the Queen that I thought she had set off. She told me she must wait until the Queen's aunt had quitted France, and afterwards see whether the plan agreed with those formed abroad.[1]

---

[1] On his return from one of the visits to St. Cloud, the King wrote to the Duchess de Polignac:

"I am returned from the country. The air has been of service to us; but how changed did the retreat appear to us! How desolate was the breakfast-room! Neither of you were there. I did not give up the hope of our meeting there again; but I know not when. How many things we shall have to say to one another! Your friend preserves her health, in spite of all the misfortunes

CHAPTER VI

First federation—Attempts to assassinate the Queen—Remarkable observations of that Princess—Affecting scene—Account of the affair of Nancy, written by Madame Campan at night in the Council Chamber, by the King's dictation—Madame Campan calumniated—Marks of confidence bestowed upon her by the Queen—Interview between that Princess and Mirabeau in the gardens of St. Cloud—He treats with the Court—Scoffs at the revolutionary party—Plan formed by the Princess for re-entering France through Lyons—Imprudence of persons attached to the Queen—Anecdote relative to M. de la Fayette—Departure of the King's aunts—Death of Mirabeau.

THERE was a meeting at Paris for the first federation on the 14th of July, the anniversary of the taking of the Bastille. What an astonishing assemblage was this of 400,000 men, amongst whom there were not perhaps 200 who did not believe that the King found

---

which press upon her. Adieu, Duchess! Speak of me to your husband and all around you; and understand that I shall not be happy until the day I find myself with my old friends again."

"The further the first National Assembly advanced in its labours," adds Montjoie, by whom this letter is given, "the more unhappy the Queen found herself." We have a proof of this in these words from another note from Louis XVI. to the Duchess de Polignac:

"For the last eighteen months we have seen and heard nothing but disagreeable things. We do not lose our temper, but we are hurt and rendered melancholy at being thwarted in everything, particularly at being misrepresented."

In a former letter from the King to the Duchess, the following passage occurs:

"Your friend is unhappy and exceedingly misrepresented; but I flatter myself that justice will one day be done to her. Still, the wicked are very active; they are more readily believed than the good; you are a striking proof of it." ("History of Marie Antoinette," by Montjoie, page 262.)—NOTE BY THE EDITOR.

happiness and glory in the order of things then being established. The love which was borne him by all, with the exception of those who meditated his ruin, still reigned in full force in the hearts of all the French of the departments; but, if I may judge from those whom I had an opportunity of seeing, it was totally impossible to enlighten them and rouse them from their enchantment. They were as much attached to the King as to the Constitution, and to the Constitution as to the King, and it was impossible to separate the one from the other in their hearts and minds.[1]

---

[1] To the particulars respecting the federation, contained in the Memoirs by Ferrières, we add the following. On one hand they describe the enthusiasm excited by that festival even among the English, and on the other characterise the far too licentious freedom of their stage:

"Two deputies from Nantes, who were sent to England to cement the fraternal union between the London Revolutionary Club and all the friends of the French Constitution, wrote the following letter:

"'From all that we have seen and known we can assure you that the people of London are at least as enthusiastic on the subject of the French Revolution as the people of France. We went yesterday to see the opera of *The Confederation of the French at the Champs de Mars*. This piece has been played daily for six weeks. The house is filled by five o'clock, though the performance does not begin till seven. When we got there there was no room, but as soon as they heard us speak French, without knowing us, they hastened to place us in the front of the boxes; they paid us every possible attention, and forced refreshments upon us.

"'The first act of this opera represents the arrival of several people at Paris to the federation.

"'The second, the works of the Champ de Mars.

"'The third, the Confederation itself.

"'In the second act capuchins are seen in grenadier caps, girls caressing abbés, the King comes in and chops with a hatchet; everybody at work and singing "Ça ira, ça ira."

"'In the third act you see the municipal officers in scarfs, the National Assembly, the National Guard, officiating ministers in pontifical dresses and priests singing. A regiment of children sing, "Moi je suis soldat pour la patrie" in French and English. All this appears to us something new upon the banks of the Thames, and every verse is encored and enthusiastically applauded.'" — "Anecdotes of the Reign of Louis XVI.," vol. iv.—NOTE BY THE EDITOR.

The Court returned to St. Cloud after the federation. A wretch named Rotondo made his way into the palace with the intention of assassinating the Queen. It is known that he penetrated to the inner gardens: the rain prevented Her Majesty from going out on that day. M. de la Fayette, who was aware of this plot, gave all the sentinels the strictest countersigns, and a description of the monster was distributed throughout the palace by order of the General. I do not know how he was saved from punishment. A counter police belonging to the King discovered that there was likewise a scheme on foot for poisoning the Queen. She spoke to me as well as to her head physician, M. Vicq-d'Azyr, about it without the slightest emotion. Both he and myself considered what precautions it would be proper to take. He relied much upon the Queen's temperance, yet he recommended me to have always a bottle of oil of sweet almonds within reach, and to renew it occasionally; oil and milk being, as is known, the most certain antidotes to the drastic action of corrosive poisons. The Queen had a habit which rendered M. Vicq-d'Azyr particularly uneasy: there was always some pounded sugar upon the table in Her Majesty's bed-chamber, and she frequently, without even calling anybody, put spoonfuls of it into a glass of water when she wished to drink. It was agreed that I should get a considerable quantity of sugar powdered; that I should always have some papers of it in my bag, and that three or four times a day, when alone in the Queen's room, I should substitute it for that in her sugar-basin. We knew that the Queen would have prevented all such precautions, but we were not aware of her motive. One day she caught me alone making such an exchange as I speak of, and told me she supposed it was an operation agreed on between myself and M. Vicq-d'Azyr, but that I gave myself very unnecessary trouble. "Remember," added she, "that not a grain of poison will be used against me. The Brinvilliers do not belong to this century. This age possesses calumny, which is a much more convenient instrument of death, and it is by that I shall perish."

While similar melancholy presentiments and the most criminal projects afflicted and rent the heart of this unfortunate Princess, the sincerest manifestations of attachment to her person and to the King's cause would frequently raise agreeable illusions in her mind, or present to her the affecting spectacle of tears shed for her sorrows. I was one day, during this same visit at St. Cloud, witness of a very touching scene, which we took great care to keep secret. It was four in the afternoon; the guard was not set; there was scarcely anybody at St. Cloud that day, and I was reading to the Queen, who was at work in a room the balcony of which hung over the courtyard. The windows were closed, yet we heard a sort of murmur from a great number of voices which seemed to articulate only stifled sounds. The Queen desired me to go and see what it was. I raised the muslin curtain, and perceived more than fifty persons beneath the balcony; this group consisted of women, young and old, perfectly well dressed in the country costume, old chevaliers of Saint Louis, young knights of Malta, and a few ecclesiastics. I told the Queen it was probably an assemblage of persons residing in the neighbourhood who wished to see her. She rose, opened the window, and appeared in the balcony. Immediately all these worthy people said to her, in an undertone, "Courage, Madame; good Frenchmen suffer for you and with you; they pray for you; Heaven will hear their prayers—we love you, we respect you, we will continue to venerate our virtuous King." The Queen burst into tears, and held her handkerchief to her eyes. "Poor Queen, she weeps!" said the women and young girls; but the dread of exposing Her Majesty, and even the persons who showed so much affection for her, prompted me to take her hand and prevail upon her to retire into her room; and, raising my eyes, I gave the excellent people to understand that my conduct was dictated by prudence. They comprehended me, for I heard, "That lady is in the right"; and afterwards, "Farewell, madam!" from several of them; and all this in accents of feeling so genuine and so mournful that I am affected at the recollection of them even after a lapse of twenty years.

A few days afterwards the insurrection of Nancy took place. Only the apparent cause of this insurrection is known; there was another, of which I might have been in full possession if the great confusion I was in upon the subject had not deprived me of the power of paying attention to it. I will endeavour to explain myself. In the early part of September the Queen, as she was going to bed, desired me to let all her people go and to remain with her myself. When we were alone she said to me, "The King will come here at midnight. You know that he has always shown you marks of distinction; he now proves his confidence in you by selecting you to write down the whole affair of Nancy from his dictation. He must have several copies of it." At midnight the King came to the Queen's apartments, and said to me, smiling, "You did not expect to become my secretary, and that, too, during the night." I followed the King into the council-chamber. I found there a blank paper book, an inkstand and pens all ready prepared. He sat down by my side and dictated to me the report of the Marquis de Bouillé, which he himself copied at the same time. My hand trembled, and I wrote with difficulty, my reflections scarcely leaving me sufficient power of attention to listen to the King. The large table, the velvet carpet, seats which ought to have been filled by none but the King's chief counsellors; what that chamber had been, and what it was at that moment, when the King was employing a woman in an office which had so little affinity with her ordinary functions; the misfortunes which had brought him to the necessity of doing so, those which my affection and my apprehension for my Sovereigns made me still dread—all these ideas made such an impression upon me that, when I had returned to the Queen's apartments, I could not sleep for the remainder of the night, nor could I remember what I had written.

The more I saw that I had the happiness to be of some service to my employers, the more scrupulously careful was I to live entirely with my family, and I never indulged in any conversation which could betray the intimacy into which I was admitted. But nothing at Court remains long concealed, and I soon saw I had numerous enemies. The means of injuring others, especially in the minds of Sovereigns, are but too easy; they were become still more so, since mere suspicion of communication with the partisans of the Revolution was sufficient to forfeit the esteem and confidence of the King and Queen. Happily my conduct protected me against the dangers of calumny. I had left St. Cloud two days when I received at Paris a note from the Queen containing these words: "Come to St. Cloud immediately; I have something concerning you to communicate." I set off without loss of time. Her Majesty told me she had a sacrifice to request of me. I answered that it was made. She said it went so far as the renunciation of a friend's society; that such a renunciation was always painful, but that it must be particularly so to me; that, for her own part, perhaps it might have suited her very well that a deputy, a man of talent, should be constantly received at my house, which might be extremely useful to her, but that, at this moment, she thought only of my welfare. The Queen then informed me that the ladies of the bed-chamber had, the preceding evening, assured her that M. de Beaumetz, deputy from the Nobility of Artois, who had taken his seat on the left of the Assembly, spent his whole time at my house. Perceiving upon what false grounds the attempt to injure me was founded, I replied respectfully, but at the same time smiling, that it was impossible for me to make the sacrifice exacted by Her Majesty; that M. de Beaumetz, a man of great judgment, had not determined to cross over to the left of the Assembly, with the intention of afterwards coming to make himself unpopular by spending his time with the Queen's first woman; that ever since the 1st of October, 1789, I had seen him nowhere but at the play or in the public walks, and even then without his ever coming to speak to me; and that this line of conduct had appeared to me perfectly consistent, for that, whether he was desirous to please the popular party or to be sought after by the Court, he could not act in any other way towards me. The Queen closed this explanation by saying, "Oh! it is clear, as clear as the day! This opportunity of attempting to do you an injury is very ill-chosen, but be cautious in your slightest actions. You perceive that the confidence placed in you by the King and myself creates you powerful enemies."

The private communications which were still kept up between the Court and Mirabeau at length procured him an interview with the Queen in the gardens of St. Cloud.[1] He left Paris on horseback on pretence of going into the country to M. de Clavières, one of our friends, but he stopped at one of the gates of the garden of St. Cloud, and was led, I know not by whom, to a spot situated in the most elevated part of the private garden, where the Queen was waiting for him. She told me she accosted him by saying, "With a common enemy, with a man who had sworn

---

[1] It was not in her apartments, as is asserted by M. de Lacretelle, that the Queen received Mirabeau, his person was too generally known. She went alone in her garden to a round tuft of ground, which is still upon the heights of the private garden of St. Cloud.—NOTE BY MADAME CAMPAN.

to destroy monarchy, without appreciating its utility among a great people, I should at this moment be guilty of a most ill-advised step, but in speaking to a Mirabeau," &c. The poor Queen was delighted at having discovered this method of exalting him above all others of his principles, and in imparting the particulars of this interview to me, she said, " Do you know that those words, ' a Mirabeau,' appeared to flatter him exceedingly." However, to the best of my judgment, it was flattering him but little, for his abilities did more harm than ever they could do good. On leaving the Queen, he said to her with warmth, " Madam, the monarchy is saved!"[1] It must have been soon afterwards that Mirabeau received very considerable sums of money. He suffered it to appear too plainly by the increase of his expenditure. Already some of his remarks upon the necessity of arresting the progress of the factions circulated in society. Being once invited to meet a person at dinner who was very much attached to the Queen, he learned that that person withdrew on hearing that he was one of the guests. The party who invited him told him this with some degree of satisfaction, but all were very much astonished when they heard Mirabeau eulogise the absent guest, and declare that in his place he would have done the same; but, he added, they had only to invite that person again in a few months and he would then dine with the restorer of the monarchy. Mirabeau forgot that it was more easy to do harm

---

[1] *Vide* the anecdote given in Weber's Memoirs, vol. ii., upon the subject of this interview.—NOTE BY THE EDITOR.

than good, and thought himself the Atlas of the whole world in politics.

Outrages and mockery were incessantly mingled with the audacious proceedings of the Revolutionists. It was customary to give serenades under the King's windows on New Year's Day, and the band of the National Guards repaired thither on that festival in 1791. In allusion to the liquidation of the debts of the State, decreed by the Assembly, they played solely and repeatedly that air from the comic opera of the *Debts*, the burden of which is: "But our creditors are paid, and that makes us easy."

On the same day some "conquerors of the Bastille," grenadiers of the Parisian guard, preceded by military music, came to present to the young Dauphin, as a New Year's gift, a box of dominoes made of some of the stone and marble of which that State prison was built. The Queen gave me this inauspicious curiosity, desiring me to preserve it, as it would be a curious illustration of the history of the Revolution. Upon the lid were engraved some bad verses, the purport of which was as follows: "*These stones from the walls which enclosed the innocent victims of arbitrary power have been converted into a toy to be presented to you, Monseigneur, as a homage of the people's love, and to teach you the extent of their power.*"

The Queen said that M. de la Fayette's thirst for popularity doomed him to lend himself, without discrimination, to all popular follies. Her aversion for the General increased daily and grew so powerful that when, towards the end of the Revolution, he seemed willing to support the tottering throne, she could never bring herself to incur so great an obligation to him.

Emigration had already removed a great many people: persons who before this period would never have dared to aspire to any office of distinction, now sought, under pretence of zeal for the King's cause, to get into the interior of the Tuileries. I knew many of them; some were mere wretched adventurers, others were well-intentioned but wanted the abilities which would have rendered them useful.

M. de J——, a colonel attached to the staff of the army, was fortunate enough to render several services to the Queen, and acquitted himself with discretion and dignity of various important missions.[1] Their Majesties had the highest confidence in him, although it frequently happened that his prudent fears, when inconsiderate projects were under discussion, brought upon him, from thoughtless persons and from enemies, the charge of following the principles of the Constitutionals. Being sent to Turin, he had some difficulty in dissuading the Princes from a scheme they had formed at that period of re-entering France, with a very weak army, by the way of Lyons; and when, in a council, which lasted till three o'clock in the morning, he showed his instructions and demonstrated that the measure would endanger the King, the Count d'Artois alone declared against the plan, which emanated from the Prince de Condé.

---

[1] During the Queen's detention in the Temple, he introduced himself into that prison in the dirty dress of a lamplighter, and there discharged his duty unrecognised. This act of attachment is still known only to his family and a few very intimate friends.—NOTE BY THE EDITOR.

Among the persons employed in subordinate situations whom the critical circumstances of the times introduced into affairs of importance was one M. de Goguelat, a geographical engineer at Versailles and an excellent draughtsman. He had made plans of St. Cloud and Trianon for the Queen; she was very much pleased with them, and got the engineer admitted into the staff of the army. At the commencement of the Revolution he was sent to Count Esterhazy, at Valenciennes, in the capacity of aide-de-camp. The latter rank was given him solely to remove him from Versailles, where he endangered the Queen, during the earlier months of the Assembly of the States-General. Making a parade of his devotion to the King's interests, he went repeatedly to the tribunes of the Assembly, and there openly railed at all the motions of the deputies, and then returned to the Queen's antechamber, where he repeated all that he had just heard or had had the imprudence to say.

I had warned the Queen of the ill effect that this officer's warmth produced; and she agreed with me in opinion respecting it. But unfortunately, at the same time that she sent away M. de Goguelat, she continued in the belief that in a dangerous predicament, and one that required great self-devotion, the man might be employed advantageously. In 1791 he was commissioned to act in concert with the Marquis de Bouillé in furtherance of the King's intended escape.[1]

Projectors in great numbers endeavoured to intro-

---

[1] Upon the subject of this officer's conduct consult the Memoirs of M. de Bouillé, those of the Duke de Choiseul, and the account of the journey to Varennes, by M. de Fontanges, in Weber's Memoirs.—NOTE BY THE EDITOR.

duce themselves not only to the Queen but to Madame Elizabeth, who had communications with many individuals who took upon themselves to lay down plans for the conduct of the Court. The Baron de Gillien and M. de Vanoise were of this description; they went to the Baroness de Mackau's, where the Princess spent almost all her evenings. The Queen did not like these meetings, from which Madame Elizabeth might adopt views in manifest opposition to the King's intentions or her own.

The Queen gave frequent audiences to M. de la Fayette. One day, when he was in her inner closet, his aides-de-camp, who waited for him, were walking up and down the great room where the persons in attendance remained. Some imprudent young women were thoughtless enough to say, with the intention of being overheard by those officers, that it was very alarming to see the Queen alone with a rebel and a brigand. I was hurt at such indiscretion, which always produced bad effects, and I imposed silence on them. One of them persisted in the appellation " brigand." I told her that, as to "rebel," M. de la Fayette well deserved the name; but that the title of leader of a party was given by history to every man commanding 40,000 men, a capital and forty leagues of country; that Kings had frequently treated with such leaders, and if it was convenient to the Queen to do the same it remained only for us to be silent and respect her action. On the morrow the Queen, with a serious air but with the greatest kindness, asked what I had said respecting M. de la Fayette on the preceding day; adding that she had been assured I had enjoined her women silence, because they did not like him, and that I had taken his part. I repeated what had passed to the Queen word for word. She condescended to tell me that I had done perfectly right.

Whenever jealousy conveyed any false reports to her respecting me, she was kind enough to inform me of them; and they had no effect on the confidence with which she continued to honour me, and which I am happy to think I have justified, even at the risk of my life.

Mesdames the King's aunts set out from Bellevue in the beginning of the year 1791.[1] I went to take

---

[1] Alexander Berthier, Prince de Neufchâtel, then a colonel on the staff of the army, and commandant of the National Guard of Versailles, favoured the departure of Mesdames. The Jacobins of that town procured his dismissal, and he ran the greatest risk, on account of having rendered this service to these Princesses.*—NOTE BY MADAME CAMPAN.

* The departure of Mesdames possessed the importance of an event. It was an actual experiment made by the Court of the means to be taken to quit Paris. We will here relate, from the Memoirs devoted to the history of these Princesses, what concerns General Berthier, and the part he took in the departure of Mesdames. In the *Historical Illustrations* (I) will be found speeches, facts and discussions which prove the suspicions conceived by the National Party, and the concealed intentions of the Administration.

"A crowd of women collected at Bellevue to oppose the setting out of Mesdames. On their arrival at the château they were told that Mesdames were no longer there, and they were gone with a suite of twenty persons. The intelligence of this departure caused a great ferment at the Palais Royal. All the clubs who were apprised of it gave orders to the leaders to put the light troops in motion. The department of Seine and Oise came to a resolution that there were no grounds for retaining the property of the Princesses. The municipality of Versailles was charged to require the commandant of the National Guard and the troops of the line to aid and assist. It was to have an understanding with the municipalities of Sèvres and Meudon to put down all obstacles.

"General Berthier justified the monarch's confidence by a firm and prudent line of conduct, which entitled him to the highest military honours and to the esteem of the warrior whose fortune, dangers and glory he afterwards shared. He went to Bellevue at midnight of the very day on which the order was made. As soon as the municipalities of Sèvres and Meudon were informed of his arrival at the château, they both came to a resolution by which they left the General full liberty to

leave of Madame Victoire. I little thought that I was then seeing that august and virtuous protectress of my earliest youth for the last time in my life. She received me alone in her closet, and assured me that she hoped and wished to return to France very soon; that the French would be much to be pitied if the excesses of the Revolution should arrive at such a pitch as to force her to prolong her absence. I knew from the Queen that the departure of Mesdames was deemed necessary, in order to leave the King free to act when he should be compelled to go away with his family. It being impossible that the Constitution of the Clergy should be otherwise than in direct opposition to the religious principles of Mesdames, they thought that their journey to Rome would be attributed to piety alone. It was, however, difficult to deceive an Assembly which would, of course, weigh the slightest

---

act for the department; but in order to leave their own sentiments relative to Mesdames uncertain, these two municipalities made the arrangement which provided that no search should be made in either the château or its dependencies.

"The posts were relieved quietly enough, but when it was necessary to send off the carriages, murmurs broke out and violent resistance was made. Part of the armed force, and the unarmed mob, declared that Mesdames should not go, and uttered horrible imprecations against those Princesses. A sapper of the National Guard of Sèvres, an officer of the same guard and an officer of chasseurs distinguished themselves by formal and obstinate disobedience. Several gunners, instead of keeping the refractory in awe by remaining at their guns, cut the traces of one of the carriages. Such was the impotence of the laws that General Berthier, although invested with full powers by reiterated acts of the departments and municipalities of Versailles and Meudon, could not send off the equipages. This officer, full of honour and gifted with the highest courage, was shut into the courtyard of Bellevue by his own troop, and ran great risk of being murdered. It was not until the 14th of March that he succeeded in executing the law. Further on may be seen what obstacles he had to overcome, and to what dangers he was exposed. He was indebted to his coolness for his preservation, and he contrived to prevent the carnage which he might have made of the factious." *Vide* the note of the following page and the explanation under letter (H). ("Memoirs of Mesdames," by Montigny, vol. i.)—NOTE BY THE EDITOR.

actions of the Royal Family, and from that moment they were more than ever alive to what was passing at the Tuileries.

Mesdames were desirous of taking Madame Elizabeth to Rome. The free exercise of religion, the happiness of taking refuge with the head of the Church and living in safety with her aunt, whom she tenderly loved—all was sacrificed by that virtuous Princess to her attachment to the King's person.[1]

The oath required of priests by the Civil Constitution of the Clergy introduced a division into France which added to the multiplied dangers by which the King was already surrounded. Mirabeau spent a whole night with the Curé de Saint-Eustache, confessor of the King and Queen, to persuade him to take the oath required by that Constitution. Their Majesties chose another confessor, who remained unknown.

---

[1] The *Chronique de Paris*, a newspaper written under the influence of the Constitutional party, contained the following article on the departure of Mesdames:

"Two Princesses, sedentary from condition, age and choice, find themselves all on a sudden seized with a mania for travelling and running all over the world. '*Tis odd, but 'tis possible*. They are going, it is said, to kiss the Pope's toe—*comical*, but *edifying*.

"Thirty-two sections, and all good citizens, interpose between them and Rome. *That's of course*.

"Mesdames, and particularly Madame Adelaide, wish to enjoy the rights of man. '*Tis natural*.

"They do not go, they say, with intentions hostile to the Revolution. *Possible*, but *doubtful*.

"These fair travellers take eighty persons in their suite—'*tis pretty;* but they carry off twelve millions—*very ugly*.

"They want change of air—*that's common enough*. But their removal makes their creditors uneasy—*that's common enough also*.

"They burn to travel (a maid's desire is a consuming fire)—*of course*. Others burn to stop them—*of course, too*.

"Mesdames insist that they are free to go wherever they please. '*Tis true*."—NOTE BY THE EDITOR.

A few months afterwards the too celebrated Mirabeau, the mercenary democrat and venal Royalist, terminated his career. The Queen regretted him, and was herself astonished when she spoke of her regret; but she had hoped that he who had possessed adroitness and weight enough to throw everything into confusion would have been able, by the same means, to repair the mischief caused by his fatal genius. Much has been said respecting the cause of Mirabeau's death. M. Cabanis, his friend and physician, denied that he was poisoned. I heard what follows said to the Queen by M. Vicq-d'Azyr the very day on which the body was opened. That gentleman assured her that the *procès-verbal* drawn up on the state of the intestines would apply just as well to a case of death produced by violent remedies as to one produced by poison. He said also that the professional people had been faithful in their report; but that it was more prudent to conclude it by a declaration of natural death, since, in the critical state in which France then was, a person innocent of any such crime might be sacrificed to public vengeance.

CHAPTER VII

Preparations for the journey to Varennes—The Queen watched and betrayed—Madame Campan's departure for Auvergne precedes that of the Royal Family for Versailles—Madame Campan hears of the King's arrest—Note written to her by the Queen immediately upon her return to Paris—Anecdotes—Measures taken for keeping the King at the Tuileries—The Queen's hair turns white from grief—Barnave gains the esteem and confidence of Marie Antoinette during the return from Versailles—His honourable and respectful conduct: she contrasts it with that of Pétion—Anecdote honourable to Barnave—His advice to the Queen—Particulars respecting the Varennes journey.

IN the beginning of the spring of 1791 the King, tired of remaining at the Tuileries, wished to return to St. Cloud. His whole household was gone, and his dinner was prepared there. He got into his carriage at one; the guard mutinied, shut the gates, and declared they would not let him pass. This event certainly proceeded from some appearances of a plan for an escape. Two persons who drew near the King's carriage were very ill treated. My father-in-law was violently laid hold of by the guards, who took his sword from him. The King and his family were obliged to alight and return to their apartments. They did not much regret this outrage in their hearts; they saw in it a justification, even in the eyes of the people, of their intentions to leave Paris.

So early as the month of March, in the same year,

the Queen began to busy herself in preparing for her departure. I spent that month with her, and executed a great number of secret orders which she gave me respecting the intended event. It was with uneasiness that I saw her thus occupied with cares which seemed to me useless and even dangerous, and I remarked to her that the Queen of France would find linen and gowns everywhere. My observations were made in vain: she determined to have a complete wardrobe with her at Brussels, as well for her children as herself. I went out alone, and almost disguised, to purchase the articles necessary and have them made up.

I ordered six chemises at the shop of one seamstress, six at that of another, gowns, combing cloths, &c. My sister had a complete set of clothes made for Madame by the measure of her eldest daughter, and I ordered clothes for the Dauphin from those of my son. I filled a mail-trunk with these things, and addressed them by the Queen's orders to one of her women, the widow of the Mayor of Arras, where she lived, by virtue of an unlimited leave of absence, in order that she might be ready to start for Brussels, or any other place, as soon as she should be directed to do so. This lady had landed property in Austrian Flanders, and could at any time quit Arras unobserved.

The Queen was to take only her first woman in attendance with her from Paris. She apprised me that if I should not be on duty at the moment of departure she would make arrangements for my joining her. She determined also to take with her

her travelling dressing-case. She consulted me upon her idea of sending it off, under pretence of making a present of it to the Archduchess Christina, Governante of the Low Countries. I ventured to oppose this plan strongly, and observed to her that, amidst so many people who watched her slightest actions, it might reasonably be foreseen that there would be found a sufficient number sharp-sighted enough to discover that the word "present" was used only as a pretence for sending away the property in question before her departure. She persisted in her intention, and all I could obtain was that the dressing-case should not be removed from her apartment, and a consent that M. de ——, *chargé d'affaires* from the Court of Vienna during the absence of the Count de Mercy, should come and ask her at her toilette, before all her people, to order one exactly like her own for the Governante of the Low Countries. The Queen therefore commanded me, before the *chargé d'affaires*, to order the article in question. This way of putting her intention in execution occasioned only the slight inconvenience of an expense of 500 louis, and appeared calculated to lull suspicion completely. If I omit no circumstance concerning this dressing-case it is because these minute details are important, since the early preparations for the journey were discovered by a woman whose conduct I had long suspected, and who I dreaded would give information of them. This was a woman belonging to the wardrobe; her duty continued uninterrupted throughout the year. As she had been placed with the Queen at the time of her marriage, Her Majesty was accustomed to see her, and was pleased with her address and intelligence. Her situation was above that to which a woman of her class was entitled; her salary and emoluments had been gradually increased until they afforded her an income of about 12,000 francs. She was handsome; she received in her apartments above the Queen's, in the little rooms between the two floors, several deputies of the Tiers Etat; and she had M. de Gouvion, an aide-de-camp of M. de la Fayette, for her lover. We shall soon see how far she carried her ingratitude.

About the middle of May, 1791, a month after the Queen had ordered me to bespeak the dressing-case, she asked me whether it would soon be finished. I sent for the ivory-turner who had it in hand. He could not complete it until the end of six weeks. I informed the Queen of this, and she told me she should not be able to wait for it, as she was to set out in the course of June. She added that as she had ordered her sister's dressing-case in the presence of all her attendants, she had taken a sufficient precaution, especially in saying that her sister was out of patience at not receiving it, and that therefore her own must be emptied and cleaned and taken to the *chargé d'affaires*, who would send it off. I executed this order without appearing to conceal it by the slightest mystery. I desired the wardrobe woman to take out of the dressing-case all that it contained, because that intended for the Archduchess could not be finished for some time, and to take great care to leave no remains of the perfumes, which might not suit that Princess. I will anticipate the order of events to show that all these precautions were no less useless than dangerous.

After the return from Varennes the Mayor of Paris put into the Queen's hands an information by the wardrobe woman, dated the 21st of May, in which she declared that preparations were making at the Tuileries for departure; that it was supposed she would not guess the true reason for the dressing-case being sent from the Queen to Brussels, but that the mention of a present made by Her Majesty to her sister was but a mere pretence; that Her Majesty liked the article in question too well to deprive herself of it, and that she had often said it would be highly useful to her in case she should have a journey to perform. She declared also that I was shut up a whole evening with the Queen busied in packing her diamonds; and that she had found them separated with cotton upon the sofa in the Queen's closet at the Tuileries. From this information the Queen concluded that this woman had, unknown to her, a duplicate key to the closet. Her Majesty did one evening, it is true, break off the arranging of her diamonds at seven o'clock to go to the card-table, and took the key of her closet, saying that she would come the next day and finish packing with me, that there was a sentinel under the window, that she had the key of her closet in her pocket, and therefore saw no danger of her jewels being stolen. It must then have been in the evening after we left the closet, or very early the next morning, that the wretch discovered the secret preparations. The box of diamonds was placed in the hands of Leonard, the Queen's hairdresser,[1] who went away with the Duke de Choiseul, and the deposit was left at Brussels. Their Majesties had already delivered up the Crown diamonds which they had in use to the commissioners of the Assembly; those which the Queen sent out of France belonged to her in her own right.

It was during these preparations for departure that the Queen told me she had a very precious charge to entrust to me, and that I must find out some person who could be relied upon in an independent situation of life, and entirely devoted to their Sovereigns, to whom I should confide a portfolio that she would place in my hands. I pitched upon Madame Valayer Coster, a member of the Academy of Painting, who lodged in the galleries of the Louvre, and in whom, as well as in her husband, I knew that all the qualifications required by the Queen were to be found. They proved as faithful as I had foretold they would be. It was not until September, 1791, after the acceptance of the Constitution, that they returned the portfolio to me. The guilty woman, of whom I have had but too much to say, made her communications respecting this fact also. She said she had seen a portfolio upon a chair, where there was not usually one placed; that the Queen, pointing to it, spoke to me in a whisper, and that it had disappeared from that time. M. Bailly, who sent two whole pages of these denunciations to

---

[1] This unfortunate man, after having emigrated for some time, returned to France and perished upon the scaffold.—NOTE BY THE EDITOR.

the Queen, made no use of them which could possibly be injurious to Her Majesty.

Madame the Duchess d'Angoulême must have come into possession of all the Queen's diamonds. Her Majesty retained nothing but a suite of pearls and a pair of earrings, composed of a ring and two drops, each formed of a single diamond. These earrings and several fancy trinkets, which were not worth the trouble of packing up, remained in Her Majesty's cabinet at the Tuileries, and were, of course, seized by the committee which took possession of the palace on the 10th of August.

After having made the preparations of which I have spoken, I had yet many private commissions, all relative to the departure, to fulfil. I was myself upon the eve of quitting Paris with my father-in-law. The Queen, apprehensive of the excesses in which the people might indulge at the moment of her flight against those whose attachment to her person was known, being unwilling that he should remain in the capital, desired M. Vicq-d'Azyr to prescribe the waters of Mont-d'Or for him. Her Majesty had also the goodness to regret that my situation about her did not admit of my going away with her, and she offered me five hundred louis for the journey I had to take, until the time when I should rejoin her. I had as much money as was necessary for myself, and I knew besides of how much consequence it was to her to keep as much as possible. I therefore did not accept them. As for the rest, she assured me that the King was only going to the frontiers, there to treat with the Assembly, and would quit France only in case his plan and proposals did not produce the effect hoped for. She relied upon a numerous party in the Assembly, many of the members of which, she said, were cured of their first enthusiasm. I set off therefore on the 1st of June, and on the 6th reached Mont d'Or, daily expecting to hear of the departure. At length the news arrived. I had already prepared what I thought would make my escape certain; but the steps taken by the Assembly after the departure of Their Majesties would have rendered that escape more difficult than the Queen had thought. I was ready to begin my journey when I heard a courier, who came from the little town of Besse, shouting to the inhabitants of Mont d'Or, with transports of joy, that the King and Queen were stopped.[1] That same evening the intelligence was confirmed, and two days afterwards we received a letter from the Queen, written under her dictation by one of her gentlemen ushers,[2] whose devotion and discretion were known to her. It contained these words: "I dictate from my bath, into which I have just thrown myself, to support, at least, my physical strength. I can say nothing of the state of my mind; we exist, that is all. Do not return here, excepting upon the receipt of a letter from myself; this is very important." This letter, unsigned, bore date the day of the Queen's arrival at Paris. We recognised the hand of him who wrote it, and were much affected at seeing that at such a

---

[1] See further on the note at page 133. See also among the *Illustrations* furnished by Madame Campan (No. 3).—NOTE BY THE EDITOR.

[2] This officer was massacred in the Queen's chamber on the 10th of August, 1792.—NOTE BY MADAME CAMPAN.

moment the unfortunate Princess had deigned to think of us. After the receipt of this letter I returned to Clermont, where the Assembly's committee *de surveillance* would have had us arrested; but as it was proved that M. Campan was really ill at the moment of his departure from Paris, that rigorous course was waived. In the early part of August the Queen desired me to return to Paris, writing word that she did not see there was any further danger in my going there, and that my speedy return would be agreeable to her. I therefore cannot give any other particulars of Their Majesties' flight than those which I have heard related by the Queen and those persons who witnessed her return home.

When the Royal Family were brought back from Varennes to the Tuileries the Queen's attendants found the greatest difficulty in making their way to her apartments. Everything had been arranged so that the wardrobe woman, who had acted as spy, should alone have the duty, and she was to be assisted in it by her sister and her sister's daughter.

M. de Gouvion, M. de la Fayette's aide-de-camp, had this woman's portrait placed at the foot of the staircase which led to the Queen's apartments, in order that the sentinel should not permit any other women to make their way in. As soon as the Queen was informed of this pitiful precaution she informed the King of it, who, not being able to credit it, sent to the bottom of the staircase to ascertain the fact. His Majesty then called for M. de la Fayette, claimed freedom in his household, and particularly in that of the Queen, and ordered him to send a woman in whom no one but himself could confide out of the palace. M. de la Fayette was obliged to comply.[1]

The measures adopted for guarding the King were at the same time rigorous with respect to the entrance into the palace and insulting as to his household. The commandants of battalion stationed in the saloon called the Grand Cabinet, which led to the Queen's bedchamber, were ordered to keep the door of it always open in order that they might have their eyes upon the Royal Family. The King shut this door one day; the officer of the guard opened it, and told him such were his orders and that he would always open it, so that His Majesty in shutting it gave himself useless trouble. It remained open even during the

---

[1] The orders by which all the women attached to the Queen's service were kept out were broken by the people in a manner which is an instance of those sudden changes which striking circumstances never fail to effect in mobs. On the day when the return of the unfortunate travellers was expected, there were no carriages in motion in the streets of Paris. Five or six of the Queen's women, after being refused admittance at all the other gates, went with one of my sisters, who had the honour to be attached to Her Majesty, to that of the Feuillans, earnestly insisting that the sentinel should admit them. The *poissardes* attacked them for their boldness in resisting the orders. One of them seized my sister by the arm, calling her slave of the Austrian. "Hear me," said my sister to her firmly and in the true accent of the feeling which inspired her; "I have been attached to the Queen ever since I was fifteen years of age; she portioned me and married me. I served her when she was powerful and happy. She is now unfortunate! Ought I to abandon her?" "She is right," cried these furies; "she ought not to abandon her mistress; let us make a passage for them." They instantly surrounded the sentinel, forced the passage, and introduced the Queen's women accompanying them to the terrace of the Feuillans. One of these furies, whom the slightest impulse would have driven to tear my sister to pieces, then taking her under her protection, gave her some advice by which she might reach the palace in safety. "But of all things, my dear friend," said she to her, "pull off that green sash; it is the sash of that D'Artois whom we will never forgive."—NOTE BY MADAME CAMPAN.

night, when the Queen was in bed; and the officer placed himself in an arm-chair between the two doors with his head turned towards Her Majesty. They only obtained permission to have the inner door shut when the Queen was rising and dressing. The Queen had the bed of her first *femme de chambre* placed very near her own; this bed, which ran on castors and was furnished with curtains, hid her from the officer's sight.

Madame de Jarjaye, my companion, who continued her functions during the whole period of my absence, told me that one night the commandant of battalion, who slept between the two doors, seeing that she was sleeping soundly and that the Queen was awake, quitted his post and went close to Her Majesty to advise her as to the line of conduct she was to pursue. Although she had the kindness to desire him to speak lower in order that he might not disturb Madame de Jarjaye's rest, the latter awoke and was near dying with the shock of seeing a man in the uniform of the Parisian guard so near the Queen's bed. Her Majesty confronted her and told her not to rise; that the person she saw was a good Frenchman, who was deceived respecting the intentions and situation of his Sovereign and herself, but whose conversation showed a sincere attachment to the King. There was a sentinel in the black corridor which runs behind the apartments in question, where there is a staircase, which was at that time a private one, and enabled the King and Queen to communicate freely. This post, which was very disagreeable because it was to be kept four-and-twenty hours, was often claimed by Saint-Prix, an actor belonging to the French theatre. He devoted himself to it, if I may use the expression, in order to facilitate short interviews between the King and Queen in this corridor. He used to leave them at a distance and give them notice if he heard the slightest noise. M. Collot, commandant of battalion of the National Guard, who was charged with the military duty of the Queen's household, in like manner softened down as far as he could with prudence all the harsh orders he received; for instance, one to follow the Queen to the very door of her wardrobe was never executed. An officer of the Parisian guard daring to speak insolently to the Queen in her own apartment, M. Collot wished to make a complaint to M. de la Fayette against him and have him removed. The Queen opposed it, and condescended to say a few words of explanation and kindness to the man; he instantly became one of her most devoted partisans.

The first time I saw Her Majesty after the unfortunate catastrophe of the Varennes journey I found her getting out of bed. Her features were not very much altered, but after the first kind words she uttered to me she took off her cap and desired me to observe the effect which grief had produced upon her hair. It became in one single night as white as that of a woman of seventy. I will not here describe the feelings which lacerated my heart. To speak of my own troubles would be quite out of place when I am retracing those of so exalted an unfortunate. Her Majesty showed me a ring she had just had mounted for the Princess de Lamballe. It contained a lock of her whitened hair with the inscription, "Bleached by sorrow." At the period of the acceptance of the Constitution the Princess wished to return to France. The Queen, who had no expectation that tranquillity would be restored, opposed this, but the attachment which Madame de Lamballe had vowed impelled her to come and tempt her own destruction.

When I returned to Paris most of the harsh precautions were abandoned. The doors were kept open, greater respect was paid to the Sovereign. It was known that the Constitution soon to be completed would be accepted, and a better order of things was hoped for.

On the day of my arrival the Queen took me into her closet to tell me that she should have great need of me in a communication she had established with Barnave, Duport and Alexandre Lameth. She informed me that M. de J——[1] was her negotiator with those remnants of the Constitutional party who had good intentions, but unfortunately too late, and told me that Barnave was a man worthy of esteem. I was astonished to hear Barnave's name pronounced with so much goodwill. When I quitted Paris a great number of persons spoke of him only with horror. I observed this to her, and she was not surprised at it, but told me he was much altered; that the young man, who was full of talent and noble feeling, belonged to that class which is distinguished by education, and was merely misled by the ambition to which

---

[1] It was the Queen who ordered M. de J—— to see to those three deputies.—NOTE BY MADAME CAMPAN.

real merit gave birth. "A feeling of pride which I cannot much blame in a young man belonging to the Tiers Etat," said the Queen, speaking of Barnave, "made him support everything which smoothed the road to rank and fame for the class in which he was born, and if we get the power into our own hands again, Barnave's pardon is beforehand written in our hearts." The Queen added that she had not the same feeling towards those Nobles who had thrown themselves into the revolutionary party, they who obtained all the marks of favour, and that very often to the injury of those of an inferior order among whom the greatest talent was to be found; in short, that the Nobles, who were born to be the safeguard of the monarchy, were too guilty in having betrayed its cause ever to obtain their pardon. The Queen astonished me more and more by the warmth with which she justified the favourable opinion she had formed of Barnave. She then told me that his conduct upon the road was perfectly correct, while Pétion's republican rudeness was disgusting; that the latter ate and drank in the King's berlin in a slovenly manner, throwing the bones of the fowls out through the window at the risk of sending them even into the King's face, lifting up his glass when Madame Elizabeth poured him out wine to show her that there was enough without saying a word; that this offensive behaviour must have been by design, because the man was not without education; and that Barnave was hurt at it. On being pressed by the Queen to take something, "Madam," replied Barnave, "on so solemn an occasion the deputies of the National

Assembly ought to engage Your Majesty's attention solely by their mission and by no means about their wants." In short, his respectful delicacy, his considerate attentions and all that he uttered gained the esteem not only of the Queen but of Madame Elizabeth also.

The King began to talk to Pétion about the situation of France and the motives of his conduct, which were founded upon the necessity of giving to the executive power a strength necessary for its action—for the good even of the Constitutional Act—since France could not be a Republic. "Not yet, 'tis true." replied Pétion, "because the French are not ripe enough for that." This audacious and cruel answer silenced the King, who said no more until his arrival at Paris. Pétion held the little Dauphin upon his knees and amused himself with curling the beautiful light hair of the interesting child round his fingers, and as he spoke with much gesticulation he pulled his locks hard enough to make the Dauphin cry out. "Give me my son," said the Queen to him, "he is accustomed to tenderness and delicacy, which render him little fit for such familiarity."

The Chevalier de Dampierre was killed near the King's carriage upon leaving Varennes. A poor village Curé, some leagues from the place where the crime was committed, was imprudent enough to draw near to speak to the King. The cannibals who surrounded the carriage rushed upon him. "Tigers," exclaimed Barnave, "have you ceased to be Frenchmen? Nation of brave men, are you become a set of assassins?" These words alone saved the Curé, who was already upon the ground, from certain death. Barnave as he spoke to them threw himself almost out of the coach window, and Madame Elizabeth, affected by this noble burst of feeling, held him by the skirt of his coat. The Queen while speaking of this event said that in the most important and momentous events whimsical contrasts always struck her, and that on this occasion the pious Elizabeth holding Barnave by the flap of his coat was a surprising sight. The deputy was astonished in another way. Madame Elizabeth's comments upon the state of France, her mild and persuasive eloquence and the noble simplicity with which she talked to him, at the same time without sacrificing her dignity in the slightest degree; indeed, everything about that divine Princess appeared to him celestial, and his heart, which was doubtless inclined to right principles if he had not followed the wrong path, was overcome by the most affecting admiration. The conduct of the two deputies convinced the Queen of the total separation between the Republican and Constitutional parties. At the inns where she alighted she had some private conversation with Barnave. The latter said a great deal about the errors committed by the Royalists during the Revolution, and declared he had found the interests of the Court so feeble and so badly defended that he had been frequently tempted to go and offer it, in himself, a courageous wrestler who knew the spirit of the age and nation. The Queen asked him what were the weapons he would have recommended her to use. "Popularity, madam." "And how could I use that," replied Her Majesty, "of which I had been deprived?" "Ah, madam, it was much more easy for you to regain it than for me to acquire it." This assertion would furnish matter for comment; I confine myself to the relation of this curious conversation.

The Queen mainly attributed the arrest at Varennes to M. Goguelat. She said he calculated the time that would be spent in the journey erroneously. He performed that from Montmédy to Paris, before taking the King's last orders, alone in a postchaise, and he founded all his calculations upon the time he spent in making that transit. The trial has been made since, and it was found that a light carriage without any courier was nearly three hours less in running the distance than a heavy carriage preceded by a courier.

The Queen also blamed him for having quitted the high road at Pont-de-Sommevelle, where the carriage was to meet the forty hussars commanded by him. She thought that he ought to have dispersed the very small number of people at Varennes, and not to have asked the hussars whether they were for the King or the nation; that particularly he ought to have avoided taking the King's orders, as he was aware of the reply M. d'Inisdal had received when it was proposed to carry off the King; and that the King having said to Goguelat, "If force should be employed will it be hot work?" he answered, "Very hot, Sire!" which was sufficient to drive the King to give twenty counter orders. Is it possible to conceive how such neglect could occur as that of sending a courier to M. de Bouillé, who would have had time to reach Varennes with an imposing force? or how nobody even thought of stopping the courier who should follow the King? Their Majesties alighted at the house of a grocer called M. Sauce, the Mayor of Varennes. The King talked to him a long time respecting his reasons for quitting Paris, and wanted to prove to him the expediency of the measure, which, far from being hostile, was suggested by his love for his subjects. This mayor could have saved the King. The Queen sat down in the shop between two piles of candles, and conversed with Madame Sauce, who seemed to be a woman of weight in her own household, and whom M. Sauce eyed, from time to time, as if to consult her; but the only reply the Queen got was, "What would you have, madam? Your situation is very unfortunate; but, you see, that would expose M. Sauce; they would cut his head off. A wife ought to think of her husband." "Well," replied the Queen, "mine is your King! He has long made you happy, and wishes to do so still." Madame Sauce went on again about the dangers of her husband: the aides-de-camp came up, and the return to Paris was decided.

The Dauphin's first *femme de chambre*, calculating that delay might give M. de Bouillé time to bring up assistance, threw herself on a bed, and began to cry out that she was dying of a dreadful colic. The Queen came up to her, and the lady squeezed her hand to give her to understand what she was aiming at. Her Majesty said she could not leave a woman who had sacrificed herself to attend her in a dangerous journey in such a condition, and that she owed her every attention; but this innocent stratagem was probably seen through, and not the slightest delay was granted.[1]

After all that the Queen had said to me respecting the mistakes made by M. Goguelat, I thought him of course disgraced. What was my surprise when, having been set at liberty after the amnesty which followed the acceptance of the Constitution, he presented himself to the Queen, and was received with marks of the greatest kindness. She said he had done his best, and that the sincerity of his zeal ought to form an excuse for all the rest.[2]

---

[1] The Queen informed me, whilst summing up all the events of that ill-omened journey, that at two leagues from Varennes, a stranger passed close to the King's carriage, full gallop, uttering aloud some words which the noise of the wheels upon the pavement prevented their hearing; but that subsequently to their arrest the King and herself, recalling the sound of the stranger's words, were almost certain that he had said to them, "You are known," or "You are discovered!"—NOTE BY MADAME CAMPAN.

[2] We have seen, at page 21 of this volume, that Madame Campan related the affair of the necklace twice, and that the two narratives, although essentially the same, differed in the nature and interest of the circumstances detailed. There are, in like manner, among her manuscripts, two accounts of the Varennes journey. The narrative, which we place among the *Illustrations* (No. 3), contains particulars relative to the preparation for the departure, the espionage to which the Queen was subjected, the value and richness of her jewels, the noble pride which she displayed at the moment of the arrest upon the journey and during the return, which we ought to preserve for history: they are materials for forming a judgment. We will add that these minute accounts of places, persons and the slightest circumstances form one of the greatest attractions of the Memoirs, and that they will be found less correct, perhaps, but in greater abundance, in the second version, which the reader may consult.—NOTE BY THE EDITOR.

CHAPTER VIII

Acceptance of the Constitution—Opinion of Barnave and his friends approved of by the Court of Vienna—Secret policy of the Court—The Legislative Assembly deliberates upon the ceremony to be observed on receiving the King—Offensive motion—Louis XVI. is received by the Assembly with transport—He gives way to profound grief when with his family—Public *fêtes* and rejoicings—M. de Montmorin's conversation with Madame Campan upon the continual indiscretions of the people about the Court—The Royal Family go to the Théâtre Français—Play changed—Personal conflicts in the pit of the Italiens—Double correspondence of the Court with foreign Powers—Maison Civile—Method adopted by the Queen respecting her secret correspondence—Madame Campan's conduct when attacked by both parties—Particulars respecting the conduct of M. Genet, her brother, *chargé d'affaires* from France to Russia—Written testimony of the Queen in favour of Madame Campan's zeal and fidelity—The King comes to see her and confirms these marks of confidence and satisfaction—Projected interview between Louis XVI. and Barnave—Attempts to poison Louis XVI.—Precautions taken—The Queen consults Pitt about the Revolution—His reply—The émigrés oppose all alliance with the Constitutionals—Letter from Barnave to the Queen.

On my arrival at Paris on the 25th of August I found the state of feeling there much more temperate than I had dared to hope; the conversation generally ran upon the acceptance of the Constitution and the *fêtes* which would be given in consequence. The Queen began to hope affairs would take a better turn. The struggle between the Jacobins and the Constitutionals on the 17th of July, 1791, nevertheless had thrown her into great terror for some moments; and the firing of the cannon from the Champ de Mars, upon a party which called for the trial of the King, and the leaders of which were in the very bosom of the Assembly, left the most gloomy impressions upon the Queen's mind.

The Constitutionals, with whom her connection was not slackened by the intervention of the three members already mentioned, had faithfully served the Royal Family during their detention.

"We hold the wire by which this popular mass is moved," said Barnave to M. de S—— one day, at the same time showing him a large volume in which the names of all those who were made to act at will by the power of gold alone were registered. It was at that time proposed to hire a considerable number of persons in order to secure loud acclamations when the King and his family should make their appearance at the play, upon the acceptance of the Constitution. That day, which afforded a glimmering hope of tranquillity, was the 14th of September. The *fêtes* were brilliant, but already new alarms too imperiously forbade the Royal Family to give way to any consolatory feeling.

The Legislative Assembly which had just succeeded the Constitutional Assembly founded their conduct upon the wildest Republican principles. Created from the midst of popular societies, it was wholly inspired by the spirit which animated them. The Constitution, as I have said, was presented to the King on the 30th of September. I return to this presentation, because it gave rise to a highly-important subject of discussion. All the ministers, with the exception of M. de Montmorin, insisted upon the necessity of accepting the Constitutional Act in all its parts. The Prince de Kaunitz was likewise of the same opinion. Malouet wished the King to express himself candidly respecting any errors or dangers that he might observe in the Constitution. But Duport and Barnave, alarmed at the spirit prevailing in the Jacobin Club and even in the Assembly, where Robespierre had already denounced them as traitors to the country, and dreading still greater evils, added their opinions to those of the majority of the ministers and M. de Kaunitz. Those who really desired that the Constitution should be maintained advised that it should not be accepted thus purely and simply; and of this number, as I have already said, were M. Montmorin and M. Malouet. The King seemed inclined to this advice, and this is one of the strongest proofs of the unfortunate monarch's sincerity.[1]

---

[1] In order to confirm the opinion Madame Campan expressed above respecting the intentions of Louis XVI., we think we ought to present the account given by Bertrand de Molleville of his first interview with that Prince.

"As it was the first time I ever had the honour of being so close to him and *tête-à-tête* with him, the most stupid diffidence so completely came over me that, if it had been my duty to speak first, it would have been impossible for me to have framed a single phrase; but I took courage when I saw the King still more embarrassed than myself, and with difficulty stammering out a few unconnected words. He in his turn became composed on seeing me at ease, and our conversation soon became highly interesting.

"After a few general observations upon the perplexities of the existing state of things, the King said to me, 'Well, have you any objection remaining?' 'No, Sire; a desire to obey and gratify Your Majesty is the only feeling I am sensible of; but in order that I may really be able to serve you, it is necessary that Your Majesty should have the goodness to inform me what is your intention with regard to the Constitution, and what is the line of conduct you would wish your Ministers to adopt.' 'That is true,' replied the King; 'this is my opinion. I do not consider the Constitution by any means a masterpiece. I think there are very great errors in it, and if I had been at liberty to comment upon it advantageous alterations would

Alexandre Lameth, Duport and Barnave, still relying on the resources of their party, hoped to have credit for controlling the King through the influence they believed they had acquired over the mind of the Queen. They also consulted people of acknowledged talent, but belonging to no council nor to any assembly. Among these was M. Dubucq, formerly Intendant of the Marine and the Colonies. He answered in one line: "Prevent disorder from organising itself."

Opinions such as those of the sententious and laconic M. Dubucq emanated from the aristocratic party, who preferred anything, even the Jacobins, to the establishment of the Constitutional laws; and who,

---

have been made in it. But the time is now gone by. Such as it is, I have sworn to maintain it; I ought to be, and I will be, strictly true to my oath, and the rather as I think the utmost exactness in executing the mandates of the Constitution is the most certain way to draw the attention of the nation to the alterations that ought to be made in it. I neither can nor ought to have any other object than this. I certainly will not abandon my intention, and I wish my Ministers to forward it.' 'Your scheme appears infinitely judicious, Sire. I feel myself in a condition to accomplish it, and I engage to do so. I have not sufficiently studied the Constitution as a whole, and in all its parts, to form a decided opinion, and I will refrain from forming one until the operation of the Constitution shall have enabled the nation to estimate it by its effects. But may I venture to ask Your Majesty whether the Queen's opinion upon this point is in accordance with your own?' 'Yes, certainly it is; she will tell you so herself.' I immediately went to the Queen, who, after assuring me, with the greatest kindness, how truly she felt the obligation under which the King lay to me for having accepted the administration in so perplexing a juncture, added, 'The King has informed you of his views with regard to the Constitution: do you not think the only way is to be faithful to the oath?' 'Yes, certainly, madam.' 'Well, then, be assured that we shall not be induced to swerve. Courage, M. Bertrand. I hope that, with patience, firmness and consistency, all is not yet lost.'" ("Private Memoirs of the Latter End of the Reign of Louis XVI.," by M. Bertrand de Molleville, Minister and Secretary of State under that Reign, vol. i., pp. 101-103.)—NOTE BY THE EDITOR.

in fact, believed that any acceptance which should have any other appearance than that of compulsion would amount to a real sanction, sufficient to uphold the new Government. The most unbridled disorders seemed preferable, because they buoyed up the hope of a total change; and twenty times over, upon occasions when persons but little acquainted with the secret policy of the Court expressed the apprehensions they entertained of the popular societies, the initiated answered that a sincere Royalist ought to favour the Jacobins. My avowal of the terror with which they inspired me often brought this answer upon me, and must even have often procured me the epithet of "Constitutional"! while all the time, through principle, and from the want of that sort of information which I think ought never to be found among persons of my sex, I was intent only upon diligently serving the unfortunate Princess with whom my destiny was united.

The letter written by the King to the Assembly, claiming to accept the Constitution in the very place where it had been created, and where he announced he would be on the 14th at midday, was received with transport, and the reading of it was repeatedly interrupted by very general plaudits. The sitting was terminated by the highest flight of enthusiasm, and M. de la Fayette obtained the release of all those who were detained on account of the King's departure, the immediate quashing of all proceedings relative to the events of the Revolution, and the discontinuance of the use of passports and of all temporary restraints upon free travelling, as well in the interior as without.

The whole was conceded by acclamation. Sixty members were deputed to go to the King and express to him fully the satisfaction His Majesty's letter had given. The Keeper of the Seals quitted the chamber in the midst of applause to precede the deputation to the King.

The King answered the speech addressed to him, and concluded by saying to the Assembly that a decree of that morning, which had abolished the Order of the Holy Ghost, had left him and his son alone permission to be decorated with it; but as an Order had no value in his eyes save for the power of conferring it, he would not use it.

The Queen, her son and Madame were at the door of the chamber into which the deputation was admitted. The King said to the deputies, "You see there my wife and children, who participate in my sentiments;" and the Queen herself confirmed the King's assurance. These apparent marks of confidence were very inconsistent with the agitated state of her mind. "These people will have no Sovereigns," said she. "We shall fall before their treacherous though well-planned tactics; they are demolishing the monarchy stone by stone."

On the day after that of the deputation the particulars of their reception by the King were reported to the Assembly, and they excited warm approbation. But the President, having put the question, whether the Assembly ought not to remain seated while the King took the oath, "Certainly," was repeated by many voices; "*and the King, standing, uncovered.*" M. Malouet observed that there was no occasion on which the nation, assembled in the presence of the King, did not acknowledge him as its head; that the omission to treat the head of the State with the respect due to him would be an offence to the nation as well as to the monarch. He moved that the King should take the oath standing, and that the Assembly should be in the same posture while he was doing so. M. Malouet's observations would have carried the decree, but a deputy from Brittany exclaimed with a shrill voice that he "had an amendment to propose, which would render all unanimous. Let us decree," said he, "that M. Malouet, and whoever else shall so please, may have leave to receive the King upon their knees, but let us stick to the decree."

The King repaired to the chamber at midday. His speech was followed by plaudits which lasted several minutes. After the signing of the Constitutional Act all sat down. The President rose to deliver his speech, but after he had begun, perceiving that the King did not rise to hear him, he sat down again. His speech made a powerful impression; the sentence with which it concluded excited fresh acclamations, cries of "Bravo!" and "Vive le Roi!" "Sire," said he, "how important in our eyes, and how dear to our hearts, how sublime a feature in our history, must be the epoch of that regeneration which gives citizens to France and a country to Frenchmen—to you, as a King, a new title of greatness and glory, and, as a man, a fresh source of enjoyment and of new feelings."

At length I hoped to see a return of that tranquillity which had so long been chased from the countenances of my august master and mistress. Their suite left them in the saloon; the Queen hastily saluted the ladies and returned much affected. The King followed her, and, throwing himself into an arm-chair, put his handkerchief to his eyes. "Ah, madam," cried he, his voice choked by his tears, "why were you present at this sitting? why did you witness it?" I heard these words and no more. Pierced at their affliction, and feeling the propriety of respecting the display of it, I withdrew, struck with the contrast between the shouts of joy without the palace and the profound grief which oppressed the Sovereigns within.[1] Half an hour afterwards the Queen sent for me. She desired to see M. Goguelat to announce to him her departure on that very night for Vienna. The new attacks upon the dignity of the throne which had been exhibited during the sitting, the spirit of an Assembly worse than the former, the monarch put upon the level of a President, without any deference to the throne—all this proclaimed but too loudly

---

1 Madame Campan, in one of her manuscripts, relates the preceding anecdote in a still more affecting manner.

"The Queen attended the sitting in a private box. I remarked her total silence, and the deep grief which was depicted in her countenance on her return.

"The King came to her apartment the private way. He was pale and his features were much changed. The Queen uttered an exclamation of surprise at his appearance. I thought he was ill; but what was my affliction when I heard the unfortunate monarch say, as he threw himself into a chair and put his handkerchief to his eyes, 'All is lost! Ah! madam, and you are witness to this humiliation! What! You are come into France to see——.' These words were interrupted by sobs. The Queen threw herself upon her knees before him and pressed him in her arms. I remained with them, not from any blamable curiosity, but from a stupefaction which rendered me incapable of determining what I ought to do. The Queen said to me 'Oh! go, go!' with an accent which expressed, Do not remain to witness the dejection and despair of your Sovereign!"—NOTE BY THE EDITOR.

that the sovereignty itself was aimed at. The Queen no longer saw any ground for hope from the interior of the country. The King wrote to the Emperor; she told me she would herself, at midnight, bring the letter which M. Goguelat was to bear to the Emperor to my room. During all the remainder of the day the castle and the Tuileries were prodigiously crowded; the illuminations were magnificent. The King and Queen were requested to take an airing in their carriage in the Champs Elysées, escorted by the aides-de-camp and leaders of the Parisian army, the Constitutional Guard not being at that time organised. Many shouts of "Vive le Roi!" were heard, but as often as they terminated, one of the mob, who never quitted the door of the King's carriage for a single instant, exclaimed with a stentorian voice, "No, don't believe them. Vive la nation!" This ill-omened cry struck terror into the Queen; she thought it not right, however, to make any complaint upon the subject, and pretended not to hear the isolated croak of this fanatic or base hireling, as if it had been drowned in the public acclamations.

A few days afterwards M. de Montmorin sent me a few lines to say he wanted to speak to me; that he would come to me if he were not apprehensive that his doing so would attract observation, and that he thought it would appear less particular if he should see me in the Queen's great closet at a time which he specified, and when nobody would be there. I went. After having made some polite observations upon the services I had already performed, and those I might yet perform, for my master and mistress under existing circumstances, he spoke to me of the King's imminent danger, of the plots which were hatching, and of the lamentable composition of the Legislative Assembly; but he particularly dwelt upon the necessity of appearing, by prudence and circumspection in conversation, as firmly attached as possible to the act the King had just recognised. I told him that could not be done without committing ourselves in the eyes of the Royalist party, which considered moderation a crime; that it was painful to hear ourselves taxed with being Constitutionals, at the same time that it was our opinion that the only Constitution which was consistent with the King's honour and the happiness and tranquillity of his people, was the entire power of the Sovereign; that this was my creed, and it would hurt me to give any room for suspicion that I was wavering in it. "Could you ever believe," said he, "that I should desire any other order of things? Have you any doubt of my attachment to the King's person and the maintenance of his rights?" "I know it, Count," replied I; "but you are not ignorant that you lie under the imputation of having adopted revolutionary ideas." "Well, madam, have resolution enough to dissemble and to conceal your real sentiments; dissimulation was never more necessary. The most strenuous endeavours are making to paralyse the evil intentions of the factious to the utmost possible extent; but we must not be counteracted here by certain dangerous expressions which are circulated in Paris, as dropping from the King and Queen." I told him that I had been already struck with an apprehension of the evil which might be done by the intemperate observations of persons who had no power to act, and that having repeatedly enjoined silence to those in the Queen's service in a very decided manner, I had felt ill consequences in so doing. "I know that," said the Count; "the Queen informed me of it, and that it was which determined me to come and request you to cherish, as much as you can, that spirit of discretion which is so necessary."

While the household of the King and Queen was a prey to all these fears, the festivities in celebration of the acceptance of the Constitution proceeded. Their Majesties went to the opera. The audience consisted entirely of persons who sided with the King, and on that day the happiness of seeing him for a short time surrounded by faithful subjects might be enjoyed. The acclamations were then sincere.

La Coquette Corrigée was selected for representation at the Théâtre Français solely because it was the piece in which Mademoiselle Contat shone most. Yet the notions propagated by the Queen's enemies coinciding in my mind with the name of the play, I thought the choice very ill-judged. I was at a loss, however, to tell Her Majesty so. But sincere attachment gives courage; I explained myself. She was obliged to me, and desired that another play might be performed. They accordingly acted *La Gouvernante*.

The Queen, Madame the King's daughter and Madame Elizabeth were all well received on this occasion. It is true that the opinions and feelings of the whole of the spectators in the boxes could not be otherwise than favourable: great pains had been taken previous to these two performances to fill the pit with proper persons. But on the other hand the Jacobins took the same precautions on their side at the Théâtre Italien, and the tumult was excessive there. The play was Grétry's *Les Evénements Imprévus*. Unfortunately, Madame Dugazon thought proper to bow to the Queen as she sang the words, "Ah! how I love my mistress!" in a duet. Above twenty voices immediately exclaimed from the pit, "No mistress! no master! liberty!" A few replied from the boxes and slips, "Vive le Roi! vive la Reine! long live the King and Queen!" Those in the pit answered, "No master, no Queen!" The quarrel increased; the pit formed into parties; they began fighting, and the Jacobins were beaten —tufts of their black hair flew about the theatre;[1] a strong guard arrived; the Faubourg of St. Antoine, hearing of what was going forward at the Théâtre Italien, flocked together and began to talk of marching towards the scene of action. The Queen preserved the coolest and calmest demeanour; the commandants of the guard surrounded and encouraged her. They conducted themselves promptly and discreetly; no accident happened. The Queen was highly applauded as she quitted the theatre. It was the last time she was ever in a playhouse.

While couriers were bearing confidential letters

---

[1] At this time none but the Jacobins had discontinued the use of hair powder.—NOTE BY MADAME CAMPAN.

from the King to the Princes his brothers and to the foreign Sovereigns, the Assembly invited him to write to the Princes in order to induce them to return into France. The King desired the Abbé de Montesquieu to write the letter he was to send. This letter, which was admirably composed in a simple and effective style suited to the character of Louis XVI., and filled with very powerful arguments in favour of the advantages to be derived from rallying round the principles of the Constitution, was confided to me by the King, who desired me to make him a copy of it.

At this period M. Mor——, one of the intendants of Monsieur's household, obtained a passport from the Assembly to join that Prince, on account of some indispensable business relative to his domestic concerns. The Queen selected him to be the bearer of this letter; she determined to give it to him herself, and to inform him of the origin of it. I was astonished at her choice of this courier. The Queen assured me he was exactly the man for her purpose; that she relied even upon his indiscretion, and it was merely necessary that the letter from the King to his brothers should be known to exist. The Princes were, doubtless, pre-informed on the subject by the private correspondence. Monsieur nevertheless manifested some degree of surprise, and the messenger returned more grieved than pleased at this mark of confidence, which had nearly cost him his life during the Reign of Terror.

Among the causes of uneasiness to the Queen there was one which was but too well founded—it was the thoughtlessness of the French whom she sent to foreign Courts. She used to say that in order to plume themselves upon the confidence with which they were honoured, they had no sooner passed the frontiers than they disclosed the most secret matters relative to the King's private sentiments, and that the leaders of the Revolution were informed of them through their agents, many of whom were Frenchmen who passed themselves off as emigrants in the cause of their King.

After the acceptance of the Constitution the formation of the King's household, military as well as civil, formed a subject of attention. The Duke de Brissac had the command of the Constitutional Guard, which was composed of officers and men selected from the regiments, and of several officers drawn from the National Guard of Paris. The King was satisfied with the feelings and conduct of this band, which, as is well known, existed but a very short time.

The new Constitution abolished what were called honours and the prerogatives belonging to them. The Duchess de Duras resigned her place of lady of the bedchamber, not choosing to lose her right to the *tabouret* at Court. This step hurt the Queen, who saw herself forsaken for obsolete privileges at a time when her rights were so warmly attacked. Many ladies of rank left the Court for the same reason. However, the King and Queen did not dare to form the civil part of their household, lest by the offices of new denominations they should confirm the dissolution of the old ones, and also lest they should admit into the highest offices persons not calculated to fill them.

Some time was spent in discussing the question, whether the household should be formed without equerrries and without ladies of honour. The Queen's constitutional advisers were of opinion that the Assembly, having decreed a civil list adequate to uphold the splendour of the throne, would be dissatisfied at seeing the King adopting only a military household, and not forming his civil household upon the new constitutional plan. "How is it, madam," wrote Barnave to the Queen, "that you will persist in giving these people even the smallest doubt as to your sentiments? When they decree you a civil and a military household, you, like young Achilles among the daughters of Lycomedes, eagerly seize the sword and scorn the mere ornaments." The Queen persisted in her determination to have no civil household. "If," said she, "this constitutional household be formed not a single person of rank will remain with us, and upon a change of affairs we shall be obliged to discharge the persons received into their place."

"Perhaps," added she, "perhaps I might find one day that I had saved the Nobility if I now had resolution enough to afflict them for a time; I have it not. When any measure which injures them is wrested from us I am mortified; nobody comes to my card-party; the King goes solitarily to bed. No allowance is made for political necessity; we are punished for our very misfortunes."

The Queen wrote almost all day and spent a part of the night in reading; her courage supported her physical strength; her temper was not at all soured by misfortune, and she was never seen in an ill-humour for a moment. She was, however, the same person who was held up to the people as a woman who was absolutely furious and mad whenever the rights of the Crown were in any way attacked.

I was with her one day at one of her windows. We saw a man plainly dressed, like an ecclesiastic, surrounded by an immense crowd. The Queen imagined it was some Abbé whom they were about to throw into the basin of the Tuileries. She hastily opened her window, and sent a *valet de chambre* to know what was going forward in the garden. It was Abbé Grégoire, whom the men and women of the tribunes were bringing back in triumph, on account of a motion he had just made in the National Assembly against the Royal authority. On the following day the democratic journalists described the Queen as witnessing this triumph, and showing, by expressive gestures at her window, how highly she was exasperated by the honours conferred upon the patriot.

The correspondence between the Queen and the foreign Powers was carried on in cipher. That to which she gave the preference can never be detected, but the greatest patience is requisite for its use. Each correspondent must have a copy of the same edition of some work. She selected "Paul and Virginia." The page and line in which the required letters, and occasionally a monosyllable, are to be found are pointed out in ciphers agreed upon. I assisted her in the operation of finding the letters, and very frequently I made an exact copy for her of all that she had ciphered without knowing a single word of its meaning.

There were always several secret committees in Paris, occupied on the part of the King in collecting information respecting the measures of the factions, and in influencing some of the committees of the Assembly.

M. Bertrand de Molleville was in close correspondence with the Queen.[1] The King employed M. Talon and others. Much money was dissipated through the latter channel on account of the expenses necessary for the secret measures. The Queen had no confidence in them. M. de Laporte, Minister of the Civil List and of the Household, also attempted to give a bias to public opinion by means of hireling publications; but these papers influenced none but the Royalist party, which needed no bias. M. de Laporte had a private police, which gave him some useful information.

I determined to sacrifice myself to my duty, but by no means to any intrigue, and I thought that, circumstanced as I was, I ought to confine myself to obedience to the Queen's orders. I frequently sent off couriers to foreign countries, and they were never discovered, so many precautions did I take. I am indebted for the preservation of my own existence to the care I took never to admit any deputy whatever to my abode, and to refuse all interviews which even people of the highest importance often requested

---

[1] About the same time Bertrand de Molleville employed himself more successfully respecting the means of counterbalancing the influence of the tribunes by spectators and applauses favourable to the Court. *Vide Historical Illustrations* (J) for the success of this experiment, and the circumstances which compelled him to give it up.—NOTE BY THE EDITOR.

of me. This line of conduct appeared to me the only one suitable to my sex and my situation at Court; but it left me exposed to every species of ill-will, and on one and the same day I saw myself denounced by Prud'homme, in his *Gazette Révolutionnaire*, as capable of making an aristocrat of the mother of the Gracchi, if a person so dangerous as myself could have got into her household, and by Gauthier's *Gazette Royaliste* as a "Monarchist," a "Constitutional," more dangerous to the Queen's interests than a Jacobin.

At this period an event with which I had nothing to do placed me in a still more critical situation. My brother, M. Genet, began his diplomatic career successfully. At eighteen he was attached to the embassy to Vienna; at twenty he was appointed Chief Secretary of Legation in England, on occasion of the peace of 1783. A memorial which he presented to M. de Vergennes, upon the dangers of the treaty of commerce then entered into with England, gave offence to M. de Calonne, a patron of that treaty, and particularly to M. Gérard de Rayneval, Chief Clerk for Foreign Affairs. So long as M. de Vergennes lived, having upon my father's death declared himself the protector of my brother, he supported him against the enemies his memorial had raised up. But upon his death, M. de Montmorin, being much in need of the long experience in business which he found in M. de Rayneval, guided himself solely by the latter and according to his instigation. The office of which my brother was the head was suppressed and added to the other offices of foreign affairs. My brother went to St. Petersburg, strongly recommended to the Count de Ségur, Minister from France to that Court, who appointed him Secretary of Legation. Some time afterwards the Count de Ségur left him at St. Petersburg, charged with the affairs of France.[1]

My brother quitted Versailles much hurt at being deprived of a considerable income for having penned a memorial which his zeal alone had dictated, and the importance of which was afterwards but too well understood. I had perceived from his correspondence that he inclined to some of the new notions, and had taken the alarm at it, when he wrote me a letter which left me no further room for doubt as to his opinions. He told me it was right he should no longer conceal from me that he sided with the Constitutional party—that the King had, in fact, commanded it, having himself accepted the Constitution; that he would proceed firmly in that course, because in this case disingenuousness would be fatal, and that he took that side of the question because he had had it proved to him that the foreign Powers would not serve the King's cause without advancing pretensions prompted by the most ancient interests, and which

---

[1] After his return from Russia M. Genet was appointed Ambassador to the United States by the party called Girondists, the deputies who headed it being from the department of the Gironde. He was shortly afterwards recalled by the Robespierre party, which overthrew the former faction on the 31st of May, 1793, and condemned to appear at the bar of the Convention—that is to say, to ascend the scaffold. Vice-President Clinton, at that time Governor of New York, offered him an asylum in his house and the hand of Cornelia Clinton, his daughter. M. Genet's crime was the execution of instructions which he had received on setting out from the party then in power. He settled in America, and lives there as a rich planter and the beloved father of a family.—NOTE BY MADAME CAMPAN.

always would remain in the spirit of their councils; that he saw no salvation for the King and Queen but from France herself, and that only by using every exertion to calm existing apprehensions and to restore harmony to the minds of men; and that he would serve the constitutional King as he served him before the Revolution had created a necessity for settling the destinies of France by a new code. And, lastly, he requested me to impart to the Queen the real sentiments of one of His Majesty's agents at a foreign Court. I immediately went to the Queen and gave her my brother's letter. She read it attentively, and said, "This is the letter of a young man led astray by discontent and ambition. I know you do not think as he does. Do not fear that you will lose the confidence of the King or mine." I offered to discontinue all correspondence with my brother. She opposed that, saying it would be dangerous. I then entreated she would permit me in future to show her my own and my brother's letters, to which she consented. I wrote warmly to my brother against the course he had adopted. I sent my letters by sure channels; he answered me by the post, and no longer touched upon anything but his family affairs. Once only he wrote to me that if I should write to him respecting the affairs of the day he would give me no answer. "Serve your august mistress with the unbounded devotion which is due from you," said he, "and let us each do our duty. I will only observe to you that at Paris the fogs of the Seine prevent people from seeing that immense capital even from the Pavilion of Flora, and I see it more clearly from

St. Petersburg." The Queen said, as she read this letter, "Perhaps he speaks but too truly. Who can decide upon so disastrous a position as ours is become?" The very day on which I gave the Queen my brother's first letter to read she had several audiences to give to ladies and other persons belonging to the Court, who came on purpose to inform her that my brother was an avowed Constitutional and revolutionist. The Queen replied, "I know it; Madame Campan came to tell me so." Persons envious of my situation, and some of ill-regulated minds, having subjected me to mortifications, and these unpleasant circumstances recurring daily, I requested the Queen's permission to withdraw from the Court. She exclaimed against the very idea; represented it to me as extremely dangerous for my own reputation, and had the kindness to add that, for my sake as well as for her own, she never would consent to it. After this conversation, during which I was at Her Majesty's knees, bathing her hands with my tears, I retired to my apartment. A few minutes afterwards a footman brought me a note from her, couched in these terms: "I have never ceased to distinguish you, nor to give you and yours proofs of my attachment. I wish to tell you in writing that I have full faith in your honour and fidelity, as well as in your other good qualities, and that I ever rely on the zeal and address you exert to serve me."[1]

---

[1] I had just received this letter from the Queen when M. de la Chapelle, Commissary-General of the King's Household and head of the offices of M. de Laporte, Minister of the Civil List, came to see me. The palace having been already forced by the brigands on the

At the very moment that I was going to express to the Queen the gratitude with which I was penetrated, I heard a tapping at the door of my room, which opened upon the Queen's inner corridor. I opened it; it was the King. I was confused; he perceived it, and said to me kindly, "I alarm you, Madame Campan; I come, however, to comfort you. The Queen has told me how much she is hurt at the injustice of several persons towards you. But how is it that you complain of injustice and calumny when you see that we also are victims of them? In some of your companions it is jealousy; in the people belonging to the Court it is anxiety. Our situation is so disastrous, and we have met with so much ingratitude and treachery, that the apprehensions of those who love us are excusable. I could quiet them

---

20th of June, he proposed that I should entrust the paper to him that he might place it in a safer situation than the apartments of the unfortunate Queen would be. When he returned into his offices he placed the letter she had condescended to write to me behind a large picture in his closet; but on the 10th of August M. de la Chapelle was thrown into the prisons of the Abbaye, and the Committee of Public Safety established themselves in his offices, whence they issued all their decrees of death. There it was that a villainous servant belonging to M. de Laporte went to declare that in the minister's apartment, under a board in the floor, a number of papers would be found. They were brought forth, and M. de Laporte was sent the first of all to the scaffold, where he suffered *for having betrayed the State by serving his master and Sovereign.* M. de la Chapelle was saved, as if by a miracle, from the massacres of the 2nd of September. The Committee of Public Safety having abolished his employments, in order to seat itself in the King's apartments at the Tuileries, M. de la Chapelle had permission to return to his closet to take away some property belonging to him. Turning up the picture behind which he had hidden the Queen's letter, he found it in the place into which he had slipped it; and, delighted to see that I was safe from the ill consequences the discovery of this paper might have brought upon me, he burnt it instantly. In troublous times a mere nothing may save life or destroy it.—NOTE BY MADAME CAMPAN.

by telling them all the secret services you perform for us daily; but I will not do it. Out of goodwill to you they would repeat all I should say, and you would be lost with the Assembly. It is much better both for you and for us that you should be thought a Constitutional. It has been mentioned to me a hundred times already. I have never contradicted it; but I come to give you my word that if we are fortunate enough to see an end of all this, I will, at the Queen's residence, and in the presence of my brothers, relate the important services you have rendered us, and I will recompense you and your son for them." I threw myself at the King's feet and kissed his hand. He raised me up, saying, "Come, come, do not grieve; the Queen, who loves you, confides in your sentiments as I do."

Occasions for mysterious and secret services recurred every moment. Barnave was the only one of the three trustworthy deputies who had not seen the King and Queen since the Varennes journey. The espionage of the Assembly was more apprehended on his account than on that of any other.

Down to the day of the acceptance it was impossible to introduce Barnave into the interior of the palace; but as the Queen was now rid of the inner guard, she said she would see him. The very great precautions which it was necessary for the deputy to take, in order to conceal his connection with the King and Queen, compelled them to spend two hours in waiting for him in one of the corridors of the Tuileries, and all in vain. The first day that he was to be admitted, having met a man whom Barnave knew to be suspicious in the courtyard of the palace, he determined to cross it without stopping, and walked in the gardens in order to lull suspicion. I was desired to wait for Barnave at a little door belonging to the *entresols* of the palace, with my hand upon the open lock. I had been in that position an hour. The King came to me frequently, and always to speak to me of the uneasiness which a servant belonging to the castle, who was a patriot, gave him. He came again to ask me whether I had heard the door called *de Décret* opened. I assured him nobody had been in the corridor, and he became easy. He was dreadfully apprehensive that his connection with Barnave would be discovered. "It would," said the King, "be a ground for capital accusations, and the unfortunate man would be lost." I then ventured to remind His Majesty that as I was not the only one in the secret of the business which brought Barnave in contact with their Majesties, one of his colleagues might be induced to speak of the communication with which they were honoured, and that, in letting them know by my presence that I also was informed of it, a risk was incurred of removing from those gentlemen part of the responsibility of the secret. Upon this observation the King quitted me hastily and returned a moment afterwards with the Queen. "Give me your place," said she; "I will wait for him in my turn. You have convinced the King. We must not increase in their eyes the number of persons informed of their communications with us."

The police of M. Laporte, Minister of the Civil List, apprised him as early as the latter end of 1791 that a man belonging to the King's offices, who had set up as a pastrycook at the Palais Royal, was about to re-enter upon the duties of his situation which had devolved upon him again on the death of one who held it for life; that he was so furious a Jacobin that he had dared to say it would be a good thing for France if the King's days were shortened. His duty was confined to the mere laying out of the pastry; he was closely watched by the head officers of the kitchen, who were devoted to His Majesty; but it is so easy to introduce a subtle poison into made dishes that it was determined the King and Queen should eat only plain roasted meat in future; that their bread should be brought to them by M. Thierry de Ville-d'Array, intendant of the smaller apartments, who was likewise to take upon himself to supply the wine. The King was fond of pastry. I was directed to order some, as if for myself—sometimes of one pastrycook and sometimes of another. The pounded sugar, too, was kept in my room. The King, the Queen and Madame Elizabeth ate together, and nobody remained to wait on them. Each had a dumb waiter and a little bell to call the servants when they were wanted. M. Thierry used himself to bring me Their Majesties' bread and wine, and I locked them up in a private cupboard in the King's closet on the ground floor. As soon as the King sat down to table I took in the pastry and bread. All was hidden under the table lest it might be necessary to have the servants in. The King thought it dangerous as well as distressing to show any apprehension of attempts against his person, or any distrust of his officers of the kitchen. As he never drank a whole bottle of wine at his meals (the Princesses drank nothing but water), he filled up that out of which he had drank about half, from the bottle served up by the officers of his buttery. I took it away after dinner. Although he never ate any other pastry than that which I brought, he took care in the same manner that it should seem that he had eaten of that served at table. The lady who succeeded found this duty all regulated, and she executed it in the same manner; the public never was in possession of these particulars, nor of the apprehensions which gave rise to them. At the end of three or four months the police of M. de Laporte gave notice that nothing more was to be dreaded from that sort of plot against the King's life; that the plan was entirely changed, and that all future attempts would be directed as much against the throne as against the person of the Sovereign.[1]

There are others besides myself who know that, about this time, one of the things about which the Queen most desired to be satisfied was the opinion of the famous Pitt. She would sometimes say to me, "I never pronounce the name of Pitt but I feel death at my shoulder." (I repeat here her very expressions.) That man is the mortal enemy of France, and he takes a dreadful revenge for the impolitic support given by the Cabinet of Versailles to the American insurgents. He wishes, by our destruction, to guarantee the maritime power of his country for ever against the efforts made by the King to increase

---

[1] The details which Madame Campan gives above add weight to the various pieces of information she took pains to collect respecting the administration of the Queen's household, the service and expenses of the table, &c. These accounts will be found among the *Historical Illustrations* (4).—NOTE BY THE EDITOR.

his navy and their happy results during the last war. He knows that it is not only the King's policy, but his private inclination, to be solicitous about his fleets, and that the most active step he has taken during his whole reign was to visit the port of Cherbourg. Pitt has served the cause of the French Revolution from the first disturbances; he will perhaps serve it until its annihilation. I will endeavour to learn to what point he intends to lead us, and I am sending M. ——[1] to London for that purpose. He has been intimately connected with Pitt, and they have often had political conversations respecting the French Government. I will get him to make Pitt speak out—at least as far as such a man can speak out."

Some time afterwards the Queen told me that her secret envoy had returned from London, and that all he had been able to wring from Pitt, whom he found alarmingly reserved, was that *he would not suffer the French monarchy to fall;* that to suffer the revolutionary spirit to erect an organised Republic in France would be a great error as regarding the tranquillity of all Europe. "Whenever," said she, "Pitt expressed himself upon the necessity of supporting a *monarchy* in France, he maintained the most profound silence upon what concerns the monarch. The result of these conversations is anything but encouraging;

---

[1] I thought for some time that this secret agent was M. Crawford. His Memoirs, which I read very eagerly, have altered my opinion, because he certainly would have mentioned this mission. I have forgotten the name of the person whom the Queen sent to London, though she condescended to entrust me with it.—NOTE BY MADAME CAMPAN.

but even as to that monarchy which he wishes to save, will he have means and strength to save it if he suffer us to fall?"

The death of the Emperor Leopold took place on the 1st of March, 1792. When the news of this event reached the Tuileries the Queen had gone out. Upon her return I put the letter containing it into her hands. She exclaimed that the Emperor had been poisoned; that she had marked and preserved a newspaper in which, in an article upon the sitting of the Jacobins, at the time when the Emperor Leopold declared for the coalition, it was said, speaking of him, that a *piecrust* would settle that matter. From this moment the Queen considered the expression as one which had involuntarily escaped the propagandists. She lamented her brother. However, the education of Francis II., which had been superintended by the Emperor Joseph, inspired her with new hopes. She thought he must have inherited the sentiments of the latter for her, and did not doubt that he had, under the care of his uncle, imbibed that valiant spirit so necessary for the support of a crown. At this period Barnave obtained the Queen's consent that he should read all the letters she should write. He was fearful of private correspondence that might hamper the plan marked out for her; he distrusted Her Majesty's sincerity upon this point; and the diversity of counsels and the necessity of yielding on the one hand to some of the views of the Constitutionals, and on the other to those of the French Princes, and even of the foreign Courts, were unfortunately the circumstances which most rapidly impelled the Court towards its ruin.

The Queen wished to have shown Barnave the letter of condolence which she wrote to Francis II. This letter was to be submitted to her "triumvirate" (for thus did she sometimes designate the three deputies whom I have named). She would not hear a single word which, from its interference with their plans, might prevent its going; she was also fearful of introducing into it anything contradictory to her private sentiments, which the Emperor might learn by other means. "Sit down at that table," said she to me, "and sketch me out a letter. Dwell upon the idea that I see in my nephew the pupil of Joseph. If yours is better than mine you shall dictate it to me." I wrote a letter. She read it, and said, "It is the very thing. I was too deeply interested to keep the true line as you have done."

The party of the Princes was much alarmed on being informed of the connection of the wreck of the constitutional party with the Queen; and the Queen on her part always dreaded the party of the Princes and the attempts of the French who composed it. She did justice to the Count d'Artois, and often said that his party would act in contravention of his sentiments towards the King his brother and herself; but that he would be led away by people over whom Calonne had a most lamentable ascendency. She reproached Count Esterhazy, whom she had loaded with favours, for having sided with Calonne so entirely that she had reason to consider him absolutely as an enemy.

However, the emigrants showed great apprehensions of the consequences which might follow in the interior from a connection with the Constitutionals, whom they described as a party existing no longer but in idea, and totally without means of repairing their errors. The Jacobins were preferred to them because, said they, there would be no treaty to be made with anyone at the moment of extricating the King and his family from the abyss in which they are plunged.

I frequently read to the Queen the letters written to her by Barnave. One among others struck me forcibly, and I think I have retained the substance of it sufficiently well to enable to me to give a faithful account of it. He told the Queen she did not rely sufficiently on the strength remaining in the constitutional party; that their flag was indeed torn, but the word "Constitution" was still legible upon it; that this word would recover its virtue if the King and his friends would rally round it sincerely; that the authors of the Constitution, enlightened with respect to their own errors, might yet amend it and restore to the throne all its splendour; that the Queen must not believe that the public mind was favourably disposed towards the Jacobins; that the weak joined them because there was no strength elsewhere, but the general opinion was for the Constitution; that the party of the French Princes, unfortunately shackled by the policy of foreign Courts, ought not to be depended on; that the majority of emigrants had already destroyed by misconduct much of the interest excited by their misfortunes; that entire confidence ought not to be reposed in the foreign Powers, guided as they were by the policy of their Cabinets and not by the ties of blood; and that the interior alone was capable of supporting the integrity of the kingdom. He concluded the letter by saying that he laid at Her Majesty's feet the only national party still in existence; that he feared to name it; but that she ought not to forget that Henry IV. was not assisted by foreign Princes in regaining his dominions, and that he ascended a Catholic throne after having fought at the head of a Protestant party.

Barnave and his friends presumed too far upon their strength; it was exhausted in the contest with the Court. The Queen was aware of this, and if she did not seem to have any confidence in them, it is probable that she was actuated by a policy which, it must be confessed, could only prove injurious to her.

CHAPTER IX

Fresh libel by Madame de Lamotte—The Queen refuses to purchase the manuscript—The King buys it—The Queen performs her Easter devotions secretly in 1792—She dares not confide in General Dumouriez—Barnave's last advice—Gross insult offered to the Queen by one of the mob—The King's dejection—The 20th of June—The King's kindness to Madame Campan—Iron closet—Louis XVI. entrusts a portfolio to Madame Campan—Importance of the documents it contained—Procedure of M. de la Fayette; why it is unsuccessful—An assassin conceals himself in the Queen's apartments.

In the beginning of the year 1792 a worthy priest requested a private interview with me. He had heard of the existence of a new libel by Madame de Lamotte. He told me he had observed in the people who came from London to get it printed in Paris nothing more than a desire of gain, and that they were ready to deliver him the manuscript for 1,000 louis if he could find any friend of the Queen disposed to make that sacrifice for her peace; that he had thought of me, and that if Her Majesty would give him the 24,000 francs he would deliver me the manuscript upon receiving them.

I communicated this proposal to the Queen, who rejected it, and desired me to answer that at the time when she had power to punish the hawkers of these libels she deemed them so atrocious and improbable that she despised the means of arresting their progress, that if she were to be imprudent and weak enough to buy a single one of them the Jacobins might possibly discover the circumstance through their espionage; that were this libel bought up it would be printed nevertheless, and would be much more dangerous when they apprised the public of the means she had used to suppress it.

The Baron d'Aubier, gentleman in ordinary to the King and my particular friend, had a strong memory and a plain and easy way of communicating the substance of the discussions, debates and decrees of the National Assembly. I went daily to the Queen's apartments to repeat all this to the King, who used to say, on seeing me, "Ah! here's the *Postillon par Calais*."[1]

M. d'Aubier came one day and said to me: "The Assembly has been much occupied with an information laid by the workmen of the Sèvres manufactory. They brought to the President's office a bundle of pamphlets, which they said were the Life of Marie Antoinette. The director of the manufactory was ordered up to the bar, and declared he had received orders to burn the printed sheets in question in the furnaces used for baking his china."

While I was relating this business to the Queen, the King coloured, and held his head down over his plate. The Queen said to him: "Do you know anything about this, Sire?" The King made no answer. Madame Elizabeth requested him to explain what all this meant—still silent. I withdrew hastily. A few minutes afterwards the Queen came to my room and informed me that the King, out of regard for her, had

---

[1] The name of a newspaper of the time.

purchased the whole edition struck off from the manuscript which I had proposed to her, and that M. de Laporte had not been able to devise any more secret way of destroying the whole of the work than that of having it burnt at Sèvres among two hundred workmen, one hundred and eighty of whom must, in all probability, be Jacobins. She told me she had concealed her vexation from the King; that he was in consternation, and that she should say nothing, since his affection and his good intentions towards her had been the cause of the accident.[1]

---

[1] Bertrand de Molleville gives the following account of this circumstance in his private Memoirs:

"M. de Laporte had, by order of the King, bought up the whole edition of the Memoirs of the notorious Madame de Lamotte against the Queen. Instead of burning them or having them pounded to atoms immediately, he shut them up in one of the closets in his house. The alarming and rapid growth of the spirit of rebellion, the arrogance of the crowd of brigands who directed and in a great measure composed the populace of Paris, and the fresh excesses daily resulting from it, rendered the Minister of the Civil List apprehensive that some mob might break into his house at a time when he should least expect it, carry off these Memoirs, and spread them among the public. In order to prevent this mischance, he gave orders for having the Memoirs burnt with every necessary precaution and secrecy; and the clerk who received the order entrusted the execution of it to a man named Riston, a dangerous intriguer and a detestable fellow, formerly an advocate of Nancy, who had a twelvemonth before escaped the gallows by favour of the new principles and the patriotism of the new tribunals, although convicted of forging the Great Seal and fabricating decrees of the Council in a proceeding instituted at the instance of the tribunal of the King's palace, in which I examined and confronted the parties at the risk of attempts at assassination, not only by the accused, who, during one of the sittings, was so enraged that he rushed at me with a knife in his hand, but also by the brigands in his pay, who filled the court and were furious at seeing that their menacing howlings did not prevent my repressing the insults incessantly offered by the accused to the witnesses who deposed against him.

"This very Riston, who a year before was labouring under a capital accusation preferred against him in the name and by the direction of the King, finding himself entrusted with a commission

Some time afterwards the Assembly received a denunciation against M. de Montmorin. The ex-minister was accused of having neglected forty despatches from M. Genet, the *chargé d'affaires* from France in Russia, without having even unsealed them, because M. Genet acted on constitutional principles. M. de Montmorin appeared at the bar to answer this accusation. Whatever distress I might feel at the moment in obeying the order I had received from the King to go and give him an account of the sitting, I thought I ought not to fail in doing so. But instead of giving my brother his family name, I merely said, " Your Majesty's *chargé d'affaires* at St. Petersburg."

The King did me the favour to say that he observed a reserve in my account, of which he approved. The Queen condescended to add a few obliging remarks to those of the King, by which I was already so much affected that I withdrew in great emotion. However, my office of journalist

---

which concerned Her Majesty, and the mystery attending which bespoke something of importance, was far less anxious to execute it faithfully than to make a parade of this mark of confidence. On the 30th of May, at ten in the morning, he had the sheets carried to the porcelain manufactory at Sèvres in a cart which he himself accompanied, and made a large fire of them before all the workmen, who were expressly forbidden to approach it. All these precautions, and the suspicions to which they naturally gave rise under such critical circumstances, gave so much publicity to this mysterious affair that it was denounced to the Assembly that very night. Brissot and the whole Jacobin party, with equal effrontery and vehemence, insisted that the papers thus secretly burnt were not, and could not be, any other than the registers and documents of the correspondence of the Austrian Committee. M. de Laporte was ordered to the bar, and there gave the most exact account of the circumstances. Riston was also called up, and confirmed M. de Laporte's deposition. But these explanations, however satisfactory, did not calm the violent ferment raised in the Assembly by this affair."—NOTE BY THE EDITOR.

gave me, in this instance, so much pain that I took an opportunity, when the King was expressing his satisfaction to me at the manner in which I gave him this daily account, to tell him that its merits belonged wholly to M. d'Aubier, who attended all the sittings to give me a summary of them; and I then ventured to request the King to suffer that excellent man to come and give him an account of the sittings himself. I went so far as to add that, at a time when the King's feelings were wounded by the conduct of so many faithless subjects, it appeared to me that men warmly devoted to him as M. d'Aubier was, deserved the honour of being about His Majesty. I assured the King that, if he would permit it, that gentleman might proceed to the Queen's apartments through mine unseen. The King consented to the arrangement. Thenceforward M. d'Aubier was admitted into the interior, and gave the King repeated proofs of zeal and attachment with much intelligence.

The Curé of Saint-Eustache ceased to be the Queen's confessor when he took the Constitutional oath. I do not remember the name of the ecclesiastic who succeeded him in that office; I only know that he was conducted into her apartments with the greatest mystery. Their Majesties did not perform their Easter devotions in public, because they could neither declare for the Constitutional clergy nor act so as to show that they were against them.

The Queen did perform her Easter devotions in 1792, but she went to the chapel attended only by myself. She desired me beforehand to request one of my relations, who was her chaplain, to perform Mass for her at five o'clock in the morning. It was still dark; she gave me her arm, and I carried a taper. I left her entirely alone at the chapel door, and she did not return to her room until the dawn of day. This piece of duty, performed with so much mystery, could not tend to edify the public, but demonstrates the Queen's religious principles.

Dangers increased daily. The Assembly was strengthened in the eyes of the people by the hostilities of the foreign armies and the army of the Princes. The communication with the latter party became more active; the Queen wrote almost every day. M. de Goguelat possessed her confidence for all correspondence with the foreign parties, and I was obliged to have him in my apartments; the Queen asked for him very frequently, and at times which she could not previously appoint.

All parties were exerting themselves either to ruin or to save the King. One day I found the Queen extremely agitated; she told me she no longer knew where she was; that the leaders of the Jacobins offered themselves to her through the medium of Dumouriez; and that Dumouriez, abandoning the Jacobins, had come and offered himself to her; that she had granted him an audience; that when alone with her he had thrown himself at her feet and told her that he had drawn the *bonnet rouge* over his head to the very ears, but that he neither was nor could be a Jacobin; that the Revolution had been suffered to extend even to that rabble of destroyers who, thinking of nothing but pillage, were ripe for anything, and might furnish the Assembly with a formidable army ready to undermine the remains of a throne already too much shaken. Whilst speaking, with the utmost ardour he seized the Queen's hand and kissed it with transport, exclaiming, "Suffer yourself to be saved." The Queen told me that the protestations of a traitor were not to be relied on; that the whole of his conduct was so well known that, undoubtedly, the wisest course was not to trust to it;[1] that, moreover, the Princes particularly recommended that no confidence should be placed in any proposition emanating from within the kingdom; that the force without became imposing, and that it was better to rely upon their success and upon the protection due from Heaven to a Sovereign so virtuous as Louis XVI. and to so just a cause.

The Constitutionals, on their part, saw that there had been nothing more than a mere pretence of listening to them. Barnave's last advice was as to the means of continuing a few weeks longer the Constitutional Guard, which had been denounced to the Assembly and was to be disbanded. The denunciation against the Constitutional Guard affected only *its staff and the Duke de Brissac*. Barnave wrote to the Queen that the staff of the guard was already attacked; that the Assembly was about to pass a decree to reduce

---

[1] The sincerity of General Dumouriez cannot be the object of a single doubt in this instance. The second volume of his Memoirs shows how unjust the distrust and reproaches of the Queen were. By rejecting his offers and refusing his services Marie Antoinette deprived herself of her only remaining support. He who saved France in the defiles of Argonne would, perhaps, have saved France before the 20th of June had he obtained the full confidence of Louis XVI. and the Queen.—NOTE BY THE EDITOR.

it, and he entreated her to prevail on the King, the very instant the decree should appear, to form the staff afresh, and to make it up of persons whose names he sent her. I did not see the list, but Barnave said that all who were set down in it passed for decided Jacobins, but were not so in fact; that they, as well as himself, were in despair at seeing the monarchical government attacked; that they had learned to dissemble their sentiments, and that it would be at least a fortnight before the Assembly could know them well, and certainly before it could succeed in make them unpopular; that it would be necessary to take advantage of that short space of time to get away from Paris, and to do so immediately after the nomination of those whom he pointed out. The Queen was of opinion that she ought not to yield to this advice. The Duke de Brissac was sent to Orleans, and the guard was reduced.

Barnave, seeing that the Queen did not follow his counsel in anything, and convinced that she placed all her reliance on assistance from abroad, determined to quit Paris. He obtained a last audience. "Your misfortunes, madam," said he, "and those which I anticipate for France, determined me to sacrifice myself to serve you. I see that my advice does not agree with the views of Your Majesties. I augur but little advantage from the plan you are induced to pursue; you are too remote from your supports; you will be lost before they reach you. Most ardently do I wish I may be mistaken in so lamentable a prediction; but I am sure to lose my head for interesting myself in your misfortunes and for the services I have sought to render you. I request, for my sole reward, the honour of kissing your hand." The Queen, her eyes suffused with tears, granted him that favour, and remained impressed with the most favourable idea of this deputy's elevated sentiments. Madame Elizabeth participated in this opinion, and the two Princesses frequently spoke of Barnave. She also received M. Duport several times, but with less mystery. Her connection with the Constitutional deputies transpired. Alexandre de Lameth was the only one of the three who survived the vengeance of the Jacobins.[1]

---

[1] After what we have just read respecting Barnave, after his well-known labours in the cause of liberty, his efforts to support the throne, his talents and his eloquence, the latter circumstances of his life possess a high degree of interest. The "Biographie de Bruxelles" relates them in these words:

"When, after the Revolution of the 10th of August, 1792, the iron closet of the castle of the Tuileries had been discovered and forced, a considerable number of documents, which had been imprudently preserved in it, and which were communicated to the Convention by Gohier, who had just succeeded Danton in the administration of justice, proved that the Court had established and maintained, during the latter months of the session of the Constituent Assembly, and from the time of the meeting of the Legislative Assembly, constant communication with the most powerful members of those Assemblies. Barnave being accused, on the 15th of August, 1792, with Alexandre de Lameth, ex-member of the Constituent Assembly, Bertrand de Molleville, Duport de Tertre, Duportail, Montmorin, and Tarbé, ex-ministers of the Marine, of Justice, of War, of Foreign Affairs, and of Public Contributions, was arrested at Grenoble, and shut up in the prison of that town. He remained there fifteen months, and his friends began to indulge the hope that he would be forgotten, when an order arrived that he should be removed to Paris. At first he was imprisoned in the Abbaye, but transferred a few days afterwards to the Conciergerie, and almost immediately taken before the revolutionary tribunal. He appeared there with wonderful firmness, summed up the services he had rendered to the cause of liberty with his usual eloquence and without losing anything of the dignity of misfortune, and made such an impression upon the numerous auditory present at the debates that, although accustomed to behold only conspirators worthy of death in all those who appeared before the tribunal, they

The National Guard, which succeeded the King's Guard, having occupied the gates of the Tuileries, all who came to see the Queen were incessantly insulted with impunity.

The most menacing cries were uttered aloud even in the Tuileries; they called for the destruction of the throne and the murder of the Sovereign. These insults assumed the character of the very lowest of the mob. The Queen one day, hearing roars of laughter under her windows, desired me to see what it was about. I saw a man almost undressed turning his back towards her apartments. My astonishment and indignation were apparent. The Queen rose to come forward; I held her back, telling her that it was a very gross insult offered by one of the rabble.

About this time the King fell into a state of despondence which amounted almost to physical helplessness. He passed ten successive days without uttering a single word, even in the bosom of his family; except, indeed, in playing at backgammon with Madame Elizabeth, when he was obliged to pronounce the words belonging to that game. The Queen roused him from this state, so fatal at a critical period, when every minute increased the necessity for action,

---

themselves considered his acquittal certain. The decree of death was read amidst the deepest silence; but Barnave's firmness was immovable. When he left the court he cast upon the judges, the jurors and the public looks expressive of contempt and indignation. He was led to his fate with the respected Duport de Tertre, one of the last ministers of Louis XVI. When he had ascended the scaffold, Barnave stamped, raised his eyes to heaven, and said, "This, then, is the reward of all that I have done for liberty!" He fell on the 29th of October, 1793, in the thirty-second year of his age; his bust is now in the Grenoble Museum. The Consular Government placed his statue next to that of Vergniaud, on the great staircase of the senatorial palace.—NOTE BY THE EDITOR.

by throwing herself at his feet, urging every idea calculated to excite alarm, and employing every affectionate expression. She represented also what he owed to his family, and went so far as to tell him that, if they were doomed to fall, they ought to fall honourably, and not wait to be both smothered upon the floor of their apartment.

About the 15th of June the King refused his sanction to the two decrees ordaining the deportation of priests and the formation of a camp of twenty thousand men under the walls of Paris. He wished himself to sanction them, and said that the general insurrection only waited for a pretence to burst forth.[1] The Queen insisted upon the *veto*, and

---

[1] This assertion contradicts the almost unanimous testimony of historians. When we reflect on the piety of Louis XVI., his respect for religion, and the deference he always manifested towards its ministers, we must hesitate to believe that Madame Campan could be well informed as to this fact. To say nothing of Dumouriez, who tells us precisely the contrary, Bertrand de Molleville enters into some particulars upon the subject which leave no room for doubt.

"The Assembly," says he, "which kept up its credit by acts of violence, passed a decree against non-Constitutional priests to oblige them to take a fresh oath or quit the kingdom. The bishops then at Paris met to draw up a petition against this decree, under a conviction that the King, who had already shown the deepest regret at having sanctioned the decrees relating to the clergy, would rejoice at having grounds pointed out to him for refusing his sanction to this. When the petition was drawn up, they applied to put it into His Majesty's hands; and the Bishop of Uzès had a private correspondence with me on this occasion; for at this period no minister could have received a bishop publicly without becoming an object of suspicion *to the nation*.

"The King appeared much moved upon reading the petition, and said to me, with all that energy which always warmed him when religion was under discussion: 'They may be very sure I will never sanction it. But the question is, whether I ought to assign a reason for my refusal, or give it plainly and simply, according to the usual formula, or whether, under all circumstances, it is not more prudent to temporise. Try

reproached herself bitterly when this last act of the Constitutional authority had occasioned the scenes of the 20th of June.

A few days previously above twenty thousand men had gone to the Commune to announce that on the 20th they would plant the tree of liberty at the door of the National Assembly, and present a petition to the King respecting the *veto* which he had placed upon the decree for the deportation of the priests. This dreadful army crossed the gardens of the Tuileries and marched under the Queen's windows. It consisted of

---

to find out what your colleagues think about it before it is discussed in council,' I observed to the King that the Constitution dispensed with any reason for his refusal to sanction, and that, although the Assembly ought to be pleased at seeing His Majesty waive so important a prerogative, they were so ill-disposed that they were capable of carrying their insolence so far as to refuse to hear the King's reasons, and would even reproach him for this departure from the Constitution as a manifest violation of his oath; that as to temporising, it would be showing weakness, and inviting the Assembly, already very enterprising, to become still more so; and therefore that a plain unexplained refusal of the sanction was the safest and most expedient course.

"This matter was discussed the next day at the council of the ministers. They all saw the unavoidable necessity for refusing the sanction, and at the following council they unanimously recommended that course to the King, who determined upon it with the greatest satisfaction. But this gleam of happiness was clouded by a proposal made to him by the Minister of the Interior immediately to form his chapel and that of the Queen of Constitutional priests, as the most certain way to shut the mouth of malevolence and completely convince the people of his sincere attachment to the Constitution. 'No, sir, no,' replied the King, in the firmest tone, 'Do not speak of that to me. Let me be left at rest upon that point. When the liberty of worship was established, it was established generally; I ought therefore to enjoy it.' The warmth with which the King spoke surprised us all, and silenced M. Cahier de Gerville."

Consult the interesting particulars contained in the latter part of these Memoirs upon the subject, and generally upon the religious sentiments of Louis XVI.—NOTE BY THE EDITOR.

people who called themselves the citizens of the Faubourgs St. Antoine and St. Marceau. Covered as they were with filthy clothes, they all bore the most terrifying appearance, and the steam from them infected the air. People asked each other whence such an army could come—nothing so disgusting had ever before appeared in Paris.

On the 20th of June this mob thronged about the Tuileries in still greater numbers, armed with pikes, hatchets and murderous instruments of all kinds, decorated with ribbons of the national colours, shouting, "The nation for ever! Down with the veto!" The King was without guards. Some of these demoniacs rushed up to his apartment. The door was about to be forced in when the King commanded that it should be opened. MM. de Bougainville, d'Hervilly, de Parois, d'Aubier, Acloque,[1] Gentil, and other courageous men who were in the apartment of M. de Septenil, the King's first *valet de chambre*, instantly ran to His Majesty's apartment. M. de Bougainville, seeing the torrent furiously advancing, cried out, "Put the King in the recess of the window, and place benches before him." Six Royalist grenadiers of the battalion of the Filles Saint Thomas made their way by an inner staircase and ranged themselves before the benches. The order given by M. de Bougainville saved the King from the blades of the assassins, among whom was a

---

[1] A citizen of Paris, commandant of battalion, who, during the whole of the Revolution was, both in virtue and conduct, in direct opposition to the regicide Santerre.*—NOTE BY MADAME CAMPAN.

* His son is now a major of the National Guard of Paris.—NOTE BY THE EDITOR.

Pole named Lazousky, who was to strike the first blow. The King's brave defenders said, "Sire, fear nothing." The King's reply is well known: "Put your hand upon my heart, and you will perceive whether I am afraid or not." M. Vanot, commandant of battalion, warded off a blow aimed by a wretch against the King's person; a grenadier of the Filles Saint Thomas parried a sword thrust made in the same direction. Madame Elizabeth ran to her brother's apartments. When she reached the door of his room she heard loud threats of death against the Queen—they called for the head of the Austrian. "Ah! let them think I am the Queen," said she to those around her, "that she may have time to escape."

The Queen could not join the King. She was in the council chamber, where the idea had also been suggested of placing her behind the great table to protect her as much as possible against the approach of the barbarians. Preserving a noble and becoming demeanour in this dreadful situation, she held the Dauphin before her seated upon the table. Madame was at her side; the Princess de Lamballe, the Princess de Tarente, Madame de la Roche-Aymon, Madame de Tourzel, and Madame de Mackau surrounded her. She had fixed a tricoloured cockade, which one of the National Guard had given her, upon her head. The poor little Dauphin was, as well as the King, shrouded in an enormous red cap.[1] The

---

[1] "One of the circumstances of the day of the 20th of June which most vexed the King's friends," says Bertrand de Molleville, "being that of the *bonnet rouge* having remained upon his head nearly three hours, I ventured to ask him for some explanation

horde passed in files before the table; the standards they carried were symbols of the most atrocious barbarity. There was one representing a gibbet, to which a dirty doll was suspended; the words "Marie Antoinette à la lanterne" were written beneath it. Another was a board to which a bullock's heart was fastened, with an inscription round it, "Heart of Louis XVI."; and then a third showed the horns of an ox, with an obscene legend.

One of the most furious Jacobin women who marched with these wretches stopped to give vent to a thousand imprecations against the Queen. Her Majesty asked her whether she had ever seen her. She replied that she had not. Whether she had done her any personal wrong. Her answer was the same; but she added, "It is you who have caused the misery of the nation." "You have been told so," answered the Queen; "you are deceived. As the

---

upon the fact, which was so strikingly in contrast with the extraordinary intrepidity and courage shown by His Majesty during that horrible day. This was his answer: 'The cries of "The nation for ever!" violently increasing around me, and seeming to be addressed to me, I replied that the nation had not a warmer friend than myself. Upon this an ill-looking man, making his way through the crowd, came up to me and said rather roughly, "Well, if you speak the truth, prove it by putting on this red cap." "I consent," replied I. One or two of them immediately came forward and placed the cap upon my hair, for it was too small for my head. I was convinced, I knew not why, that his intention was merely to place the cap upon my head for a moment, and then to take it off again; and I was so completely taken up with what was passing before me that I did not feel whether the cap did or did not remain upon my hair. I was so little aware of it that when I returned to my room I knew only from being told so that it was still there. I was very much surprised to find it upon my head; and was the more vexed at it, because I might have taken it off immediately without the smallest difficulty. But I am satisfied that if I had hesitated to consent to its being placed upon my head the drunken fellow who offered it to me would have thrust his pike into my stomach.'"— NOTE BY THE EDITOR.

12—2

wife of the King of France, and mother of the Dauphin, I am a Frenchwoman. I shall never see my own country again. I can be happy or unhappy only in France. I was happy when you loved me." The fury began to weep, asked her pardon, and said, "It was because I did not know you; I see that you are good."

Santerre, the monarch of the faubourgs, made his subjects file off as quickly as he could; and it was thought at the time that he was ignorant of the object of this insurrection, which was the murder of the Royal Family.[1] However, it was eight o'clock in the evening before the palace was completely cleared. Twelve deputies, impelled by their attachment to the King's person, came and ranged themselves near him at the very commencement of the insurrection; but the deputation from the Assembly did not reach the Tuileries until six in the evening. All the doors of the apartments were broken. The Queen pointed out to the deputies the state of the King's palace, and the disgraceful manner in which his asylum had been violated under the very eyes

---

[1] Montjoie, one of the most decided Royalist writers, thus expresses himself respecting Santerre in the "History of Marie Antoinette" (pp. 295 and 296); and this testimony of his appears the more remarkable as it was the less to be expected:

"The muscular expansion of his tall person, the sonorous hoarseness of his voice, his rough manners, and his easy and vulgar eloquence, of course made him a hero among the lower rabble. And in truth he had gained a despotic empire over the dregs of the faubourgs. He moved them at will, but that was all he knew how to do, or could do; for, as to the rest, he was neither wicked nor cruel. He engaged blindly in all conspiracies, but he was never guilty of the execution of them, either by himself or by those who obeyed him. He was always concerned for an unfortunate person, of whatever party he might be. Affliction and tears disarmed his hands."
—NOTE BY THE EDITOR.

of the Assembly. She saw that Merlin de Thionville was so much affected as to shed tears while she spoke. "You weep, M. Merlin," she said to him, "at seeing the King and his family so cruelly treated by a people whom he always wished to make happy."

"True, madam," replied Merlin; "I weep for the misfortunes of a beautiful and feeling woman, the mother of a family; but do not mistake—not one of my tears falls for either King or Queen. I hate kings and queens; it is the only feeling they inspire me with: it is my religion." The Queen could not understand this madness, and saw all that was to be apprehended from persons who were seized with it.

All hope was gone, and nothing was thought of but succour from abroad. The Queen entreated her family and the King's brothers; her letters probably became more pressing, and expressed her apprehensions upon the tardiness of relief. Her Majesty read me one to herself from the Archduchess Christina, Gouvernante of the Low Countries. She reproached her for some of her expressions, and told her that those out of France were at least as much alarmed as herself at the King's situation and her own; but that the manner of attempting to assist her might either save her or endanger her safety; and that the members of the Coalition were bound to act prudently, entrusted as they were with interests so dear to them.

The 14th of July, fixed by the Constitution as the anniversary of the independence of the nation, drew near. The King and Queen were compelled to make their appearance on the occasion. Aware that the plot of the 20th of June had for its object their assassination, they had no doubt but that their death was determined on for the day of this national festival. The Queen was recommended, in order to give the King's friends time to defend him if the attack should be made, to guard him against the first stroke of a dagger by making him wear a breastplate. I was directed to get one made in my apartments: it was composed of fifteen folds of Italian taffety, formed into an under-waistcoat and a wide belt. This breastplate was tried; it resisted all thrusts of the dagger, and several balls fired for the purpose were turned aside by it. When it was completed, the difficulty was to let the King try it on without running the risk of being surprised. I wore the immense heavy waistcoat as an under-petticoat for three days without being able to find the favourable moment. At length the King found an opportunity one morning to pull off his coat in the Queen's chamber and try on the breastplate.[1]

The Queen was in bed. The King pulled me gently by the gown and drew me as far as he could from the Queen's bed, and said to me in a very low tone of voice, "It is to satisfy her that I submit to this inconvenience; they will not assassinate me; their scheme is changed; they will put me to death another way." The Queen heard the King whispering to me, and when he was gone out she asked me what he had said. I hesitated to answer; she insisted that I should, saying that nothing must be concealed

---

[1] M. Gentil, the first valet of the wardrobe, assisted me to try on this under-waistcoat which the King wore on the 14th of July, 1792, but M. de Paris had a second made a few days before the 10th of August.—NOTE BY MADAME CAMPAN.

from her, and that she was resigned upon every point. When she was informed of the King's remark she told me she had guessed it; that he had long since observed to her that all which was going forward in France was an imitation of the revolution in England in the time of Charles I.; and that he was incessantly reading the history of that unfortunate monarch, in order that he might act better than Charles had done at a similar crisis.[1] "I begin to be fearful of the King being brought to trial," continued the Queen; "as to me, I am a foreigner; they will assassinate me. What will become of my poor children?" These

---

1 A passage in Bertrand de Molleville shows by what gloomy presentiments the unfortunate Prince was overwhelmed, and proves with what courageous resignation he foresaw his fate and prepared to undergo it. His family were his only care. He had no apprehension but for them. The feelings of the friend, the husband and the father constantly weakened or usurped the resolutions of the King.

"His usual book was the 'History of Charles I.,' and his principal attention was directed to avoiding in all his actions everything that it appeared to him would serve as a pretence for a judicial accusation. He would readily have sacrificed his life, but not the glory of France, which an assassination, that would have been only the crime of a few individuals, would not have tarnished.

"It was not until the private conversation which I had with the King, at nine o'clock on the evening of the 21st of June, that I was able to judge how far he was governed by these dismal anticipations. To all my congratulations upon his good fortune in escaping the dangers of the preceding day, His Majesty answered with the utmost indifference: 'All my uneasiness was about the Queen and my sister; for as to myself——' 'But it appears to me,' said I, 'this insurrection was directed chiefly against Your Majesty.' 'I know it well; I saw that they wished to assassinate me, and I cannot tell how it was that they did not do so. But I shall not escape them another time, so that I am no better off; there is but little difference in being assassinated two months earlier or later.' 'Good heavens, Sire!' exclaimed I, 'can Your Majesty, then, so steadfastly believe that you will be assassinated?' 'Yes, I am certain of it. I have long expected it, and have made up my mind. Do you think I fear death?' 'No, surely; but I should be glad to see Your Majesty less determined to expect that event, and more disposed to adopt vigorous measures, which are now become the only means by

sad ejaculations were followed by a torrent of tears.¹
I wished to give her an antispasmodic; she refused it,
saying that it was only for women who were happy
to feel nervous, and that the cruel situation to which she
was reduced rendered these remedies useless. In fact
the Queen, who during her happier days was frequently
attacked by hysterical disorders, enjoyed a more uniform
state of health when all the faculties of her soul were
called forth to support her physical strength.

---

which Your Majesty can look to be rescued.' 'I believe that; but still there would be many chances against me, and I am not fortunate. I should be at no loss if I had not my family with me. It would soon be seen that I am not so weak as they think me; but what will become of my wife and children if I do not succeed?' 'But does Your Majesty think that if you were assassinated your family would be more secure?' 'Yes, I do think so; at least I hope so. And if it happened otherwise I should not have to reproach myself with being the cause of their misfortunes. Besides, what could I do?' 'I think Your Majesty might at this moment leave Paris with greater ease than ever; because the events of yesterday but too clearly prove that your life is not safe in the capital.' 'Oh! I will not fly a second time; I suffered too much before.' 'I am of opinion, too, that Your Majesty should not think of it, at least at this moment; but it seems to me that existing circumstances, and the general indignation which the affair of yesterday appears to have excited, present the King with the most favourable opportunity that can possibly offer for leaving Paris publicly, and without any opposition, not only with the consent of the great majority of the citizens, but with their approbation. I ask Your Majesty's permission to reflect upon this step, and to give you my ideas upon the mode and means of executing it.' 'Do so; but it is a more difficult matter than you imagine.'"—NOTE BY THE EDITOR.

1 These distressing scenes were often renewed. There is nothing in history to which the misfortunes of Marie Antoinette can be compared, but those of Henrietta of France, the daughter of Henry IV., wife of Charles I., and mother of Charles II. Like Henrietta, she was accused of having exercised too much control over the King's mind. Like her she was haunted by continual fears for the lives of her husband and her children. They were both most deeply afflicted; but she had not, like Henrietta, the consolation, after protracted misfortunes, of seeing her family reascend the throne. The tragic and deplorable end of Mary Stuart awaited her who had experienced all the griefs of Henrietta of France.—NOTE BY THE EDITOR.

I had prepared a corset for her, for the same purpose as the King's under-waistcoat, without her knowledge, but she would not make use of it; all my entreaties, all my tears, were in vain. "If the rebels assassinate me," she replied, "it will be a fortunate event for me; they will deliver me from a most painful existence." A few days after the King had tried on his breastplate I met him upon a back staircase, and drew back to let him pass. He stopped and took my hand. I wished to kiss his; he would not suffer it, but drew me towards him by the hand and kissed both my cheeks without saying a single word. This silent mark of his approbation so confused me that I should afterwards have confounded the remembrance of it with the dreams which frequently brought my unhappy Sovereigns again before me, if my sisters had not reminded me that I had communicated this proof of the King's goodness to them shortly after he had given it.

The fear of another attack upon the Tuileries occasioned the most scrupulous searches among the King's papers. I burnt almost all those belonging to the Queen. She put her family letters, a great deal of correspondence which she thought it necessary to preserve for the history of the era of the Revolution, and particularly Barnave's letters and her answers, of which she had preserved copies, into a portfolio, which she entrusted to M. de J——. That gentleman was unable to save this deposit, and it was burnt. The Queen left a few papers in her *secrétaire*. Among them was a paper of instructions to Madame de Tourzel, respecting the dispositions of her children, and the characters and abilities of the governesses under that lady's orders. This paper, which the Queen drew up at the time of Madame de Tourzel's appointment, with several letters from Maria Theresa, filled with the best advice and the most laudable instructions, were printed after the 10th of August by order of the Assembly in the collection of papers found in the *secrétaires* of the King and Queen.

Her Majesty had still, without reckoning the current money of the month, 140,000 francs in gold. She was desirous of depositing the whole of it with me; but I advised her to retain 1,500 louis, as a sum of rather considerable amount might the next moment be very necessary for her. The King had an immense quantity of papers, and unfortunately conceived the idea of privately making a place of concealment in an inner corridor of his apartments, with the assistance of a locksmith who had worked with him above ten years. The place of concealment, but for the man's information, would have been long undiscovered.[1] The wall in which it was made was painted to imitate stone-work, and the opening was entirely concealed among the brown grooves which formed the shaded part of these painted stones. But even before this locksmith had denounced what was afterwards called "the iron closet" to the Assembly, the Queen was aware that he had talked of it to some of his friends,

---

[1] See Note (M) of the first volume upon the subject of this workman, who was named Gamin, the confidence placed in him by Louis XVI., and even the kind of familiarity into which that Prince had admitted him. It is remarkable that Soulavie himself, from whom those particulars are extracted, makes use of the expression, *the infamous Gamin*, and reproaches him with the pension of 1,200 francs, given him by the Convention when he accused Louis XVI. of having wished to poison him.—NOTE BY THE EDITOR.

and that this man, in whom the King, from long habit, placed too much confidence, was a Jacobin. She warned the King of it, and prevailed on him to fill a very large portfolio with all the papers he was most interested in preserving, and entrust it to me. She entreated him, in my presence, to leave nothing in this closet; and the King, in order to quiet her, told her that he had left nothing there. I would have taken the portfolio and carried it to my apartment, but it was too heavy for me to lift. The King said he would carry it himself. I went before him to open the doors. When he placed the portfolio in my inner closet he merely said, "The Queen will tell you what it contains." Upon my return to the Queen I put the question to her, deeming from what the King had said that it was necessary I should know. "They are," the Queen answered me, "such documents as would be most dangerous to the King should they go so far as to proceed to a trial against him. But what he most wishes me to tell you is, no doubt, that the portfolio contains a *procès-verbal* of a cabinet council, in which the King gave his opinion against war. He had it signed by all the ministers, and, in case of a proceeding, he trusts that this document will be very useful to him." I asked the Queen to whom she thought I ought to commit the portfolio. "To whom you please," answered she; "*you alone are answerable for it.* Do not quit the palace, even during your vacation months; there may be circumstances under which it would be very desirable that we should be able to have it instantly."

At this period M. de la Fayette, who had probably

given up the idea of establishing a republic in France similar to that of the United States, and was desirous to support the first Constitution, which he had sworn to defend, quitted his army and came to the Assembly for the purpose of supporting by his presence and by an energetic speech a petition, signed by twenty thousand citizens, against the late violation of the residence of the King and his family. The General found the Constitutional party powerless, and saw that he himself had lost his popularity. The Assembly disapproved of the step he had taken; the King, for whom it was taken, showed no satisfaction at it, and he saw himself compelled to return to his army as quickly as he could. He thought he could rely on the National Guard; but on the day of his arrival those officers who were in the King's interest enquired of His Majesty whether they were to forward the views of General de la Fayette by joining him in such measures as he should pursue during his stay at Paris. The King enjoined them not to do so. From this answer M. de la Fayette perceived that he was abandoned by the remainder of his party in the Paris Guard.

Upon his arrival a plan was presented to the Queen in which it was proposed, by a junction between La Fayette's army and the King's party, to rescue the Royal Family and convey them to Rouen. I did not learn the particulars of this plan; the Queen only said to me upon the subject that "M. de la Fayette was offered to them as a resource, but that it would be better for them to perish than to owe their safety to the man who had done them the most mischief, or to place themselves under the necessity of treating with him."

I passed the whole month of July without going to bed; I was fearful of some attack by night. There was one plot against the Queen's life which has never been made known. I was alone by her bedside at one o'clock in the morning; we heard somebody walking softly along the corridor which passes along the whole line of her apartments, and which was then locked at each end. I went out to fetch the *valet de chambre;* he entered the corridor, and the Queen and myself soon heard the noise of two men fighting. The unfortunate Princess held me locked in her arms, and said to me, "What a situation! insults by day and assassins by night!" The *valet de chambre* cried out to her from the corridor, "Madam, I know the wretch; I have him." "Let him go," said the Queen; "open the door to him; he came to murder me; the Jacobins would carry him about in triumph to-morrow." The man was a servant of the King's toilette, who had taken the key of the corridor out of His Majesty's pocket, after he was in bed, no doubt with the intention of committing the crime suspected. The *valet de chambre*, who was a very strong man, held him by the wrists and thrust him out at the door. The wretch did not speak a word. The *valet de chambre* said, in answer to the Queen, who spoke to him gratefully of the danger to which he had exposed himself, that "he feared nothing, and that he had always a pair of excellent pistols about him for no other purpose than to defend Her Majesty."

On the next day M. de Septeuil had all the locks

of the King's inner apartments changed; I did the same by those of the Queen.

We were every moment told that the Faubourg St. Antoine was preparing to march against the Palace. At four o'clock one morning, towards the latter end of July, a person came to give me information to that effect. I instantly sent off two men on whom I could rely, with orders to proceed to the usual places for assembling and to come back speedily and give me an account of the state of the city. We knew that at least an hour must elapse before the populace of the faubourgs assembled upon the site of the Bastille could reach the Tuileries. It seemed to me sufficient for the Queen's safety that all about her should be awakened. I went softly into her room; she was asleep; I did not awaken her. I found General de W—— in the great closet; he told me the meeting was for this once dispersing. The General had endeavoured to please the populace by the same means that M. de la Fayette had employed. He saluted the lowest *poissarde*, and lowered his hat down to his very stirrup. But the populace, who had been flattered for three years, required far different homage to its power, and the poor man was unnoticed. The King had been awakened, and so had Madame Elizabeth, who had gone to him. The Queen, yielding to the weight of her griefs, slept till nine o'clock on that day, which was very unusual with her. The King had already been to know whether she was awake. I told him what I had done, and the care I had taken not to disturb her rest. He thanked me, and said, " I was awake and so was the whole Palace;

she ran no risk. I am very glad to see her take a little rest. Alas! her griefs double mine!" added the King as he left me. What was my chagrin when, upon awaking and learning what had passed, the Queen began to weep bitterly from regret at not having been called, and to upbraid me, on whose friendship she ought to have been able to rely, for having served her so ill under such circumstances! In vain did I reiterate that it had been only a false alarm, and that it was necessary for her to recruit her strength. "It is not diminished," said she; "misfortune gives us additional strength. Elizabeth was with the King, and I was asleep!—I who am determined to perish by his side. I am his wife; I will not suffer him to incur the smallest risk without my sharing it."

CHAPTER X

Madame Campan's communications with M. Bertrand de Molleville for the King's service—Hope of a speedy deliverance—The Queen's reflections upon the character of Louis XVI.—Insults—Enquiry set on foot by the Princess de Lamballe respecting the persons of the Queen's household—The Tenth of August—Curious particulars—Battle—Scenes of carnage—The Royal Family at the Feuillans.

DURING the month of July the correspondence of M. Bertrand de Molleville with the King and Queen was most active. M. de Marsilly, formerly a lieutenant of the *Cent Suisses* of the Guard, was the bearer of the letters.[1] He came to me the first time with a note from the Queen directed to M. Bertrand himself. In this note the Queen said: "Address yourself with full confidence to Madame Campan; the conduct of her brother in Russia has not at all influenced her

---

[1] Bertrand de Molleville thus relates the measures adopted for his communications with the Queen and Louis XVI.:

"I received by night only the King's answer, written with his own hand in the margin of my letter. Such was the usual form of my correspondence with him. I always sent him back with the day's letter that to which he had replied the day before; so that my letters and his answers, of which I contented myself with taking notes only, never remained with me twenty-four hours. I proposed this arrangement to His Majesty to remove all uneasiness from his mind; my letters were generally delivered to the King or the Queen by M. de Marsilly, captain of the King's Guard, whose attachment and fidelity were known to Their Majesties. I also sometimes employed M. Bernard de Marigny, who had left Brest, entirely for the purpose of facing the dangers which threatened the King, and sharing with all His Majesty's faithful servants the honour of forming a rampart round him with their bodies." ("Private Memoirs," vol. ii., page 12.)—NOTE BY THE EDITOR.

sentiments; she is wholly devoted to us; and if hereafter you should have anything to say to us verbally, you may rely entirely upon her self-devotion and discretion."

The mobs which gathered almost nightly in the faubourgs alarmed the Queen's friends; they entreated her not to sleep in her room on the ground floor of the Tuileries. She removed to the first floor, to a room which was between the King's apartments and those of the Dauphin. Being awake always from daybreak, she ordered that neither the shutters nor the window blinds should be closed, that her long, sleepless nights might be the less weary. About the middle of one of these nights, when the moon was shining into her bed-chamber, she gazed at it, and told me that in a month she should not see that moon, unless freed from her chains and beholding the King at liberty. She then imparted to me all that was being done to deliver them, but said that the opinions of their intimate advisers were alarmingly at variance—that some vouched for complete success, while others pointed out insurmountable dangers. She added that she possessed the itinerary of the march of the Princes and the King of Prussia; that on such a day they would be at Verdun; on another day at such a place; that Lisle was about to be besieged, but that M. de J——, whose prudence and intelligence the King as well as herself highly valued, alarmed them much respecting the success of that siege, and made them apprehensive that, even were the commandant devoted to them, the civil authority, which by the Constitution gave great power to the mayors of towns, would overrule the military commandant. She was also very uneasy as to what would take place at Paris during the interval, and spoke to me upon the King's want of energy, but always in terms expressive of her veneration of his virtues and her attachment to himself. "The King," said she, "is not a coward; he possesses abundance of passive courage, but he is overwhelmed by an awkward shyness, a distrust of himself, which proceeds from his education as much as from his disposition. He is afraid to command, and above all things dreads speaking to assembled numbers. He lived like a child, and always ill at ease, under the eyes of Louis XV., until the age of twenty-one. This constraint confirmed his timidity.[1] Circumstanced as we are, a few well-

---

[1] The following extract points out the causes to which the extreme timidity of Louis XVI. is to be attributed, and in what circumstances he succeeded in overcoming it. It adds also some interesting and faithful particulars to those we have already collected respecting the disposition, qualifications and mind of that Prince.

"One of the most remarkable features of the King's character and of the nature of his mind was that his natural timidity and the difficulty which he generally felt in expressing himself were never perceptible when religion, the relief of the people or the welfare of the French were the subjects in question; he would then speak with a facility and an energy which astonished new ministers in particular, who almost invariably came at first to the Council possessed with the generally received opinion that the King had a very limited intellect. I do not mean to say that Louis XVI. was a genius; but I am convinced that if he had received a different education and his abilities had been cultivated and exercised, he would have been taught to do himself credit by them; he would have shown as much talent as those Princes who have had the reputation of possessing the most. This, however, is certain, that we saw him daily, and with the greatest ease, do a thing which is considered an exploit for people who have the greatest talent, and which it is impossible to perform without talent, and that is to read a letter, a newspaper, or a memorial, and at the same time to listen to the relation of some affair, and yet to understand both perfectly well. The King's constant practice was to come to the Council with the

delivered words addressed to the Parisians, who are devoted to him, would multiply the strength of our party a hundredfold. He will not utter them. What can we expect from those addresses to the people which he has been advised to post up? Nothing but fresh outrages. As for myself, I could do anything, and would appear on horseback if necessary. But if I were really to begin to act, that would be furnishing arms to the King's enemies; the cry against the Austrian and against the sway of a female would become general in France, and moreover, by showing myself, I should render the King a mere cipher. A Queen who is not Regent ought, under these circumstances, to remain passive and prepare to die."

The garden of the Tuileries was filled with a mob, who insulted all who seemed to side with the Court.

Journal du Soir, and the letters or memorials which had been presented to him during the day, in his hand. He spent the first half-hour of each sitting in reading them, handed the memorials which required attention to the proper ministers, lighted the others and the newspaper at the taper next to him, and threw them in flames upon the floor. During all this time the ministers reported the business of their respective departments, and the King understood them so well that in an affair of some delicacy, reported while he was reading by M. Cahier de Gerville, and adjourned for a week for consideration, His Majesty astonished us upon the second report of the same affair by the exactness with which he fixed upon the omission of a fact extremely important to the decision, and which M. Cahier de Gerville no longer remembered. True it is that none of us could cope with the King in point of memory—I never knew one so true. His judgment was not less sound, not only in business, but in the composition of proclamations or of letters or speeches addressed to the Assembly. In fact, I can bear witness that all the important documents of that nature which appeared during my administration were submitted to the King's examination in particular, after having been discussed and frequently settled at the committee of the ministers, and that there are few of them in which His Majesty did not make some corrections which were perfectly proper." ("Memoirs by Bertrand de Molleville," vol. i.) —NOTE BY THE EDITOR.

The "Life of Marie Antoinette" was cried under the Queen's windows; infamous plates were annexed to the book, which hawkers showed to the passers-by.[1] On all sides were heard the jubilant outcries of a people in a state of delirium almost as frightful as the explosion of their rage. The Queen and her children being unable to breathe the open air any longer, it was determined that the garden of the Tuileries should be closed. As soon as this step was taken the Assembly decreed that the whole length of the terrace of the Tuileries belonged to it, and fixed the boundary between what was called the "National ground" and the "Coblentz ground" by a tricoloured ribbon stretched from one end of the terrace to the other. All good citizens were ordered, by notices affixed to it, not to go down into the garden, under pain of being treated in the same manner as Foulon and Berthier.[2] The shutting-up of the Tuileries did not enable the Queen and her children to walk in the garden. The people on the terrace sent forth dreadful

---

[1] The Editor who pens these notes has seen these obscene engravings and read these detestable pamphlets. He has expressed the impression of sorrow and disgust he retains respecting them in the Biographical Notice. What he has to add here, and which gives rise to a painful degree of astonishment, is that among these writings, and particularly among the verses, are to be found some which bespeak a very considerable extent of talent; some passages recall the force of Rousseau's epigrams and the libertine *point* of Piron. What a scandalous and criminal abuse of endowments of mind!—NOTE BY THE EDITOR.

[2] A young man who did not perceive this written order went down into the garden. Furious outcries, threats of "La lanterne," and the crowd of people which collected upon the terrace, warned him of his imprudence and the danger which he ran. He immediately pulled off his shoes, took out his handkerchief and wiped the dust from off their soles. The people cried out, "Bravo! the good citizen for ever!" He was carried off in triumph.—NOTE BY MADAME CAMPAN.

howls, and she was twice compelled to return to her apartments.

In the early part of August many zealous persons offered the King money. He refused considerable sums, being unwilling to injure the fortunes of individuals. M. de la Ferté, Intendant of the Menus Plaisirs, brought me a thousand louis, requesting me to lay them at the feet of the Queen. He thought she could not have too much money at so perilous a time, and that every good Frenchman should hasten to place all his ready money in her hands. She refused this sum, and others of much greater amount which were offered to her.[1] However, a few days afterwards she told me that she would accept of M. de la Ferté's 24,000 francs, because they would make up a sum which the King had to expend. She therefore directed me to go and receive those 24,000 francs, to add them to the 100,000 francs she had placed in my hands, and to change the whole into assignats to increase their amount. Her orders were executed and the assignats were delivered to the King. The Queen informed me that Madame Elizabeth had found a well-meaning man, who had engaged to gain over Pétion by the bribe of a large sum of money, and that that deputy would, by a preconcerted signal, inform the King of the success of the project. His Majesty soon had an opportunity of seeing Pétion, and on

---

[1] M. Auguié, my brother-in-law, Receiver-General of the Finances, offered her, through the medium of his wife, a portfolio containing 100,000 crowns in paper money. On this occasion the Queen said the most affecting things to my sister expressive of her happiness at having contributed to the fortunes of such faithful subjects as herself and her husband, but declined accepting her offer.—NOTE BY MADAME CAMPAN.

the Queen asking him before me if he was satisfied with him, the King replied: "Neither more nor less satisfied than usual; he did not make the concerted signal, and I believe I have been cheated." The Queen then condescended to explain the whole of the enigma to me. "Pétion," said she, "was, while talking to the King, to have kept his finger fixed upon his right eye for at least two seconds." "He did not even put his hand up to his chin," said the King. "After all, it is but so much money stolen; the thief will not boast of it, and the affair will remain a secret. Let us talk of something else." He turned to me and said, "Your father was an intimate friend of Mandat, who now commands the National Guard. Describe him to me; what ought I to expect from him?" I answered that he was one of the most faithful subjects of His Majesty, but that, while he possessed a great deal of loyalty, he had likewise very little sense, and that he was involved in the constitutional vortex. "I understand," said the King; "he is a man who would defend my palace and my person because that is enjoined by the Constitution which he has sworn to support, but who would fight against the party in favour of Sovereign authority; it is well to know this with certainty."

On the next day the Princess de Lamballe sent for me very early in the morning. I found her sitting upon a sofa opposite to a window looking out upon the Pont-Royal. She then occupied that apartment of the Pavilion of Flora which was on a level with that of the Queen. She desired me to sit down by her. Her Highness had a writing-desk upon her knees. "You have had many enemies," said she. "Attempts have been made to deprive you of the Queen's favour; they have been far from successful. Do you know that even I myself, not being so well acquainted with you as the Queen, was rendered suspicious of you, and that upon the arrival of the Court at the Tuileries I gave you a companion to be a spy upon you,¹ and that I had another belonging to the police placed at your door! I was assured that you received five or six of the most virulent deputies of the Tiers Etat, but this report came from that woman belonging to the wardrobe who was lodged above you. In short," said the Princess, "persons of integrity have nothing to fear from the evil-disposed when they belong to so upright a Prince as the King. As to the Queen, she knows you and has loved you ever since she came into France. You shall judge of the King's opinion of you. It was yesterday evening decided in the family circle that, at a time when the Tuileries is likely to be attacked, it was necessary to have the most faithful account of the opinions and conduct of all the individuals composing the Queen's service. The King takes the same precaution on his part respecting all who are about him. He said there was with him a person of great integrity to whom he would commit this enquiry, and that with regard to the Queen's household you

---

¹ This was M. de P——, who afterwards owned it to me, telling me that, though he did accept of this base employment, it was because he was sure that my acquaintance consisted only of Royalists, and that, moreover, he did not doubt the sincerity of my sentiments.—NOTE BY MADAME CAMPAN.

must be spoken to; that he had long studied your character, and that he esteemed your veracity."

The Princess had the names of all who belonged to the Queen's chamber upon her desk. She asked me for information respecting each individual. At such a moment honour and duty efface even the recollection of enmity. I was fortunate in having none but the most favourable information to give. I had to speak of my avowed enemy in the Queen's chamber, of her who most wished to make me responsible for my brother's political opinions. The Princess, as the head of the chamber, could not be ignorant of this circumstance, but as the woman in question, who idolised the King and Queen, would not have hesitated to sacrifice her life in order to save theirs, and as possibly her attachment to them, united to considerable narrowness of intellect and a limited education, contributed to her jealousy of me, I spoke of her in the highest terms.

The Princess wrote as I dictated, and occasionally looked at me with astonishment. When I had done I entreated Her Highness to write down in the margin that the lady alluded to was my declared enemy. She embraced me, saying, "Ah! write it! we should not record an injustice which ought to be forgotten." We came to the name of a man of genius, who was much attached to the Queen. I described him as a man born solely for disputation, showing himself, out of a mere spirit of contradiction, an aristocrat with democrats and a democrat among aristocrats, but still a man of probity and well affected to his Sovereign. The Princess said she knew many persons of that disposition, and that she was delighted I had nothing to say against this man, because she herself had placed him about the Queen.

The whole of Her Majesty's chamber, which consisted entirely of persons of fidelity, gave throughout all the dreadful convulsions of the Revolution proofs of the greatest prudence and the most absolute self-devotion. The same cannot be said of the ante-chambers. With the exception of three or four, all the servants of that class were outrageous Jacobins; and I saw on those occasions the necessity of composing the private household of Princes of persons completely separated from the class of the people.

The situation of the Royal Family was so unbearable during the months which immediately preceded the 10th of August that the Queen longed for the coming of the crisis whatever might be its issue. She frequently said that a long confinement in a tower by the seaside would seem to her less intolerable than those feuds in which the weakness of her party daily threatened an inevitable catastrophe.[1]

Not only were Their Majesties prevented from breathing the open air, but they were also insulted at the very foot of the altar. The Sunday before the

---

[1] A few days before the 10th of August the squabbles between the Royalists and Jacobins, and between the Jacobins and the Constitutionals, increased in warmth; among the latter, those men who defended the principles they professed with the greatest talent, courage and constancy were at the same time the most exposed to danger. Montjoie relates the following anecdote:

"The question of abdication was discussed with a degree of frenzy in the Assembly. Such of the deputies as voted against that scandalous discussion were abused, ill-treated and surrounded by assassins. They had a battle to fight at every step they took; and

last day of the monarchy, while the Royal Family went through the gallery to the chapel, half the soldiers of the National Guard exclaimed, "Long live the King!" and the other half, "No! no King! down with the veto!" and on that day, at vespers, the choristers preconcerted to increase the loudness of their voices threefold, in an alarming manner, when they chanted the words, "Deposuit potentes de sede," in the *Magnificat*. Incensed at such an infamous proceeding, the Royalists, in their turn, thrice exclaimed, " Et reginam" after the " Domine salvum fac regem." The tumult during the whole time of Divine service was excessive.

At length arrived that terrible night of the 10th of August. On the preceding evening Pétion went to the Assembly and informed it that preparations were making for a great insurrection on the following day; that the tocsin would sound at midnight; and that he feared he had not sufficient means for resisting the attack which was about to take place. Upon this information the Assembly passed to the order of the day. Pétion, however, gave an order for repelling force by force. M. Mandat was armed with this order, and, finding his fidelity to the King's person supported by what he considered the law of the State, he conducted himself, in all his operations, with the

---

at length they did not dare to sleep in their own houses. Of this number were Regnault de Beaucaron, Frondière, Girardin and Vaublanc.

"Girardin complained of having been struck in one of the lobbies of the Assembly; a voice cried out to him, 'Say where you were struck?' 'Where?' replied Girardin; 'what a question! Behind. *Do assassins ever strike otherwise?*'" ("History of Marie Antoinette.")—NOTE BY THE EDITOR.

greatest energy. On the evening of the 9th I was present at the King's supper. While His Majesty was giving me various orders we heard a great noise at the door of the apartment. I went to see what was the cause of it, and I found the two sentinels fighting. One said, speaking of the King, that he was hearty in the cause of the Constitution, and would defend it at the peril of his life; the other maintained that he was an incumbrance to the only Constitution suitable to a free people. They were near destroying each other. I returned with a countenance which betrayed my emotion. The King desired to know what was going forward at his door: I could not conceal it from him. The Queen said she was not at all surprised at it, and that more than half the guard belonged to the Jacobin party.

The tocsin sounded at midnight. The Swiss were drawn up like real walls; and, in the midst of their soldier-like silence, which formed a striking contrast to the perpetual din of the town guard, the King informed M. de J———, an officer of the staff, of the plan of defence laid down by General Vioménil. M. de J—— said to me, after this private conference, "Put your jewels and money into your pockets. Our dangers are unavoidable; the means of defence are unavailing; safety might be obtained from some degree of energy in the King, but that is the only virtue in which he is deficient."

An hour after midnight the Queen and Madame Elizabeth said they would lie down on a sofa in a closet in the *entresols*, the windows of which commanded the courtyard of the Tuileries.

The Queen told me the King had just refused to put on his quilted under-waistcoat; that he had consented to wear it on the 14th of July because he was merely going to a ceremony, where the blade of an assassin was to be apprehended; but that on a day on which his party might fight against the revolutionists he thought there was something cowardly in preserving his life by such means.

During this time Madame Elizabeth disengaged herself of some of her clothing which encumbered her in order to lie down on the sofa: she took a cornelian pin out of her tippet, and before she laid it down on the table she showed it to me, and desired me to read a motto engraved upon it round a stalk of lilies. The words were, "*Oblivion of injuries—pardon for offences.*" "I much fear," added that virtuous Princess, "that this maxim has but little influence among our enemies; but it ought not to be less dear to us on that account."[1]

The Queen desired me to sit down by her. The two Princesses could not sleep; they were conversing mournfully upon their situation when a musket was

---

[1] The Princess did not take this precious trinket when she quitted the Queen's *entresol*. Into what hands did it fall? It would adorn the richest treasury.

The exalted piety of Madame Elizabeth gave to all she said and did a noble character, descriptive of that of her soul. On the day on which this worthy descendant of St. Louis was sacrificed, the executioner, in tying her hands behind her back, raised up one of the ends of her handkerchief in front. Madame Elizabeth, with calmness, and with a voice which seemed not to belong to earth, said to him, "In the name of modesty, cover my bosom." I learned this trait of heroism from Madame de Serilly, who was condemned the same day as the Princess, but who obtained a respite at the moment of the execution, Madame de Montmorin, her relation, declaring that her cousin was pregnant.—NOTE BY MADAME CAMPAN.

discharged in the courtyard. They both quitted the sofa, saying, "There is the first shot; unfortunately it will not be the last. Let us go up to the King." The Queen desired me to follow her; several of her women went with me.

At four o'clock the Queen came out of the King's chamber and told us she had no longer any hope, that M. Mandat, who had gone to the Hôtel de Ville to receive further orders, had just been assassinated, and that the people were at that time carrying his head about the streets. Day came; the King, the Queen, Madame Elizabeth, Madame and the Dauphin went down to pass through the ranks of the sections of the National Guard: the cry of "Vive le Roi!" was heard from a few places. I was at a window on the garden side; I saw some of the gunners quit their posts, go up to the King and thrust their fists in his face, insulting him by the most brutal language. MM. de Salvert and M. de Bridges drove them off in a spirited manner. The King was as pale as a corpse. The Royal Family came in again; the Queen told me that all was lost; that the King had shown no energy, and that this sort of review had done more harm than good.[1]

---

[1] Montjoie, in his "History of Marie Antoinette," gives an account of the affair of the Château, which he says was furnished by an eye-witness. The narrator thus expresses himself:

"M. Mandat being gone, the command devolved on M. de la Chesnaye.

"I then perceived a considerable degree of bustle in the interior of the castle.

"The National Guard and the Swiss Guards being called to their posts, all went to them in the greatest order. The interior of the apartments, the staircases and vestibules were occupied by soldiers; the posts of the courtyards were distributed, and cannon

I was in the billiard-room with my companions; we placed ourselves upon some high benches. I then saw M. d'Hervilly, with a drawn sword in his hand, ordering the usher to open the door to the French *noblesse*. Two hundred persons entered the room which was nearest to that in which the family were; others also drew up in two lines in the preceding rooms. I saw a few people belonging to the Court, many others whose features were unknown to me, and a few who figured ridiculously enough among what was called the *noblesse*, but whose self-devotion ennobled them at once. They were all so badly armed that even in that situation the French vivacity, which yields to nothing, indulged in jests upon that which was no jesting matter. M. de Saint-Souplet, one of the King's equerries, and a page, instead of muskets, carried upon their shoulders the tongs belonging to the King's ante-chamber, which they had broken and divided between them. Another page, who had a pocket-pistol in his hand, stuck the end of it against the back of the person who stood before him, and who begged he would be good enough to rest it elsewhere. A sword and a pair of pistols were the only arms of those who had had the precaution to provide themselves with arms at all. Meanwhile

---

were brought from different parts of the great court. All these preparations announced the most terrible resolves; they seemed to express a determination to offer a vigorous resistance. I turned my eyes away and lamented first the manner and then the inefficiency of the means employed; the manner, because I saw a scene of bloodshed and murders without number in preparation; the inefficiency, because, in spite of the wild and criminal scheme of an unavailing resistance, I was convinced beforehand that there was no fence strong enough to stem the impetuous torrent."— NOTE BY THE EDITOR.

the numerous bands from the faubourgs, armed with pikes and cutlasses, filled the Carrousel and the streets adjacent to the Tuileries. The sanguinary Marseillais were at their head, with cannon pointed against the castle. In this emergency the King's council sent M. Dejoly, the Minister of Justice, to the Assembly to request they would send the King a deputation which might serve as a safeguard to the executive power. Its ruin was resolved on—they passed to the order of the day. At eight o'clock the department repaired to the castle; the *procureur-syndic*, seeing that the guard within was ready to join the assailants, went into the King's closet and requested to speak to him in private. The King received him in his chamber; the Queen was with him. There M. Rœderer told him that the King, all his family and the people about them would inevitably fall unless His Majesty immediately determined to go to the National Assembly. The Queen at first opposed this advice; but the *procureur-syndic* told her that she rendered herself responsible for the deaths of the King, her children and all who were in the palace; upon this she no longer objected. The King then consented to go to the Assembly. As he set out he said to the minister and persons who surrounded him, "Come, gentlemen, there is nothing more to be done here."[1]

---

[1] The informant cited by Montjoie thus relates the efforts made by M. Rœderer with the people and the National Guard, and the conversation he afterwards had with the King in his closet. This account of the 10th of August contains also several other important particulars; but we refer them all to the *Historical Illustrations* (K), not to interrupt Madame Campan's narrative.

"M. Rœderer, it must be said to his praise, tried all means. At last, being unable to subdue the fury of the people, he calmed it

The Queen said to me as she left the King's chamber, "Wait in my apartments; I will come to you, or I will send for you, to go—I know not whither." She took with her only the Princess de Lamballe and Madame de Tourzel. The Princess de Tarente and Madame de la Roche-Aymon were inconsolable at being left at the Tuileries. They, and all who belonged to the chamber, went down into the Queen's apartments.

We saw the Royal Family pass between two lines formed by the Swiss grenadiers and those of the battalions of the Petits Pères and the Filles Saint Thomas. They were so pressed upon by the crowd that during that short passage the Queen was robbed of her watch

for a few minutes; they granted him half an hour, and the depositaries of the law instantly returned into the castle-yard.

"Here they met with obstacles of another kind, the National Guard seemed perfectly resolute and well disposed.

"M. Rœderer called their attention to the extent of the danger; he made them promise to remain firm at their posts; he exhorted them not to attack their fellow citizens, their brethren, as long as they should remain inactive; but he foresaw the approaching moment when the Château would be attacked. He explained to them the principles of the lawful defence, and made the requisition prescribed by the law of the month of May, 1791, relative to the public force. The National Guard, however, remained silent, and the gunners discharged their cannon.

"What could the authorities of the department then do? They joined the King's ministers, and all with one consent conjured him to save himself with his family and take refuge in the bosom of the National Assembly. 'There only, Sire,' said M. Rœderer, 'in the midst of the representatives of the people, can Your Majesty, the Queen and the Royal Family be in safety. Come, let us fly; in another quarter of an hour, perhaps, we shall not be able to command a retreat.'

"The King hesitated; the Queen manifested the highest dissatisfaction. 'What!' said she; 'are we alone; is there nobody who can act——?' 'Yes, madam, alone; action is useless—resistance is impossible.' One of the members of the department, M. Gerdret, resolved to add his voice; he insisted upon the prompt execution of the proposed measure. 'Silence! sir,' said the Queen to him; 'silence! you are the only person who ought to be silent here. When the mischief is done, those who did it should not pretend to wish to remedy it.'"—NOTE BY THE EDITOR.

and purse. A man of frightful height and atrocious appearance—one of such as were to be seen at the head of all the insurrections—drew near the Dauphin, whom the Queen was leading by the hand, and took him up in his arms. The Queen uttered a scream of terror, and was ready to faint. The man said to her, "Don't be frightened; I will do him no harm"; and he gave him back to her at the entrance of the chamber.

I leave to history all the details of that too memorable day, confining myself to retracing a few of the frightful scenes enacted in the interior of the Tuileries after the King had quitted the palace.

The assailants did not know that the King and his family had betaken themselves to the bosom of the Assembly; and those who defended the palace on the court side were equally ignorant of it. It is supposed that if they had been aware of the fact the siege would never have taken place.

The Marseillais began by driving from their posts several Swiss, who yielded without resistance. A few of the assailants fired upon them. Some of the Swiss officers, unable to contain themselves at seeing their men fall thus, and perhaps thinking the King was still at the Tuileries, gave the word to a whole battalion to fire. The aggressors were thrown into disorder, and the Carrousel was cleared in a moment; but they soon returned, spurred on by rage and revenge. The Swiss were but 800 strong; they fell back into the interior of the castle. Some of the doors were battered in by the guns, others broken through with hatchets; the populace rushed from all quarters into the interior of the palace; almost all the Swiss were massacred. The Nobles, flying through the gallery which leads to the Louvre, were either stabbed or pistolled, and the bodies were thrown out of the windows. M. Pallas and M. de Marchais, ushers of the King's chamber, were killed in defending the door of the council chamber; many others of the King's servants fell, victims of their attachment to their master. I mention these two persons in particular because, with their hats pulled over their brows and their swords in their hands, they exclaimed, as they defended themselves with unavailing but praiseworthy courage: "We will not survive. This is our post—our duty is to die at it." M. Diet acted in the same manner at the door of the Queen's bed-chamber; he experienced the same fate. The Princess de Tarente had fortunately opened the door of the entrance into the apartments, otherwise the dreadful band, seeing several women collected in the Queen's saloon, would have fancied she was among us, and would immediately have massacred us if their rage had been increased by resistance. However, we were all about to perish, when a man with a long beard came up, exclaiming, in the name of Pétion, "Spare the women! don't disgrace the nation!" A particular circumstance placed me in greater danger than the others. In my confusion I imagined, a moment before the assailants entered the Queen's apartments, that my sister was not among the group of women collected there, and I went up into an *entresol*, where I supposed she had taken refuge, to induce her to come down, fancying it of consequence to our safety that we should not be separated. I did not find her in the room in question; I saw there only our two *femmes de chambre* and one of the Queen's two *heydukes*—a man of great height and a perfectly military aspect. I cried out to him, "Fly! the footmen and our people are already safe." "I cannot," said the man to me; "I am dying of fear." As he spoke, I heard a number of men rushing hastily up the staircase. They threw themselves upon him, and I saw him assassinated. I ran towards the staircase, followed by our women. The murderers left the *heyduke* to come to me. The women threw themselves at their feet and held their sabres. The narrowness of the staircase impeded the assassins, but I had already felt a horrid hand thrust down my back to seize me by my clothes, when someone called out from the bottom of the staircase, "What are you doing up there?" The terrible Marseillais who was going to massacre me answered by a "*Heu!*" the sound of which will never escape my memory. The other voice replied with these words, "We don't kill women."

I was on my knees. My executioner quitted his hold of me, and said, "Get up, you jade; the nation pardons you."

The brutality of these words did not prevent me from suddenly experiencing an indescribable feeling, which partook almost equally of the love of life and the idea that I was going to see my son and all that was dear to me again. A moment before I had thought less of death than of the pain which the steel suspended over my head would occasion me. Death is seldom seen so close without striking his blow. I can assert that upon such an occasion the organs, unless fainting ensues, are in full activity, and that I heard every syllable uttered by the assassins just as if I had been calm.

Five or six men seized me and my women, and having made us get upon benches placed before the windows, ordered us to call out, "The nation for ever!"

I passed over several corpses. I recognised that of the old Viscount de Broves, to whom the Queen had sent me, at the beginning of the night, to desire him and another old gentleman in her name to go home. These brave men desired I would tell Her Majesty that they had but too strictly obeyed the King's orders in all circumstances under which they ought to have exposed their own lives in order to preserve his, and that for this once they would not obey, but would cherish the recollection of the Queen's goodness.

Near the *grille*, on the side next the bridge, the men who conducted me asked whither I wished to go. Upon my asking in my turn whether they were at liberty to take me wherever I wished to go, one of them, who was a Marseillais, asked me, giving me at the same time a push with the butt end of his musket, whether I still doubted the power of the people? I answered "No," and I mentioned the number of my father-in-law's house. I saw my sister ascending the steps of the parapet of the bridge, surrounded by men of the National Guard. I called to her, and she turned round.

"Would you have her go with you?" said my guardian to me. I told him I did wish it; they then called to the people who were leading my sister to prison, and she joined me.

Madame de la Roche-Aymon and her daughter, Mademoiselle Pauline de Tourzel, Madame de Ginestoux, lady to the Princess de Lamballe, the other women of the Queen, and the old Count d'Affry, were led off together to the prisons of the Abbaye.

Our progress from the Palace of the Tuileries to my sister's house was most distressing. We saw several Swiss pursued and killed, and musket shots were crossing each other in all directions. We passed under the walls of the gallery of the Louvre; they were firing from the parapet into the windows of the gallery, to hit the "Knights of the dagger," for thus did the populace designate those faithful subjects who had assembled at the Tuileries to defend the King.

The brigands broke some vessels of water in the Queen's first ante-chamber; the mixture of blood and water stained the bottoms of our white gowns. The *poissardes* screamed after us in the streets that we were attached to "the Austrian." Our protectors then showed some consideration for us, and made us go up a gateway to pull off our gowns; but our petticoats being too short and making us look like persons in disguise, other *poissardes* began to bawl out that we were young Swiss dressed up like women. We then saw a tribe of female cannibals enter the street carrying the head of poor Mandat. Our guards hurriedly made us enter a little wine-shop, called for some wine, and desired us to drink with them. They assured the landlady that we were their sisters and good patriots. Happily the Marseillais had quitted us to return to the Tuileries. One of the men who remained with us said to me in an undertone, "I am a gauze-worker in the faubourg; I was forced to march; I am not for all this. I have not killed anybody, and have rescued you. You ran a great risk when we met the mad women who are carrying Mandat's head. These horrible women said yesterday, at midnight, upon the site of the Bastille, that they must have their revenge for the 6th of October at Versailles, and that they had sworn to kill the Queen and all the women attached to her. The danger of the action saved you all."

As I crossed the Carrousel I saw my house in flames; but as soon as the first moment of affright was over I thought no more of my personal misfortunes. My ideas turned solely upon the dreadful situation of the Queen.

On reaching my sister's we found all our family in despair, believing they should never see us again. I could not remain at her house; some of the mob around the door exclaimed that Marie Antoinette's confidante was in the house, and that they must have her head. I disguised myself, and was concealed at the house of M. Morel, secretary for the lotteries. On the morrow I was enquired for there in the name of the Queen. A deputy, whose sentiments were known to her, took upon himself to find me out.

'I borrowed clothes and went with my sister to

the Feuillans. We got there at the same time with M. Thierry de Ville-d'Avry, the King's first *valet de chambre*. We were taken into an office, where we wrote down our names and places of abode, and we received tickets for admission into the rooms belonging to Camus, the Keeper of the Archives, where the King was with his family.

As we entered the first room a person who was there said to me, "Ah! you are a good creature; but where is that Thierry[1]—that man loaded with his master's bounties?" "He is here," said I; "he is following me; and I perceive that even scenes of death do not banish jealous feelings from among you."

Having belonged to the Court from my earliest youth, I was known to many persons whom I did not know. As I traversed a corridor above the cloisters which led to the cells inhabited by the unfortunate Louis XVI. and his family, several of the grenadiers spoke to me, calling me by my name. One of them said to me, "Well! the poor King is lost! The Count d'Artois would have managed it better." "Not a bit," said another.

The Royal Family occupied a small suite of apartments consisting of four cells, formerly belonging to the ancient monastery of the Feuillans. In the first were the men who had accompanied the King: the Prince de Poix, the Baron d'Aubier, M. de Saint-Pardou, equerry to Madame Elizabeth, MM. Goguelat, Chamilly and Huë. In the second we found the King;

---

1 M. Thierry, who never ceased to give his Sovereign proofs of the most respectful and unalterable attachment, was one of the victims of the 2nd of September.—NOTE BY MADAME CAMPAN.

he was having his hair dressed. He took two locks of it, and gave one to my sister and one to me. We offered to kiss his hand; he opposed it, and embraced us without saying anything. In the third was the Queen, in bed, and in an indescribable state of affliction. We found her accompanied only by a bulky woman, who appeared tolerably civil; she was the keeper of the apartments; she waited upon the Queen, who as yet had none of her own people about her. Her Majesty stretched out her arms to us, saying, "Come, unfortunate women; come and see one still more unhappy than yourself, since she has been the cause of all your misfortunes. We are ruined," continued she; "we are arrived at that point to which they have been leading us for three years through all possible outrages; we shall fall in this dreadful revolution, and many others will perish after us. All have alike contributed to our downfall; the reformers have urged it like mad people, and others through ambition, for their own interests; for the wildest Jacobin seeks wealth and distinction, and the mob is eager for plunder—there is not one lover of his country among all this infamous horde. The emigrant party had their intrigues and schemes; foreigners sought to profit by the dissensions of France; everyone had a share in our misfortunes."

The Dauphin came in with Madame and the Marchioness de Tourzel. On seeing them the Queen said to me, "Poor children! how heartrending it is, instead of handing down to them so fine an inheritance, to say, 'It ends with us!'" She afterwards conversed with me about the Tuileries and the persons who had fallen; she condescended also to mention the burning of my house. Without the smallest affectation I say it, I looked upon that loss as a mischance which ought not to dwell in her mind, and I told her so. She spoke of the Princess de Tarente, whom she greatly loved and valued, of Madame de la Roche-Aymon and her daughter, of other persons whom she had left at the palace, and of the Duchess de Luynes, who was to have passed the night at the Tuileries. Respecting her she said, "Hers was one of the first heads turned by the rage for that mischievous philosophy; but her heart brought her back, and I again found a friend in her."[1] I asked the Queen what the ambassadors from foreign Powers had done under existing circumstances. She told me that they could do nothing; and that the wife of the English ambassador had just given her a proof of the private interest she took in her welfare by sending her linen for her son.

I informed her that in the pillaging of my house all my accounts with her had been thrown into the Carrousel, and that every sheet of my month's expenditure was signed by her, sometimes leaving four or five inches of blank paper above her signature —a circumstance which rendered me very uneasy, from an apprehension that an improper use might be made of those signatures. She desired me to demand

---

[1] During the Reign of Terror I withdrew to the Château de Coubertin, near that of De Dampierre. The Duchess de Luynes frequently came to request I would repeat to her what the Queen had said about her at the Feuillans. We wept together, and she would say as she went away, "I have often need to request you to repeat those words of the Queen."—NOTE BY MADAME CAMPAN.

admission into the Committee of General Safety and to make this declaration there. I repaired thither instantly and found a deputy, with whose name I have never yet become acquainted. After hearing me, he said that "he would not receive my deposition, that Marie Antoinette was now nothing more than any other Frenchwoman, and that if any of those detached papers bearing her signature should be misapplied, she would have, at a future period, a right to make a complaint, and to support her declaration by the facts which I had just related." The Queen regretted having sent me, and entertained an apprehension that she had, by her very caution, pointed out a method of fabricating forgeries which might be dangerous to her. Then, again, she exclaimed, "My apprehensions are as absurd as the step I made you take. They need nothing more for our ruin—all is over." She gave us an account of what had taken place subsequently to the King's arrival at the Assembly. It is all well known, and I have no occasion to repeat it. I will merely mention that she told us, though with much delicacy, that she was not a little hurt at the King's conduct since he had been at the Feuillans; that his habit of laying no restraint upon himself, and his great appetite, had prompted him to eat as if he had been at his palace; that those who did not know him as she did, did not feel the piety and the magnanimity of his resignation—all which produced so bad an effect that deputies who were devoted to him had warned him of it, but that no change could be effected.

I still see in imagination—and shall always see—

that narrow cell at the Feuillans, hung with green paper; that wretched couch whence the dethroned Queen stretched out her arms to us, saying that our misfortunes, of which she was the cause, aggravated her own! There, for the last time, I saw the tears, I heard the sobs of her whom her high birth, the endowments of Nature, and, above all, the goodness of her heart, had seemed to destine for the adornment of a throne and the happiness of her people! It is impossible for those who have lived with Louis XVI. and Marie Antoinette not to be fully convinced, even doing all justice to the King's virtues, that if the Queen had been, from the moment of her arrival in France, the object of the care and affection of a Prince of decision and authority, she would have greatly contributed to the glory of his reign.

What affecting things I have heard the Queen say in the depth of her affliction, occasioned by the ill-founded opinion of a part of the Court and the whole of the people, that she did not love France! How did that opinion shock those who knew her heart and her sentiments! Twice did I see her on the point of going forth from her apartments in the Tuileries into the gardens, for the purpose of addressing the immense throng constantly assembled there to insult her. "Yes," exclaimed she, as she paced her chamber with hurried steps; "I will say to them, 'Frenchmen, they have had the cruelty to persuade you that I do not love France! I, the mother of a Dauphin who will reign over this noble country! I, whom Providence has seated upon the most powerful throne of Europe! Of all the daughters of

Maria Theresa, am I not that one whom fortune has most highly favoured? And ought I not to feel all these advantages? What should I find at Vienna? Nothing but sepulchres! What should I lose in France? Everything which flatters honourable pride and sensibility!'"

I protest I only repeat her own words here; but if, prompted by existing circumstances, her noble heart did at first send forth this burst of feeling, the soundness of her judgment soon pointed out to her the dangers of such a proceeding with regard to the people. "I should descend from the throne," said she, "merely, perhaps, to excite a momentary sympathy, which the factious would soon render more injurious than beneficial to me."

Yes, not only did Marie Antoinette love France, but few women possessed in greater vigour than herself that feeling of pride which the courage of Frenchmen must inspire. I could adduce a multitude of proofs of this; I will relate two traits which demonstrate the noblest national enthusiasm. The Queen was telling me that at the period of the coronation of the Emperor Francis II., that Prince, in bespeaking the admiration of a French general officer, who was then an emigrant, in favour of the fine appearance of his troops, said to him, "There are the men to beat your *sans-culottes!*" "That remains to be seen, Sire," instantly replied the officer. The Queen added, "I don't know the name of the brave Frenchman, but I will learn it; the King ought to be in possession of it." As she was reading the public papers a few days before the 10th of August, she observed that mention was made of the courage of a man who died in defending the flag he carried and shouting "Vive la nation!" "Ah! the fine fellow!" said the Queen; "what a happiness it would have been for us if such men had never left off crying 'Vive le Roi!'"

In all that I have hitherto said of this most unfortunate of woman and of queens, those who did not live with her, those who knew her but partially—and especially the majority of foreigners, prejudiced by infamous libels—may imagine I have thought it my duty to sacrifice truth on the altar of gratitude. Fortunately there are still in existence unexceptionable witnesses whom I can invoke; they will declare whether what I assert that I have seen and heard appears to them either untrue or improbable.

CHAPTER XI

Pétion refuses Madame Campan permission to be confined in the Temple with the Queen—She excites the suspicions of Robespierre—Domiciliary visits—Madame Campan opens the portfolio she had received from the King—Papers in it, with the Seals of State—Mirabeau's secret correspondence with the Court—It is destroyed, as well as the other papers—The only document preserved—It is delivered to M. de Malesherbes, upon the trial of the unfortunate Louis XVI.—End of the Memoirs.

THE Queen having lost her watch and purse as she was passing from the Tuileries to the Feuillans, requested my sister to lend her twenty-five louis.[1]

I spent part of the day at the Feuillans, and Her Majesty told me she would ask Pétion to let me be with her in the place which the Assembly should decree for the prison. I then returned home to prepare everything that might be necessary for me to accompany her thither.

---

[1] On being interrogated, the Queen declared that these five-and-twenty louis had been lent to her by my sister; this formed a pretence for arresting her and myself, and led to the death of that virtuous mother of a family.*—NOTE BY MADAME CAMPAN.

* Madame Auguié, who was remarkable for her height and beauty, was a woman of the greatest resolution. Death had no terrors for her; but the idea of perishing innocently upon a scaffold aroused her indignation. "Never," said she, "shall the executioner lay his hand on me." Her religious sentiments would, perhaps, have inspired her with more resignation, but she was a mother, and the desire of preserving her property to her family suffered her to think of nothing but the means of anticipating an arrest otherwise inevitable. At the instant when the officers presented themselves for the purpose of arresting her, she precipitated herself from a third floor. This last sacrifice of maternal tenderness renders her end as honourable as her self-devotion to the Queen had been praiseworthy and affecting.—NOTE BY THE EDITOR.

On the same day (the 11th of August), at nine in the evening, I returned to the Feuillans, and found there were orders at all the gates forbidding my being admitted. I claimed a right to enter by virtue of the first permission which had been given to me, and was again refused. I was told that the Queen had as many people as were requisite about her. My sister was with her as well as one of my companions, who came out of the prisons of the Abbaye on the 11th. I renewed my solicitations on the 12th; my tears and entreaties moved neither the keepers of the gates nor even a deputy to whom I addressed myself.

I soon heard of the transfer of Louis XVI. and his family to the Temple. I went to Pétion accompanied by a man for whom I had procured a place in the post-office,[1] and who was much disposed to serve me. He determined to go up to Pétion alone; he supplicated and told him that those who requested to be confined could not be suspected of evil designs, and that no political opinion could afford a ground of objection to these solicitations. Seeing that the well-meaning man did not succeed, I thought to do more in person; but Pétion persisted in his refusal, and threatened to send me to the prison of La Force. He was still more cruel when, thinking to give me a sort of consolation, he added that I might be certain that all those who were then with Louis XVI. and his family would not stay with them long. And in fact, two or three days afterwards, the Princess de Lamballe, Madame de Tourzel, her daughter, the Queen's first woman, the first woman

---

[1] M. Valadon.

of the Dauphin and Madame, M. de Chamilly and M. Huë were carried off during the night and transferred to La Force.

After the departure of the King and Queen for the Temple, my sister was detained a prisoner for twenty-four hours in the apartments Their Majesties had quitted.

From this time I was reduced to the misery of having no further intelligence of my august and unfortunate mistress but through the medium of the newspapers or the National Guard, who did duty at the Temple.

The King and Queen said nothing to me at the Feuillans about the portfolio which had been deposited with me. No doubt they expected to see me again. The Minister Roland and the deputies composing the Provisional Government were very intent on search for papers belonging to Their Majesties. They had the whole of the Tuileries ransacked. The infamous Robespierre bethought himself of M. Campan, the Queen's private secretary, and said that his death was feigned, that he was living unknown in some obscure part of France, and was doubtless the depositary of all the important papers. In a great portfolio belonging to the King there had been found a solitary letter from the Count d'Artois, which, by its date and the subjects of which it treated, indicated the existence of a continued correspondence. (This letter appears among the documents used at the trial of Louis XVI.) A former preceptor of my son's had studied with Robespierre. The latter meeting him in the street, and knowing the connection which had subsisted between him and the family of M. Campan, required him to say, upon his honour, whether he was certain of the death of the latter. The man replied that M. Campan had died at La Briche in 1791, and that he had seen him interred in the cemetery of Epinay. "Well, then," resumed Robespierre, "bring me the certificate of his burial at twelve tomorrow; it is a document for which I have pressing occasion." Upon hearing the deputy's demand, I instantly sent for a certificate of M. Campan's burial, and Robespierre received it at nine o'clock the next morning. But I considered that in thinking of my father-in-law they were coming very near me, the real depositary of these important papers. I passed days and nights in considering what I could do for the best, or what would be the most prudent under such circumstances.

I was thus situated when the order to inform against what were called the *attentats* of the 10th of August led to domiciliary visits. My servants were informed that the people of the quarter in which I lived talked much of the search that would be made in my house, and came to apprise me of it. I heard that fifty armed men would make themselves masters of M. Auguié's house, where I then was. I had just received this intelligence when M. Gougenot, the King's *maître d'hôtel* and receiver-general of the household, a man much attached to his Sovereign, came into my room, wrapped in a riding-cloak, under which with great difficulty he carried the King's portfolio which I had entrusted to him. He threw it down at my feet, and said to me, "There is your deposit. I did not receive it from our unfortunate King's own hands; in delivering it to you I have executed my trust." After saying this he was about to withdraw. I stopped him, praying him to concert with me what I ought to do in such a trying emergency. He would not listen to my entreaties, or even hear me describe the course I intended to pursue. I told him my abode was about to be surrounded; I imparted to him what the Queen had said to me about the contents of the portfolio. To all this he answered, "There it is; decide for yourself; I will have no hand in it." Upon that I remained a few seconds buried in thought, and I remember that my conduct was founded upon the following reasons. I spoke aloud, although to myself; I walked about the room with agitated steps. The unfortunate Gougenot was thunderstruck. "Yes," said I, "when we can no longer communicate with our King and receive his orders, however attached we may be to him, we can only serve him according to the best of our own judgment. The Queen said to me, 'This portfolio contains scarcely anything but documents of a most dangerous description in the event of a trial taking place, if it should fall into the hand of revolutionary persons.' She mentioned, too, a single document which would under the same circumstances be useful. It is my duty to interpret her words and consider them as orders. She meant to say, 'You will save such a paper; you will destroy the rest if they are likely to be taken from you.' If it were not so, was there any occasion for her to enter into any particulars of what the portfolio contained? The order to keep it was sufficient. Probably it contains, moreover, the letters of that part of the family which has emigrated. There is nothing which may have been foreseen or decided upon that can be useful now, and there can be no political thread which has not been cut by the events of the 10th of August and the imprisonment of the King. My house is about to be surrounded. I cannot conceal anything of such bulk. I might, then, through my want of foresight give up that which would possibly cause the condemnation of the King. Let us open the portfolio, save the document alluded to, and destroy the rest." I took a knife and cut open one side of the portfolio. I saw a great number of envelopes endorsed with the King's own hand. M. Gougenot found there the ancient seals of the King,[1] such as they were before the Assembly had changed the inscription. At this moment we heard a great noise. He agreed to tie up the portfolio, take it again under his cloak, and go to a safe place to execute what I had taken upon myself to determine. He made me swear by all I held most sacred that I would affirm, under every possible emergency, that the course I was pursuing had not been dictated to me by anybody, and that whatever might be the result I would take all the credit or all the blame upon myself. I lifted up my hand and took the oath he required; he went out. Half an hour afterwards a great number of armed men came to

---

[1] No doubt it was in order to have the ancient seals ready at a moment's notice in case of a counter-revolution that the Queen desired me not to quit the Tuileries. M. Gougenot threw the seals into the river, one from off the Pont Neuf and the other from near the Pont Royal.—NOTE BY MADAME CAMPAN.

my house. They placed sentinels at all the outlets, they broke open *secrétaires* and closets of which they had not the keys, they searched the garden pots and boxes, they examined the cellars, and the commandant repeatedly said, "Look particularly for papers." In the afternoon M. Gougenot returned. He had still the seals of France about him, and he brought me a statement of all that he had burnt.

The portfolio contained twenty letters from Monsieur, eighteen or nineteen from the Count d'Artois, seventeen from Madame Adelaide, eighteen from Madame Victoire, a great many letters from Count Alexandre de Lameth, and many from M. de Malesherbes, with documents annexed to them. There were also some from M. de Montmorin and other ex-ministers or ambassadors. Each correspondence had its title written in the King's own hand upon the blank paper which contained it. The most voluminous was that from Mirabeau. It was tied up with a scheme for an escape, which he thought necessary. M. Gougenot, who had skimmed over these letters with more attention than the rest, told me they were of so interesting a nature that the King had no doubt kept them as documents exceedingly valuable for a history of his reign, and that the correspondence with the Princes, which was entirely relative to what was going forward without in concert with the King, would have been fatal to him had it been seized. After he had finished he placed in my hands the *procès-verbal* signed by all the ministers, to which the King attached so much importance, because he had given his opinion against the declaration of war; a copy of the letter written by the King to the Princes, his brothers, inviting them to return to France; an account of the diamonds which the Queen had sent to Brussels (these two documents were in my handwriting), and a receipt for 400,000 francs under the hand of a celebrated banker. This sum was part of the 800,000 francs which the Queen had gradually saved during her reign out of her pension of 300,000 francs per annum and out of the 100,000 francs given by way of present on the birth of the Dauphin. This receipt, written on a very small piece of paper, was in the cover of an almanac. I agreed with M. Gougenot, who was obliged by his station to reside in Paris, that he should retain the *procès-verbal* of the Council and the receipt for the 400,000 francs, and that we should wait either for orders or for the means of transmitting these documents to the King or Queen, and I set out for Versailles.

The strictness of the precautions taken to guard the illustrious prisoners was daily increased. The idea that I could not inform the King of the course I had adopted of burning his papers, and the fear that I should not be able to transmit him that which he had pointed out as necessary to him, tormented me to such a degree that it is wonderful my health endured the trial. I was, moreover, harassed every morning by the fears and projects of a very worthy person, who proved to me that in times of civil tumults terror causes the commission of actions which assist the factious, and that secrets of importance should be entrusted to none but persons of strong minds incapable of fear. The poor seamstress, who had been shut up a week in my apartment at the Tuileries to make the King's breastplate there, was very pious and very much attached to the Royal Family. I thought I could rely upon her, but the poor woman persuaded herself that she, her children and her husband were in danger of destruction if she did not go to the Assembly and declare that at such a time she had been sent for to the Castle of the Tuileries for a purpose which she thought it her duty to denounce. She came every morning as soon as I awoke to inform me that she was going to Paris, and that she would not ruin her whole family. I calmed her, and brought her to her senses. I proved to her that I had merely used her as she would her own needle, that the affair could not transpire unless she disclosed it, and that in case it did, which, however, appeared to me impossible, the unfortunate monarch would be first attacked for having ordered the work; and next, that I should be called in question for having caused it to be executed; but that she, who had only worked by the day under my direction, had nothing to fear. She would leave me in a more quiet state, but would return on the morrow fraught with new fears. Nor were visions wanting in the case: the Virgin had told her that her children and husband were not to be sacrificed for any human being whomsoever. I remained at least a fortnight tormented by this perpetual uneasiness. Happily, time set her weak head at rest. When the Assembly held up to the people Louis XVI. and Marie Antoinette as having wished to put all Paris to the sword, they would not have failed to impute weakness to the King on account of this breastplate, which he had at first consented to wear merely in compliance with the Queen's entreaties, and of which he had refused to make use on the night of the 10th of August.

The dreadful trial drew near. Official advocates were granted to the King; the heroic virtue of M. de Malesherbes induced him to brave the most imminent dangers, either to save his master or to perish with him. I hoped also to be able to find some means of informing His Majesty of what I had thought it right to do. I sent a man on whom I could rely to Paris to request M. Gougenot to come to me at Versailles; he came immediately. We agreed that he should see M. de Malesherbes without availing himself of any intermediate person for that purpose.

M. Gougenot awaited his return from the Temple at the door of his hotel, and made a sign that he wished to speak to him. A moment afterwards a servant came to introduce him into the magistrates' room. He imparted to M. de Malesherbes what I had thought right to do with respect to the King's papers, and placed in his hands the *procès-verbal* of the Council, which His Majesty had preserved in order to serve, if occasion required it, for a ground of his defence. However, this paper is not mentioned in either of the speeches of his advocate; probably it was determined not to make use of it.

I pause at that terrible period which is marked by the assassination of a King whose divine virtues are well known, but I cannot refrain from relating what he deigned to say in my favour to M. de Malesherbes:

"Let Madame Campan know that she did what I should myself have ordered her to do. I thank her for it; she is one of those whom I regret I have it not in my power to recompense for their fidelity to my person and for their good services." I did not hear of this until the morning after he had suffered, and I think I should have sunk under my despair if I had not been consoled by this honourable testimony.

※ ※ ※ ※ ※ ※

[Madame Campan's Memoirs terminate here. Her recital ends with her services about the unfortunate Princess, who fully appreciated her zeal and her self-devotion. She was unwilling to speak of anything but what she had seen with her own eyes or learnt from the mouth of the Queen herself, and her silence respecting the lamentable events which succeeded the 10th of August gives greater weight to her testimony upon all that goes before.—NOTE BY THE EDITOR.]

CHAPTER XII

FROM THE COMMITTAL TO THE TEMPLE TO THE DEATH OF LOUIS XVI.

Committal of the Royal Family to the Temple—Removal of the Princess de Lamballe — Description of the Temple — Apartments occupied—Attendance—Expenses—Extract from Clery's Journal—Habits of the Royal Family—Studies—Massacres in the prisons of Paris—Murder of the Princess de Lamballe—Brutality of the mob—Sufferings of the Royal Family—Abolition of Royalty—Trial of Louis XVI.—Separation from his family — His execution — Destruction of his remains.

THE faithful and eloquent relation of the weaknesses, the sorrows, the sufferings, attributable to nothing less than the sins of the unfortunate Royal Family of France, terminates abruptly with the separation of their illustrious narrator, Madame Campan, from the august victim whom she had served so faithfully through such vicissitudes of splendour and despair, of magnificence and misery.

That separation occurred on Monday, the 13th day of August, 1792, when Louis, with Marie Antoinette, Madame Elizabeth (the King's sister), Madame Royale (the King's daughter, afterwards Duchess d'Angoulême), and the Dauphin, the Princess de Lamballe, one male and two or three female attendants, were conveyed to the Temple, and when Pétion, the infamous Mayor of Paris, refused to

Madame Campan the sad consolation of sharing the imprisonment and endeavouring at least to alleviate the sufferings of her Royal mistress.

This cruelty was speedily followed by worse barbarities. On pretence of suspicious circumstances, the Princess de Lamballe and all the female attendants were removed by the order of the insurrectionary Commune, now the executive, or rather, sole supreme power of France, the former to be confined in the common prison called l'Abbaye, whence she was never to issue until the day of her atrocious murder.

The Temple, in which the Royal Family was now immured, is no other than the old castellated pile, half monastery, half fortress, formerly the possession and abode of the celebrated order of Knights Templars, from which they had been driven out to the gibbet, the faggot and the rack five centuries before, on a false charge of necromancy and magic, by the then ancestor of its present tenant. It consisted of two parts, one called the Palace, into which the Royal Family were placed in the first instance; the other, known as the Tower, the ancient keep or donjon of the place, to which they were consigned on the very night of their arrival.

This prison was composed of "a high, square tower" (we quote from the "History of the French Revolutions" published by Messrs. Chambers: People's Edition), "flanked by two turrets, in one of which was a winding staircase leading to a terrace on the top. In each story of the tower were three rooms, one being simply the size of the turret and very small. The first story was occupied by guards and municipal officers, the second by the Queen and the Princesses, and the third by the King and the faithful Cléry,[1] the only attendant left to wait on the whole family after the removal of M. Huë, who was carried off on the 2nd of September and narrowly escaped the murders of that period. A municipal officer was constantly on guard in each of the upper stories. During the day he sat in the same room with the prisoners, and by his presence prevented them from holding confidential intercourse, a restraint they found of all others the most irksome and galling; during the night, one lay at the door of the King's room with the bed in sight. The other watched over the Queen in like manner, but had the decency to allow the door to be closed. The life led by the prisoners was pretty uniform, except when disturbed by the caprice of municipals with a larger share of vulgar arrogance than was usual with their fellows."

At first it would appear that some degree of decency was observed towards the unfortunate Royal Family, although restrictions, the more cruel because utterly unnecessary — such as the constant presence of the rudest and most brutal of the populace as superintendents and watchers—were inflicted on them day and night.

Although but one personal attendant was permitted to the whole Royal Family, a measure attributed to the jealousy of extreme precaution, thirteen are said to have been employed in the kitchens allowed to the establish-

---

[1] Cléry did not in truth enter the Temple until after Huë's dismissal.

ment—though it is very difficult to conceive how so many could be employed in preparing food for three adults and two children, and though the fact rests only on the authority of M. Thiers, who never gives his data and must be admitted a most partial, or rather partisan, historian—and 28,745 livres (about £1,100) were the expenses of the table during two months. No news of any kind was, however, permitted to enter the precincts of the Temple, save the tidings of victories gained by the Republic over the invading Austrian and Prussian forces, which were regularly sent into the prison by the representatives of the commune, not as an act of mercy, but as a refinement of cruelty, since these tidings, proving the inability of their friends to rescue them by force of arms, served only to deprive them of every hope.

Up to the period when the trial and punishment of the Royal prisoner Louis began to be very seriously mooted, the lives of the prisoners were as uniform as they were sad and monotonous, and are thus simply, and therefore the more touchingly, related by the faithful attendant Cléry, who devoted himself, with a fidelity more like that of the canine than of the human species, to alleviate the miseries of his hapless master, from whom he parted only at the foot of the scaffold which he was soon to ascend, the best, if the weakest, of dethroned and decapitated kings.

"The largest room was the Queen's bed-chamber, in which the Dauphin also slept. The second, which was separated from the Queen's by a small ante-chamber almost without light, was occupied by Madame Royale and Madame Elizabeth. This chamber was the only way to the turret room of this story, and the turret room was the only place of office for this whole range of building, being in common for the Royal Family, the municipal officers and the soldiers. The King's apartments were on the third story. He slept in the great chamber, and made a study of the turret closet. There was a kitchen separated from the King's chamber by a small dark room, which had been successively occupied by MM. de Chantilly and de Huë, and on which the seals were now fixed. The fourth story was closed, and on the ground-floor there were kitchens, of which no use was now made. The King usually rose at six in the morning. He shaved himself, and I dressed his hair; he then went to his reading-room, which being very small, the municipal officer remained on duty in the bed-chamber, that he might always keep the King in sight. His Majesty continued praying, on his knees, till seven or eight o'clock, and then read till nine. During that interval, after putting his chamber to rights and preparing the breakfast,[1] I went down to the Queen, who never opened her door till I arrived, in order to prevent the municipal officer from going into her apartment. At nine o'clock the Queen, the children and Madame Elizabeth went up to the King's chamber to breakfast. At ten the King and his family went down to the Queen's chamber. and there passed the day. He employed himself in educating his son, made him recite passages from Corneille and Racine,

---

[1] This, and the previous statement concerning the kitchens on the ground-floor being closed, appear utterly to contradict the statement of M. Thiers, and we regard the words of the faithful domestic as far more credible than that of the revolutionary partisan.

gave him lessons in geography, and exercised him in colouring the maps. The Queen, on her part, was employed in the education of her daughter, and these different lessons lasted till eleven o'clock. The remaining time till noon was passed in needlework, knitting, or making tapestry. At one o'clock, when the weather was fine, the Royal Family were conducted to the garden by four municipal officers and a commander of a legion of the National Guard. At two we returned to the tower, where I served the dinner, at which time Santerre regularly came to the Temple attended by two aides-de-camp. The King sometimes spoke to him, the Queen never. In the evening, the family sat round a table, while the Queen read to them books of history or other works proper to instruct and amuse the children. Madame Elizabeth took the book in her turn, and in this manner they read till eight o'clock. After the Dauphin had supped, I undressed him, and the Queen heard him say his prayers. At nine the King went to supper, and afterwards went for a moment to the Queen's chamber, shook hands with her and his sister, kissed his children, and then retired to the turret room, where he sat reading till midnight.

"The Queen and the Princesses locked themselves in, and one of the municipal officers remained in the little room which parted their chamber, where he passed the night. The other followed His Majesty. In this manner the time was passed as long as the King remained in the little tower."

We learn from other authorities that the favourite authors of Louis XVI. were Plato, Hume, Bossuet,

Fénélon, Montesquieu and the French tragedians, Corneille, Racine and Voltaire; and from the same source, that the turret chamber of the suite used as dining and sitting rooms contained a small library of from twelve to fifteen hundred volumes, which proved the greatest solace to the captives.

Thus things passed on with a monotonous tranquillity, interrupted only by the anticipations of their future fate, and the occasional insults of their brutal keepers and yet more brutal visitors from the commune—insults endured by the King with a calm and patient dignity, which would have been absolute heroism had it not been attributable in some degree to the natural indifference of an impassive temper; by the Queen with a haughty scorn, interrupted by occasional bursts of feminine spirit—until the hideous massacres of the prisoners in all the places of detention throughout the metropolis, from the 2nd to the 7th of September.

These massacres—which Carlyle attempts to palliate by representing them as no more horrible or detestable than any other equal number of deaths, whether resulting from famine, war or pestilence, and which other apologists of the revolutionary crimes have attempted to ascribe entirely to the casual fury of the mob—were in reality planned deliberately by Danton, Marat and other members of the Mountain party, as is proved by the fact that pits filled with quicklime were prepared for the reception of the corpses, in *anticipation* of their slaughter by the orders of Manuel and Pétion.

In the course of these deliberate slaughters, the

prisoners being arraigned before mock tribunals and then slaughtered with every species of torture, insult and indignity, even to the maiming of corpses; slaughters interrupted by regular intervals, during which the corpses were removed while the *workmen* (*ouvriers*, as they were then termed) quietly sat down, ate their dinners (brought to them in baskets by their wives and daughters), drank wine supplied to them by the authorities, and received wages from the commune; slaughters gloated over by the fiendish women of the period, who insisted on having the streets illuminated by night, that they might feast their woman-eyes on the sufferings and the carnage which ceased not day or night. In the course of these slaughters, it is variously computed that prisoners of both sexes, of all ages and ranks, from the wanton in the hospital of Bicêtre to the Princess in the Abbaye, were deliberately butchered by authority, to the number of eight and up to fourteen thousand. Of all these none was more hideous or brutal than that of the Princess de Lamballe.

She was young, very beautiful, gentle, kindly disposed to all, moderate in her opinions, had never taken any part in politics; but she was beloved by the Queen, was the friend of the King, and with these crimes against her what could her virtues avail in her behalf with a revolutionary mob?

On her mock trial she consented to swear fealty to "Liberty and Equality," but refused to swear hatred to "the King, the Queen, and loyalty." This was her condemnation; with the by-word, "Let Madame be *set at liberty*," the fatal sentence at the

Abbaye, she was consigned to her murderers. The atrocities which followed are thus described by eye-witnesses, and though they may probably cause the blood to run cold and the hair to bristle with horror, it is yet good to contemplate them in order to perceive more clearly of what the populace is capable when controlled by no laws, human or divine, and left to the guidance of its own unbridled temper.

"The Princess de Lamballe, having been spared on the night of the 2nd, flung herself on her bed, oppressed with every species of anxiety and horror. She closed her eyes, but only to open them in an instant, startled with frightful dreams. About eight o'clock next morning two national guards entered her room to inform her that she was going to be removed to the Abbaye. She slipped on her gown and went downstairs into the sessions-room. When she entered this frightful court, the sight of weapons stained with blood, and of executioners whose hands, faces and clothes were smeared over with the same red dye, gave her such a shock that she fainted several times. At length she was subjected to a mock examination, after which, just as she was stepping across the threshold of the door, she received on the back of her head a blow with a hanger, which made the blood spout. Two men then laid fast hold of her, and obliged her to walk over dead bodies, while she was fainting every instant. They then completed her murder by running her through with their spears on a heap of corpses. She was afterwards stripped, and her naked body exposed to the insults of the populace. In this state it remained more than two hours. When any blood gushing from its wounds stained the skin some men, placed there for the purpose, immediately washed it off to make the spectators take more particular notice of its whiteness. I must not venture to describe the excesses of barbarity and lustful indecency with which this corpse was defiled. I shall only say that a cannon was charged with one of the legs. Towards noon the murderers determined to cut off her head, and carry it in triumph round Paris. Her other scattered limbs were also given to troops of cannibals who trailed them along the streets. The pike that supported the head was planted under the very windows of the Duke of Orleans. He was sitting down to dinner at the time, but rose from his chair, and gazed at the ghastly spectacle without displaying the least symptom of uneasiness, terror or satisfaction.

"Madame de Lamballe's sincere attachment to the Queen was her only crime. In the midst of our commotions she had played no part; nothing could render her suspected by the people, to whom she was only known by repeated acts of beneficence. When summoned to the bar of La Force many among the crowd besought pardon for her, and the assassins for a moment stood doubtful, but soon murdered her. Immediately they cut off her head and her breasts; her body was opened; her heart torn out, and the tigers who had so mangled her took a barbarous pleasure in going to show her head and heart to Louis XVI. and his family at the Temple. Madame de Lamballe was beautiful, gentle, obliging and moderate."

Even the cynical Pantagruelist Carlyle—who, in his strange admiration for whatever is strong, stringent, energetic and decisive, whether in man or masses, apologises for every crime and cruelty, and who grins and gibbers with grim exultation over all suffering and sorrow of the feeble-minded great in his bitter scorn of all that is weak—is moved by this fiendish deed to an eloquence as nigh akin to pity as his stern and hard nature is capable of.

What followed is thus related by Mr. Redhead, in Chambers' popular edition of the "French Revolutions," which I prefer to the narrative of M. Thiers, as it is fuller and far more circumstantial. While he states honestly both sides of the picture, the historian of the Revolution carefully conceals all the darker features of the scene and exposes all the gentler and more redeeming traits.

"The murder of the Princess de Lamballe recalled to memory the illustrious captives of the Temple, who seemed to have been forgotten up to that moment. A detachment of the assassins employed at La Force now moved towards their prison bearing aloft the head and heart of the Princess and followed by a tumultuous rabble. The King and his family were at dinner when they heard the tumult caused by their arrival. They rose from the table in great alarm, but the municipal officers on guard over them maintained a dogged silence and refused to satisfy their anxious enquiries. The outer gate meanwhile was besieged by the multitude, who demanded admittance and access into the interior of the Temple to lay the head of Lamballe, as the ringleader expressed it, *at the foot of the throne.* Certain commissioners of the commune who had been deputed to protect the asylum of the national hostages, for such Louis and his family were denominated, parleyed with the assailants, and agreed to admit them into the court and garden of the Tower on their promising to proceed no farther. Such a promise was, of course, purely derisory, and it is certain that the lives of the Royal Family were abandoned to the mercy or discretion of these murderers. 'Resistance,' the commissioners had resolved amongst themselves, 'would be impolitic, dangerous and, perhaps, unjust.' And in fact the muskets of the national guards had been purposely left unloaded and their bayonets taken from them. Therefore no material obstacle opposed the assassins; the way was made smooth for them; but they had undoubtedly secret instructions, and pretended to respect a tricoloured ribbon which the municipal officers had hung across the door of the Tower, in accordance with a stale device which furnished orators with the theme of much lively bombast. They insisted, however, that the King and Queen should show themselves at the windows that they might see the head of the Princess and 'learn the fate that was in store for the enemies of the people.' Finding that their interpellations were not regarded—for the officers with the King happening to be men of some humanity[1] kept him and the Queen from going

---

[1] *One* municipal in the Temple with the Royal prisoners at the moment said, "Look out." Another eagerly whispered, "Do not look."—CARLYLE.

to the window—they asserted that the Royal Family had been removed from the Temple and claimed that a deputation should be permitted to enter and verify the fact. To this demand the commissioners were fain to accede, and four of the ruffians were taken to the room in which the Royal Family were assembled. One of these, more forward than the rest, was urgent that the King and Queen should show themselves, but the municipal officers positively refused to allow them, whereupon he turned to the Queen and said, 'It is Lamballe's head they want to keep you from seeing, but I advise you to show yourself if you would not have the avengers come up here.' On hearing these words the Queen immediately fainted. The King advanced to the wretch and rebuked him with sternness. 'We are prepared, sir, for anything,' he observed to him; 'but you might have spared the Queen the relation of this horrible disaster.' The deputation then hastily withdrew, and guaranteed to the mob without that the hostages were, at all events, safe within their dungeons; but for several hours gangs of miscreants continued around the prison, bellowing with fearful howls, beating with furious discordance loud, resonant drums, and renewing every moment the dread of a violent irruption. It was eight in the evening before tranquillity was restored in the neighbourhood of the Temple and the Royal captives left to snatch some repose after the cruel agitations of the day."

From this fearful moment the sufferings, no less than the fears, of the Royal Family were cruelly augmented. Their restrictions and the impertinent annoyances of their democratic visitors increased daily.

The King's sword was taken from him, and then the penknives and scissors of the Princesses were demanded, as if they would have committed suicide. When they went out to walk in the garden the guards insulted them with obscene language, puffed smoke in their faces and purposely obstructed their way, treading on their feet and otherwise pressing on their persons. In fact, nothing that low-bred cruelty could devise was omitted for their torture; for what torture can be greater to the high-minded and delicately bred and nobly nurtured than the endurance of obscenity and insult from the low and profane rabble!

It is related by Cléry in his journal, that one of the soldiers on guard within the Tower wrote one day on the King's chamber door, and that on the inside, "The guillotine is permanent, and ready for the tyrant Louis XVI." The King read the words, which I made an attempt to rub out, but His Majesty prevented me.

Up to this period the Royal Family had been detained merely, as it was expressed, as "national hostages," and Royalty was considered as not being abolished, but merely suspended. The time had now, however, come when this farce was to be brought to a termination; accordingly—we quote as before from Cléry's journal of the sufferings of the Royal captives:

"On the 21st of September, at four o'clock in the afternoon, Lubin, a municipal officer, attended by horsemen and a great mob, came before the Tower to make a proclamation. Trumpets were sounded and a dead silence ensued. Lubin's voice was of the stentorian kind. The Royal Family could distinctly hear the proclamation of the abolition of Royalty and of the establishment of a Republic. Hebert, so well known by the name of Père Duchesne, and Destournelles, since made Minister of the Public Contributions, were then on guard over the family. They were sitting at the time near the door, and rudely stared the King in the face. The monarch perceived it, but, having a book in his hand, continued to read, without suffering the smallest alteration to appear in his countenance. The Queen displayed equal resolution. At the end of the proclamation the trumpets sounded again, and I went to the window. The eyes of the populace were immediately turned upon me; I was taken for my Royal master and overwhelmed with abuse. The same evening I informed the King that curtains and more clothes were wanting for the Dauphin's bed as the weather began to be cold. He desired me to write the demand for them, which he signed. I used the same expressions that I had hitherto done, 'The King requires for his son,' and so forth. 'It is a great piece of assurance in you,' said Destournelles, 'thus to persist in a title abolished by the will of the people, as you have just heard.' I replied that I had heard a proclamation, but was unacquainted with the object of it. 'It is,' rejoined he, 'for the abolition of Royalty; and you may tell the *gentleman*,' pointing to the King, 'to give over taking a title no longer acknowledged by the people.' I told him I could not alter this note, which was already signed, as the King would ask me the reason and it was not my part to tell him. 'You will do as you like,' continued Destournelles, 'but I shall not certify the demand.'"

From this period forward their sufferings were, if possible, yet augmented, until at length they were brought to a climax by the announcement to the hapless captives that, in the words of M. Thiers:

"The unfortunate monarch was thus about to appear before the National Convention and to undergo an examination concerning all the acts of his reign. This intelligence had reached Cléry by the secret means of correspondence which he had secured outside the prison, and it was with trembling that he imparted it to the disconsolate family. Not daring to tell the King himself, he had communicated it to Madame Elizabeth, and had, moreover, informed her that during the trial the commune had determined to separate Louis XVI. from his family. He agreed with the Princess upon a method of correspondence during this separation. This method consisted in a handkerchief which Cléry, who was to remain with the King, was to transmit to the Princesses if Louis XVI. should be ill. This was all that the unfortunate prisoners could calculate upon communicating to one another. The King was apprised by his sister of his speedily-required appearance, and of the separation which they were to undergo during the trial. He received the tidings with perfect resignation, and prepared to encounter with firmness that painful scene.

"The commune had given directions that early in the morning of the 11th of December all the administrative bodies should meet; that all the sections should be under arms; that the guard of all the public places, chests, depôts, &c., should be augmented by two hundred men for each post; that numerous reserves should be stationed at different points with a strong artillery; and that an escort of picked men should accompany the carriage.

"Accordingly, on the morning of the 11th of December, the *générale* announced to the capital this novel and melancholy scene. Numerous troops surrounded the Temple, and the din of arms and the tramp of horses reached the prisoners, who affected ignorance of the cause of all this bustle. At nine in the morning the family repaired as usual to the King's apartment to breakfast. The municipal officers, more vigilant than ever, prevented by their presence any outpouring of affection. The family was at length separated. In vain the King desired that his son should be left with him for a few moments. In spite of his entreaties the young Prince was taken away, and he remained alone for about two hours. The Mayor of Paris and the *procureur* of the commune then arrived, and communicated to him the decree of the Convention, summoning him to its bar by the name of Louis Capet. 'Capet,' replied the Prince, 'was the name of one of my ancestors, but it is not mine.' He then rose, and entered the carriage of the mayor, which was waiting for him. Six hundred picked men surrounded the vehicle. It was preceded by three pieces of cannon and followed by three more. A numerous body of cavalry formed the advance and the rear guard. A great concourse of people surveyed in silence this sad cavalcade, and suffered this rigour as it had long submitted to that of the old Government. There were some shouts, but very few. The Prince was not moved by them, and calmly conversed upon the objects that presented themselves on the way. Having arrived at the Feuillans, he was placed in a room to await the orders of the Assembly."

The cruel circumstance of the deprivation of his son is thus related by Cléry, on whose simple narrations we place the highest confidence.

"At eleven o'clock, when the King was hearing the Dauphin read, two municipal officers walked in, and told His Majesty that they were come to carry the young Louis to his mother. The King desired to know why he was taken away. The commissioners replied that they were executing the orders of the council of the commune. The King tenderly embraced his son, and charged me to conduct him. On my return, I assured His Majesty that I had delivered the Prince to the Queen, which appeared a little to relieve his mind. His Majesty afterwards for some minutes walked about his room in much agitation, then sat down in an arm-chair at the head of the bed. The door stood ajar, but the officer did not like to go in, wishing, as he told me, to avoid questions; but half an hour passing thus in dead silence, he became uneasy at not hearing the King move, and went softly in; he found him leaning with his head upon his hand, apparently in deep thought. The King, upon being disturbed, said, 'What do you want with me?' 'I was afraid,' answered the officer, 'that you were unwell.' 'I am obliged to you,' replied the King, in an accent replete with anguish; 'but the manner in which they have taken my son from me cuts me to the heart.' The municipal officer withdrew without saying a word."

From this time forth, with a barbarity inconceivable in those human fiends, and days of merciless and more than devilish crime, the wretched Louis was refused all access to his miserable family. The use of a razor was denied him, so that he suffered actual pain from the irritation of his face, until, on the eve of his execution, he was allowed to shave in the presence of a municipal officer.

He was permitted, it is true, the aid of counsel and the use of pens and paper, but what availed either when his sentence was predetermined and his death-warrant almost signed before he was brought to the bar? He named Tronchet and Target as his advocates, but the latter dastardly refused the perilous but honourable office; and the vacancy occasioned by his baseness was nobly filled by the venerable Malesherbes, who volunteered to act in his defence, for which most honourable action he suffered in after days, with nearly his whole family, by the same fatal instrument from which he vainly strove to preserve his King.

On the 11th of December the King was first brought before the Assembly. For more than a month the strife between life and death continued; and on the 15th of January, 1793, the voting commenced on these three questions:

1st. Is Louis Capet guilty of conspiracy against

liberty and of attempts against the general safety of the State?

2nd. Shall the definitive judgment on Louis be referred to the primary assemblies?

3rd. What punishment shall be inflicted on Louis?

On all these points judgment was pronounced adverse to the King, the Girondins basely sacrificing their opinions, which were in favour of Louis, to their personal fears. It is consolatory to know that they all shortly followed him down the one dark road which must be trodden by the monarch and the slave, by the victim and his assassin, and that, too, by the same bloody death; and it is almost painful to consider that, by the courage and dignity they showed in their last hours, they have in some sort redeemed in popular opinion their cowardice and guilt in yielding to the bloodthirsty faction who in after days wreaked on them the same vengeance which they now voted against their guiltless King.

A majority of fifty-three pronounced for the death of this weak man but blameless King—the Duke of Orleans, his near kinsman, among the number. All efforts to obtain a reconsideration, a reference or delay were fruitless; the majority were bent on death, and "the Executive Council was charged with the melancholy commission of carrying the sentence into execution. All the ministers were assembled in the hall where they met, and they were struck with consternation. Garat, as Minister of Justice, had the most painful of all tasks imposed upon him, that of acquainting Louis XVI. with the decrees of the Convention. He repaired to the Temple, accompanied by Santerre, by a deputation of the commune and the criminal tribunal and by the secretary of the Executive Council. Louis XVI. had been for four days expecting his defenders and applying in vain to see them. On the 20th of January, at two in the afternoon, he was still awaiting them, when all at once he heard the sound of a numerous party. He stepped forward and perceived the envoys of the Executive Council. He stopped with dignity at the door of his apartment, apparently unmoved. Garat then told him sorrowfully that he was commissioned to communicate to him the decrees of the Convention. Grouvelle, secretary of the Executive Council, read them to him. The first declared Louis XVI. guilty of treason against the general safety of the State; the second condemned him to death; the third rejected any appeal to the people; and the fourth and last ordered his execution in twenty-four hours. Louis looked calmly around upon all those who were about him, took the paper from the hand of Grouvelle, put it in his pocket, and read Garat a letter in which he demanded from the Convention three days to prepare for death, a confessor to assist him in his last moments, liberty to see his family, and permission for them to leave France. Garat took the letter, promising to submit it immediately to the Convention. The King gave him at the same time the address of the ecclesiastic whose spiritual assistance he wished to have in his last moments.

"Louis XVI. went back into his room with great composure, ordered his dinner, and ate as usual. There were no knives on the table, and his attendants refused to let him have any. 'Do they think me so weak,' he exclaimed, 'as to lay violent hands on myself? I am innocent, and I am not afraid to die.' He was obliged to dispense with a knife. On finishing his repast he returned to his apartment and calmly awaited the answer to his letter.

"The Convention refused the delay, but granted all the other demands which he had made. Garat sent for Edgeworth de Firmont, the ecclesiastic whom Louis XVI. had chosen, and took him in his own carriage to the Temple. He arrived there at six o'clock, and went to the great Tower, accompanied by Santerre. He informed the King that the Convention allowed him to have a minister and to see his family alone, but that it rejected the application for delay. Garat added that M. Edgeworth had arrived, that he was in the council-room, and should be introduced. He then retired, more astonished and more touched than ever by the calm magnanimity of the Prince."

In the whole history of the world there is, perhaps, no sadder scene than the meeting of Louis with his family, from whom he had been so barbarously and so unnecessarily separated during the dreadful crisis of his fate—separated solely, as it would appear, for the hideous purpose of depriving him of any consolation, and rendering his last hours as miserable as they could be rendered. That meeting was but preparatory to an immediate and eternal separation. A single day's delay had been refused him; and on the evening of the very day on which his sentence was announced to him, the eve of his last earthly morrow, the following scene occurred, which shook even the hearts of the stern and savage functionaries who beheld it. Again we quote from Cléry:

"At eight o'clock the King came out of his closet, and desired the municipal officers to conduct him to his family. They replied that could not be, but his family should be brought down if he desired it. 'Be it so,' said His Majesty; and accordingly, at half-past eight, the door opened, and his wife and children made their appearance. They all threw themselves into the arms of the King. A melancholy silence prevailed for some minutes, only broken by sighs and sobs. The Queen made an inclination towards His Majesty's chamber. 'No,' said the King, 'we must go into this room; I can only see you there.' They went in, and I shut the glass door. The King sat down; the Queen was on his left hand, Madame Elizabeth on his right, Madame Royale nearly opposite, and the young Prince stood between his legs. All were leaning on the King, and often pressed him to their arms. This scene of sorrow lasted an hour and three-quarters, during which it was impossible to hear anything. It could, however, be seen that after every sentence uttered by the King, the agitation of the Queen and Princesses increased, lasted some minutes, and then the King began to speak again. It was plain from their gestures that they received from himself the first intelligence of his condemnation. At a quarter-past ten the King rose first; they all followed. I opened the door. The Queen held the King by his right arm; their Majesties gave each a hand to the Dauphin. Madame Royale, on the King's left, had her arms round his body; and behind her Madame Elizabeth, on the same side, had taken his arm. They advanced some steps towards the entry door, breaking out into the most agonising lamentations. 'I assure you,' said the King, 'that I will see you again to-morrow morning at eight o'clock.' 'You promise,' said they all together. 'Yes, I promise.' 'Why not at seven o'clock?' asked the Queen. 'Well—yes, at seven,' replied the King; 'farewell!' He pronounced 'farewell' in so impressive a manner that their sobs were renewed, and Madame Royale fainted at the feet of the King, round whom she had clung. His Majesty, willing to put an end to this agonising scene, once more embraced them all most tenderly, and had the resolution to tear himself from their arms. 'Farewell! farewell!' said he, and went into his chamber. The Queen, Princesses and Dauphin returned to their own apartments; and though both the doors were shut, their screams and lamentations were heard for some time on the stairs. The King went back to his confessor in the turret closet."

On the following morning, pursues Cléry:

"On hearing five o'clock strike, I began to light the fire. The noise I made awoke the King, who, drawing his curtains, asked if it had struck five. I said it had by several clocks, but not yet by that in the apartment. Having finished with the fire, I went to his bedside. 'I have slept soundly,' said His Majesty, 'and I stood in need of it; yesterday was a trying day to me. Where is M. Edgeworth?' I answered, 'On my bed.' 'And where were you all night?' 'On this chair.' 'I am sorry for it,' said the King, and gave me his hand, at the same time tenderly pressing mine. I then dressed His Majesty, who, as soon as he was ready, bade me go and call M. Edgeworth, whom I found already risen, and he immediately attended the King to the turret. Meanwhile, I placed a chest of drawers in the middle of the chambers, and arranged it in the form of an altar for saying Mass. The necessary articles of dress had been brought at two o'clock in the morning. The priest's garments I carried into my chamber, and when everything was ready I went and informed His Majesty. He had a book in his hand, which he opened, and finding the place of the Mass, gave it me; he then took another book for himself. The priest meanwhile was dressing. Before the altar I had placed an arm-chair for His Majesty, with a large cushion on the ground; the cushion he desired me to take away, and went himself to his closet for a smaller one, made of hair, which he commonly used at his prayers. When the priest came in, the municipal officer retired into the ante-chamber, and I shut one fold of the door. The Mass began at six o'clock. There was profound silence during the awful ceremony. The King, all the time on his knees, heard Mass with the most devout attention, and received the Communion. After the service he withdrew to his closet, and the priest went into my chamber to put off his official attire.

"In the course of the morning the King said to me, 'You will give this seal to my son, and this ring to the Queen, and assure her that it is with pain I part with it. This little packet contains locks of the hair of all my family; you will give her that also. Tell the

Queen, my dear sister and my children that, although I promised to see them again this morning, I have resolved to spare them the pang of so cruel a separation. Tell them how much it costs me to go away without receiving their embraces once more!' He wiped away some tears, and then added in the most mournful accents, 'I charge you to bear them my last farewell.'

"All the troops in Paris had been under arms from five o'clock in the morning. The beat of drums, the sound of trumpets, the clash of arms, the trampling of horses, the removal of cannon, which were incessantly carried from one place to another—all resounded in the tower. At half-past eight o'clock the noise increased; the doors were thrown open with great clatter, and Santerre, accompanied by seven or eight municipal officers, entered at the head of ten soldiers, and drew them up in two lines. At this movement the King came out of his closet, and said to Santerre, 'You are come for me?' 'Yes,' was the answer. 'Wait a moment,' said His Majesty, and went into his closet, whence he instantly returned, followed by his confessor. I was standing behind the King, near the fireplace. He turned round to me, and I offered him his great-coat. 'I shall not want it,' said he; 'give me only my hat.' I presented it to him, and his hand met mine, which he pressed for the last time. His Majesty then looked at Santerre and said, 'Lead on.' These were the last words he spoke in his apartments."

"On quitting the tower," says the Abbé Edgeworth, "the King crossed the first court, formerly the garden, on foot; he turned back once or twice towards the tower, as if to bid adieu to all most dear to him on earth; and by his gestures it was plain that he was trying to collect all his strength and firmness. At the entrance of the second court a carriage waited; two gendarmes held the door; at the King's approach one of these men entered first and placed himself in front, His Majesty followed and placed me by his side at the back of the carriage; the other gendarme jumped in last and shut the door. The procession lasted almost two hours; the streets were lined with citizens, all armed; and the carriage was surrounded by a body of troops, formed of the most desperate people of Paris. As soon as the King perceived that the carriage stopped, he turned and whispered to me, 'We have arrived, if I mistake not.' My silence answered that we had. On quitting the vehicle, three guards surrounded His Majesty, and would have taken off his clothes, but he repulsed them with haughtiness; he undressed himself, untied his neckcloth, opened his shirt and arranged it himself. The path leading to the scaffold was extremely rough and difficult to pass; the King was obliged to lean on my arm, and from the slowness with which he proceeded I feared for a moment that his courage might fail; but what was my astonishment when he arrived at the last step! I felt that he suddenly let go my arm, and I saw him cross with a firm foot the breadth of the whole scaffold, silence by his look alone fifteen or twenty drums that were placed opposite to him, and in a loud voice heard him pronounce distinctly these memorable words: 'I die innocent of all the crimes laid to my charge; I pardon those who have occasioned my death, and I pray to God that the blood which you are now going to shed may never be visited on France.' He was proceeding, when a man on horseback, in the national uniform, waved his sword and ordered the drums to beat. Many voices were at the same time heard encouraging the executioners, who immediately seized the King with violence, and dragged him under the axe of the guillotine, which with one stroke severed his head from his body."

It was on Monday, the 21st of January, 1793. His age was thirty-eight years, four months and twenty-eight days.

Of the sorrows of the Royal Family during that fatal day the Duchess of Angoulême gives the following brief statement. Whose heart will not sympathise with the griefs of these noble mourners, three out of the four of whom were so soon to follow to the tomb the adored and faithful husband, the beloved brother, the pious and devoted father?

"On the morning of this terrible day the Princesses rose at six o'clock. The Queen the night before had scarcely strength enough to put her son to bed. She threw herself dressed as she was upon her own bed, where she remained shivering with cold and grief all night long! At a quarter past six the door opened; the Princesses believed they were sent for to see the King, but it was only the officers looking for a prayer-book for his Mass. They did not, however, abandon the hope of seeing him till the shouts of joy of the unprincipled populace announced to them that all was over."

It has been said that, as the axe fell, the Abbé Edgeworth took leave of the King in the following memorable words: "Son of St. Louis, ascend to heaven!" but on being questioned in after days, he declared himself unconscious of anything that passed relative to himself at that awful moment.

Alison informs us that after this legalised murder of a good King and pious man, whose only faults were an amiable weakness and an over-regard for the lives of a wicked and ungrateful people, "One person actually tasted the blood, with a brutal exclamation that it was 'shockingly bitter,' and the hair and pieces of the dress were sold by the attendants. No strong emotion was evinced at the moment; the place was like a fair; but, a few days after, Paris, and those who had voted for the death of the monarch, began to feel serious and uneasy at what they had done.

"The body of Louis was, immediately after the execution, removed into the ancient cemetery of the Madeleine. Large quantities of quicklime were thrown into the grave, which occasioned so rapid a decomposition that, when his remains were sought after in 1815, it was with great difficulty that any part could be recovered. Over the spot where he was interred Napoleon commenced the splendid Temple of Glory, after the battle of Jena, and the superb edifice was completed by the Bourbons, and now forms the church of the Madeleine, the most beautiful of the many beautiful structures in Paris. Louis was executed on the same ground where the Queen, the Princess Elizabeth and so many other noble victims of the

Revolution perished, where Robespierre and Danton afterwards suffered, and where the Emperor Alexander and the allied Sovereigns took their station when their victorious troops entered Paris in 1814! The history of modern Europe has not a scene fraught with equally interesting recollections to exhibit. It is now marked by the colossal obelisk of blood-red granite which was brought from Thebes, in Upper Egypt, in 1833 by the French Government."

Thus ends the first act of the horrid tragedy—never, we trust, to be repeated—the second of which was the slaughter of all the prisoners save one, and the *dénouement*, the terrible retribution wrought on the guilty nation during the devastating wars of that Child of the Revolution, Napoleon the Emperor, in the course of which three millions of native Frenchmen fattened the plains of foreign countries by their gore, and the final subjugation of France and occupation of the regicidal capital by the descendants of the Saxon, the Goth, the Vandal and the Hun, whom the "*grande nation*" ever regarded with such contemptuous loathing.

Verily a great lesson to guilty nations, that *their* retribution is in *this* world; and that, in the words of the old tragedian, "Crime begets crime, and of guilt, Guilt is for ever the avenger."

CHAPTER XIII

FROM THE DEATH OF LOUIS XVI. TO THE RELEASE OF MADAME ROYALE.

Increased sufferings of the Royal Family after the execution of Louis XVI.—Extract from Thiers' History—The Dauphin committed to the care of Simon, the shoemaker—Separation of the Family—Marie Antoinette committed to the Conciergerie —Her privations—She is brought before the revolutionary tribunal—Accusations against her—Her conviction—Execution —Joy of the Jacobins—Execution of Madame Elizabeth— Extract from the Memoirs of the Duchess d'Angoulême; from Alison—Death of the Dauphin—Release of his sister— Successors of Louis XVI.

AFTER the decapitation of the Sixteenth Louis some weary months elapsed, during which the condition of the hapless survivors of that most unfortunate of kings gradually but continually deteriorated; they were stripped one by one of every resource that might tend to cheer or alleviate the sad monotony of confinement, and they were now to endure the last extremities to which the fury of their persecutors could subject them. The only comfort still left to them was that of living together, and that was speedily taken from them.

A part of the enormities which they endured are thus described by one whose known partiality for the Revolution and tenderness toward the motives and memories of its worst monsters—such as Robespierre, Pétion, and Fouché—are too well known to require comment, and who in consequence deserves implicit confidence when he feels compelled to state anything against them—we allude of course to the celebrated author of the "History of the French Revolution" and the "History of the Consulate and Empire."

"That wretch Hebert, the deputy of Chaumette, editor of the disgusting paper *Père Duchesne*, and a writer of the party of which Vincent, Ronsin, Varlet and Leclerc were the leaders, had made it his particular business to torment the unfortunate remnant of the dethroned family. He asserted that the family of the tyrant ought not to be better treated than any *sans-culotte* family; and he had caused a resolution to be passed, by which the sort of luxury in which the prisoners in the Temple were maintained was to be suppressed. They were no longer to be allowed either poultry or pastry; they were reduced to one sort of aliment for breakfast, and to soup, or broth, and a single dish for dinner, to two dishes for supper, and half a bottle of wine apiece. Tallow candles were to be furnished instead of wax, pewter instead of silver plate, and Delft ware instead of porcelain. The wood and water carriers alone were permitted to enter their room, and that only accompanied by two commissioners. Their food was to be introduced to them by means of a turning box. The numerous establishment was reduced to a cook and an assistant, two men-servants, and a woman-servant to attend to the linen.

"As soon as this resolution was passed, Hebert repaired to the Temple, and inhumanly deprived the unfortunate prisoners of even the most trifling articles to which they attached a high value. Eighty louis which Madame Elizabeth had in reserve, and which she had received from Madame de Lamballe, were also taken away. No one is more dangerous and more cruel than the man without acquirements, without education, clothed in the garb of authority. If, above all, he possesses a base nature; if, like Hebert, who was checktaker at the door of a theatre and embezzled money out of the receipts, he be destitute of natural morality; and if he leaps all at once from the mud of his condition into power, he is as mean as he is atrocious. Such was Hebert in his conduct at the Temple. He did not confine himself to the annoyances which we have mentioned, but with some others conceived the idea of separating the young Prince from his aunt and sister. A shoemaker, named Simon, and his wife were the instructors to whom it was deemed right to consign him, for the purpose of giving him a *sans-culotte* education. Simon and his wife were shut up in the Temple, and, becoming prisoners with the unfortunate child, were directed to bring him up in their own way. Their food was better than that of the Princesses, and they shared the table of the municipal commissioners who were on duty. Simon was permitted to go down, accompanied by two commissioners, to the court of the Temple, for the purpose of giving him a little exercise."

This wretch Simon, to whom was entrusted the care of the miserable child, who, born to so high promise, speedily fell to so sad a reality, is described in these words by Cléry—and no person can doubt that it was for his brutal qualities alone, and the certainty that he would exercise them to the utmost for the torture of his captives, that he was indebted for his situation as gaoler and tutor to the infant hitherto so sedulously nurtured:

"A man named Simon, a shoemaker and municipal officer, was one of the six commissioners appointed to inspect the works and the expenses of the Temple. This man, whenever he appeared in the presence of the Royal Family, always treated them with the vilest insolence; and would frequently say to me, so near the King as to be heard by him, 'Cléry, ask Capet if he wants anything, that I mayn't have the trouble of coming up twice.'"

On the 3rd of July, however, even the last wretched consolation of suffering in common was thought too great a boon by the wretches who composed the National Convention of France, for those who had committed no offence toward God or against man; unless it be a crime—as assuredly it seems a misfortune—to be born to elevated station.

A decree was passed on that day that the young Dauphin or King should be torn from the arms of his mother. Marie Antoinette struggled against the efforts of the officers, who would literally have forced him violently from her embrace, until threatened by those fiends—for men they cannot be called—that they would kill both him and her daughter before her eyes. She released him—never to see him on earth again—in an agony of tenderness and grief so touching that even her iron gaolers melted and, according to their own confession, wept.

They wept at sufferings which they themselves had enhanced, if not actually created, and which they still persisted in enhancing to the utmost of their ability, so strangely inconsistent is French—if we should not rather say, human—nature.

With the child, for the present, we have done; choosing rather to present the sad tale of the Queen's last days in an unbroken thread, than to interrupt them in order to treat of other matters which can in another place be more fitly treated.

For one month longer she was suffered to remain with her sister-in-law, Madame Elizabeth, and her daughter Madame Royale; but on the 2nd of August she was separated from these also, and consigned to the common prison of the Conciergerie, as the subject of her trial, or summary condemnation, was already in contemplation. She was then, as we learn from Du Broza, "lodged in a room called the council chamber, which was considered the most unwholesome apartment in the Conciergerie, on account of its dampness and the bad smells by which it was continually affected. Under pretence of giving her a person to wait upon her, they placed near her a spy—a man of a horrible countenance and hollow, sepulchral voice. This wretch, whose name was Barassin, was a robber and murderer by profession. Such was the chosen attendant on the Queen of France! A few days before her trial this wretch was removed, and a gendarme placed in her chamber, who watched over her night and day, and from whom she was not separated, even when in bed, but by a ragged curtain. In this melancholy abode Marie Antoinette had no other dress than an old black gown, stockings with holes, which she was forced to mend every day; and she was entirely destitute of shoes."

The only furniture in this miserable cell was a straw bed covered by a ragged mattress and an old worn-out coverlet, and the veriest necessaries and decencies of life were denied to *the woman*, in which light at least, if not even as *the Princess*, she was entitled to them.

But what were all bodily sufferings compared to the mental tortures which she must have endured. She, the fairest and most favoured Princess of the proudest and most ancient House of Europe, that great House of Hapsburg, which had for so many centuries filled the Imperial throne of the West—who had exchanged those maiden honours only to become the bride of the most powerful king in Europe!

Yet mental sufferings and bodily afflictions served only to bring forth the native dignity and firmness of her virtue. If she had failed somewhat of the highest standard while seated on the pinnacle of human splendour and magnificence, she soared even above it from the squalor and obscenity of her foul prison-house. If not in all things equal to prosperity, she proved herself superior to the direst adversity.

Her serene dignity, her proud self-possession, her majestic mildness, awed those whom it could not move. Yet let it be recorded that it did move Robespierre, for so deep need has that monstrous blot on the escutcheon of humanity of one redeeming trait, that it must be recorded of him that he did strive to avert the trial, tantamount to the condemnation, of the Queen. His resistance was, however, of no avail; he was overpowered by a huge majority, and the trial of the Queen was decided. Accordingly, on the 14th of October, she was led before the revolutionary tribunal.

At first the Queen, consulting her own sense of dignity, had resolved at her trial to make no other reply to the question of her judges than, "Assassinate me, as you have already assassinated my husband!" Afterwards she determined to follow the example of the King, exert herself in her defence, and leave her judges without any excuse or pretext for putting her to death.

The revolutionary tribunal had determined to sacrifice the Queen; but still even they "felt it necessary," as Thiers states, "to produce witnesses. Lecointre, deputy of Versailles, who had seen what had passed on the 5th and 6th of October; Hebert, who had frequently visited the Temple; various clerks in the ministerial offices, and several domestic servants of the old Court were summoned. Admiral d'Estaing, formerly commandant of the guard of Versailles; Manuel, the ex-procureur of the commune; Latour du Pin, Minister of War in 1789; the venerable Bailly, who it was said had been, with La Fayette, an accomplice in the journey to Varennes; lastly, Valazé, one of the Girondins destined to the scaffold, were taken from their prisons and compelled to give evidence.

"No precise fact was elicited. Some had seen the Queen in high spirits when the life-guards testified their attachment; others had seen her vexed and dejected while being conducted to Paris or brought back from Varennes; these had been present at splendid festivities which must have cost enormous sums; those had heard it said in the ministerial offices that the Queen was adverse to the sanction of the decrees. An ancient waiting-woman of the Queen had heard the Duke de Coigny say, in 1788, that the Emperor had already received two hundred millions from France to make war upon the Turks.

"The cynical Hebert, being brought before the unfortunate Queen, dared at length to prefer the charges wrung from the young Prince. He said that Charles Capet had given Simon an account of the journey to Varennes, and mentioned La Fayette and Bailly as having co-operated in it. He then added that this boy was addicted to odious and very premature vices for his age; that he had been surprised by Simon, who, on questioning him, learned that he derived from his mother the vices in which he indulged. Hebert said that it was no doubt the intention of Marie Antoinette, by weakening thus early the physical constitution of her son, to secure to herself the means of ruling him in case he should ever ascend the throne.

"The rumours which had been whispered for twenty years by a malicious Court had given the people a most unfavourable opinion of the morals of the Queen. That audience, however, though wholly Jacobin, was disgusted at the accusations of Hebert.

He nevertheless persisted in asserting them. The unhappy mother made no reply. Urged anew to explain herself, she said with extraordinary emotion, 'I thought that human nature would excuse me from answering such an imputation; but I appeal from it to the heart of every mother here present.' This noble and simple reply affected all who heard it. In the depositions of the witnesses, however, all was not so bitter for Marie Antoinette. The brave D'Estaing, whose enemy she had been, would not say anything to inculpate her, and spoke only of the courage which she had shown on the 5th and 6th of October, and of the noble resolution which she had expressed to die beside her husband rather than fly. Manuel, in spite of his enmity to the Court during the time of the Legislative Assembly, declared that he could not say anything against the accused. When the venerable Bailly was brought forward, who formerly had so often predicted to the Court the calamities which its imprudence must produce, he appeared painfully affected; and when he was asked if he knew the wife of Capet, 'Yes,' said he, bowing respectfully, 'I have known *Madame*.' He declared that he knew nothing, and maintained that the declarations extorted from the young Prince relative to the journey to Varennes were false. In recompense for his deposition he was assailed with outrageous reproaches, from which he might judge what fate would soon be awarded to himself.

"In the whole of the evidence there appeared but two serious facts, attested by Latour du Pin and Valazé, who deposed to them because they could not help it. Latour du Pin declared that Marie Antoinette had applied to him for an accurate statement of the armies while he was War Minister. Valazé, always cold but respectful towards misfortune, would not say anything to incriminate the accused, yet he could not help declaring that, as a member of the Commission of Twenty-Four, being charged with his colleagues to examine the papers found at the house of Septeuil, treasurer of the Civil List, he had seen bonds for various sums signed 'Antoinette,' which was very natural; but he added that he had also seen a letter in which the minister requested the King to transmit to the Queen the copy of the plan of campaign which he had in his hands. The most unfavourable construction was immediately put upon these two facts—the application for a statement of the armies, and the communication of the plan of campaign; and it was concluded that they could not be wanted for any other purpose than to be sent to the enemy, for it was not supposed that a young Princess should turn her attention, merely for her own satisfaction, to matters of administration and military plans. After these depositions several others were received respecting the expenses of the Court, the influence of the Queen in public affairs, the scene of the 10th of August, and what had passed in the Temple; and the most vague rumours and most trivial circumstances were eagerly caught as proofs.

"Marie Antoinette frequently repeated, with presence of mind and firmness, that there was no precise fact against her; that besides, though the wife of Louis XVI., she was not answerable for any of the acts of his reign. Fouquier nevertheless declared her to be sufficiently convicted; Chaveau-Lagarde made unavailing efforts to defend her; and the unfortunate Queen was condemned to suffer the same fate as her husband.

"Conveyed back to the Conciergerie, she there passed the night preceding her execution in tolerable composure, and on the morning of the following day, the 16th of October,[1] she was conducted, amidst a great concourse of the populace, to the fatal spot where, ten months before, Louis XVI. had perished. She listened with calmness to the exhortations of the ecclesiastic who accompanied her, and cast an indifferent look at the people who had so often applauded her beauty and her grace, and who now as warmly applauded her execution. On reaching the foot of the scaffold she perceived the Tuileries, and appeared to be moved; but she hastened to ascend the fatal ladder, and gave herself up with courage to the executioner.[2] The infamous wretch exhibited her

---

[1] "At four o'clock in the morning of the day of her execution, the Queen wrote a letter to the Princess Elizabeth. 'To you, my sister,' said she, 'I address myself for the last time. I have been condemned, not to an ignominious death — it is so only to the guilty—but to rejoin your brother. I weep only for my children; I hope that one day, when they have regained their rank, they may be reunited to you, and feel the blessing of your tender care. May my son never forget the last words of his father, which I now repeat from myself—Never attempt to revenge our death. I die true to the Catholic religion. Deprived of all spiritual consolation, I can only seek for pardon from Heaven. I ask forgiveness of all who know me. I pray for forgiveness to all my enemies.'"—ALISON.

[2] "Sorrow had blanched the Queen's once beautiful hair; but her features and demeanour still commanded the admiration of all who beheld her. Her cheeks, pale and emaciated, were occasionally tinged with a vivid colour at the mention of those she had lost. When led out to execution, she was dressed in white,

head to the people, as he was accustomed to do when he had sacrificed an illustrious victim."

The Jacobins were overjoyed. "Let these tidings be carried to Austria," said they. "The Romans sold the ground occupied by Annibal; we strike off the heads that are dearest to the Sovereigns who have invaded our territory."

It is a little remarkable—or, perhaps, we should say, *not* a little remarkable—that all the Girondins who signed and sealed their own *just* condemnation, by their signing and sealing the *unjust* condemnation of Louis, shortly followed her to the same scaffold.

We know not wherefore Carlyle, who so detests all human weakness, defends and *shrieks*, as he would term it, over the weakness and the guillotining of the murderers, Vergniaud, Valazé and their confederates, while he has no *shriek* for their murdered victims.

It was not until the 22nd of April following that, after the Girondins, after Danton himself and others of the Mountain, had been decapitated—some weeping, some bellowing, all blaspheming—by the hands of the impassive Samson, the King's surviving sister, Madame Elizabeth, was sent to death.

"Her trial," says Carlyle, "was like the rest; for plots, for plots. She was among the kindliest, most innocent of women. There sat with her, amid four-

---

she had cut off her hair with her own hands. Placed in a tumbrel, with her arms tied behind her, she was taken by a circuitous route to the Place de la Révolution, and she ascended the scaffold with a firm and dignified step, as if she had been about to take her place on a throne by the side of her husband."
—LACRETELLE.

and-twenty others, a once timorous Marchioness de Crussol; courageous now; expressing towards her the liveliest loyalty. At the foot of the scaffold, Elizabeth, with tears in her eyes, thanked this Marchioness; said she was grieved she could not reward her. 'Ah, Madame, would your Royal Highness deign to embrace me my wishes were complete.' 'Right willingly, Madame de Crussol, and with all my heart.' Thus they at the foot of the scaffold. The Royal Family are now reduced to two; a girl and a little boy. This boy, once named Dauphin, was taken from his mother while she yet lived, and given to one Simon, by trade a cordwainer on service then about the Temple, to bring him up in the principles of Sansculottism."

From Carlyle we will quote no further, for in this very passage which he begins so nobly and pathetically, before the end he degenerates into his usual Pantagruelistic cynicism, and grins and sneers like a hyena over the corpse of fallen Royalty. What right has he to pretend to the title of philosopher who, puissant to destroy, is powerless to build up; who, the habitual admirer of strong vice and derider of innocent weakness, has no plan or counsel for giving power to innocence or depriving strength of its vice?

Two very brief extracts, one from the Memoirs of the Duchess d'Angoulême, the other from the pages of Alison, sum up this brief and sad tale:

"The young Prince was taken to that part of the Tower which Louis XVI. had previously occupied; and the manner in which Simon educated him may be judged by the statement of his sister (afterwards the Duchess d'Angoulême), in her interesting history of the confinement of the Royal Family. She says: 'We sometimes received intelligence of my brother through the municipal officers, but even that did not last long. We heard him every day singing, in company with Simon, the song of " La Carmagnole," the " Marseillaise Hymn," and a thousand other horrible compositions of the sort. Simon dressed him in a red cap and a *carmagnole* (a small tight jacket), and made him sing at the windows so as to be heard by the guard, and taught him to utter the most dreadful blasphemies and curses against God, his family and the aristocrats. . . . Simon gave him the coarsest food to eat, and made him by force drink a quantity of wine, which he naturally detested.' "

"The 9th of Thermidor came too late to save the infant King of France, Louis XVII. His gaoler, Simon, was indeed beheaded, and a less cruel tyrant substituted in his place; but the temper of the times would not at first admit of any decided measures of indulgence in favour of the heir to the throne. The barbarous treatment he had experienced from Simon had alienated his reason, but not extinguished his feelings of gratitude. On one occasion that inhuman wretch had seized him by the hair and threatened to dash his head against the wall; the surgeon, Naulin, interfered to prevent him, and the child next day presented him with two pears which had been given him for his supper the preceding evening, lamenting at the same time that he had no other means of testifying his gratitude. Simon and Hebert had put him to the torture to extract from him an avowal of crimes connected with his mother which he was too young to understand; after that cruel day he almost always preserved silence lest his words should prove fatal to some of his relations. This resolution, and the closeness of his confinement, soon preyed upon his health. In February, 1795, he was seized with a fever, and visited by three members of the Committee of Public Safety; they found him seated at a little table making castles of cards. They addressed him with words of kindness, but could not obtain any answer. In May the state of his health became so alarming that the celebrated surgeon Desault was directed by the Convention to visit him. His generous attentions assuaged the sufferings of the child's latter days, but could not prolong his life."

He died of a tumour in the knee, as it was said, arising from a scrofulous affection, but in reality from the miseries he endured in his confinement, the horrible nature of his food and the filth amid which he was intentionally forced to live by his tormentors.

After his death the sufferings of his sister gradually diminished; she was detained in prison, indeed, but was treated with some sort of humanity and decorum, not as a wild beast, but as a woman, if not as a Princess.

It was at length agreed with Austria that she should be released from captivity and placed in the hands of that Power, in exchange for the deputies placed in her hands by Dumouriez, as also La Fayette and his associates. She was removed from the Temple on the 19th of December, 1795. The Minister of the

Interior himself went to fetch her, and conducted her with the greatest respect to his own hotel, whence she set out accompanied by persons of her own selection. An ample provision was made for her journey, and she was thus conveyed to the frontiers.

She afterwards married her cousin, the Duke d'Angoulême, and obtained by her conduct at Bordeaux, in 1815, the highest praise for her courage. Napoleon is said to have observed with regard to her that "she was the only man in the family."

By the death of the child Dauphin, otherwise Louis XVII., the crown hereditary of France devolved on the head of the Count of Provence, who became, on the Restoration in 1815, King Louis XVIII. of France. On his death without heirs male he was succeeded by his brother, Charles X., who lost his throne in the three days of July, 1830, and subsequently died in exile.

Thus ends this awful history of crime and sorrow—a lesson both to Sovereigns and nations, if either would give ear to the teachings of history. But of a verity the course of human events, as they occur age after age, so similar as almost to seem the same, go far to show the truth of the old Roman's saying, that "whom God willeth to destroy He first dementeth."

RECOLLECTIONS,
SKETCHES AND ANECDOTES
BY
MADAME CAMPAN

PREFACE

There are already so many books that ordinary talents for writing are by no means a sufficient excuse for increasing the number. Convinced as I am that the mania for publishing is both censurable and ridiculous, I am far from being weak enough to suffer it to affect me; but destiny having formerly placed me near crowned heads, I now amuse my solitude with recording a variety of facts which may prove interesting to my family when I shall be no more. I have already collected all that concerned the domestic life of an unfortunate Princess, whose reputation is not yet cleared of the stains it suffered from the attacks of calumny, and who justly merited a different lot in life, a different place in the opinion of mankind after her downfall. These Memoirs, which were finished ten years since, have met with the approbation of some persons; and my son may, perhaps, think proper to print them after my decease.[1] I know not whether my Recollections will be thought worthy to see the light; but whilst I am occupied in writing them my mind is diverted; I pass calmer hours; and I seem removed from the melancholy scenes by which I am now surrounded, as far as the sensibility of my heart will permit me to forget the present. The idea of collecting all the interesting materials which my memory affords, occurred to me from reading the work entitled "Paris, Versailles and the Provinces in the Eighteenth Century." That work, composed by a man accustomed to the best society, is full of piquant anecdotes, nearly all of which have been recognised

---

[1] When Madame Campan wrote these lines, she little thought that the death of her son would precede her own. See the Biographical Notice of Madame Campan.—Note by the Editor.

as true by the contemporaries of the author. Such compilations are at least as valuable as those collections of *bons mots* and puns which were in vogue fifty years ago. They give facts; they introduce personages who have performed distinguished parts. They are also, in some degree, capable of affording experience, that most valuable acquisition, which we gain only by our errors, which age renders almost useless and which can be transmitted but very imperfectly.

ANECDOTES OF THE REIGN OF LOUIS XIV.

Previous to the Revolution there were customs and even words in use at Versailles with which few people were acquainted. The King's dinner was called *the King's meat*. Two of the body-guard accompanied the attendants who carried the dinner; every one rose as they passed through the halls, saying, "There is the King's *meat*." All precautionary duties were distinguished by the words—*in case*. Some chemises and handkerchiefs, kept in readiness in a basket in the King's or Queen's apartments in case Their Majesties should wish to change their linen without sending to the wardrobe, constituted the packet *in case*. Their clothes, brought in great baskets, or clothes of green taffety, were called the King's or Queen's *ready*. Thus the attendants would ask; "Is the King's *ready* come?" One of the guards might be heard to say, "I am *in case* in the forest of St. Germain." In the evening they always brought the Queen a large bowl of broth, a cold roast fowl, one bottle of wine, one of orgeat, one of lemonade and some other articles, which were called the *in case* for the night. An old medical gentleman, who had been physician in ordinary to Louis XIV., and was still living at the time of the marriage of Louis XV., told M. Campan's father an anecdote which seems too remarkable to have remained unknown; nevertheless, he was an intelligent, honourable man, and incapable of inventing this story. His name was Lafosse. He said, that Louis XIV. was informed that the officers of his table evinced, in the most disdainful and offensive manner, the mortification they felt at being obliged to eat at the table of the comptroller of the kitchen along with Molière, *valet de chambre* to His Majesty, because Molière had performed on the stage; and that this celebrated author consequently declined appearing at that table. Louis XIV., determined to put an end to insults which ought never to have been offered to one of the greatest geniuses of the age, said one morning to Molière, at the hour of his private levee, "They say you live very poorly here, Molière; and that the officers of my chamber do not find you good enough to eat with them. Perhaps you are hungry; for my part, I awoke with a good appetite this morning; sit down at this table. Serve up my *in case* for the night there." The King, cutting up the fowl and ordering Molière to sit down, then helped him to a wing, at the same time taking one for himself, and ordered the persons entitled to familiar entrance—that is to say, the most distinguished and favourite people at Court—to be admitted. "You see me," said the King to them, "engaged in entertaining Molière, whom my *valets de chambre* do not consider sufficiently good company for them." From that time Molière never had occasion to appear at the *valets*' table; the whole Court was forward enough to send him invitations.[1]

The same M. de Lafosse used also to relate that a

---

[1] This anecdote is, perhaps, one of the most honourable to the character of Louis XIV. that is extant. It is pleasing to see this haughty monarch behaving thus graciously to the player Molière, as the author of "Tartuffe" and the "Misanthrope." These are the acts by which a truly great Prince knows how to avenge injured genius on malignant dulness, and also to reward its labours.

Louis XV. was also desirous of encouraging literature; but he was only capable of affording it a cold and supercilious protection, unaccompanied by any demonstration of grace, affability or kindness, and more humiliating than obliging.

In the entertaining Memoirs of Madame du Hausset, one of Madame de Pompadour's *femmes de chambre*, we meet with the following passage:

"The King, who admired all that was connected with the age of Louis XIV., recollecting that the Boileaus and Racines had been protected by him, and that part of the splendour of that reign was attributed to his own, was flattered with the idea that a Voltaire flourished in his own Court; but he feared that author, and did not esteem him. He could not, however, help saying, 'I have treated him as well as Louis XIV. behaved to Racine and Boileau; I gave him the place of gentleman in ordinary, and a pension, as Louis XIV. did to Racine. If he is presumptuous enough to aim at being a chamberlain, wearing a cross and supping with the King, it is not my fault. It is not the fashion in France; and as there are more wits and great lords here than in Prussia, I should have occasion for an immense table to entertain them all together.' He then counted on his fingers: 'Maupertuis, Fontenelle, La Motte, Voltaire, Piron, Destouches, Montesquieu, Cardinal de Polignac.' 'Your Majesty forgets,' said someone, ' D'Alembert and Clairault.' 'And Crébillon,' said he, 'and La Chaussée.' 'Crébillon, the son,' said another, 'who must be more agreeable than his father; and there is the Abbé Prevôt and the Abbé Olivet.' 'Very well,' said the King, 'all these people would have dined or supped with me for the last five-and-twenty years.'"

brigade-major of the body-guard, being ordered to place the company in the little theatre at the Palace of Versailles, very roughly turned out one of the King's comptrollers, who had taken his seat on one of the benches, a place to which his newly-acquired office entitled him. In vain he insisted on his quality and his right. The altercation was ended by the brigade-major in these words, "Gentlemen body-guards, do your duty." In this case their duty was to take the man and put him out at the door. This comptroller, who had paid sixty or eighty thousand francs for his place, was a man of a good family, and had had the honour of serving His Majesty five-and-twenty years in one of his regiments. Thus disgracefully driven out of the hall, he placed himself in the King's way, in the great hall of the guards, and, bowing to His Majesty, requested him to repair the honour of an old soldier, who had wished to end his days in his Prince's civil employment, now that age had obliged him to relinquish his military service. The King stopped, heard the tale he told in accents of grief and truth, and then ordered him to follow him. His Majesty attended the representation in a sort of amphitheatre, in which his armchair was placed. Behind him was a row of stools for the captain of the guards, the first gentlemen of the chamber and other great officers. The brigade-major was entitled to one of these places. The King stopped opposite the seat which ought to have been occupied by that officer, and said to the comptroller, "Take, sir, for this evening, the place near my person of him who has offended you, and let the expression of my displeasure at this unjust affront satisfy you instead of any other reparation."

During the latter years of the reign of Louis XIV., he never went out but in a chair carried by porters, and he showed much partiality for a man of the name of d'Aigremont, one of these porters, who always went in front and opened the door of the chair. The slightest preference shown by Sovereigns, even to the meanest of their servants, never fails to excite observation.[1] The King had done some-

---

[1] This reflection is justified by an anecdote which was probably unknown to the author. People of the very first rank did not disdain to descend to the level of D'Aigremont. "Lauzun," says the Duchess d'Orleans, in her Memoirs, "sometimes affects stupidity in order to tell the people their own with impunity, for he is very malicious. In order to make Marshal Tessé feel the impropriety of his familiarity with people of the common sort, he called out, in the drawing-room at Marly, 'Marshal, give me a pinch of snuff; some of your best, such as you take in a morning with M. d'Aigremont, the chair-man.'"—NOTE BY THE EDITOR.

thing for this man's numerous family, and frequently talked to him. An abbé belonging to the chapel thought proper to request D'Aigremont to present a memorial to the King, in which he petitioned His Majesty to grant him a benefice. Louis XIV. did not approve of the liberty thus taken by his chair-man, and said to him, in a very angry tone, "D'Aigremont, you have been made to do a very unbecoming act, and I am sure there must be *simony* in the case." "No, Sire, there is not the least *ceremony* in the case, I assure you," answered the poor man, in great consternation; "the abbé only said he would give me a hundred louis." "D'Aigremont," said the King, "I forgive you, on account of your ignorance and candour. I will give you the hundred louis out of my privy purse, but I will discharge you the very next time you venture to present a memorial to me."

Louis XIV. was very kind to those of his servants who were nearest his person; but the moment he assumed his Royal deportment those who were most accustomed to see him in his domestic character were as much intimidated as if they were appearing in his presence for the first time in their lives. Some of the members of His Majesty's civil household, then called *commensalité*, enjoying the title of equerry and the privileges attached to officers of the King's household, had occasion to claim some prerogatives, the exercise of which the municipal body of St. Germain, where they resided, disputed with them. Being assembled in considerable numbers in that town, they obtained the consent of the Minister of the Household to allow them to send a deputation to the King, and for that purpose chose from amongst themselves two of His Majesty's *valets de chambre* named Bazire and Soulaigre. The King's levee being over, the deputation of the inhabitants of the town of St. Germain was called in. They entered with confidence; the King looked at them, and assumed his imposing attitude. Bazire, one of these *valets de chambre*, was about to speak; but Louis the Great was looking on him. He no longer saw the Prince he was accustomed to attend at home; he was intimidated, and could not find words. He recovered, however, and began, as usual, with the word *Sire*. But timidity again overpowered him, and finding himself unable to recollect the slightest particle of what he came to say, he repeated the word *Sire* several times over, and at length concluded by saying, "*Sire*, here is Soulaigre." Soulaigre, who was very angry with Bazire and expected to acquit himself much better, then began to speak. But he also, after repeating *Sire* several times, found his embarrassment increase upon him until his confusion equalled that of his colleague. He therefore ended with "*Sire*, here is Bazire."

The King smiled, and answered, "Gentlemen, I have been informed of the business upon which you have been deputed to wait on me, and I will take care that what is right shall be done. I am highly satisfied with the manner in which you have fulfilled your functions as deputies."[1]

ANECDOTES OF THE REIGN OF LOUIS XV.

THE first event which made any impression on me in my earliest childhood was the attempt of Damiens to assassinate Louis XV. This occurrence struck me so forcibly that the most minute details relating to the confusion and grief which prevailed at Versailles on that day seem as completely present to my imagination as the most recent events. I had dined with my father and mother, in company with one of their friends. The drawing-room was lighted up with a number of tapers, and four card-tables were already occupied, when a friend of the gentleman of

---

[1] In this pleasantry there is nothing bitter or harsh, as in most of those of Louis XV. It leaves only the impression of an agreeable piece of wit. Louis XIV. never indulged in an expression capable of offending anyone, and his repartees, which were almost always full of meaning, often disclose a refined and delicate tact. Generally speaking, wit, either poignant and caustic or pleasant and lively, has never been wanting in the descendants of Henry IV. In the Memoirs of Madame de Hausset there is a striking observation by Duclos on this subject.

"M. Duclos was at Dr. Quesnay's, haranguing with his usual warmth. I heard him say to two or three persons, 'The world is always unjust towards great men, ministers and princes; nothing is more common than to deny them all claims to wit. A few days ago I surprised one of these gentlemen of the *infallible brigade* by telling him that there has been more wit in the House of Bourbon than in any other.' 'Did you prove that?' said someone with a sneer. 'Yes,' said Duclos, 'and I will prove it to you. I presume you allow that the great Condé was no fool, and the Duchess de Longueville is celebrated as one of the most brilliant of women. The Regent was unrivalled for wit of every kind. The Prince de Conti, who was elected King of Poland, was distinguished for this quality, and his verses are equal to those of La Fare and Saint-Aulaire. The Duke of Burgundy was learned and enlightened. The Duchess, Madame, daughter of Louis XV., was an eminent wit, and made epigrams and couplets. The Duke de Maine is in general known only by his weakness; but no one could have more agreeable talents for conversation. His wife was a giddy creature, but she was fond of literature, understood poetry, and possessed a brilliant and inexhaustible imagination. I have now mentioned enough of them,' continued he; 'and as I am not given to flattery, and hate even the appearance of it, I shall say nothing of the living.' This list excited astonishment, and everyone subscribed to the truth of his assertions."

the house came in with a pale and terrified countenance and said, in a voice scarcely audible, "I bring you terrible news. The King has been assassinated!" Two ladies in company instantly fainted; a brigadier of the body-guards threw down his cards and cried out, "I do not wonder at it; it is those rascally Jesuits." "What are you saying, brother?" cried a lady, flying to him; "would you get yourself arrested?" "Arrested! for what? for unmasking those wretches who want a bigot for a King?" My father came in. He recommended circumspection, saying that the blow was not mortal, and that all meetings ought to be suspended at so critical a moment. He had brought a chaise for my mother, who placed me on her knees. We lived in the Avenue de Paris, and throughout our drive I heard incessant cries and sobs from the footpaths. At last I saw a man arrested. He was an usher of the King's chamber who had gone mad, and was crying out, "Yes, I know them, the wretches! the villains!" Our chaise was stopped by this bustle; my mother recognised the unfortunate man who had been seized, and gave his name to the brave trooper who had stopped him. This faithful servant was merely conducted to the gendarmes' station, which was then in the avenue. In times of public calamities or national events the slightest acts of imprudence may be fatal. When the people take part in an opinion or occurrence we ought to avoid coming in contact with them, or even alarming them. Informations are no longer the result of an organised police, and punishments cease to emanate from impartial justice. At the period of which I am speaking, the love of the Sovereign was a sort of religion, and this attempt against the life of Louis XV. brought on a multitude of groundless arrests.[1] M. de la Serre, then governor of the Invalides, his wife, his daughter, and some of his domestics were taken up because Mademoiselle de la Serre, who was that very day come from her convent to pass the holiday of the King's birthday with her family, said, in her father's drawing-room, on hearing this news from Versailles, "It is not to be wondered at. I have often heard Mother N—— say that it would certainly happen because the King is not sufficiently attached to religion." Mother N——, the director and several of the nuns of this convent were

---

[1] At this period Louis XV. was still beloved. In the *Historical Illustrations* (V) will be found a notice relative to this attempt to assassinate the King, together with some curious facts related by Madame de Hausset on the momentary disgrace of Madame de Pompadour, and her subsequent triumph on the King's recovery.—NOTE BY THE EDITOR.

interrogated by the lieutenant of police. The public animosity against the Jesuits, kept up by the partisans of Port Royal and the adepts of the new philosophy, did not conceal the suspicions which they directed against the Jesuits; and, although there was not the slightest proof against that order, the attempt to assassinate the King was certainly made use of against it, a few years afterwards, by the party which affected the destruction of the Company of Jesus. The wretch Damiens avenged himself on several persons whom he had served in several provinces by getting them arrested; and when they were confronted with him, he said to some of them, "It was out of revenge for your ill-treatment of me that I put you into this fright." To some women he said, "That he had amused himself in his prison with the thoughts of the terror they would feel." This monster confessed that he had murdered the virtuous La Bourdonnaye, by giving him a *lavement* of aquafortis. He had also committed several other crimes. People are too careless about those whom they take into their service; such examples prove that too many precautions cannot be used in ascertaining the character of strangers before we admit them into our houses.

I have often heard M. de Landsmath, equerry and master of the hounds, who used to come frequently to my father's, say that, on the news of the attempt on the King's life, he instantly repaired to His Majesty. I cannot repeat the coarse expressions he made use of to encourage His Majesty; but his account of the affair, long afterwards, used to entertain the parties in which he was prevailed on to relate it, when all apprehensions respecting the consequences of this event had subsided. This M. de Landsmath was an old soldier who had given proofs of extraordinary valour. Nothing had been able to soften his manners or subdue his excessive bluntness to the respectful customs of the Court. The King was very fond of him. He possessed prodigious strength, and had often contended with Marshal Saxe, renowned for his great bodily power, in trying the strength of their respective wrists.¹ M. de Landsmath had a thundering voice. When he came into the King's apartment, he found the Dauphin and

---

1 One day, when the King was hunting in the forest of St. Germain, Landsmath, riding before him, wanted a cart, filled with mud from a pond that had just been cleansed, to draw up out of the way. The carter resisted, and even answered with impertinence. Landsmath, without dismounting, seized him by the breast of his coat, lifted him up, and threw him into his cart.—NOTE BY MADAME CAMPAN.

Mesdames His Majesty's daughters there; the Princesses, in tears, surrounded the King's bed. "Send out all these weeping ladies, Sire," said the old equerry, "I want to speak to you alone." The King made a sign to the Princesses to withdraw. "Come," said De Landsmath, "your wound is nothing; you had plenty of waistcoats and flannel on." Then uncovering his breast, "Look here," said he, showing four or five great scars, "these are something like wounds. I received them thirty years ago; now cough as loud as you can." The King did so. Then taking up a *vase de nuit*, he desired His Majesty in the most unceremonious way to make use of it, which he did. "'Tis nothing at all," said Landsmath; "you must laugh at it; we shall hunt a stag together in four days." "But suppose the blade was poisoned," said the King. "Old grandame's tales," replied De Landsmath; "if it had been so, the waistcoats and flannels would have rubbed the poison off." The King was tranquillised, and passed a very good night.

This same M. de Landsmath, who, by his military and familiar language, thus calmed the fears of Louis XV. on the day of Damiens' horrible crime, was one of those people who, in the most haughty Courts, often tell the truth bluntly. It is remarkable that there is a person of this description to be found in almost every Court, who seems to supply the place of the ancient King's jester, and to claim the right of saying whatever he pleases.

His Majesty one day asked M. de Landsmath how old he was? He was aged, and by no means fond of thinking of his age, so evaded the question. A fortnight after Louis XV. took a paper out of his pocket and read aloud, "On such a day in the month of * * *, one thousand six hundred and eighty * * *, was baptised by me, rector of * * *, the son of the high and mighty Lord, &c." "What's that?" said De Landsmath, angrily; "has Your Majesty been procuring the certificate of my baptism?" "There it is, you see, Landsmath," said the King. "Well, Sire, hide it as fast as you can; a Prince entrusted with the happiness of twenty-five millions of men ought not to hurt at pleasure the feelings of one individual."

The King learned that De Landsmath had lost his confessor, a missionary priest of the parish of Notre Dame. It was the custom of the Lazarists to expose their dead with the face uncovered. Louis XV. wished to try his equerry's firmness. "You have lost your confessor, I hear," said the King. "Yes, Sire." "He will be exposed with his face bare?"

"Such is the custom." "I command you to go and see him." "Sire, my confessor was my friend; it would be very painful to me." "No matter; I command you." "Are you really in earnest, Sire?" "Quite so." "It would be the first time in my life that I had disobeyed my Sovereign's order. I will go." The next day the King, at his levee, as soon as he perceived De Landsmath, said, "Have you done as I desired you, Landsmath?" "Undoubtedly, Sire." "Well, what did you see?" "Faith, I saw that Your Majesty and I are no great things!"[1]

At the death of Queen Maria Leckzinska, M. Campan, who was afterwards secretary of the closet to Marie Antoinette, and at that time an officer of the chamber, having performed several confidential duties at the time of that Queen's decease, the King asked Madame Adelaide how he should reward him. She requested him to create an office in his household of master of the wardrobe, with a salary of a thousand crowns, for M. Campan. "I will do so," said the King, "it will be an honourable title; but tell Campan not to add a single crown to his expenses, for you will see they will never pay him."

The manner in which Mademoiselle de Romans, mistress to Louis XV. and mother of the Abbé Bourbon, was presented to him deserves, I think, to be related. The King had gone with a grand cavalcade to Paris to hold a bed of justice. As he passed the terrace of the Tuileries he observed a chevalier de St. Louis, dressed in a faded lustring coat, and a woman of a pretty good figure, holding on the parapet of the terrace a young girl strikingly beautiful, much adorned, and dressed in a rose-coloured taffety frock. The King's notice was involuntarily attracted by the marked manner in which he was pointed out to the girl. On returning to Versailles he called Le Bel, the minister and confidant of his secret pleasures, and ordered him to seek in Paris a young female about twelve

---

[1] "The King often talked about death, burials, and cemeteries," says Madame du Hausset; "nobody could be more melancholy by nature. Madame de Pompadour has often told me that he felt a painful sensation whenever he was forced to laugh, and that he often requested her to put an end to a diverting story. He smiled, and that was all. He had, in general, the most gloomy ideas on all events. When a new minister came into office the King would say, 'He spread out his goods, like the rest, and promised the finest things in the world, none of which will ever happen. He does not know how the land lies; he will see.' When schemes for increasing the naval force were proposed to him he used to say, 'I have heard it talked of continually for the last twenty years; France will never have a navy, I believe.' I had this from M. de Marigny."—NOTE BY THE EDITOR.

or thirteen years of age, describing her as I have just done. Le Bel assured him he saw no probability of the success of such a commission. "Pardon me," said Louis XV., "this family must live in the neighbourhood of the Tuileries, on the side of the Faubourg St. Honoré, or at the entrance of the Faubourg St. Germain. These people certainly go on foot; they did not make the girl, of whom they seemed so fond, cross all Paris. They are poor; the clothes of the child were so new that I have no doubt they were made for the very day I was to go to Paris. She will wear that dress all the summer; they will walk in the Tuileries on Sundays and holidays. Apply to the man who sells lemonade at the terrace of the Feuillans; children take refreshment there; you will discover her by these means."

Le Bel fulfilled his master's orders; and within a month discovered the dwelling of the girl; he found that Louis XV. was not in the least mistaken with respect to the intentions which he supposed to exist. All conditions were easily agreed on; the King contributed, by considerable presents, to the education of Mademoiselle de Romans for the space of two years. She was kept totally ignorant of her future destiny; and, when she had completed her fifteenth year, she was taken to Versailles on the pretence of going to see the palace. Between four and five o'clock in the afternoon, she was conducted into the mirror gallery. All the grand apartments were usually deserted at that hour. Le Bel, who waited for them, opened the glass door which led from the gallery into the King's closet, and invited Mademoiselle de Romans to go in and examine its beauties. Encouraged by the sight of a man whom she knew, and excited by the curiosity so excusable at her age, she eagerly accepted the offer, but insisted on Le Bel procuring the same pleasure for her parents. He assured her that it was impossible, that they were going to sit down in one of the windows of the gallery and wait for her, and that when she had seen the inner apartments he would bring her back to them. She consented; the glass door closed on her. Le Bel showed her the chamber, the council-room, and talked with enthusiasm of the monarch who possessed the magnificence with which she was surrounded; and at length conducted her to the private apartments, where Mademoiselle de Romans found the King himself awaiting her arrival with all the impatience and eagerness of a Prince who had been two years engaged in bringing about the moment of this interview.

What painful reflections are excited by all this immorality! The art with which this intrigue had been carried on, and the genuine innocence of the youthful De Romans, were doubtless the motives of the King's particular attachment to this mistress. She was the only one who prevailed on him to allow her son to bear the name of Bourbon. At the moment of his birth she received a note in the King's handwriting, containing the following words: "The Rector of Chaillot, when he baptizes the child of Mademoiselle de Romans, will give him the following names: Louis N. de Bourbon." A few years afterwards, the King being dissatisfied at the importance which Mademoiselle de Romans assumed on account of her good fortune in having given birth to an acknowledged son, and seeing by the splendid way in which she was bringing him up that she entertained the idea of causing him to be legitimatised, had him taken out of his mother's hand. This commission was executed with great severity. Louis XV. had vowed never to legitimatise a natural child. The great number of Princes of this description which Louis XIV. had left was burdensome to the State, and made this determination of Louis XV. truly laudable. The Abbé Bourbon was very handsome, and exactly resembled his father. He was much beloved by the Princesses, the King's daughters, and his ecclesiastical elevation would have been carried by Louis XV. to the highest degree. A cardinal's hat was intended for him, as well as the abbey of St. Germain des Prés and the bishopric of Bayeux. Without being considered one of the Princes of the Blood, he would have enjoyed a most happy lot. He died at Rome of confluent small-pox. He was generally regretted there; but the unfortunate events by which his family have since been afflicted afford reason to regard his death as a merciful dispensation of Providence. Mademoiselle de Romans married a gentleman named Cavanac. The King was displeased at it, and she was universally blamed for having in some degree abandoned by this alliance the plain title of mother of the Abbé de Bourbon.[1]

---

[1] This anecdote is calculated to excite mournful reflections; but its impression is heightened by the fact that many similar adventures took place. In the *Historical Illustrations* (W) will be found two anecdotes—the one related by Soulavie, the other by Madame du Hausset,—which, although the names of the parties differ, are but too similar to this of Mademoiselle de Romans.

The following article, written with extraordinary impartiality by M. de Lacretelle, leaves no possible doubt as to the origin and extent of these scandalous practices:

"Louis, satiated with the conquests which the Court offered him, was led by a depraved imagination to form an establishment for his pleasures of such an infamous description that, after having depicted the debaucheries of the Regency, it is difficult to find terms appropriate to an excess of this kind. Several elegant houses, built in an enclosure called the Parc-aux-Cerfs, were used for the reception of

The monotonous habits of Royal greatness too frequently inspire Princes with the desire of procuring for themselves the enjoyments of private individuals; and then they vainly flatter themselves with the hope of remaining concealed in mysterious obscurity. They ought to be warned against these transient errors, and accustomed to support the tediousness of greatness, as well as to enjoy its extensive advantages, which they well know how to do. Louis XV., by his noble carriage, and the mild yet majestic expression of his features, was perfectly worthy to succeed Louis the Great. But he too frequently indulged in secret pleasures, which at last were sure to become known. During several winters he was passionately fond of *candles' end balls*, as he called those parties amongst the very lowest classes of society. He got intelligence of the picnics given by little dealers, milliners and seamstresses of Versailles, whither he repaired in a black domino and masked, accompanied by the captain of his guards masked like himself. His great delight was to go *en brouette*.[1] Care was always taken to give notice to five or six officers of the King's or Queen's chamber to be there, in order that His Majesty might be surrounded by safe people without perceiving it or finding it troublesome. Probably the captain of the guards also took other precautions of this description on his part. My father-in-law, when the King

---

women, who there awaited the pleasure of their master. Hither were brought young girls sold by their parents, and sometimes forced from them. They left this place loaded with gifts, but almost certain of never more beholding the King who had dishonoured them, even when they bore with them a pledge of his base passion. Hence corruption found its way into the most peaceful and obscure habitations. It was skilfully and patiently fostered by those who ministered to the debaucheries of Louis. Whole years were occupied in the seduction of girls not yet of marriageable age, and in undermining the principles of modesty and fidelity in young women. Some of these victims were so unhappy as to feel a true affection and sincere attachment to the King. For a few minutes he would seem moved by their fidelity, but he quickly repressed such feelings, and persuaded himself that it was all artifice intended to govern him; and he himself became the informer against them to the Marchioness, who soon forced her rivals back into their original obscurity. Mademoiselle de Romans was the only one who procured her son to be acknowledged as the King's child. Madame de Pompadour succeeded in removing a rival who seemed to have made so profound an impression on the King's heart. Mademoiselle de Romans had her son taken from her; he was brought up by a peasant, and his mother durst not protest against this outrage until after the King's death. Louis XVI. restored her son to her, and took him under his protection; he was afterwards known under the name of the Abbé de Bourbon. ("History of France," by Lacretelle, vol. iii.)—NOTE BY THE EDITOR.

1 In a kind of sedan chair, running on two wheels, and drawn by a chair-man.

and he were both young, has often made one amongst the servants desired to attend masked at these parties, assembled in some garret, or parlour of a tavern. In those times, during the carnival, masked companies had a right to join the citizens' balls; it was sufficient that one of the party should unmask and name himself.

These secret excursions, and his too habitual intercourse with ladies more distinguished for their personal charms than the advantages of education, were no doubt the means by which the King acquired many vulgar expressions which otherwise would never have reached his ears.

Yet, amidst the most shameful excesses, the King sometimes resumed suddenly the dignity of his rank in a very noble manner. The familiar courtiers of Louis XV. had one day abandoned themselves to the unrestrained gaiety of a supper after returning from the chase. Each boasted and described the beauty of his mistress. Some of them amused themselves with giving a particular account of their wives' personal defects, and in claiming extraordinary merit for their performance of marital duties. An imprudent word, addressed to Louis XV. and applicable only to the Queen, instantly dispelled all the mirth of the entertainment. The King assumed his regal air, and, knocking with his knife on the table twice or thrice, "Gentlemen," said he, "here is the King."[1]

Three young men of the College of St. Germain, who had just completed their course of studies, knowing no person about the Court, and having heard that strangers were always well treated there, resolved to dress themselves completely in the Armenian costume, and thus clad to present themselves to see the grand ceremony of the reception of several knights of the Order of the Holy Ghost. The stratagem met with all the success with which they had flattered themselves. While the procession was passing through the long mirror gallery, the Swiss of the apartments placed them in the first row of spectators, recommending everyone to pay all possible attention to the strangers. The latter, however, were imprudent enough to enter the "bull's-eye," where were MM. Cardonne and Ruffin, interpreters of Oriental languages, and the first clerk of the consul's department, whose business it was to attend to everything which related to the natives of the East who were in France. The three scholars were

---

[1] No anecdote could more completely expose the excessive corruption of the times than this shameful conduct of married men, although that of their wives was probably no better. According to facts mentioned by Soulavie, there were women audacious enough to demand evidence of their own infamy in order to effect a separation from their husbands.—NOTE BY THE EDITOR.

immediately surrounded and questioned by these gentlemen, at first in modern Greek. Without being disconcerted, they made signs that they did not understand it. They were then addressed in Turkish and Arabic. At length, one of the interpreters, losing all patience, exclaimed. "Gentlemen, you certainly must understand some of the languages in which you have been addressed; what country can you possibly come from, then?" "From St. Germain-en-Laye, sir," replied the boldest amongst them. "This is the first time you have put the question to us in French." Then they confessed the motive of their disguise; the eldest of them was not more than eighteen years of age. Louis XV. was informed of the affair. He laughed heartily; ordered them a few hours' confinement and a good admonition, after which they were to be set at liberty.

Louis XV. liked to talk about death, though he was extremely apprehensive of it; but his excellent health and his Royal dignity probably made him imagine himself invulnerable. He often said to people who had very bad colds, "You've a churchyard cough there." Hunting one day in the forest of Sénard, in a year in which bread was extremely dear, he met a man on horseback carrying a coffin. "Whither are you carrying that coffin?" "To the village of ———," answered the peasant. "Is it for a man or a woman?" "For a man." "What did he die of?" "Hunger," bluntly replied the villager. The King spurred his horse and asked no more questions.

When I was young I often met in company Madame de Marchais, the wife of the King's first *valet de chambre*. She was a very well-informed woman, and had enjoyed the favour of Louis XV., being a relation of Madame de Pompadour. M. de Marchais was rich and much respected; had served in the army, was a chevalier de St. Louis, and, besides being principal *valet de chambre*, was governor of the Louvre. Madame de Marchais was visited by the whole Court; the captains of the guards came there constantly, and many officers of the body-guard. Eminent officers of every kind used to get introduced to her, as to Madame Geoffrin. She possessed some influence, particularly in soliciting votes for the candidates for the academicians' chairs. I have seen all the celebrated men of the age at her house: La Harpe, Diderot, D'Alembert, Duclos, Thomas, &c. She was remarkable for her wit and studied display, as was her husband for his good-nature and simplicity. He was fond of spoiling her most innocent schemes for obtaining admiration. No one could describe an academical speech, a sermon, or the subject of a new piece with so much precision and grace as Madame de Marchais. She had also the art of turning the conversation at pleasure upon any ancient or modern work, and her husband often delighted in saying to those who sat near him, "My wife read that this morning." Count d'Angiviller, charmed with the graces of her mind, paid assiduous court to her, and, when she became the widow of M. de Marchais, married her. She was still living at Versailles in the early part of the reign of Napoleon, but never left her bed. She had retained her fondness for dress, and although unable to rise, always had her hair dressed as people used to wear it twenty years before that period. She disguised the ravages of time under a prodigious quantity of white and red paint, and seemed, by the feeble light which penetrated through her closed blinds and drawn curtains, nothing but a kind of doll—but a doll which spoke in a charming and most spirited manner. She had retained a very beautiful head of hair to an advanced age; it was said that the celebrated Count Saint-Germain, who had appeared at the Court of Louis XV. as one of the most famous alchemists of the day, had given her a liquor which preserved the hair and prevented it from turning white through age.

Louis XV. had, as it is well known, adopted the whimsical system of separating Louis de Bourbon from the King of France. As a private individual, he had his personal fortune, his own distinct financial interests. He used to deal as an individual in all the contracts and bargains he engaged in; he had bought a tolerably handsome house at the Parc-aux-Cerfs at Versailles, where he used to keep one of those obscure mistresses whom the indulgence or the policy of Madame de Pompadour tolerated so long as she herself retained the title of his declared mistress. After the King had relinquished this custom, he wished to sell the house. Sevin, first clerk of the War Office, offered to purchase it; the notary instructed to effect the sale informed the King of his proposals. The contract for the sale was made out between Louis de Bourbon and Pierre Sevin; and the King sent word to the purchaser to bring him the money himself in gold. The first clerk collected 40,000 francs in louis d'or, and being introduced by the notary of the King's private cabinet, delivered the purchase-money of the house into His Majesty's own hands.

Out of his private funds the King paid the household expenses of his mistresses, those of the education of his illegitimate daughters, who were brought up in convents at Paris, and their dowries when they married.

Men of the most dissolute manners are not, on that account, insensible to virtue in women. The Countess de Périgord was as beautiful as she was virtuous. During some excursions she made to Choisy, whither she had been invited, she perceived that the King took great notice of her. Her demeanour of chilling respect, her cautious perseverance in shunning all serious conversation with the monarch, were insufficient to extinguish this rising flame; and he at length addressed a letter to her worded in the most passionate terms. This excellent woman instantly formed her resolution: honour forbade her returning the King's passion, whilst her profound respect for the Sovereign made her unwilling to disturb his tranquillity. She therefore voluntarily banished herself to an estate she possessed, called Chalais, near Barbezieux, the mansion of which had been uninhabited for nearly a century; the porter's lodge was the only place in a condition to receive her. From this seat she wrote to His Majesty, explaining her motives for leaving Court; and she remained there several years without visiting Paris. Louis XV. was speedily attracted by other objects, and regained the composure to which Madame de Périgord had thought it her duty to make so great a sacrifice. Some years afterwards the Princesses' lady of honour died; many great families solicited the place. The King, without answering any of their applications, wrote to the Countess de Périgord: "My daughters have just lost their lady of honour; this place, madam, is your due, no less on account of your eminent virtues than of the illustrious name of your family."

Count d'Halville, sprung from a very ancient Swiss house, commenced his career at Versailles in the humble rank of ensign in the regiment of Swiss Guards. His name and distinguished qualities gained him the patronage of some powerful friends, who, in order to support the honour of the ancient name he bore by a handsome fortune, obtained for him in marriage the daughter of a very rich financier named M. de la Garde. The offspring of this union was an only daughter, who married Count Esterhazy. Amongst the estates which belonged to Mademoiselle de la Garde was the Château des Trous, situate four leagues from Versailles, where the Count was visited by many people attached to the Court. The young ensign of the body-guards, who had obtained that rank on account of his name and of the favour which his family enjoyed, and possessed all the confidence which usually accompanies unmerited success, but of which the progress of time fortunately relieves young people, was one day taking it upon himself to give his opinion of the Swiss nobility, although he knew nothing of the great families of Switzerland. Without the least delicacy or consideration for the Count, his host, he asserted boldly that there were no ancient families in Switzerland. "Excuse me," said the Count very coolly, "there are several of great antiquity." "Can you name them, sir?" answered the youth. "Yes," said M. d'Halville; "for instance, there is my House, and that of Hapsburg, which now reigns in Germany." "Of course you have your reasons for naming your own family first," replied the imprudent ensign. "Yes, sir," said M. d'Halville, sternly; "because the House of Hapsburg dates from the period when its founder was page to my ancestors. Read history, study the antiquities of nations and families, and in future be more circumspect in your assertions."

Weak as Louis XV. was, the Parliaments would never have obtained his consent to the convocation of the States-General. I heard an anecdote on this subject from two officers attached to that Prince's household. It was at the period when the remonstrances of the Parliaments and the refusals to register the decrees for levying the taxes produced alarm with respect to the state of the finances. This became the subject of conversation one evening at the *coucher* of Louis XV., "You will see, Sire," said a courtier, whose office placed him in close communication with the King, "that all this will make it absolutely necessary to assemble the States-General." The King, roused by this speech from his habitual apathy, seized the courtier by the arm, and said to him in a passion, "Never repeat those words. I am not sanguinary; but had I a brother, and he were to dare to give me such advice, I would sacrifice him within twenty-four hours to the duration of the monarchy and the tranquillity of the kingdom."

Natural causes of the Death of the Dauphin, the father of Louis XVI., and of the Dauphiness, Princess of Saxony, in answer to all the reports spread by Soulavie about poison.[1]

SEVERAL years prior to his death, the Dauphin had a confluent small-pox which endangered his life; and after his convalescence he was long troubled with a malignant ulcer under the nose. He was injudiciously advised to get rid of it by the use of extract of lead, which proved effectual; but from that time the Dauphin, who was corpulent, insensibly grew thin; and a short, dry cough evinced that the humour, driven in, had fallen on the lungs. Some persons also suspected him of having taken acids in too great a quantity for the purpose of reducing his bulk. The state of his health was not, however, such as to excite alarm at the time of the camp at Compiègne, in July, 1764. The Dauphin reviewed the troops, and exerted much activity in the performance of his duties; it was even observed that he was seeking to gain the attachment of the army. He presented the Dauphiness to the soldiers, saying, with a simplicity which at that time made a great sensation, "My children, here is my wife." Returning late on horseback to Compiègne, he found himself cold. The heat of the day had been excessive; the Prince's clothes had been wet with perspiration. An illness followed this accident; the Prince began to spit blood. His principal physician wished to have him bled; the consulting physicians insisted on purgation, and their advice was followed. The pleurisy being ill-cured, assumed and retained all the symptoms of consumption; the Dauphin languished from that period until December, 1765, and died at Fontainebleau, where the Court, on account of his condition, had prolonged its stay, which usually ended on the 2nd of November.

---

[1] We leave the title of this piece as it stands; but it is proper to remark that the reproach here applied to Soulavie is not perfectly well founded. He has only done that which is the duty of every impartial chronicler. He has, indeed, stated the odious accusations which were made against the Duke de Choiseul, and which we believe to be unfounded; but at the same time he brings forward testimony in defence of the memory of M. de Choiseul which seems to us sufficiently protected by his character. The Duke de Choiseul disliked the Dauphin; he even defied him, which was wrong. His violent rage was undoubtedly reprehensible when he forgot himself so far as to say, "I may one day be condemned to the misfortune of being your subject, but I will never be your slave." But there is a wide interval between this audacious fury of the moment, and the blackest of crimes: an interval which M. de Choiseul was incapable of passing.

The Dauphiness, his widow, was excessively afflicted, but the immoderate despair which characterised her grief induced many to suspect that the loss of the crown was an important part of the calamity she lamented. She long refused to eat enough to support life; she encouraged her tears to flow by placing portraits of the Dauphin in every retired part of her apartments. She had him represented pale and ready to expire, in a picture placed at the foot of her bed, under draperies of grey cloth, with which the chambers of the Princesses were always hung in court mournings. Their grand cabinet was hung with black cloth, with an alcove, a canopy, and a throne, on which they received compliments of condolence after the first period of the deep mourning. The Dauphiness, some months before the end of her life, regretted her conduct in abridging it; but it was too late; the fatal blow had been struck. It may also be presumed that living with a consumptive man had contributed to her complaint. This Princess had no opportunity of displaying her qualities; living in a Court in which she was eclipsed by the King and Queen, the only characteristics that could be remarked in her were her extreme attachment to her husband and her great piety.

The Dauphin was little known, and his character has been much mistaken. He himself, as he confessed to his intimate friends, sought to disguise it. He one day asked one of his most familiar servants, "What do they say in Paris of that great fool of a Dauphin?" The person interrogated seeming confused, the Dauphin urged him to express himself sincerely, saying, "Speak freely; that is positively the idea which I wish people to form of me."

As he died of a disease which allows the last moment to be anticipated long beforehand, he wrote much, and transmitted his affections and his prejudices to his son by secret notes.[1] This was really what prevented the Queen from recalling M. de Choiseul at the death of Louis XV., and what promoted M. de Muy, the intimate friend of the Dauphin, to the place of Minister of War. The destruction of the Jesuits, effected by M. de Choiseul, had given the Dauphin's hatred of him that character of party spirit which induced him to transmit it to his son. Had he ascended the throne, he would have supported the Jesuits and priests in general, and kept down the philosophers. Maria Leckzinska, the wife of Louis XV., placed her highest merit in abstaining from public affairs and in the strict observance of her religious duties, never asking for anything for herself, and

---

[1] The *Historical Illustrations* (X) contain some particulars of the disposition and manners of Louis XVI. in his youth.

sending all she possessed to the poor. Such a life ought to secure a person against all danger of poison, but has not preserved the memory of this Princess from that venom which Soulavie makes the Duke de Choiseul deal around him indiscriminately.

ANECDOTES RELATIVE TO MARIA LECKZINSKA.[1]

MARIA LECKZINSKA, wife of Louis XV., often spoke of the situation, even below mediocrity, in which she stood at the time when the policy of the Court of Versailles caused the marriage of the King with the young Infanta to be broken off, and raised a Polish Princess, daughter of a dethroned monarch, to the rank of Queen of France. Before this unhoped-for event changed the destiny of this virtuous Princess, there had been some idea of marrying her to the Duke d'Estrées; and when the Duchess of that name came to pay her court to her at Versailles, she said to those who surrounded her, "I might have been in that lady's place myself, and curtseying to the Queen of France." She used to relate that the King, her father, informed her of her elevation in a manner which might have made too strong an impression on her mind; that he had taken care, to avoid disturbing her tranquillity, to leave her in total ignorance of the first negotiations set on foot relative to her marriage; and that when all was definitely arranged and the ambassador arrived, her father went to her apartment, placed an arm-chair for her, had her set in it, and addressed her thus: "Allow me, madam, to enjoy a happiness which far overbalances all I have suffered; I wish to be the first to pay my respects to the Queen of France."

Maria Leckzinska was not handsome, but she possessed much intelligence, an expressive countenance, a simplicity of manner, and all the gracefulness of the Polish ladies. She loved the King, and found his first infidelities very grievous to endure. Nevertheless, the death of Madame de Châteauroux, whom she had known very young and who had even been honoured by her kindness, made a painful impression on her. This good Queen still suffered from the bad

---

[1] "In some esteemed Memoirs of the Reign of Maria Leckzinska it is said that she was to have been married to the Duke de Bourbon. I know not whether this be certain; but I can affirm that she has often conversed with Madame Campan, my mother-in-law, on the project of her marriage with the Duke d'Estrées."—NOTE BY MADAME CAMPAN.

effects of an early superstitious education. She was fearful of ghosts. The first night after she heard of this almost sudden death she could not sleep, and made one of her women sit up, who endeavoured to calm her restlessness by telling her stories, which she would in such cases call for, as children do with their nurses. This night nothing could overcome her wakefulness; her *femme de chambre*, thinking she was asleep, was leaving her bed on tiptoe; the slightest noise on the floor roused the Queen, who cried, "Whither are you going? Stay, go on with your story." As it was past two in the morning, this woman, whose name was Boirot, and who was somewhat unceremonious, said, "What can be the matter with Your Majesty to-night? Are you feverish? Shall I call up the physician?" "Oh! no, no, my good Boirot, I am not ill; but that poor Madame de Châteauroux—if she were to come again!" "Jesus, madam!" cried the woman, who had lost all patience, "if Madame de Châteauroux should come again, it certainly will not be Your Majesty that she will look for." The Queen burst into a fit of laughter at this observation, her agitation subsided, and she soon fell asleep.

The nomination of Madame le Normand d'Etioles, Marchioness de Pompadour, to the place of lady of the bedchamber to the Queen, offended the dignity as well as the sensibility of this Princess. Nevertheless, the respectful homage paid by the Marchioness, the interest which certain great personages, who were candidates for her favour, had in procuring her an indulgent reception from Her Majesty, the respect of Maria Leckzinska for all the King's wishes, all conspired to secure her the Queen's favourable notice. Madame de Pompadour's brother received patents of high birth from His Majesty, and was appointed superintendent of the buildings and gardens. He often presented to Her Majesty, through the medium of his sister, the rarest flowers, pine-apples and early vegetables from the gardens of Trianon and Choisy. One day when the Marchioness came into the Queen's apartment, carrying a large basket of flowers, which she held in her two beautiful arms, without gloves, as a mark of respect, the Queen loudly declared her admiration of her beauty, and seemed as if she wished to defend the King's choice by praising her various charms in detail in a manner that would have been as suitable to a production of the fine arts as to a living being. After applauding the complexion, eyes and fine arms of the favourite with that haughty condescension which renders approbation more offensive than flattering, the Queen at length requested her to sing in the attitude in which she stood, being desirous of hearing the voice and musical talent by which the King's Court had been charmed in the performances of the private apartments, and thus to combine the gratification of the ear with that of the eyes. The Marchioness, who still held her enormous basket, was perfectly sensible of something offensive in this request, and tried to excuse herself from singing. The Queen at last commanded her. She then exerted her fine voice in the solo of *Armida*, " At length he is in my power." The change in Her Majesty's countenance was so obvious that the ladies present at this scene had the greatest difficulty to keep theirs.

The Queen received visitors with much grace and dignity, but it is very common with the great to reiterate the same questions; a sterility of ideas is very excusable on public occasions, when there is so little to say. The lady of an ambassador, however, made Her Majesty feel that she did not choose to give way to her forgetfulness in matters concerning herself. This lady was pregnant, but, nevertheless, constantly appeared at the Queen's drawing-rooms, who never failed to ask her whether she was in the state alluded to, and on receiving an answer in the affirmative, always enquired how many months of her time had elapsed. At length the lady, weary of the eternal repetition of the same question, and of the total forgetfulness which betrayed the insincerity of the Queen in pretending to take interest in her affairs, replied to the usual enquiry, "No, madam." This answer instantly recalled to Her Majesty's recollection those which the lady had so often given before. "How, madam," said she, "it appears to me that you have several times answered me that you were so. Have you been brought to bed?" "No, madam; but I was fearful of fatiguing Your Majesty by constantly repeating the same thing." This lady was from that day very coldly received by Maria Leckzinska, and had Her Majesty possessed more influence the ambassador might have suffered for his wife's indiscretion. The Queen was affable and modest, but the more thankful she was in her heart to heaven for having placed her on the first throne in Europe, the more unwilling she was to be reminded of her elevation. This sentiment induced her to insist on the observation of all the forms of respect due to Royal birth; whereas in other Princes the consciousness of that birth often induces them to disdain the ceremonies of etiquette, and to prefer habits of ease and simplicity. There was a striking contrast in this respect between Maria Leckzinska and Marie Antoinette, as has been justly and generally thought. The latter unfortunate Queen carried her disregard of everything belonging to the strict forms of etiquette too far.[1] One day, when the Maréchale de Mouchy was teasing her with questions relative to the extent to which she would allow the ladies the option of taking off or wearing their cloaks, and of pinning up the lappets of their caps or letting them hang down, the Queen replied to her, in my presence, "Arrange all those matters, madam, just as you please; but do not imagine that a Queen, born Archduchess of Austria, can attach that importance to them which might be felt by a Polish Princess who had become Queen of France."

The Polish Princess, in truth, never forgave the slightest deviation from the respect due to her person and to all belonging to her. The Duchess of ———, a lady of her bed-chamber, who was of an imperious and irritable temper, often drew upon herself such petty slights as are constantly shown towards haughty and ill-natured people by the servants of Princes when they can justify those affronts by the plea of their duty or of the customs of the Court.

---

[1] Marie Antoinette has been so often reproached for having derogated from the strictness of old custom, that it is extremely necessary to answer this accusation, once for all, by facts. No Prince was ever more jealously observant of the laws of etiquette than Louis XIV, in whose latter years the prudery of Madame de Maintenon rather tended to increase than to weaken this inclination. Let those, therefore, who cannot excuse the slightest infraction of ceremony in Marie Antoinette compare her conduct with that of the Duchess of Burgundy:

"This Princess," says the Duchess d'Orleans in her Memoirs, "was often entirely alone in her château, unattended by any of her people; she would take the arm of one of the young ladies, and walk out without equerries, lady of honour or tire-woman. At Marly and Versailles she went on foot without a corset; would go into the church and sit down by the *femmes de chambre*. At Madame de Maintenon's no distinction of rank was observed, and the whole company seated themselves indiscriminately; she contrived this purposely that her own rank might not be remarked. At Marly the Dauphiness walked in the garden all night with the young people until three or four in the morning. The King knew nothing of these nocturnal excursions."

Is not this clear and positive enough? Whence then the blame so unjustly thrown on Marie Antoinette, whilst a profound silence is maintained respecting the imprudence, to say no worse, of the Duchess of Burgundy? It is because the excessive mildness of Louis XVI. encouraged audacity and calumny amongst the courtiers, whilst under Louis XIV., on the contrary, the most prompt chastisement would have been the lot of any daring individual who had ventured to point his malignant slanders at a personage placed near the throne. The Duchess d'Orleans makes this sufficiently evident. "Madame de Maintenon," she adds, "had prohibited the Duchess du Lude from annoying the Duchess of Burgundy, that she might not put her in an ill-humour, because when out of temper the Dauphiness could not divert the King. She had also threatened with her eternal anger whomsoever should dare to accuse the Dauphiness to His Majesty."
—NOTE BY THE EDITOR.

Etiquette, or indeed I might say a sense of propriety, prohibited all persons from laying things belonging to them on the seats of the Queen's chamber. At Versailles one had to cross this chamber to reach the play-room. The Duchess de —— laid her cloak on one of the folding-stools which stood before the balustrade of the bed. The usher of the chamber, whose duty it was to attend to whatever occurred in this room, whilst they were at play, saw this cloak, took it and carried it into the footman's ante-chamber. The Queen had a large favourite cat, which was constantly running about the apartments. This satin cloak, lined with fur, appeared very convenient to the cat, who took possession of it accordingly. Unfortunately, he left very unpleasant marks of his preference, which remained but too evident on the white satin of the pelisse, in spite of all the pains that were taken to efface them before it was given to the Duchess. She perceived them, took the cloak in her hand, and returned in a violent passion to the Queen's chamber, where Her Majesty remained surrounded by almost all the Court. "Only see, madam," said she, "the impertinence of *your people*, who have thrown my pelisse on a bench in the ante-chamber, where Your Majesty's cat has served it in this manner." The Queen, displeased at her complaints and familiar expressions, said to her, with the coldest look imaginable, "Know, madam, that it is you, not I, who keep *people;* I have officers of my chamber who have purchased the honour of serving me, and are persons of good breeding and education. They know the dignity which ought to belong to a lady of the bed-chamber; they are not ignorant that you, who have been chosen from amongst the first ladies of the kingdom, ought to be accompanied by a gentleman, or at least a *valet de chambre* as his substitute, to receive your cloak, and that had you observed the forms suitable to your rank you would not have been exposed to the mortification of seeing your things thrown on the benches of the ante-chamber."

I have read in several works written on the life of Queen Maria Leckzinska that she possessed great talents. Her religious, noble and resigned conduct, and the refinement and judiciousness of her understanding, sufficiently prove that her august father had promoted with the most tender care the development of all those excellent qualities with which Heaven had endowed her.

The virtues and information of the great are always evinced by their conduct. Their accomplishments, coming within the scope of flattery, are never to be ascertained by any authentic proofs, and those who have lived near them may be excused for some degree of scepticism with regard to their attainments of this kind. If they draw or paint, there is always an able artist present, who, if he does not absolutely guide the pencil with his own hand, directs it by his advice. He sets the palette, and mixes the colours on which the tones depend. If a Princess attempt a piece of embroidery in colours, of that description which ranks amongst the productions of the arts, a skilful embroideress is employed to undo and repair whatever has been spoilt, and to cover the neglected tints with new threads. If a Princess be a musician, there are no ears that will discover when she is out of tune; at least there is no tongue that will tell her so. This imperfection in the accomplishments of the great is but a slight misfortune. It is sufficiently meritorious in them to engage in such pursuits, even with indifferent success, because this taste and the protection it extends produce abundance of talent on every side. The Queen delighted in the art of painting, and imagined she herself could draw and paint. She had a drawing-master, who passed all his time in her cabinet. She undertook to paint four large Chinese pictures, with which she wished to ornament her private drawing-room, already richly furnished with rare porcelain and the finest marbles. This painter was entrusted with the landscape and background of the pictures. He drew the figures with a pencil. The faces and arms were also left by the Queen to his execution. She reserved to herself nothing but the draperies and the least important accessories. The Queen every morning filled up the outline marked out for her with a little red, blue or green colour, which the master prepared on the palette and with which he even filled her pencil, constantly repeating, "Higher up, madam — lower down, madam—a little to the right—more to the left." After an hour's work, the time for hearing Mass or some other family or pious duty would interrupt Her Majesty; and the painter, putting the shades into the draperies she had painted, softening off the colour where she had laid too much, &c., finished the small figures. When the work was completed, the private drawing-room was decorated with Her Majesty's work; and the firm persuasion of this good Queen that she had painted it herself was so entire that she left this cabinet, with all its furniture and paintings, to the Countess de Noailles, her lady of honour. She added to the bequest, "The pictures in my cabinet, being my own work, I hope the Countess de Noailles will preserve them for my sake." Madame de Noailles, afterwards Maréchale de Mouchy, had a new additional pavilion constructed in her hotel in the Faubourg St. Germain, in order to form a suitable receptacle for the Queen's legacy, and had the following inscription placed over the door in letters of gold: "The innocent falsehood of a good Princess."

The Queen had selected as her intimate friends the Duke, the Duchess and the worthy Cardinal de Luynes. She called them her good folks. She often did the Duchess the honour to spend the evening and sup with her. The President Hénault was the charm of this pious and virtuous society. This magistrate combined the weighty qualifications of his functions in society with the attainments of a man of letters and the polish of a courtier. The Queen one day surprised the Duchess writing to the President, who had just published his "Chronological Abridgment of the History of France." She took the pen from Madame de Luynes, and wrote at the bottom of the letter this postscript: "I think that M. de Hénault, who says a great deal in few words, cannot be very partial to the language of women, who use a vast number of words to say very little." Instead of signing this, she added, "Guess who." The President answered this anonymous epistle by these ingenious lines:

> "This sentence, written by a heavenly hand,
>   Fills with perplexing doubts my conscious mind:
> Presumptuous, if I dare to understand;
>   Ungrateful, if I fail the truth to find."[1]

One evening the Queen, having entered the cabinet of the Duke de Luynes, took down several books successively to read the titles. A translation of Ovid's "Art of Love" having fallen into her hands, she replaced it hastily, exclaiming, "Oh, fie!" "How, madam," said the President; "is that the way in which Your Majesty treats the art of pleasing?" "No, Monsieur Hénault," answered the Queen, "I should esteem the art of pleasing; it is the art of seducing that I throw from me."

Madame de Civrac, daughter of the Duke d'Aumont, lady of honour to the Princesses, belonged to this intimate circle of the Queen's. Her virtues and amiable character pro-

---

[1] "Ces mots, tracés par une main divine,
  Ne peuvent me causer que trouble et qu'embarras:
C'est trop oser, si mon cœur les devine;
  C'est être ingrat, s'il ne les devine pas."

cured her equal esteem and affection in that connection, and in her family, from which a premature death removed her. The President Hénault paid her a respectful homage, or rather, delighted in being the medium of that which this distinguished circle eagerly rendered to her talents, her virtues and her sufferings. Some time before the death of Madame de Civrac she was ordered to try the mineral waters; she left Versailles much debilitated and in very bad health. The wish to amuse her during a journey which removed her to a distance from all that was dear to her, inspired the President with the idea of an entertainment, which was given to her at every place she stopped to rest. Her friends set out before her, in order to be a few posts in advance and prepare their disguises. When she stopped at Bernis the interesting traveller found a group of lords dressed in the costume of ancient French knights, accompanied by the best musicians of the King's chapel. They sang Madame de Civrac some stanzas composed by the President, the first of which began thus:

> "Can naught your cruel flight impede?
> Must distant climes your charms adore?
> Why thus to other conquests speed,
> And leave our hearts, enslaved before?"[1]

At Nemours the same persons, dressed as village swains and nymphs, presented her with a rural scene, in which they invited her to enjoy the simple pleasures of the country. Elsewhere they appeared as burgesses and their wives, with the bailiff and town clerk; and these disguises, continually varied and enlivened by the amiable ingenuity of the President, followed Madame de Civrac as far as the watering-place to which she was going. I read this ingenious and affecting entertainment when I was young; I know not whether the manuscript has been preserved by the heirs of the President Hénault. The candour and religious simplicity of the good Cardinal formed a striking contrast to the gallant and agreeable character of the President; and people would sometimes divert themselves with his simplicity, without forgetting the respect due to him. One of these instances, however, produced such happy results as to justify the good Cardinal in a singular misapplication of his well-meant piety. Unwilling to forget the homilies which he had composed in his youth, and as jealous of his

---

[1] "Quoi! vous partez sans que rien vous arrête!
Vous allez plaire en de nouveaux climats!
Pourquoi voler de conquête en conquête?
Nos cœurs soumis ne suffisent-ils pas?"

works as the Archbishop of Granada, who discharged Gil Blas, the Cardinal used to rise at five in the morning every Sunday during the residence of the Court at Fontainebleau (which town was in his diocese), and go to officiate at the parish church, where, mounting the pulpit, he repeated one of his homilies, all of which had been composed to exhort people of rank and fashion to return to the primitive simplicity suitable to true Christians. A few hundred peasants sitting on their sabots, surrounded by the baskets in which they had carried vegetables or fruit to market, listened to His Eminence without understanding a single word of what he was saying to them. Some people belonging to the Court, happening to go to Mass previous to setting out for Paris, heard His Eminence exclaiming, with truly pastoral vehemence, "My dear brethren, why do you carry luxury even to the foot of the sanctuary? Wherefore are these velvet cushions, these bags covered with laces and fringe, carried before you into the temple of the Lord? Abandon these sumptuous and magnificent customs, which you ought to regard as a cumbrous appendage to your rank, and to put away from you when you enter the presence of your Divine Saviour." The fashionable hearers of these homilies mentioned them at Court; everyone wished to hear them; ladies of the highest rank would be awakened at break of day to hear the Cardinal say Mass; and thus His Eminence was speedily surrounded by a congregation to which his homilies were perfectly adapted.

Maria Leckzinska could never look with cordiality on the Princess of Saxony, who married the Dauphin; but the attention, respect and cautious behaviour of the Dauphiness at length made Her Majesty forget that the Princess was daughter to a King who wore her father's crown. Nevertheless, when the great entertain a deep resentment, some marks of it will occasionally be observed by those who constantly surround them; and, although the Queen now saw in the Princess of Saxony only a wife beloved by her son, and the mother of the Prince destined to succeed to the throne, she never could forget that Augustus wore the crown of Stanislaus. One day an officer of her chamber having undertaken to ask a private audience of her for the Saxon minister, and the Queen being unwilling to grant it, he persisted in his request, and ventured to add that he should not have ventured to ask this favour of the Queen had not the minister been the ambassador of a member of the family. "Say of an *enemy* of the family," replied the Queen, angrily; "and let him come in."

The Queen was very partial to the Princess de Tallard, governess of the children of France. This lady, having attained an advanced age, came to take leave of Her Majesty, and to acquaint her with the resolution she had taken to quit the world and to place an interval between her life and dissolution. The Queen expressed much regret, endeavoured to dissuade her from this scheme, and, much affected at the thoughts of the sacrifice on which the Princess had determined, asked her whither she intended to retire: "To the *entresols* of my hotel, madam," answered Madame de Tallard.

Count Tessé, father of the last Count of that name, who left no children, was first equerry to Queen Maria Leckzinska. She esteemed his virtues, but often diverted herself at the expense of his simplicity. One day, when the conversation turned on the noble military actions by which the French nobility were distinguished, the Queen said to the Count, "And your family, M. de Tessé, has been famous, too, in the field." "Ah! madam, we have all been killed in our masters' service!" "How rejoiced I am," replied the Queen, "that you are left to tell me of it." The son of this worthy M. de Tessé was married to the amiable and highly-gifted daughter of the Duke d'Ayen, afterwards Marshal de Noailles; he was excessively fond of his daughter-in-law, and never could speak of her without emotion. The Queen, to please him, often talked to him about the young Countess; and one day asked him which of her good qualities seemed to him most conspicuous. "Her gentleness, madam; her gentleness," said he, with tears in his eyes; "she is so mild, so soft—as soft as a good carriage." "Well," said Her Majesty, "that's an excellent comparison for a first equerry."

In 1730 Queen Maria Leckzinska, going to Mass, met old Marshal Villars leaning on a wooden crutch not worth fifteen pence; she rallied him about it, and the Marshal told her that he had used it ever since he had received a wound which obliged him to add this article to the equipments of the army. Her Majesty, smiling, said she thought this crutch so unworthy of him that she hoped to induce him to give it up. On returning home she despatched M. Campan to Paris, with orders to purchase at the celebrated Germain's the handsomest cane, with a gold enamelled crutch, that he could find, and carry it without delay to Marshal Villars' hotel, and present it to him from her. He was announced accordingly, and fulfilled his commission. The Marshal, in attending him to the door, requested him to express his gratitude to the Queen, and said that he had nothing fit to offer to an officer who had the honour to belong to Her Majesty, but he begged him to accept of his old stick, and that his grandchildren would probably some day be glad to possess the cane with which he had commanded at Marchiennes and Denain. The known character of Marshal Villars appears in this anecdote; but he was not mistaken with respect to the estimation in which his stick would be held. It was thenceforth kept with veneration by M. Campan's family. On the 10th of August, 1792, a house which I occupied on the Carrousel, at the entrance of the court of the Tuileries, was pillaged and nearly burnt down; the cane of Marshal Villars was thrown into the Carrousel, as of no value, and picked up by my servant. Had its old master been living at that period we should not have witnessed such a deplorable day.

The Queen's father died in consequence of being severely burnt by his fireside. Like almost all old men, he disliked those attentions which imply the decay of the faculties, and had ordered a *valet de chambre* who wished to remain near him to withdraw into the adjoining room; a spark set fire to a taffety dressing-gown, wadded with cotton, which his daughter had sent him. The poor old Prince, who entertained hopes of recovering from the frightful state into which this accident reduced him, wished to inform the Queen of it himself, and wrote her a letter evincing the mild gaiety of his disposition, as well as the courage of his soul, in which he said, "What consoles me is the reflection that I am burning for you." To the last moment of her life Maria Leckzinska never parted with this letter, and her women often surprised her kissing a paper, which they concluded to be this last farewell of Stanislaus.[1]

---

[1] This anecdote does honour to the heart and filial piety of Maria Leckzinska. That Princess was equally gifted with wit and sensibility, if we may judge by many expressions which fell from her lips in conversation, and which have been collected by the Abbé Proyart. Many of them are remarkable for the depth of thought they display, and frequently for an ingenious and lively turn of expression.

"We should not be great but for the little. We ought to be so only for their good."—(Page 240.)

"To be vain of one's rank is to declare oneself beneath it."—(*Ibid.*)

"A King who enforces respect to God has no occasion to command homage to be paid to himself."—(*Ibid.*)

"The mercy of Kings is to do justice, and the justice of Queens is to exercise mercy."—(Page 241.)

ANECDOTES OF THE REIGN OF LOUIS XVI. AND OF MARIE ANTOINETTE

In a tranquil and happy Court, such as Versailles was previous to the fatal period of the Revolution, the most trifling events engage attention, and those that are uncommon afford a particular delight. In the beginning of the reign of Louis XVI., a person who associated with the Duchess de Cossé, the Queen's dresser, discovered, in a village near Marly, a female living retired in a cottage more neatly arranged and better furnished than those of the other peasants in the vicinity. She had a cow, which, however, she knew not how to milk, and requested her neighbours to render her that service. One thing seemed still more surprising: it was a library of about two hundred volumes, which formed the principal ornament of her retreat. The Duchess spoke of this interesting recluse to the Queen. By her account she was a "Sarah Th——," like the heroine of a novel which the Chevalier de Saint-Lambert had just published at the conclusion of the poem of the Seasons.

For several days nothing was talked of but this Sarah of Marly; it was observed that she was only known in the village by the name of Marguerite; that she went to Paris but twice a year, and alone; that she seldom spoke to her neighbours, unless to thank them for any little services they had rendered her; that she regularly heard low Mass on Sundays and holidays, but was not religious; that the works of Racine, Voltaire and Jean-Jacques had been seen in her cottage. At length the interest thus excited increased to such a degree that Marie Antoinette desired to be acquainted with the object of it, and directed her ride towards the place of her retreat. The Queen quitted her carriage before she reached the village, and, taking the arm of the Duchess de Cossé, entered the cottage. "Good day, Marguerite," she said; "your cottage

---

" Good **Kings are slaves, and their subjects are free."**—(*Ibid.*).
" Content **seldom travels with fortune, but follows virtue even in** adversity."—(*Ibid.*)
" Solitude can **be** delightful only to **the** innocent."—(*Ibid.*)
"To consider oneself great on account of rank and wealth is to imagine that the pedestal makes the hero."—(*Ibid.*)
" Many Princes when dying have lamented having made war. We hear of none who **at** that moment have regretted having loved peace."—(*Ibid.*)
" Sensible people judge of **a** head by what **it** contains; frivolous **women** by what is on the outside of it."—(Page 245.)
"Courtiers **cry out to us,** 'Give **us,** without reckoning!' and the **people,** ' Reckon what we give you!'"

is extremely pretty." "Nothing to speak of, madam; but I keep it neat." "Your furniture is good." "I brought it from Paris when I came to fix myself here." "They say you go there very little?" "I have no occasion." "You have a cow that you do not attend to yourself?" "My health requires me to drink a good deal of milk; and, having always lived in town, I am unable to milk my cow, and my neighbours do me this service." "You have books?" "As you see, madam." "What, Voltaire!" said the Queen, taking up a volume of that author; "have you read the whole of his works?" "I have read those volumes which I possess, 'The Age of Louis XIV.,'.' The Reign of Charles XII.,' 'The Henriade,' and his tragedies." "What taste in the selection!" exclaimed the Duchess; "it is really surprising! You read a great deal, it is said." "I have nothing better to do; I like it; it kills time, and the evenings are long." "How did you obtain these books?" resumed the Queen; "did you purchase them?" "No, madam," replied Marguerite, "I was housekeeper to a physician, who died and left me by will his furniture, his books and an annuity of eight hundred livres from the Hôtel de Ville, which I go to receive every half-year." The Queen was highly amused at seeing all the reports about the recluse of Marly overturned by a narrative so simple and so little deserving of attention.

The new "Sarah Th——" was, in fact, a retired cook.

Marie Antoinette while she was yet Dauphiness could ill endure the yoke of etiquette. The Abbé de Vermond had in some degree contributed to encourage this disposition in her. When she became Queen he endeavoured openly to induce her to shake off the restraints, the ancient origin of which she still respected. If he chanced to enter her apartment at the time she was preparing to go out, "For whom," he would say in a tone of raillery, "for whom is this detachment of warriors which I found in the Court? Is it some general going to inspect his army? Does all this military display become a young Queen adored by her subjects?" He would take this opportunity to call to her mind the simplicity with which Maria Theresa lived; the visits she made without guards or even attendants to the Prince d'Esterhazy, to the Count de Palfi, to pass whole days there far from the fatiguing ceremonies of the Crown. The Abbé thus flattered with baleful address the inclination of Marie Antoinette. He showed her by what expedients she might disguise even from herself her aversion for the haughty but venerated habits followed by he descendants of Louis XIV.

The theatre, that fruitful and convenient resource of shallow minds, was the constant source of conversation at Court.[1] It was invariably the subject of discourse at the Queen's toilette. She wished to be informed of everything that occurred at a performance when she had not been present. The question "Was it well attended?" was never omitted. I have seen more than one courteous Duke reply, with a bow, "There was not even a cat." This did not mean, as might be thought, that the theatre was empty; it was even possible that it might be full; but in that case it expressed that it was only filled with financiers, honest citizens and gentry from the country. The nobility—I should rather say the high nobility—knew none but their equals. It was necessary to have been presented to be admitted to their society. There were, moreover, among persons of this class a privileged few; these were called persons of quality, and the persons of quality, who lived at Versailles and who were admitted to the King and Queen, were not without some feeling of contempt for those who only paid their respects once a week. Under these circumstances, a woman of quality who had been presented, and who was of the most illustrious family, might be disdainfully classed among those who were called "Sunday ladies."

The retirement of Madame Louise and her removal from Court had only served to give her up entirely to the intrigues of the clergy. She received incessant visits from bishops, archbishops and ambitious priests of every rank; she prevailed on the King her father to grant many ecclesiastical preferments, and probably looked forward to play an important part at the time when the King, weary of his pleasures and his licentious course of life, should begin to think of his salvation. This, perhaps, might have been the case had not a sudden and unexpected death put an end to his career. The project of Madame Louise fell to the ground in consequence of this event. She remained in her convent, from whence she continued to solicit favours, as I could well ascertain from the complaints of the Queen, who often said to me, "Here is another letter from my aunt Louise. She

---

[1] A well-told story, a *bon mot*, an instance of laughable simplicity in a countryman, were also fortunate hits of which everyone hastened to avail himself. There were courtiers who were constantly in search of new incidents to relate, and it must be confessed that they had carried the agreeable art of narrating gracefully to a great extent. It was delightful to hear them; but, without possessing a talent equal to theirs, it was difficult to repeat what they had been telling; the tone and the style taken away, nothing remained.—NOTE BY THE EDITOR.

is certainly the most intriguing little Carmelite that exists in the kingdom." The Court went to visit her about three times a year; and I recollect that the Queen, intending to take her daughter there, ordered me to get a doll dressed like a Carmelite for her, that the young Princess might be accustomed, before she went into the convent, to the habit of her aunt the nun.

In a situation where ambition keeps every passion awake, a word, a single reflection, may give rise to prejudice and excite hatred, and I cannot help thinking that the known aversion that existed between the Queen and Madame de Genlis originated in a reply of Marie Antoinette to the Duchess d'Orleans respecting that lady. On the day for paying respects to the Queen after the birth of the Dauphin, the Duchess d'Orleans approached the couch to apologise for Madame de Genlis not appearing on an occasion when the whole Court hastened to congratulate Her Majesty on the birth of an heir. Indisposition had prevented her. The Queen replied that the Duchess de Chartres would have caused an apology to be made in such a case; that the celebrity of Madame de Genlis might, indeed, have caused her absence to be noticed, but that she was not of a rank to send an apology for it. This proceeding on the part of the Princess, influenced by the talents of the governess of her children, proves, at any rate, that at this time she still desired the regard and the friendship of the Queen; and from this very moment unfavourable reflections on the habits and inclinations of the Sovereign, and sharp criticisms on the works and the conduct of the female author, were continually interchanged between Marie Antoinette and Madame de Genlis. At least, I am sure that the songs and epigrams that appeared against the governess of the Duke d'Orleans' children never failed to be brought to the Queen; and it is most likely that the malice of courtiers transmitted with equal rapidity to the Palais Royal all that might have been said in the Queen's apartments to the disadvantage of Madame de Genlis.

M. de Maurepas died on the 21st of November, one month after the birth of the Dauphin. The King seemed much affected at this loss. Whatever might be the indifference and levity of this guide, habit had rendered him necessary. The King denied himself, at the time of his death, several gratifications, such as the chase and a dinner-party at Brunoy with Monsieur. He visited him several times when ill, and showed marks of real sensibility. M. de Vergennes, without inheriting the title of Prime Minister, completely occupied the place of M. de Maurepas about the King.[1] Political historians will decide on his talents and the errors which M. de Vergennes may have committed. But plain reason has led me to give him credit for having contrived to conceal the weakness of his master's character from the eyes of all Europe. It cannot be denied that as long as he lived he covered Louis XVI. with a veil of respectability, of which the King seemed immediately deprived on the death of this minister.[2]

---

[1] See among the *Illustrations* (M) some historical particulars of the means used by M. de Maurepas to maintain himself in the administration and to render the Duke de Choiseul more and more odious to Louis XVI.—NOTE BY THE EDITOR.

[2] "The manners of this minister," says Rhulières in an article relating to M. de Vergennes, "were neither amiable nor polished, but sufficiently imposing. And why? Because every man who can seclude himself in the midst of a Court and make his indifference for women and ostentation pass for a virtue resulting from reflection; who can assume the grave exterior of a man of application, and obtain the reputation of being free from all kind of shuffling, will create the belief that he is devoted to public affairs, and never for an instant neglects the business of the State. M. de Vergennes had acquired this reputation so completely that, in one of those humorous conceits invented at Court as a refuge from *ennui*, he was figured as borne down by the pressure of labour. It was intended to represent the ministers and other distinguished personages in masquerade. The Queen was to guess and discover the masks. The Count de Vergennes was represented bearing the globe on his head, a map of America on his breast, and that of England on his back. There are ministers who might be pictured holding in their hands the girdle of Venus and playing with the quiver of her son.

"Upon another occasion a lady of the Court, old and ill-favoured, having approached the King's table dressed with more splendour than became her age and person, Monsieur asked her what she wanted. 'Ah! what do I want? I wish to beseech the King to obtain for me an audience from M. de Vergennes.' The King, joining heartily in the laugh with those around him, promised the old lady to procure her an interview with the minister before she died.

"These events, however trifling they may appear, disclose what was the state of opinion, particularly at Court, where even their sports are never without some aim, some malicious points." (*See* Note N.)

Rhulières adds, some pages further on: "The Duke de Choiseul possessed great talents; M. Turgot, much information; M. de Vergennes, an imposing mediocrity; M. de Maupeou, a despotic firmness; M. de Calonne, an unpardonable degree of complaisance."

This portrait of M. de Vergennes is, in general, too satirical, and we do not think that the reproach of mediocrity has any foundation. But a more serious charge is made against him: that of having consented to the treaty which ruined our manufactures.—NOTE BY THE EDITOR.

Winter of 1788.

The gratitude of the Parisians for the succours poured forth by the King and Queen was very lively and sincere. The snow was so abundant that since that period there has never been seen such a prodigious quantity in France. In different parts of Paris pyramids and obelisks of snow were erected, with inscriptions expressive of the gratitude of the people. The pyramid in the Rue d'Angiviller was particularly deserving of attention: it was supported by a base of five or six feet high by twelve broad; it rose to the height of fifteen feet, and was terminated by a globe. Four posts placed at the angles corresponded with the obelisk, and gave it an appearance not devoid of elegance. Several inscriptions in honour of the King and Queen were affixed to it.

I went to see this singular monument, and recollect the following inscription:

"To Marie Antoinette.

"Lovely and good, to tender pity true,
  Queen of a virtuous King, this trophy view;
Cold ice and snow sustain its form,
  But every grateful heart to thee is warm.
Oh, may this tribute in your hearts excite,
Illustrious pair, more pure and real delight
(Whilst thus your virtues are sincerely praised)
Than pompous domes by servile flattery raised."

The theatres generally rang with praises of the beneficence of the Sovereigns. *La Partie de Chasse de Henri IV.* was represented for the benefit of the poor. The receipts were very considerable, and the audience vehemently called for the repetition of the following verses:

"A virtuous King's benignant reign
  Relieves the sufferings of the poor;
The Queen and all her brilliant train
  Drive sorrow from the cottage door;
The sons of labour cease their cries,
  Nor dread disease or famine's sting;
The country with the palace vies
  To celebrate our bounteous King."[1]

I have not inserted these lines for their literary merit, but as showing the opinion most commonly entertained in

---

[1] Once, during the absence of the King, M. d'Angiviller caused an unfrequented room in the interior apartments to be repaired. This repair cost 30,000 francs. The King, being informed of the expense on his return, made the palace resound with exclamations and complaints against M. d'Angiviller. "I could have made thirty families happy," said Louis XVI.—Note by the Editor.

Paris with respect to the King and Queen, just five years before the general and fatal shock which the French monarchy suffered.

In order, then, to produce so complete a change in the long-cherished love of the people for their rulers, it required the union of the principles of the new philosophy with the enthusiasm for liberty imbibed in the plains of America; and that this eagerness for change and this enthusiasm should be seconded by the weakness of the monarch, the incessant corruption of English gold, and by projects, either of revenge or of ambition, in the Duke d'Orléans. Let it not be thought that this accusation is founded on what has been so often repeated by the heads of the French Government since the Revolution. Twice, between the 14th of July, 1789, and the 6th of October in the same year, the day on which the Court was dragged to Paris, the Queen prevented me from making little excursions thither of business or pleasure, saying to me, "Do not go on such a day to Paris; the English have been scattering gold; we shall have some disturbance."

The repeated visits of this Prince to England had excited the Anglomania to such a pitch that Paris was no longer distinguishable from London. The French, constantly imitated by the whole of Europe, became on a sudden a nation of imitators, without considering the evils that arts and manufactures must suffer in consequence of the change. Since the treaty of commerce made with England at the peace of 1783, not merely equipages, but everything, even to ribbons and common earthenware, were of English make. If this predominance of English fashions had been confined to filling our drawing-rooms with young men in English frock-coats instead of the French dress, good taste and commerce might alone have suffered; but the principles of English government had taken possession of these young heads—*Constitution, Upper House, Lower House, National guarantee, balance of power, Great Charter, Law of Habeas Corpus;* all these words were incessantly repeated, rarely understood; but they were of fundamental importance to a party which was then forming.

The taste for dress which the Queen had indulged during the first years of her reign had given way to a love of simplicity, carried even to an impolitic extent, the splendour and magnificence of the throne being in France to a certain degree inseparable from the interests of the nation.

Except on those days when the assemblies at Court were particularly attended, such as the 1st of January and the 2nd of February, devoted to the procession of the Order of the Holy Ghost, and on the festivals of Easter, Whitsuntide and Christmas, the Queen no longer wore any dresses but muslin or white Florentine taffety. Her head-dress was merely a hat—the plainest were preferred; and her diamonds never quitted their caskets but for the dresses of ceremony, confined to the days I have mentioned.

The Queen was not yet five-and-twenty, and already began to apprehend that she might be induced to make too frequent use of flowers and of ornaments, which at that time were exclusively reserved for youth.

Mademoiselle Bertin having brought a wreath composed of roses for the head and neck, the Queen, in trying them, was fearful that the brightness of the flowers might be disadvantageous to her complexion. She was unquestionably too severe upon herself, her beauty having as yet experienced no alteration—it is easy to conceive the concert of praise and compliment that replied to the doubt she had expressed. The Queen, approaching me, conceived the idea of promising to refer to my judgment the time when she should abandon the use of flowers in the way of ornament. "Think well of it," said she; "I charge you from this day to give me notice when flowers shall cease to become me." "I shall do no such thing," I replied immediately; "I have not read Gil Blas without profiting in some degree from it, and I find Your Majesty's order too much like that given him by the Archbishop of Granada to warn him of the moment when he should begin to fall off in the composition of his homilies." "Go!" said the Queen; "you are less sincere than Gil Blas; and I would have been more liberal than the Archbishop of Granada."

The indiscreet zeal of courtiers is frequently prejudicial to the true interests of Princes. An erroneous proceeding on the part of M. Augeard, secretary to the *Queen's orders*, and farmer of the revenue, had greatly contributed to make it publicly believed that the Queen disposed of all the offices of finance. He had required the committee of farmers-general, without any authority to that effect, to inform him of the vacancies in any of the offices at all lucrative, assuring them that they would be acting in a manner very agreeable to the wishes of the Queen. The members of the committee acceded to this demand of M. Augeard, but not without complaining of it at their different meetings. The Queen at first only attributed to the zeal of her secretary the care he took to inform her of every vacancy; but when she became acquainted with the proceeding he had adopted in the society he belonged to, she highly disapproved of it, caused this to be made known to the farmers of the revenue, and abstained from asking for financial situations. At the last lease of the taxes renewed by M. de Calonne she made but one request of this kind, and that was as a marriage portion to a young woman of family among her attendants. There was, however, at this period a great number of important situations to dispose of. Deeply afflicted at seeing the general conviction that the Queen disposed of all employments without distinction, and having had information of some who were deprived of places to which they had good claims, under the pretext of demands made by the Queen, I advised them to write to Her Majesty to entreat her to let them know if she had asked for the situations to which they had just pretensions. The Queen was well satisfied with the confidence these individuals had placed in her, and caused an official answer to be returned to them, "that she had made no demand of the places they were soliciting, and that she authorised them to make use of her letter." These persons obtained the situations they desired.

There was frequently seen in the gardens and the apartments at Versailles a veteran captain of the grenadiers of France, called the Chevalier d'Orville, who, during four years, had been soliciting of the Minister of War a majority, or the post of King's lieutenant. He was known to be very poor, but he supported his lot without ever complaining of this vexatious delay in rewarding his honourable services. He attended regularly upon the Marshal de Ségur, at the hour appointed by the minister for receiving the numerous solicitations in his department. One day the Marshal said to him, "You are still at Versailles, M. d'Orville?" "Sir," replied this brave officer, "you may observe that by this board of the flooring, where I regularly place myself; it is already worn down several lines by the weight of my body." This reply was circulated at Versailles; I heard of it.

The Queen frequently stood at the window of her bedchamber to observe with her glass the people who were walking in the park. Sometimes she enquired of her attendants the names of those persons who were unknown to her. One day she saw the Chevalier d'Orville passing, and asked me the name of that knight of Saint-Louis, whom she had seen everywhere and for a long time past. I knew who he was, and related his history. "That must be put an end to," said the Queen, with some degree of vivacity. "With all due deference to our Court patrons, such an example of indifference is calculated to discourage the military: a man may be extremely brave and yet have no protector." "That affair will be settled whenever Your Majesty shall please to take it in hand," I replied. "Yes, yes," said the Queen without explaining herself further, and she turned her glass towards some other persons who were walking. The next day, in crossing the gallery to go to Mass, the Queen perceived the Chevalier d'Orville. She stopped and went directly towards him. The poor man fell back in the recess of a window, looking to the right and left to discover the person towards whom the Queen was directing her steps, when she addressed him: "M. d'Orville, you have been several years at Versailles, soliciting a majority or a King's lieutenancy. You must have very powerless patrons." "I have none, madam," replied the Chevalier, in great confusion. "Well! I will take you under my protection. To-morrow, at the same hour, be here with a petition and a memorial of your services." A fortnight after M. d'Orville was appointed King's lieutenant, either at La Rochelle or at Rochefort.[1]

The genuine sensibility of the Queen furnished her upon the instant with the most flattering and honourable expres-

---

[1] It seems that Louis XVI. vied with his Queen in benevolent actions of this kind. An old officer had in vain solicited a pension during the administration of the Duke de Choiseul. He had returned to the charge in the times of the Marquis de Monteynard and the Duke d'Aiguillon. He had urged his claims to Count de Muy, who had made a note of them, with the best intentions in the world to serve him; but the effect did not correspond with the minister's wishes. Tired of so many fruitless efforts, he at last appeared at the King's supper, and having placed himself so as to be seen and heard, cried out, at a moment when silence prevailed, "*Sire!*" The people near him said, "What are you about? That is not the way to speak to the King." "I fear nothing," said he; and, raising his voice, repeated, "*Sire!*" The King, much surprised, looked at him and said, "What do you want, sir?" "Sire," answered he, "I am seventy years of age; I have served my King more than fifty years, and I am dying of want." "Have you a memorial?" replied the King. "Yes, Sire, I have." "Give it to me;" and His Majesty took it without saying anything more. The next morning an exempt of the guards was sent by the King into the great gallery to look for the officer, who was walking there. The exempt said to him, "The King desires to see you, sir;" and he was immediately conducted into the King's closet. His Majesty said, "Sir, I grant you an annuity of 1,500 livres out of my privy purse; and you may go and receive the first year's payment, which is become due." ("Secret Correspondence of the Court: Reign of Louis XVI.")—NOTE BY THE EDITOR.

sions towards those she esteemed. When M. Loustonneau, first surgeon to the Princes of France, was appointed to the reversion of the situation of M. Andouillé, first surgeon to the King, he came, at the Queen's breakfast hour, to make his acknowledgments. This worthy man was generally beloved at Versailles; he had devoted himself to the care of the poorer class, and expended upon indigent invalids nearly 30,000 francs a year. His excessive modesty could not prevent such extensive charities from eventually becoming known. After receiving from the benevolent Loustonneau the homage of his gratitude, the Queen said to him, "You are satisfied, sir; but I am far from being so with the inhabitants of Versailles. Upon the news of the favour the King has just conferred on you the town should have been illuminated." And why so, madam?" said the first surgeon, with an air of anxious astonishment. "Ah!" replied the Queen, in a tone of sensibility, "if all the poor whom you have succoured for twenty years past had but each placed a single candle in their window, it would have been the most beautiful illumination ever witnessed."

The very day on which the King announced that he gave his assent to the convocation of the States-General, the Queen left the public dinner and placed herself in the recess of the first window of her bed-chamber, with her face towards the garden. Her chief butler followed her, to present her coffee, which she usually took standing as she was about to leave the table. She made me a sign to come near her. The King was engaged in conversation with someone in his room. When the attendant had served her he retired; and she addressed me, with the cup still in her hand, "Good God! what fatal news goes forth this day! The King assents to the convocation of the States-General." Then she added, raising her eyes to heaven, "I dread it; this important event is a first fatal signal of discord in France." She cast her eyes down; they were filled with tears. She could not take the remainder of her coffee, but handed me the cup and went to join the King. In the evening, when she was alone with me, she spoke only of this momentous decision. "It is the Parliament," said she, "that has reduced the King to the necessity of having recourse to a measure long considered as fatal to the repose of the kingdom. These gentlemen wish to restrain the power of the King; but this at least is certain, that they give a great shock to the authority of which they make so bad a use, and that they will bring on their own destruction. That, perhaps, is the only favourable view that can be taken of such an alarming proceeding."

Extract from different Letters of Madame Campan, First Femme de Chambre to the Queen, from the 5th of October to the 31st of December, 1789.

I know not whether I shall have strength to give you a description of the afflicting scenes that have lately taken place almost under my very eyes. My scattered senses are not yet collected, my dreams are horrid, my slumbers painful. My sister was with the Queen during the night of the 5th; I obtained from her part of the circumstances I am about to relate. When M. de la Fayette had left the King, saying that he was going to quarter his troops as well as he could, everyone in the palace hoped to enjoy the consolation of repose. The Queen herself went to bed, and when my sister had done waiting on her, she retired into the chamber immediately before the Queen's; there, giving way to accents of grief, she burst into tears, and said to her companions, "Is it a time to retire to bed when the town is occupied by thirty thousand troops, ten thousand ruffians, and two-and-forty pieces of cannon?" "Surely not," they replied; "we must not think of committing so great an error." They all, therefore, remained dressed, and took their rest reclining on their beds. It was then four o'clock. Exactly at six the host of ruffians, having forced the barriers, took their course towards Her Majesty's apartment. My sister was the first who heard these dreadful words: "*Save the Queen.*" The body-guard who pronounced them received thirteen wounds at the very door from whence he gave us the alarm. Had the Queen's women gone to bed Her Majesty would have been lost; they had only time to rush into her chamber, snatch her out of bed, throw a covering over her, carry her into the King's apartment, and close in the best manner they could the door of the gallery that leads to it. She fell senseless into the arms of her august husband. You know what has happened since: the King, yielding to the wishes of the capital, went thither with his whole family on the morning of the 6th. The journey occupied seven hours and a half, during which we heard incessantly a continued noise of thirty thousand muskets, loaded with ball, which were charged and discharged in token of joy for the happiness of conducting the King to Paris. They cried out, but in vain, "Fire straight!" In spite of this notice, the balls sometimes struck the ornaments of the carriages; the smell of the powder almost suffocated us, and the crowd was so immense that the people, pressing the coaches on all sides, gave them the motion of a boat. If you wish to form an idea of this march, conceive a multitude of half-clad ruffians, armed with sabres, pistols, spits, saws; old partisans, marching without order, shouting, yelling, headed by a monster, a tiger, whom the municipality of Paris sought out with the utmost care, a man with a long beard, who till now served as a model at the Academy of Painting, and who, since the troubles, has yielded to his desire for murder, and has himself cut off the heads of all the wretched victims of popular frenzy. When we consider that it was this very mob that, at six in the morning, had forced the barrier of the marble staircase, broken open the doors of the ante-chamber, and penetrated even to the spot where that brave guard made a resistance sufficiently long to give us time to save the Queen—when we recollect that this dreadful army filled the streets of Versailles during the whole night, we still find that Heaven has protected us; we perceive the power of Providence, and this danger passed gives us hopes for the future. Moreover, it was now ascertained that all these terrible events, of which I have only been able to give you a faint sketch, were the horrid result of the foulest, the most abominable conspiracy. The city of Paris is engaged in discovering the authors; but I doubt whether they will be all brought to light, and I believe that posterity alone will be fully informed of these dreadful secrets.

The severity of military law, the great activity of the commanders of the militia and city guard, the attachment, the veneration of all citizens in the capital for the august family that has come within its walls, and is fully determined to remain there till the new Constitution shall be completed—these afford the only prospect capable of affording any consolation to our bosoms.

Since the Queen has been at Paris her Court is well attended; she dines three times a week in public with the King; her card-rooms are open on those days. Though the apartments are small, all Paris is to be found there. She converses with the commanders of districts; she finds familiar opportunities of saying obliging things even to the private soldiers, among whom citizens of the first class are to be found, as well as the lowest artisans: mildness, resignation, courage, affability, popularity, everything is made use of, and sincerely, to reconcile people's minds and concur in the re-establishment of order. Everyone does justice to such affecting attentions, and that is a reparation for the cruel sufferings that have been endured and the dreadful risks that had been encountered. Upon the whole, nothing can be more prudent or more consistent than the conduct of the King and Queen, and therefore the number of their partisans increases daily. They are spoken of with enthusiasm in almost every company. I have lost much on the score of the happiness, the enjoyments and the hopes of life, but I am exceedingly flattered in being attached to a Princess who in moments of adversity has displayed a character so generous and so elevated; she is an angel of mildness and of goodness; she is a woman particularly gifted with courage. I am in hopes that the clouds accumulated about her by the impure breath of calumny will dissipate; and at the Queen's age, and with her virtues, she may still expect to resume in history and in the eyes of posterity that rank from which she cannot be removed without injustice. Princes assailed by imbecility and vice towards their decline have in vain displayed some virtues in early youth; their latter years efface the splendour of their earlier, and they carry to the tomb the hatred and contempt of their subjects. How many happy years has our amiable Queen yet to pass?—and when she acts of her own accord she is always sure of the most complete success. She has given proofs of it in the most critical moments; and Paris, replete with the most seditious opinions—Paris, continually reading the most disgusting libels, could not refuse her the admiration due to true courage, presence of mind and courteousness. Her bitterest enemies confine themselves to saying, "It must be confessed that she is a woman of strong mind." I cannot express to you how anxious I am with respect to the opinion that is entertained of this interesting Princess in foreign Courts: have those shameless libels been sent thither? Is it believed in Russia that one Madame de Lamotte was ever the favourite of the Queen? Do they give credit to all the abominable reports of that infernal schemer? I hope not: the justice, the reparation that are due to this Princess never cease to engage my thoughts. I should lose my senses if I were a little younger, and if my imagination were as lively as my heart is sensitive. I, who have seen her for fifteen years attached to her august husband, to her children, gracious to her servants—unfortunately, too affable, too unaffected, too much on a level with the people of the Court—I cannot endure to see her character vilified. I wish I had a hundred mouths, I wish I had wings, that I might inspire that confidence in listening to truth which is so readily yielded to falsehood. Let us still pray that time will bring about this important object.

The Queen's Opinions of the Nobility.

The Queen has frequently said to me, "The nobility will ruin us; but I believe we cannot save ourselves without them. We act sometimes in a manner that offends them, but only with good intentions towards them. Nevertheless, when I encounter angry looks from those who surround us, I am grieved at it; then we adopt some proceeding, or impart something in confidence to encourage all these poor people, who really have a great deal to suffer. They spread it abroad; the revolutionists are informed of it, and take the alarm; the Assembly becomes more urgent and more malignant, and dangers increase."

The power of Louis XIV. had long ceased to exist at Versailles, yet all the exterior forms of this absolute authority still prevailed in 1789.

This monarch, in the latter years of his reign, had paid for his warlike ambition by reverses from which the nation had suffered greatly. Become old, his remorse and the devotion of his last mistress rendered him weak and bigoted.

The priests governed, and obtained from him violent edicts against his subjects of the Reformed Churches. A multitude of industrious Frenchmen, manufacturers, abandoned their country and carried their useful labours among neighbouring people. The decree which produced so fatal an effect to France is called the Revocation of the Edict of Nantes.

For the Edict of Nantes the nation was indebted to Henry IV.; it secured to all the various churches the free exercise of their religion.

Louis XIV. died. He left, as heir to the Crown, his great-grandson, five years of age. This Prince had for Regent his uncle, the Duke d'Orleans, witty, volatile and licentious. He ventured on systems of finance which ruined France, and addicted himself to public debauchery, and a contempt for every sentiment and duty of religion, by which licentiousness quickly succeeded to hypocrisy. The Government of Louis XV. was weak. During the first years of his reign his youth, his beauty, and some success in arms made him beloved by the French; shortly after, the most unbridled libertinism caused him to lose this early affection of the people, and even deprived him of the esteem of his Court.

On the death of Louis XV., Louis XVI. ascended the throne, with all the virtues of a man but few of those which become a great monarch, and which are indispensable in times when the people are agitated by the spirit of faction.[1]

---

[1] Louis XVI. had not the qualities of a great King, yet with a firm and able minister who had known how to fix his wavering resolution, defeat the intrigues of courtiers and overpower their resistance, he would have evinced the virtues and reigned with the character of a good King. No Prince was ever more anxious for the public good; and even in 1791, when the overthrow of his power and the contempt of his authority presented to his mind the most painful reflections, his chief

The Queen was amiable, sensible, handsome and of a good disposition. The slanders that have been cast on this Princess are the fruit of the spirit of discontent which prevailed at that time. But she loved pleasure, and was too fond of exciting admiration of her beauty. Amusements and festivals lulled the Court into security, until the very moment of the dreadful shock prepared by opinions introduced into France during the preceding half-century, and which had already obtained an imposing influence.

Three ministers, who had calculated the danger of this fermentation of ideas, endeavoured successively to operate a reform of abuses — in a word, to repair the worn-out machinery of absolute power by new laws of reformation and regeneration. They could not do it without attacking the

---

affliction arose from the calamities which the nation then suffered, and the evils which he foresaw it was destined to endure.

"We witnessed, in the Council," says Bertrand de Molleville, "during the Legislative Assembly, a scene much too interesting to be passed over in silence. M. Cahier de Gerville read a draft of a proclamation relative to the murders and robberies which were committed in many departments upon the nobles and their property, under the condemnatory pretext of 'aristocracy.' In this draft was the following expression: '*These disorders interrupt the happiness we enjoy in the most grievous manner.*' 'Alter that phrase,' said the King to M. Cahier de Gerville, who, after reading it again, answered that he did not perceive what there was to alter. 'Do not make me talk about my happiness, sir; I cannot lie at that rate; how can I be happy, M. de Gerville, when no one in France is so? No, sir, the French are not happy; I see it but too plainly; I hope they will be so one day; I ardently wish it; then I shall be so likewise, and may talk of my happiness.'

"These words, which the King pronounced with extreme feeling, and with tears in his eyes, made the most lively impression on us, and were followed by a general silence of emotion, which lasted two or three minutes. His Majesty, doubtless fearing lest this burst of sensibility, which he had not been able to restrain, should raise any doubt of his attachment to the Constitution, seized, with much address, shortly afterwards, an opportunity of evincing, at least, his scrupulous fidelity to the oath he had taken to maintain it, by adopting the course most conformable to the Constitution in a matter brought forward by M. Cahier de Gerville, who advised the opposite proceeding, and was amazed to find the King more constitutional than himself.

"This religious probity of the King with respect to the fatal oath which had been wrested from him, and his tender concern for the welfare of a nation of which he had so much reason to complain, at once excited our astonishment and our admiration."

Louis XVI. had imbibed his love of the people and this desire to render them happy from the works of Fénélon. The writings of Nicole and the "**Telemachus**" were continually read by him. He had extracted from them maxims of government by which he wished to abide; and the particulars given in the *Historical Illustrations* (O) on this subject, and on the methodical habits of this Prince, will be found interesting.—NOTE BY THE EDITOR.

privileges of the nobility and the clergy; these classes considered them imprescriptible, and do so still, even after the torrent of a most terrible revolution has swept away the last traces of their privileges and their wealth.

The three ministers, Turgot,[1] Malesherbes, and Necker,[2] were overthrown by the power of those ancient classes.

The impolitic desire of diminishing the power of England had induced Louis XVI. to embrace the cause of the American insurgents against the mother-country. Our youth flew to the wars waged in the New World for liberty and against the rights of thrones. Liberty prevailed; they returned triumphant to France, and brought with them the seeds of independence. Letters from various military men were frequently received at the Palace of Versailles, the seals of which bore the thirteen stars of the United States surrounding the cap of Liberty; and the Chevalier de Parny, one of the most esteemed poets of the day, brother to one of the Queen's equerries and himself attendant on the Court, published an epistle to the citizens of Boston, in which were found the following lines:

> " You, happy people, freed from Kings and Queens,
> Dance to the rattling of the chains that bind,
> In servile shame, the rest of human kind."

Soon after, financial embarrassments, the stubborn opposition of the Parliaments and the unskilfulness of the Minister De Loménie de Brienne led to the convocation of the States-General. Notwithstanding the excesses which sullied this epoch, notwithstanding the subversion of all the ancient institutions, good might still have been accomplished if the Constituent Assembly had yielded to the advice and intelligence of that party which demanded not only a guarantee for national liberty, but the advantages of an hereditary nobility, by the formation of an Upper Chamber, composed of nobles, who should no longer be exposed to see talents rendered

---

1 When M. de Maurepas proposed Turgot as a minister to Louis XVI., the King said to him, with a degree of candour highly respectable, " It is said that M. Turgot never goes to Mass." " Well, Sire," replied Maurepas, " the Abbé Terray goes to it every day." This was enough to remove all the King's prejudices. (" Universal Biography," vol. xxvii.)—NOTE BY THE EDITOR.

2 M. Necker wished for the support of the favour and confidence of the people; and, resembling M. Turgot so far, he could not be agreeable to the clergy, or the nobility, who were absolute strangers to the personal predilections of the Genevese minister. The clergy murmured at the choice of a Protestant minister. " I will give him up to you if you will pay the National Debt," said M. de Maurepas to an archbishop who was scandalised at his nomination. (" History of Marie Antoinette," by Montjoie.)—NOTE BY MADAME CAMPAN.

useless to the welfare of the State, from the will of a Sovereign or the hatred of a favourite. Names worthy of respect were found at the head of this party: the Marquis de Lally-Tollendal, the Viscount de Noailles, the Marquis de la Fayette, Malouet, Mounier, &c. The Duke d'Orleans ranked among them for a short time, but only as a factious, discontented man, ready to shift successively into every party that was most extravagant. At that time, to speak at Court of the English Constitution, to place the King of France on a level with a King of England, appeared as criminal as if it had been proposed to dethrone the King and to destroy the crown adorned with lilies. The rejection by the Court of that party which desired two chambers, afforded time for a more Republican party to form itself and obtain the support of popular influence. M. de la Fayette, imbued with the American principles which he had served with so much glory, found himself placed at the head of this party. After the 6th of October, 1789, six months subsequent to the opening of the States-General, almost the whole of the partisans of the English Constitution emigrated and withdrew from the horrors that threatened France.

A man unhappily worthy of the fame of the orators of Greece and Rome, Mirabeau, embraced the cause of a more Republican Constitution. The Court was naturally still more opposed to this than to the former wishes of the friends of the English Constitution.

The revolutionists inflamed the people, called them to their assistance, armed them. Mansions were burnt or pillaged, all the nobles compelled to quit France. The Palace of Versailles was besieged by the populace of Paris; the King was dragged to the capital in a cruel and degrading manner, his carriage, preceded by a horde who carried in triumph the heads of two of his guards. The deputies, amid the storm, laboured to complete the Constitutional Act; the King, as the executive power, was too much deprived of authority by it. He foresaw the impossibility of carrying on such a Constitution, and fled with his family. His organised flight, and his intentions, being betrayed, afforded time to the Assembly to have him arrested as he approached the frontiers of the kingdom; he was brought back with the unfortunate Marie Antoinette, the virtuous Elizabeth, Madame and the Dauphin. On the road they endured every insult from a licentious mob.

As this period the Jacobins, a furious and sanguinary faction, at whose head were Robespierre and Marat, wished to obtain a declaration of the deposition of the King, and to found a republic. The Constitutional party, though much

weakened, had still sufficient strength to oppose it. The
Constitution was finished; the King, who since the failure of
his flight had remained in arrest, was restored to liberty, and
came to take, on this new charter, the oath to maintain and
defend it. Brilliant festivals were held, which preceded by
a very short interval days of mourning and despair. Two
decrees which the King rejected—that which menaced the
priests, and that relative to forming a camp round Paris—
served as a pretext for the most violent attacks directed
against him. Unfortunately the King thought that, without
altering his course, he should be withdrawn from his restrictions and released from his forced engagements. He was
deceived: the whole nation advanced; the foreign troops
were repulsed; the Palace of the Tuileries besieged; the
King and his family confined in the Temple, which they
never quitted but to mount the scaffold, with the exception
of Madame and the young Prince, the latter of whom died a
victim to the ill-treatment to which he was subjected.

The Emperor Joseph II. evinced, in November, 1783, and
still more in May, 1784, pretensions of a perplexing nature on
the Republic of the United Provinces. He demanded the
opening of the Scheldt, the cession of Maestricht with its
dependencies, of the country beyond the Meuse, the county
of Vroenhoven and a sum of 70,000,000 florins.

The first gun was fired by the Emperor, on the Scheldt,
the 5th of November, 1784.

Peace was concluded and signed the 8th of November,
1785, between the Emperor and the United Provinces, under
the mediation of France.

The singular part was the indemnification granted to the
Emperor; this was a sum of 10,000,000 Dutch florins; the
Articles 15, 16 and 17 of the treaty stipulated the quotas of
it. Holland paid 5,500,000, and France, under the direction
of M. de Vergennes, 4,500,000 florins—that is to say, 9,045,000
francs, according to M. Soulavie.

M. de Ségur, in his work entitled "Policy of Cabinets"
(vol. iii.), says, in a note on a Memoir by M. de Vergennes,
relative to this affair:

"M. de Vergennes has been much blamed for having
terminated by a sacrifice of seven millions the contest that
existed between the United Provinces and the Emperor.
In that age of philosophy men were still very uncivilised;
in that age of commerce they made very erroneous calculations, and those who accused the Queen of sending the gold
of France to her brother would have been better pleased if,

to support a Republic void of energy, the blood of two hundred thousand men and three or four hundred millions of francs had been sacrificed, and incurred the risk of losing the advantage of the peace concluded with England at the same time. It is grievous and humiliating to see in what manner, and by whom, such criticisms are made; those who call to mind all the violent declamations then indulged in against the policy of the Cabinet of Versailles will see, in the Memoirs of M. de Vergennes, with what prudence the ministers, accused by ignorance, presumption and folly, then deliberated."

MISCELLANEOUS ANECDOTES

The collection of celebrated trials has rendered the important service of inducing in the world a salutary mistrust of appearances of criminality. What advantage would not society derive from a collection of all the accounts of these impostors; from those who, passing themselves off for Sovereigns, or heirs of Sovereign power, have formed parties, and involved credulous people in difficulties, down to those who, born in an obscure rank, have assumed the names of persons of a superior class, or have obtained credit for intimate connections with the great, and even with crowned heads. Alas! the unheard-of misfortunes of Marie Antoinette are to be attributed, in a great degree, to the audacious falsehoods of a woman whose person even was unknown to her; and who had found means to persuade the Cardinal de Rohan that she was an intimate and secret friend of that illustrious and unfortunate Princess. There is no class in which these ingenious and dangerous characters do not succeed in disturbing the peace of society, and carrying misery and desolation into the most respectable families. If their mischievous genius leads them to have recourse to legal and judicial forms to support their impudent falsehoods, the marvellous, which always accompanies statements destitute of probability, engages and amuses the indifferent, and generally excites the self-conceit of some lawyer, who believes, no doubt, that he is defending the cause of persons oppressed by fraud, avarice or power. The most prudent feeling is to have a mistrust of the wonderful, and to say of a thing which is opposed to the laws of honour, of probity and propriety—it is likely that this is not true. This valuable mistrust would be generally promoted by the collection which I should like to see entrusted to the care of some eminent lawyer. These reflections precede the history, but little known, of a female intriguer of the lowest class in society, and whose audacious falsehoods involved the most illustrious and most estimable characters.

My father had provided for me a sort of governess, or rather upper nurse, who had a niece of the same age as mine. Till the period of our receiving the first Sacrament she was accustomed to pass her holidays with her aunt, and to play with me. When she had reached the age of twelve years, my father, whose caution was not influenced by any feeling of pride, declared that he would no longer permit her to come to play with me and my sisters. Desirous of educating us in the most careful manner, he dreaded our forming an intimate connection with a young person destined to the situation of a seamstress or embroiderer. The girl was pretty, fair and of a very modest demeanour. Six years after the period at which my father had forbidden her entrance into his house, the Duke de la Vrillière, then M. le Comte de Saint-Florentin, sent to enquire of my father, "Have you," he said, "in your service, an old woman named Paris?" My father replied that she had brought us up, and was still in his family. "Do you know her young niece?" rejoined the minister. Then my father told him what the prudence of a parent, desirous that his children should never have any but useful connections, had suggested to him six years before. "You have acted very prudently," said M. de Saint-Florentin to him. "During the forty years I have been in the government I never met with a more impudent impostor than this little hussy; she has implicated in her fabrications our illustrious monarch, our virtuous Princesses, Mesdames Adelaide and Victoire, and the worthy M. Baret, Curé of St. Louis, who at this moment is suspended from his clerical functions until this infamous charge is perfectly cleared up. The little baggage is now in the Bastille. Only conceive," added he, "that by means of her crafty misrepresentations, she has obtained more than 60,000 francs from several credulous people at Versailles; to some she affirmed that she was the King's mistress; suffered them to accompany her to the glass door that opens into the gallery, and entered the King's apartment by the private door, it being opened for her by some of the pages in the palace, who received her favours. Nearly at the same time she sent for Gauthier, the surgeon to the light-horse, to attend a woman in labour at her house, whose face was covered with a black crape; and she provided the surgeon with the napkins that were necessary, and which were all marked with the crown, according to the depositions of Gauthier. She also brought him a warming-pan with the arms of the Princesses on it, to warm the bed for this female; and a silver basin marked in the same way. In consequence of the investigations entered upon with respect to this affair, we also know that it was a young man, a servant in the family of Mesdames, who procured her these articles; but she put this odious and wicked lie in circulation among people of her own class, and it has extended even to some whose opinions are of more importance. This is not yet all," said the minister; "she has confessed all her crimes; but in the midst of tears and sobs of penitence, she declared that she was born with virtuous inclinations, and had been led into the path of vice by her confessor, the curate M. Baret, who had seduced her at the age of fourteen. The curate has been confronted with her. The wretch, whose air and demeanour were far from indicating the perverseness of her disposition and habits, had the effrontery to maintain in his presence what she had declared, and even dared to support this declaration by a circumstance which seemed to imply the most intimate connection, by telling the worthy priest that he had a mark on his left shoulder. At these words the curate desired that a *valet de chambre*, formerly in his service, and whom he had discharged for his bad conduct, might be immediately arrested. The subsequent interrogatories have shown that this rascal had also been in the number of the girl's favourites, and that it was from him that she got the information as to the mark which she had the impudence and audacity to refer to." The poor curate Baret suffered a serious illness from the anxiety he underwent during this troublesome and unmerited proceeding. However, the King had the kindness to receive him on his return to Versailles, and to say to him that he ought to consider that nothing could be held sacred by such an impudent wretch. When the matter was fully cleared up, the minister removed this vile impostor from the Bastille, and she was sent to pass the remainder of her days in confinement in St. Pélagie.

The Courtly Abbé.

The day on which the Queen received the first visit of the Grand Duke and Grand Duchess of Russia at Versailles, a multitude, eager to obtain a sight, filled the palace and besieged the doors. The Queen had assigned to me the care of her inner closets, with the order to suffer no one to pass that way but the daughter of the Duchess de Polignac, then a child, and who was to place herself near her couch within the balustrade, to be present at the reception of the Grand Duke. A young abbé slipped into the closets, crossed the library, and opened the door communicating with the interior of this balustrade. I hastened towards him, and stopped him; he stepped back a few paces and said to me, " Pardon me, madam; I am fresh from college; I am not acquainted with the interior of the Palace of Versailles; the only direction my father gave me was this: " My son, continue to go straight forward till you are stopped, then submit respectfully to the order. You stop me, madam; I withdraw, and beg you to excuse me." This young man certainly knew how to advance with confidence and to stop with prudence.

On the Court.

The art of war is incessantly exercised at Court. Ranks, dignities, private audiences, but above all favour, keep up an uninterrupted strife, which excludes thence all idea of peace. Those who give themselves up to the service of the Court often speak of their children, of the sacrifices they make for them, and their language is sincere. The courtier most in favour, of the highest credit, only finds strength to resist the anxiety he endures in the idea that he devotes himself for the advancement or the fortune of those who belong to him; he who is not supported by these laudable sentiments thinks of the honour of being able to pay his debts, or the gratification he derives from the pleasure of shining in the eyes of those who are ignorant of his secret griefs.

La Fontaine has said of favour: " It is preserved with trouble and anxiety, to be lost with despair."

Never could a better definition be given of the splendid and harassing yoke borne by the man in favour. The moment the Prince utters a word that indicates his esteem or admiration of anyone, the first impulse of the courtiers is to be the echo of the Prince's sentiments; but this first step is only made to put them in a situation to ruin him who has been favourably noticed. Then begins the game of intrigue; if it can be accomplished, they destroy this new object of uneasiness by calumny; the favourable idea of the Prince is diverted or destroyed, and they enjoy this easy victory. But if the Sovereign, persevering in his opinion and his sentiments, selects from the ranks the man whom he has noticed, and in whom he believes he has recognised useful talents or amiable qualities, and introduces him among his favourites, the attack becomes incessant; years do not abate the ardour of it; they assume all forms, all means to ruin him. The public then come to the assistance of the courtiers; it is no longer these who speak. On the contrary, officious attentions and respect respond immediately to the favour of the monarch; and with these they charm, they bewilder the head of their victim; they disguise their jealousy, they leave it to Time to weaken the fascination of the Prince; they know that men's sentiments are disposed to change; they perceive the moment when the first warmth of prepossession decays; they begin their attack. If these first attempts awaken the attention of the monarch and enable him to observe the manœuvres of the courtiers, if he give some new mark of favour to the object of their envy, they fall back immediately and adjourn their project.

The man of the greatest merit will have some failings or commit some errors; they reckon upon them, look out for them, exaggerate them, circulate them in society, and they are reported to the Prince under the mask of zeal and perfect devotion to his interests; in the end they generally succeed in the object. Favour only saves from these cruel and persevering attacks those who, from their place at Court, never quit the Prince, and are able to defend themselves at all hours, both by day and by night. The labours of ministers do not allow them this facility; they can only appear at Court for short intervals; for this reason they are easily attacked and displaced when the King has not made it a principle, whatever he may hear said, to make as few changes as possible. Employments which leave intervals of repose never obtain any great favour because they afford time for the indefatigable underminers at Court. While the action is thus warm within the palace, they take care to direct some arrows, even to a distance, against everyone who has merit; they know that merit affords means of rising from the multitude, and that it is easier to attack it while it is still in the crowd. To see anyone disgraced never gives pain; he is a man fallen back into the ranks. Death and disgrace excite only the same idea at Court: by whom will he who is fallen be replaced?

Reply to M. de Lacretelle the Younger on the Subject of his Work.

The letter you have done me the honour to address to me reached me at Coudreaux, the seat of the Duchess d'Elchingen, where I went to spend a few days. You do not give me your address; nevertheless I desire to have the honour of thanking you for the obliging manner in which you have written to me in consequence of some reflections I ventured to transmit to you relative to your "History of France."

Everyone should hasten to communicate actual facts to an author who knows how to render them so interesting, to combine them with so much art, to narrate them with so much taste, and to deduce from them such just and luminous results; but in occupying yourself with history in general, you must, sir, have studied that of the human heart; you must have observed that constant carelessness with regard to the success of the most laudable undertakings which is only equalled by a no less persevering disposition to criticise them. I think, then, that you should not have waited for useful information, but have taken more trouble to obtain it. The Baron de Breteuil was much broken when he returned to France; but old men have a lively memory for old anecdotes, and he knew an infinite number of private events. Madame de Narbonne, lady of honour to Madame Adelaide, who had considerable influence during the first years of the reign of Louis XVI., would have been very useful to you. Lastly, I was dining with a very great nobleman, who has infinite talent. Your book was spoken of and was praised; but many errors were pointed out with reference to the administration of the Duke de Choiseul. You are deceived when you state it as doubtful that M. de Machault was on the eve of being appointed in the room of M. de Maurepas. The letter of the King was written, was given to the page, he had his foot in the stirrup, when my father-in-law, by order of Louis XVI., descended the great staircase of Choisy to recall the page. The Queen, who had already studied the King's character, then told my father-in-law that if he had not been in such haste to execute the King's command M. de Machault would have been appointed; that the King would never have had the courage to write a letter contrary to his first intention. I have been moved even to tears by the manner in which you re-establish the Queen's character in a more favourable light; but never accuse her of prodigality—she had the contrary failing. She never in her life drew the smallest sum from the Treasury; the Duchess, her favourite, had scarcely what would maintain her at Court, her situation requiring an expense far exceeding what she derived from her husband's places and her own. The Queen ordered some little edifices, in the style suited to an English garden, to be erected at Trianon; all Paris exclaimed against it, while M. de Saint-James was expending 150,000 livres at Neuilly for a grotto. The Queen was so far from allowing large sums to be expended on her favourite habitation, that when she quitted this villa, in 1789, she still left there the ancient furniture of Louis XV.: it was not till after soliciting her, for six years together, not to use any longer an old painted bedstead that had belonged to the Countess du Barry, that I obtained leave from the Queen to order another. Never was any person more slandered; all the blows by which it was intended to assail the throne were for a long time directed against her solely. I have a multitude of anecdotes of a nature to make her better known; but they are only suited to my Memoirs. I will not allow them to be printed during my life; my son will have them after me. In my Recollections I do not go beyond the details which I did and must know. Presumption ruins all the writers of Memoirs; if they know what passed in the chamber, they will also relate the deliberations of the Council, and these are very different matters. M. Thierry de Villedavray was ignorant of what the ministers knew, and they would often have been delighted to discover what he was acquainted with. In history, as in poetry, we must recur to what Boileau has said about truth.

The Memoirs of Laporte are valued, because he says, "The Queen sent me to such a place," "I said to the Cardinal," &c., and those of Cléry are most deeply interesting because he repeats, word for word, what he heard, and finishes his recital with the roll of the drum, which separated him from his unfortunate Sovereign.

Sincerity, sir, accompanies the highest esteem, and it is that which emboldens me to enter into these details with you, and to express to you the regret I feel to see you engaged in your second edition before you have patiently consulted the greatest possible number of contemporaries well informed of the facts which form your two last volumes.

Portrait of Maria Theresa.

A lady bought at the Marquis de Marigny's sale a large miniature portrait of the Empress Maria Theresa. It was in a gilt metal frame, and at the back the Marchioness's brother had caused these words to be engraved: "The Empress-Queen made a present of this portrait to my sister; it was surrounded with superb Brazil diamonds." This lady thought she was offering the Queen what would be very agreeable to her; she was deceived. Her Majesty considered that she ought not to appear insensible to her attention, but as soon as the lady had withdrawn the Queen said to me, "Take this proof of my mother's policy out of my sight quickly. Perhaps I am indebted to her in some degree for the honour of being Queen of France, but, in truth, Sovereigns are sometimes constrained to very mean actions."

HISTORICAL ILLUSTRATIONS

COLLECTED AND ARRANGED

BY MADAME CAMPAN

Note No. 1, page 21.

THE Queen brought the Duke of Normandy into the world, and the birth of a second son appeared to add to the happiness she enjoyed. She had also a second Princess, named Sophie. The quiet and regular habits of the Royal Family, now past the age of turbulent pleasures, make me look back on the years which elapsed between the peace of 1783 and the birth of the second Princess as the most happy period of the reign of Louis XVI. That happiness was soon to be disturbed by an unforeseen storm, increased by error, by the vilest corruption, and by the blackest calumny.

The Cardinal de Rohan, who was involved in Madame de Lamotte's intrigues in a manner not yet entirely explained, made some overtures to M. de Saint-James, the Treasurer of the War Extraordinaries, for the loan of a considerable sum. He communicated to him some particulars of the bargain he had made with Bœhmer to procure his magnificent necklace for the Queen. The financier, whose fortune was at that time shaken, and who soon after failed for an enormous sum, lent no money. He could not understand how the Cardinal, who was avowedly at enmity with the Queen, should be deputed to execute such a commission; and felt himself called upon to speak to Her Majesty respecting what he had heard. I know not how lightly this information may have been communicated; I only know that it made very little impression upon the Queen. Standing, as she did, upon the pinnacle of happiness and honour, how should she imagine that such an object should be the basis of an intrigue sufficient to raise the direst storm? The Queen merely told me they were talking again about that tiresome necklace; that M. de Saint-James had informed her that Bœhmer still entertained the hope of persuading her to buy it of him. She requested me to mention it to him the first time I should see him, merely by way of asking him what he had done with that ornament.

On the following Sunday I met Bœhmer in one of the halls

of the principal apartments as I was going to the Queen's Mass. I called to him; he accompanied me to my threshold. I asked him whether he had at last got rid of his necklace or not. He answered that it was sold. I asked him in what Court. He replied, "At Constantinople, and it is at this moment the property of the favourite Sultana." I congratulated him on the occasion. My real ground of satisfaction, however, was that the Queen would no longer be molested on the subject. In the evening I gave an account of my meeting with the jeweller, and the conversation I had had with him. The Queen was really rejoiced at it. She did, however, show some surprise that a necklace made to ornament a Frenchwoman should have been carried to the seraglio, and dwelt on the belief that the beauty of the collection of diamonds had been the sole inducement for purchasing it. She spoke a long time upon the subject, and upon the total change which took place in the tastes and desires of women between the ages of twenty years and thirty. She told me that when she was ten years younger she was excessively fond of diamonds; but that she had now no taste but for private society, for the country, for work, and for the cares which the education of her children would demand. From that time to the fatal exposure nothing more was said about the necklace.

The baptism of the Duke d'Angoulême took place in 1785. The Queen ordered the shoulder-knot, buckles and sword, of which the King and herself made him presents upon the occasion, of Bœhmer. When Bœhmer delivered these articles to Her Majesty, he presented her a note, which is faithfully copied into one of the memorials printed in the course of the Cardinal's trial. The Queen came into her library, where I was reading. She held the note in her hand. She read it to me, saying that, as I had in the morning guessed the enigmas of the *Mercure*, I could no doubt find her the meaning of that which that madman Bœhmer had just handed to her. These were her very expressions. She read me the note, which, like that in the memorial, contained a request "not to forget him," and expressions of his happiness at seeing her in the possession of the most beautiful diamonds that could be found in Europe. As she finished reading it she twisted it up and burnt it at a taper which was standing lighted in her library for sealing letters, and merely recommended me, when I should see Bœhmer, to request an explanation of it. "Has he assorted some other ornaments?" added the Queen. "I should be quite vexed at it, for I do not intend to make use of his services any longer. If I wish to change the setting of my diamonds I will employ my *valet de chambre* who takes care of my jewels, for he will have no ambition to sell me a single carat."

After this conversation I set off for my country-house at Crespy. My father-in-law had company to dine there every Sunday. Bœhmer had been there once or twice in the summer time. As soon as I was settled he came there.

I repeated to him faithfully what the Queen had desired me to tell him. He seemed petrified, and asked how it was that the Queen had been unable to understand the meaning of the paper

VOL. II 22

he had presented to her. "I read it myself," said I, "and I understood nothing of it." "I am not surprised at that as far as concerns you, madam," replied Bœhmer. He added that there was a mystery in all this with which I was not made acquainted, and requested of me an interview, wherein he would inform me fully of what had passed between the Queen and himself. I could only promise it him for the evening, when the people from Paris would be gone. When I had got rid of the persons who required my company in the drawing-room, I went with Bœhmer down into one of the garden walks. I think I can repeat verbatim the conversation which took place between this man and myself. I was so struck with horror the very instant I discovered this most base and dangerous intrigue that every word which passed between us is deeply engraven in my memory. I was so absorbed in grief, I perceived so many dangers in the manner in which the Queen would have to disengage herself from such a fabrication, that a storm of thunder and rain came on while I was talking to Bœhmer without exciting my attention.

Being alone, then, with Bœhmer, I began thus:

"What is the meaning of the paper which you gave to Her Majesty on Sunday as she left the chapel?"

B. "The Queen cannot be ignorant of it, madam."

"I beg your pardon; nay, more, she has desired me to ask you."

B. "That is a feint of hers."

"And, pray, what feint can there be in so plain a matter between you and the Queen? The Queen very seldom appears in full dress, and you know it. You told me yourself that the extreme plainness of the Court of Versailles was injurious to your trade. She is afraid you are projecting something new, and she expressly ordered me to tell you that she would not add a diamond of the value of twenty louis to those which she possesses."

B. "I believe it, madam; she has less need of them than ever; but what said she about the money?"

"You were paid long ago."

B. "Ah! madam, you are greatly mistaken! There is a very large sum due to me."

"What do you mean?"

B. "I must disclose all to you. The Queen deals mysteriously with you; she has purchased my grand necklace."

"The Queen! she refused you personally; she refused it of the King, who would have given it to her."

B. "Well, she changed her mind."

"If she had changed her mind, she would have told the King so. I have not seen the necklace among the Queen's diamonds."

B. "She was to have worn it on Whit-Sunday. I was very much astonished that she did not."

"When did the Queen tell you she had determined to buy your necklace?"

B. "She never spoke to me upon the subject herself."

"Through whom, then?"

B. "The Cardinal de Rohan."

"She has not spoken to him these ten years! By what contrivance I know not, my dear Bœhmer, but you are robbed, that's certain."

B. "The Queen pretends to be at variance with His Eminence, but he is upon very good terms with her."

"What do you mean? The Queen pretends to be at variance with a person so conspicuous at Court! Sovereigns rather pretend the other way. She pretended for four successive years that she would neither buy nor accept of your necklace! She buys it, and pretends not to remember that, since she does not wear it! You are mad, my poor Bœhmer, and I see you entangled in an intrigue which makes me shudder for you, and distresses me for Her Majesty's sake. When I asked you, six months ago, what was become of the necklace and where you had sent it, you told me you had sold it to the favourite Sultana."

B. "I answered as the Queen wished. She ordered me to make that reply through the Cardinal."

"But how were Her Majesty's orders transmitted to you?"

B. "By written documents signed with her own hand; and I have for some time been obliged to show them to people who have lent me money, in order to keep them quiet."

"You have received no money, then?"

B. "I beg your pardon; on delivery of the necklace I received a sum of 30,000 francs in notes of the Caisse d'Escompte, which Her Majesty sent to me by the Cardinal; and you may rely on it, he sees Her Majesty in private, for as he gave me the money he told me that she took it from a portfolio which was in her Sèvres china *secrétaire* in her little boudoir."

"That was all a falsehood; and you, who have sworn faithfully to serve the King and Queen in the offices you hold about their persons, are much to blame for having treated for the Queen without the King's knowledge when so important a matter was in question, and with her without having received her orders directly from herself."

The latter remark struck this dangerous fool. He asked me what he was to do. I advised him to go to the Baron de Breteuil, who was the minister of his department, inasmuch as he held the office of keeper of the crown diamonds, to tell him candidly all that had passed, and to be ruled by him. He assured me he would prefer deputing me to explain to the Queen. That, however, I declined, perceiving from his account that there existed a multiplicity of intrigues, which prudence warned me to avoid. I spent ten days at my country house without hearing a word of this affair. The Queen then sent for me to Little Trianon, to rehearse with me the part of Rosina, which she was to perform in the *Barber of Seville*. I was alone with her, sitting upon her couch; no mention was made of anything but the part. After we had spent an hour in the rehearsal, Her Majesty asked me why I had sent Bœhmer to her, saying he had been in my name to speak to her, and that she would not see him. It was thus that I learned he had not, in the slightest degree, followed my advice. The change in my countenance when I heard the man's name was very perceptible; the Queen perceived it and questioned me. I entreated her to see him, and assured her it was of the utmost importance for her peace of mind; that there was a plot going on of which she was not aware; and that it was a serious one, since engagements signed by herself were shown about to people who had lent Bœhmer money. Her astonishment and vexation were excessive. She desired me to remain at Trianon, and sent off a courier to Paris, ordering Bœhmer to come to her upon some pretence which has escaped my recollection. He came the next morning; in fact, it was the day on which the play was performed, and that was the last time that the Queen indulged in such amusements at that seat.

The Queen took him into her closet and asked him by what fatality it was that she was still doomed to hear of his foolish pretensions about selling her an article which she had steadily refused for several years? He replied that he was compelled, being unable to pacify his creditors any longer. "What are your creditors to me?" said Her Majesty. Bœhmer then regularly related to her all that, according to his deluded imagination, had passed between the Queen and himself, through the intervention of the Cardinal. She was equally thunderstruck, incensed and surprised at everything she heard. In vain did she speak. The jeweller, equally importunate and dangerous, repeated incessantly, "Madam, this is no time for feigning; condescend to confess that you have my necklace, and order me some assistance, or else a bankruptcy will soon bring the whole to light."

It is easy to imagine how much the Queen must have suffered. On Bœhmer's going away I found her in an alarming condition. The idea that anyone could have believed that such a man as the Cardinal possessed her full confidence, and that she should have bargained through him with a tradesman, without the King's knowledge, for a thing which she had refused from the King himself, drove her to desperation. She sent first for the Abbé de Vermond and then for the Baron de Breteuil. Their hatred and contempt for the Cardinal made them too easily forget that the lowest vices do not prevent the higher orders of the empire from being defended by those to whom they have the honour to belong; that a Rohan, a Prince of the Church, however culpable he might be, would be sure to have a considerable party, which would, of course, be joined by all the discontented persons of the Court and all the censorious people of Paris.

It was too easily believed that he would be stripped of all the advantages of his rank and order, and given up to the disgrace due to his irregular conduct; disappointment was the consequence.

I saw the Queen after the departure of the Baron and the Abbé; her agitation made me shudder. "Hideous vices must be unmasked," said she, "when the Roman purple and the title of Prince cover a mere sharper, a cheat, who dares to compromise the wife of his Sovereign; Europe and all France should know it." It is evident that from that moment the fatal plan was decided on. The Queen perceived my alarm; I did not conceal it from her. I was too well aware that she had many enemies not to be apprehensive on seeing her attract the attention of the whole world to an intrigue which would prove of the most intricate description. I entreated her to seek the most prudent and moderate advice. She silenced me by desiring me to make myself easy, and to rest satisfied that no imprudence would be committed.

On the following Sunday, being the Assumption, at twelve o'clock, at the very moment when the Cardinal, dressed in his pontifical garments, was about to proceed to the chapel, the King sent for him into his closet where he was with the Queen. "You have purchased some diamonds of Bœhmer," said the King to him. "Yes, Sire." "What have you done with them?" "I thought they had been delivered to the Queen." "Who commissioned you to make the purchase?" "A lady called the Countess de Lamotte-Valois, who handed me a letter from the Queen, and I thought I was acting agreeably to Her Majesty's wishes when I took this negotiation upon myself." The Queen interrupted him with warmth, in order to ask him how he could possibly believe that he, to whom she had not spoken for above eight years, had been selected for such a commission, and that through a woman whom she did not even know. "I see very plainly," said the Cardinal, "that I have been deceived." He then took out of his pocket a note from Her Majesty, signed *Marie Antoinette de France.* The King uttered an exclamation, and told him that a Grand Almoner ought to know that Queens of France signed only their baptismal names; that even the daughters of France had no other signature; and that if the Royal Family added anything to that signature it would not be *de France.* The writing was no more like the original signature than the body of the paper; the King remarked this to him. His Majesty afterwards showed him a copy of a letter addressed to Bœhmer, asking him if he had written any such letter. The Cardinal, after looking at it, replied that he did not remember having written it. "If you were to be shown such a letter, signed by yourself?" said the King to him. "If the letter be signed by me," said the Cardinal, "it is genuine." He was extremely confused, and repeated several times, "I have been deceived, Sire; I will pay for the necklace. I ask pardon of Your Majesties." The King desired him to compose himself, and to go into the adjoining closet, where he would find writing implements and might pen down his avowal or his answers. M. de Vergennes and the Keeper of the Seals were of opinion that the affair ought to be hushed up, in order that the scandal attending it might be avoided. The Baron de Breteuil's opinion prevailed; the Queen's resentment favoured it. The Cardinal came in again and handed the King a few lines, which were almost as unintelligible as what he had said. He was ordered out, and was accompanied by the Baron, who had him arrested by M. d'Agoult, the mayor of the Court. He confided the care of conducting the Cardinal to his apartments to a young ensign of the guards who had been arrested a few days before for debt. The order to accompany the Cardinal, with the information that he would be responsible for his person, and the word *arrest,* so perplexed the young man that he lost all power of reflecting upon the importance of his charge. The Cardinal met his *heyduke* in the gallery of the chapel, and spoke to him in German. Wishing to write down his orders, and having no pencil about him, he asked the ensign if he could lend him one. He had one, handed it to the Cardinal, and waited patiently while his Eminence wrote upon a piece of paper his orders to the Abbé Georgel, his grand vicar, to burn the whole of his correspondence with Madame de Lamotte which was in his closet at Paris. From that moment all proofs of this intrigue disappeared. Madame de Lamotte was apprehended at Bar-sur-Aube; her husband was already gone to England. From the beginning of this fatal affair all the proceedings of the Court appear to have been prompted by imprudence and want of foresight; the obscurity resulting left scope for the fables of which the voluminous memorials written on one side and the other consisted. The Queen so little imagined what could have given rise to the intrigue, of which she was about to become the victim, that at the moment when the King was interrogating the Cardinal, a terrific idea entered her mind. With that rapidity of thought caused by personal interest and extreme agitation, she fancied that if the design to ruin her in the eyes of the King and the French people was the concealed motive of this intrigue, the Cardinal would, perhaps, affirm that she had the necklace; that he had been honoured with her confidence for this purchase, made without the King's knowledge; and point out some secret place in her apartment, where he might have got some villain to hide it. Want of money and the meanest swindling were the sole foundations of this criminal affair. The necklace was by this time taken to pieces and sold, partly in London, partly in Holland, and the rest in Paris.

From the moment the Cardinal's arrest was known a universal clamour arose. Every memorial that appeared during the trial increased the outcry, and nothing tended to develop the hidden facts. On this occasion the clergy took that course, which a little wisdom, and the least knowledge of the spirit of such a body, ought to have foreseen. The Rohans and the House of Condé, as well as the clergy, complained in all quarters. The King agreed to the legal judgment, and early in September he addressed letters patent to the Parliament, in which His Majesty said that, "penetrated with the most just indignation on seeing the means which, by the confession of His Eminence the Cardinal, had been employed in order to inculpate his most dear and most honourable spouse and companion, he had," &c.

Fatal moment! in which the Queen found herself, in consequence of this highly impolitic error, opposed to a subject who ought to have been dealt with by the power of the King alone. Erroneous principles of equity, ignorance and hatred united with the confusion of ill-digested advice to form a course of conduct which was injurious alike to the Royal authority and to public morals.

The Princes and Princesses of the House of Condé, and of the Houses of Rohan, Soubise and Guéménée, put on mourning, and were seen ranging themselves in the way of the members of the Great Chamber, to salute them as they proceeded to the Palace, on the days of sitting upon the Cardinal's trial; and Princes of the Blood openly canvassed against the Queen of France.

The Pope wished to claim, on behalf of the Cardinal de Rohan, the right belonging to his ecclesiastical rank, and demanded that he should be judged at Rome. The Cardinal de Bernis, ambassador from France to His Holiness, formerly Minister for Foreign Affairs, blending the wisdom of an old diplomatist with the principles of a Prince of the Church, wished that this scandalous affair should be hushed up.

The King's aunts, who were on very intimate terms with the Ambassador, adopted his opinion; and the conduct of the King and Queen was equally and loudly censured in the apartments of Versailles and in the hotels and coffee-houses of Paris.

It is easy to refer to this transaction, alike fatal and unexpected, hastily entered into and weakly and dangerously followed up, the disorders which furnished so many weapons to the party opposed to authority.

In the early part of the year 1786 the Cardinal was fully acquitted, and came out of the Bastille; Madame de Lamotte was condemned to be whipped, branded and confined. The Court, following up the false views which had guided its measures, conceived that the Cardinal and the woman De Lamotte were equally culpable and unequally judged, and sought to restore the balance of justice by exiling the Cardinal to the abbey of La Chaise-Dieu, and suffering Madame de Lamotte to escape a few days after her entrance into the hospital.

This new error confirmed the Parisians in the idea that the low wretch, who had never been able to make her way into the room appropriated to the Queen's women, had really interested that unfortunate Princess. Cagliostro, one of those dabblers in pretended sciences or secret discoveries who appear every twenty-five or thirty years to give the most consequential idlers of Paris something to do, a capuchin, and a girl of the Palais Royal were implicated in this trial; no person of any note appeared upon the stage. The man named Declos, a servant of the Queen's chamber and a singer at the chapel, was the only man attached to the service of the Court that Madame de Lamotte dare to cite. He appeared upon the Cardinal's trial. It was to him that she said she had given the necklace. She named him because she had spent an evening with him at the house of the wife of a petty surgeon-accoucheur of Versailles. Thus the pretended friend of the Queen, when she went to pay her court to her, lived at the Belle-Image, and moved in the circle of the humblest townspeople of that place.

As soon as I heard of the sentence passed on the Cardinal I went to the Queen. She heard my voice in the room preceding her closet. She called to me; I found her very much agitated. In a faltering voice, she said to me, "Condole with me; the sharper who wished to ruin me, or get money by misusing my name and adopting my signature, has just being fully acquitted; but," added she, with warmth, "as a Frenchwoman, let me pity you. Unfortunate indeed are a people who have for their supreme tribunal a set of men who consult only their passions; and some of whom are capable of being corrupted, and others of an audacity which they have always manifested against authority, and which they have just suffered to break out against those who are invested with it."[1] At this moment the King entered, and I wished to withdraw. "Stay," said he to me; "you are one of those who sincerely participate in the grief of your mistress." He went up to the Queen and took her by the hand. "This affair," said he, "has been decided contrary to all principle; however, that is very easily accounted for. To be able to cut this Gordian knot it is not necessary to be an Alexander. In the Cardinal the Parliament saw only a Prince of the Church, a Prince de Rohan, the near relation of a Prince of the Blood, while they ought to have looked upon him as a man unworthy of his ecclesiastical character, a spendthrift, a great nobleman degraded by his shameful connections, a young fashionable trying expedients, like many in Paris, and grasping at everything. He thought he would pay Bœhmer on account sums large enough to discharge the price of the necklace within a moderate time; but he knew the customs of the Court well enough, and was not so silly as to believe that Madame de Lamotte was admitted by the Queen and deputed to execute such a commission."

In giving the King's opinion, I do not pretend to speak decisively on the Cardinal's credulity or dishonesty; but it got abroad, and I am bound to report the exact particulars of a conversation in which he declared it with so little reserve. He still continued to speak of that dreadful trial, and condescended to say to me, "I have saved you a mortification, which you would have experienced without any advantage to the Queen; all the Cardinal's papers were burnt, with the exception of a little note written by him, which was found by itself at the bottom of a drawer; it is dated in the latter end of July, and says that Bœhmer has seen Madame Campan, who told him to beware of the intrigue of which he would become the victim; that she would lay her head upon the block to maintain that the Queen had never wished to have the necklace, and that she had certainly not purchased it secretly. Had you any such conversation with the man?" the King continued. I answered that I remembered having said nearly those very words to him, and that I had informed the Queen of it. "Well," continued he, "I was asked whether it would be agree-

---

[1] "M. d'Espreménil, a councillor of the Parliament," says the Abbé Georgel in his Memoirs, "but who was not a judge in the affair, found secret means to inform us of very interesting particulars, the knowledge of which was of the greatest utility to us. I owe here this homage to his zeal and condescension."

He adds, in another place, speaking of the moment in which the decree was pronounced: "The sittings were long and multiplied; it was necessary to read the whole proceeding; more than fifty judges sat; a master of requests, a friend of the Prince, wrote down all that was said there, and sent it to his advisers, who found means to inform the Cardinal of it, and to add the plan of conduct he ought to pursue."

D'Espreménil, and other young councillors, in fact, showed upon that occasion but too much audacity in braving the Court, too much eagerness in seizing an opportunity of attacking it. They were the first to shake that authority which their functions made it a duty in them to render respectable. We ought to note errors, which their misfortunes have since but too entirely expiated.—NOTE BY THE EDITOR.

able to me that you should be summoned to appear, and I replied that it was not absolutely indispensable. I should rather that a person so intimately connected with the Queen as yourself should not be summoned. How could it, for instance, be explained," added the King, "that this man wrote the note in question three weeks before the day on which I spoke to him, without taking any step either with the Queen or myself?"

M. Pierre de Laurence, the Attorney-General's substitute, sent the Queen a list of the names of the members of the Great Chamber, with the means made use of by the Cardinal to gain their votes during the trial. I had this list to keep among the papers which the Queen deposited in the house of M. Campan, my father-in-law, and which at his death she ordered me to preserve. I burnt this statement, and I remember upon this occasion ladies performed a part not very creditable to their morals; it was by them, and in consideration of large sums which they received, that some of the oldest and most respectable heads were seduced. I did not see a single name among the whole Parliament that was gained over directly.

At this period the Queen's happy days terminated. Farewell for ever to the quiet and unostentatious excursions to Trianon, to the entertainments where the magnificence, the wit and the good taste of the Court of France shone forth at the same time; farewell, especially farewell, to that deference and to that respect, the outward shows of which wait upon the throne, while the reality alone is its solid basis.

Note No. 2, Page 64.

Short Account of the Departure of Louis XVI. for Paris, on the 6th of October, 1789,[1] by M. de Saint-Priest.

I think I ought to commence the narrative of what took place at Versailles, on the 5th and 6th of October, 1789, by relating the contents of a letter written to me by M. de la Fayette, a few days before. I was unable to preserve it, as my papers were burnt in France during my emigration; but I have copied it from Bailly's Journal, printed after his death.

"The Duke de la Rochefoucauld will have informed you of the idea, put into the grenadiers' heads, of going to Versailles this night. I wrote to you not to be uneasy about it, because I rely upon their confidence in me in order to divert them from this project. I owe them the justice to say that they had intended to ask my permission to do so, and that many of them thought it was a very proper step, and one ordered by me. Their very slight inclination has been destroyed by four words which I said to them. The affair is off my mind, except as to the idea of the inexhaustible resources of the plotters of mischief.

---

[1] Interested as we are for the cause of truth, which is confirmed by contradictory testimonies, we cannot too strongly recommend the reader to compare this interesting account with the details contained in the Memoirs of Ferrières, Dusaulx and Bailly, and the explanation annexed to those of Weber.—NOTE BY THE EDITOR.

You should not consider this circumstance as anything more than an indication of a design, and by no means as dangerous."

M. de la Fayette did not rely so much as he told me he did upon the obedience of these grenadiers who had formerly belonged to the French guards, since he posted detachments of the unpaid National Guards at Sèvres and at St. Cloud, to guard those passages of the River Seine. He informed me of it, and ordered the commandant of those posts to apprise me, if there should be any occasion.

These arrangements appeared to me insufficient for the safety of the Royal residence. I took M. de la Fayette's letter to the Council of State, and made it the ground of a proposal to reinforce Versailles with some regular troops. I observed that M. de la Fayette's letter afforded a plausible reason for it, and offered the means of literally complying with the decree sanctioned by the King, which gave the municipal authorities the first right to direct the action of regular troops. The King, by the advice of his Council, approved of my proposal, and charged me to execute it. I consequently addressed M. de la Fayette's letter to the municipality of Versailles, after having apprised the mayor of it. This document was entered in the register, and a resolution was made for demanding a reinforcement of troops for the executive power. Invested with this authority, I observed to the Minister of War that the Flanders regiment of foot being on the march, escorting a convoy of arms destined for the Parisian National Guard, from Douai to Paris, it would be well to draw that body to Versailles as soon as its mission should be fulfilled, in order to prevent, at least in part, the ferment which the arrival of a corps of soldiers of the line in the Royal residence would not fail to occasion at Paris and in the National Assembly. This measure was adopted by the Council. Bailly, in his journal, says that he wrote to me respecting the uneasiness it gave the districts of Paris. He adds that I replied that "the arrival of armed men in the Royal residence, announced by circumstantial reports, had determined the King to call in the Flanders regiment, and to take military measures upon the subject."

I am the less able to recollect what I could have meant by that, inasmuch as I am certain I never took any step of a military nature, beyond that of desiring the Flanders regiment to march in a military manner, without turning aside from their destination.

It is true that the civic authorities of Paris, in pursuance of my answer to Bailly, had the insolence to send four deputies to Versailles, to learn from the King's ministers their reasons for calling in the Flanders regiment. These deputies alighted at my house, and one of them, M. Dusaulx, a member of the Académie des Belles Lettres, was the spokesman. He interrogated me upon the matter in question in the most imperious manner, informing me that carrying it into execution would be followed by fatal consequences. I answered with all the moderation I could command, that this demand of a regiment of the line was a natural consequence of the information communicated by a letter from M. de la Fayette. I added that I gave him this answer as from myself, the King not having authorised me to answer a question which His Majesty could never have imagined anyone would dare to put to his minister. M. Dusaulx and his three brother deputies returned much dissatisfied. M. de Condorcet was one of them. Some factious members of the National Assembly likewise meddled in the matter. M. Alexandre Lameth and M. Barnave spoke to me and endeavoured to persuade me to induce the King to revoke his call for this regiment of the line. I answered them in such a manner as to leave them no hope of it. The regiment arrived at Versailles without meeting the smallest obstacle. The conspirators gave the old French guards to understand that it was destined to guard the King in their stead, which was untrue; but that served to make them resume their project of coming to Versailles. I am ignorant whether they had any other view than to take their post again, or whether they had already determined to bring the King back to Paris. However that may have been, the event soon took place.

The body-guards gave a regimental entertainment to the officers of the Flanders regiment, and invited a few subaltern officers and soldiers, as well as some of the National Guards of Versailles. It was an old custom for the military corps quartered at any place to pay this compliment to others which arrived there. Upon such occasions many healths will, of course, be drunk, and the repasts must, of necessity be always noisy; and this was the case with the present. The regimental band had been invited, and the air beginning, "O Richard! O my King!" from the play of *Richard Cœur de Lion*, excited the liveliest enthusiasm. It was thought right to go and fetch the Queen, to increase the fervour. And, in fact, Her Majesty came with the Dauphin, which prompted fresh acclamation. When the company left the dining-hall, a few soldiers, perhaps affected by wine, appeared in the marble court below the apartments of the King, who had returned from hunting. Shouts of "Vive le Roi!" were heard; and one of the soldiers, with the assistance of his comrades, climbed up on the outside as high as the balcony of the chamber of His Majesty, who did not show himself. I was in my closet, and I sent to know what occasioned the noise, and was informed. I have, however, no reason to believe that the national cockade was trampled under foot; and it is less likely, because the King wore it at that time and it would have been a want of respect to His Majesty himself. It was a lie invented to irritate the minds of the Parisian National Guard.

The Count d'Estaing commanded the National Guard of Versailles at that time. The King gave him, also, the command of all the regular troops there. They consisted of the two battalions of the Flanders regiment, two hundred chasseurs des Evéchés, eight hundred mounted body-guards, and the Swiss guard on duty. On the 5th of October, at about eleven in the morning, one of my *valets de chambre* came from Paris to apprise me that the Parisian National Guard, both paid and unpaid, accompanied by a numerous populace of men and women, had set out for Versailles. The King was hunting on the heights of Meudon, and I wrote to tell him of it. His Majesty returned promptly, and ordered that the Council of State should be summoned for half-past three. The Council then consisted of eight ministers: the Marshal de Beauvau, the Archbishop of Vienna, the Archbishop of Bordeaux, Keeper of the Seals, M. Necker, Minister of the Finances, and the Counts de Montmorin, de la Luzerne, de Latour du Pin and de Saint-Priest, Secretaries of State.

I laid before the Council the information I had received, and which had been subsequently confirmed by several other reports. I represented the danger that would attend the waiting for this multitude at Versailles, and I proposed measures to be pursued on this emergency. They were, that detachments should be sent to guard the bridges across the Seine, a battalion of the Flanders regiment for that at Sèvres, another for that at St. Cloud, and the Swiss guard for that at Neuilly, and that the King should send the Queen and the Royal Family to Rambouillet, where the chasseurs of the regiment of Lorraine were, while His Majesty himself should go and meet the Parisians with the two hundred chasseurs des Évêchés and his eight hundred body-guards. The thousand horse being drawn up in order of battle beyond the bridge of Sèvres, the King was to order the Parisian band to retire, and in case they should disobey, was to make a few charges of cavalry to endeavour to disperse them. Then, if this should be unsuccessful, the King would have time to regain Versailles at the head of his troops and march immediately to Rambouillet. My advice was approved of by Marshal de Beauvau, M. de la Luzerne, and M. de Latour du Pin; and warmly opposed by M. Necker, seconded by Count de Montmorin and the Archbishops of Vienna and Bordeaux. M. Necker insisted that there was no danger in suffering the multitude to come to Versailles, where its object was, probably, only to present some petition to the King; and should the worst happen, if His Majesty should find it necessary to reside at Paris, he would be venerated and respected there by his people, who adored him.

I replied by opposing to this reasoning the origin and the features of this proceeding, which completely contradicted all these pretented dispositions of the people of Paris.

The King did not declare himself as to the course he should pursue; he broke up the Council and that we knew he went to consult the Queen. She declared that she would not upon any consideration whatever separate herself from him and her children, which rendered the execution of the measure I had proposed impossible. Thus perplexed, we did nothing but wait. However, I sent an order to the Swiss barracks at Courbevoie that all belonging to the regiment of guards who were then there, should immediately repair to Versailles, which was promptly done.

The National Assembly was sitting when information of the march of the Parisians was given to it by one of the deputies who came from Paris. A certain number of the members were no strangers to this movement. It appears that Mirabeau wished to avail himself of it to raise the Duke of Orleans to the throne. It was then that Mounier, who presided over the National Assembly, rejected the idea with horror. "*My good man*," said Mirabeau to him, "*what difference will it make to you to have Louis XVII. for your King instead of Louis XVI.?*" The Duke of Orleans was baptised Louis.

Mounier, seeing the urgency of the case, proposed that the Assembly should declare itself permanent and inseparable from His Majesty; which was decreed. Mirabeau then insisted that the deputation which should carry up this decree to the King should demand his sanction to some others which had remained in arrear; among others, that of the rights of man, in which some alterations were desired. But existing circumstances carried the King's sanction. A few female citizens then presented themselves to offer civic gifts. It seems they were sent to keep the Assembly employed until the arrival of the Parisians. They were admitted, and the scene was ridiculous enough.

The Count d'Estaing had ordered the mounted body-guards to horse, and stationed them in the Place d'Armes, in advance of the post of the French guard, which was occupied by a detachment of the National Guard of Versailles, commanded by a man named Lecointre, a draper, and a man of very bad disposition. He was displeased that the body-guards left his soldiers in the second line, and tried to raise some quarrel in order to dislodge them. For that purpose he sent persons, who slipped between the ranks of the soldiers, to annoy the horses. M. de Savannières, an officer of the body-guards, while giving chase to these wretches, received a musket-shot from the National Guard, of which he died. A short time afterwards, M. d'Estaing, who had received a secret order from the King not to make any attack, sent the body-guard back to their hotel. They were saluted, as they went off, by a few musket-shots from the National Guard of Versailles, by which some men and horses were wounded. When they reached their hotel they found it pillaged by the populace of Versailles, which brought them back to their former position.

The Flanders regiment was under arms at the end of the avenue of Versailles. Mirabeau and some other deputies mingled among the ranks of the soldiery. It is asserted that they distributed money to them. The soldiers dispersed themselves in the public-houses in the town, and reassembled in the evening, when they were shut up in the King's stables.

As to the body-guards, M. d'Estaing knew not what to do beyond bringing them into the courtyard of the ministers and shutting the gratings. Thence they proceeded to the castle terrace, then to Trianon, and, lastly, to Rambouillet.

I could not refrain from expressing to M. d'Estaing, when he came to the King, my astonishment at not seeing him make any military disposition. "Sir," replied he, "I await the orders of the King" (who did not open his mouth). "When the King gives no orders," pursued I, "a general should decide for himself in a soldierlike manner." This observation remained unanswered. About seven o'clock in the evening a kind of advanced guard from Paris, consisting of ill-armed men and women of the rabble, arrived at the gates of the ministers' courtyard, which those within refused to open. The mob then demanded that a few women should be permitted to go and present a supplication to the King. His Majesty ordered that six should be let in, and desired me to go into the "bull's-eye" and there hear what they had to say. I accordingly went. One of these women, whom I afterwards found to be a common strumpet, spoke to acquaint me that a scarcity of bread existed in Paris, and that the people came to ask bread of His Majesty. I answered that the King had taken all the steps which could depend on him for preventing the injurious effects of the failure in the last harvest; and I added that calamities of this nature ought to be borne with patience, as drought was borne when there was a dearth of rain. I dismissed the women, telling them to return to Paris, and to assure their fellow-citizens of the King's affection for the people of his capital. It was then that a private individual, whom I did not know at that time, but whom I have since found to have been the Marquis de Favras, proposed to me to mount a number of gentlemen then present upon horses from the King's stables, and that they should meet the Parisians and force them to retreat. I answered him that the King's horses, not being trained to the kind of service which he proposed, would be but ill-adapted to it, and would only endanger their riders, without answering any purpose. I returned to the King to give him an account of my conversation with the women. Shortly afterwards the King assembled the Council. It was dark; we were scarcely seated when an aide-de-camp of M. de la Fayette, named Villars, brought me a letter written to me by that General from near Auteuil, half a league from Paris. He informed me that he was on his march with the National Guard of Paris, both paid and unpaid, and a part of the people of Paris, who came to make remonstrances to the King. He begged me to assure His Majesty that no disorder would take place, and that he vouched for it. Notwithstanding this tone of confidence, it is certain that La Fayette had been dragged to Versailles against his will at the moment when he endeavoured to stop the old French guards, who were already on their march, upon the Pont Royal. It is not the less true that he had become familiar with the idea of marching to Versailles since the first time he had written to me about it. He had even spoken to me on the subject, as believing it at that time preferable that the King should reside at Paris instead of Versailles; but undoubtedly he would have preferred the adoption of some other method of taking His Majesty thither.

After I had read M. de la Fayette's letter to the Council, I recapitulated my advice of the afternoon, observing, however, that it was now impossible to resort to the measures I had then proposed, but that it was of importance that the King, with his family and regular troops, should set off for Rambouillet. The contest between M. Necker and myself now grew warmer than upon the former occasion. I explained the risks which the King and his family would incur if they did not avoid them by departing. I dwelt upon the advantages that would be gained by quitting Versailles for Rambouillet, and I concluded by saying to the King, "*Sire, if you are taken to Paris to-morrow, your crown is lost!*" The King was shaken, and he arose to go and speak to the Queen, who this time consented to the departure. M. Necker says, in one of his works: "*He alone* (the King) *was to determine, and he determined to remain at Versailles. Out of a considerable number of persons, one alone, as far as I remember, was for the departure, and without any modification.*"

It is probably to myself that M. Necker attributes this isolated opinion, but his memory has failed him, for it is a fact that M. de Beauvau, M. de la Luzerne and M. de Latour du Pin were constantly of my opinion.

M. Necker passes over in silence the order which the King gave me on re-entering the council chamber, to have his carriages got ready, which broke up the Council. I told His Majesty that I would execute his orders, send off my wife and children to Rambouillet, and proceed thither myself, to be ready to receive him upon his arrival. I deputed the Chevalier de Cubières, equerry, to carry to the stables the order for getting the carriages ready, and I went home to make my own arrangements. After regulating everything with Madame de Saint-Priest for her departure, I got on horseback, wrapped up in my cloak, that I might not be observed, and succeeded in keeping myself concealed. I had scarcely proceeded half a league when my wife's carriage overtook me. She informed me that M. de Montmorin had sent her word that the King was no longer willing to set out; "but," added she, "I would not countermand the arrangements you had made." I begged she would proceed on her journey, most happy in the reflection that she and my children would be far from the scene which I then anticipated would take place on the morrow. As for myself, I retraced my steps and re-entered by one of the park gates, where I dismissed my horses and went through the gardens to the King's apartments. There I found M. de la Fayette, who had just arrived. He personally confirmed to His Majesty all the assurances which he had by letter desired me to give him, and went to bed, extremely fatigued by the events of the day, without making any fresh arrangement for the safety of the castle. The King, as he withdrew, gave orders to the captain of his guards to prohibit his subalterns from making any attack.

I never knew perfectly what made the King change his mind respecting his departure. I returned home in great anxiety, and threw myself, dressed as I was, upon my bed. It was impossible for me to close my eyes on account of the noise made by the mob from Paris, with which the streets of Versailles were filled. At daybreak I went into my closet, the windows of which commanded the courtyard of the ministers; at that very moment I saw the gates open, and a frenzied multitude of banditti, armed with pikes and bludgeons, and some of them with sabres and muskets, rush into the courtyard and run with the utmost speed to the courtyard of the Princes, wherein the staircase leading to the apartments of Their Majesties is situated. They all passed below my windows without seeing me. I waited about a quarter of an hour, and saw a considerable number of them bringing back a dozen of the body-guards, whom they had seized in the Queen's guard-room and were going to massacre in the Place d'Armes. Fortunately for these unhappy men M. de la Fayette appeared with some soldiers of the guards, whom he employed to drive off the banditti. It is known that they immediately went up to the Queen's apartments; that the body-guard suffered them to enter their guard-room without opposition, in pursuance of the King's orders; that, however, those who stood sentinels at the door of the Queen's ante-chamber made some resistance, and gave the footmen time to awaken the Queen and barricade the door with trunks and chairs; and that Her Majesty, alarmed by the noise, took refuge in the King's rooms through the communication between their apartments. The rioters then made their way in, and, finding their prey escaped, committed no violence in the apartments. But they had assassinated two of the body-guards, and wounded many others in the guard-room, which was the result of the King's order of the preceding day to make no opposition. M. de la Fayette went up to the King's rooms, and found the door of the ante-chamber, called the "bull's-eye," closed and barricaded. He parleyed with the body-guards, who had taken refuge there to preserve His Majesty's apartments. Upon M. de la Fayette's assurances the door was opened. He then stationed there some grenadiers, who, in conjunction with the body-guards, kept that entry closed until the King's departure for Paris. The door by which the King generally went out to get into his carriage remained constantly free—the people of Paris were not aware of its existence. I wrapped myself in a great-coat to make my way through the crowd which filled the courtyard, and went up to the King's apartments. I found him with the Queen and the Dauphin in the balcony of his bedroom, protected by M. de la Fayette, who harangued the rabble from time to time; but all his speeches could not stop their shouts of "*To Paris, to Paris!*" There were even a few musket-shots fired from the courtyard, which fortunately struck nobody. The King occasionally withdrew into his room to sit down and rest himself; he was in a state of stupefaction, which it is difficult to describe or even to imagine. I accosted him repeatedly, and represented to him that delay in yielding to the wishes of the mob was useless and dangerous; that it was necessary he should promise to go to Paris, and that this was the only way of getting rid of these savages, who might the very next moment proceed to the utmost extremities, to which there were not wanting persons to excite them. To all this the King did not answer one single word. The Queen, who was present, said to me, "*Ah! Monsieur de Saint Priest, why did we not go away last night!*" I could not refrain from saying in reply, "*It is no fault of mine.*" "*I know that well,*" answered she.

These remarks proved to me that she had no share in His Majesty's change of determination. He made up his mind at last, about eleven o'clock, to promise to go to Paris. Some cries of "Vive le Roi!" were then heard, and the mob began to quit the courtyards and take the road to the capital. Care had been taken to send cartloads of bread from Paris during the night to feed the multitude. I left the King in order to be at the Tuileries before him, and as I took the St. Cloud road I met with no obstacle. I dined with the Ambassador of the Two Sicilies, and proceeded to the Tuileries, ready for the arrival of Their Majesties. I had not calculated that their unfortunate journey, which was a real martyrdom, would have occupied so much time. Their carriage was preceded by the heads of two murdered body-guards carried upon pikes. The carriage was surrounded by ruffians, who contemplated the Royal personages with a brutal curiosity. A few of the body-guards on foot and unarmed, covered by the former French guards, followed dejectedly; and to complete the climax, after six or seven hours spent in travelling from Versailles to Paris, Their Majesties were led to the Hôtel de Ville as if to make the *amende honorable*. I know not who ordered this. The King ascended the Hôtel de Ville, and said that he came freely to reside in his capital. As he spoke in a low tone of voice, "Tell them, then," said the Queen, "that the King comes freely to reside in his capital." "*You are more fortunate than if I had uttered it*," said Bailly, "*since the Queen herself has given you this favourable assurance*." This was a falsehood, in which His Majesty was obviously contradicted by facts; never had he acted less freely. It was near ten at night when the King reached the Tuileries. As he got out of his carriage I told him that if I had known he was going to the Hôtel de Ville I would have waited for him there. "*I did not know it myself*," replied the King in a tone of dejection.

On the morrow the body-guard, who had passed the night upon benches in the Castle of the Tuileries, were dismissed. M. de la Fayette filled up all the posts with the National Guard of Paris, which was commanded by himself, and hence he became the keeper of the Royal Family.

Thus was fulfilled what I had told the King on the preceding day at Versailles, namely, that if he suffered himself to be dragged to Paris he would lose his crown. I did not then suspect that the life also of the unhappy monarch depended upon that false step.

When I reflect how many favourable consequences would have resulted from a more steadfast resolution to quit Versailles, I feel myself even at this day filled with regret.

In the first place M. de Villars, M. de la Fayette's aide-de-camp, who brought me the letter from the latter to Versailles on the 5th of October, told me that he had been sent by his general to the bridge of Sèvres to know whether it was defended, and that if it had been he would have retreated. Secondly, Madame de Saint-Priest, on her arrival at Rambouillet, saw there a deputation from the city of Chartres, which is in its neighbourhood. They came in the name of their fellow-citizens to entreat His Majesty would make their city his asylum, to assure him they abhorred the insolence of the Parisians, and that they would lay down their lives and property in support of His Majesty's authority—an example which would infallibly have been followed by the other towns one after another, and in particular by Orleans, which was wholly devoted to the Royal cause. The Mayor of Rambouillet has since assured me that the request of the deputation from Chartres was transcribed into the registers of the municipality of Rambouillet. It must be there still. Thirdly, the National Assembly, under the presidency of Mounier, a man of integrity, who had the welfare of the State at heart, had declared itself inseparable from His Majesty. It would therefore have followed him to Rambouillet and Chartres. It is probable, moreover, that the factious leaders would not have ventured themselves there, and that the National Assembly, purified by their absence, would have knit itself to the King, whose intentions were pure, and that useful reforms would have been the results without an overthrow of the monarchical Constitution. Fourthly, and lastly, if it had been necessary to come to extremities for the reduction of Paris, what advantages would not the Royal party have possessed over that city, which at that time subsisted only upon the corn carried up the Seine! By stopping the convoys at Pontoise, Paris would have been starved. Besides, the King would easily have collected round him 10,000 men in four days, and 40,000 in five, secure of being able to concentrate still more considerable forces if circumstances should require it. The army under M. de Bouillé, in his district of Metz, would have been ready to march in a very short time, and under such a general the insurgents would speedily have been subdued.

Such is the correct narrative which I determined to give, as an eye-witness, and even as an actor, on the days of the 5th and 6th of October. It may one day contribute to the history of that remarkable period which, by its consequences, has perhaps decided the fate of the universe.

Note No. 3, Page 133.

Four or five months before the ill-omened journey to Varennes the Queen secretly began preparing for it. She was anxious to send before her several things very useful at ordinary times, but which it would then have been more prudent to look upon as superfluous.

I was ordered to prepare, with the utmost secrecy, a complete wardrobe for the Queen, her daughter and the Dauphin. The espionage of the Assembly was at that time carried to such a pitch, and the most indifferent actions of persons known to possess the confidence of Their Majesties were scrutinised with so much care, that I was obliged to go on foot, and almost disguised, to purchase all the necessary articles.

My sister prepared the clothes intended for Madame and the Dauphin, under pretence of sending a present into the country. The trunks went to the frontiers as belonging to one of my aunts, Madame Candon, widow of the Mayor of Arras, who proceeded to Brussels under an order to wait there for the Queen, and who did not return to France until after the acceptance of the Constitution in September, 1791. A *nécessaire* of enormous size, containing various articles, from a warming-pan to a silver porringer, was considered indispensable. The Queen was devising some way of forwarding her *necessaire* to Brussels. She had ordered it at the time of the first insurrections in 1789, to be made use of *in case of precipitate flight*. The moment for using it was come. She would not be deprived of it.

I opposed the execution of this resolution with every effort of reasoning. A piece of furniture of great bulk, and adapted for travelling, could not be sent out of the Queen's chamber without giving rise to much suspicion, and perhaps to a denunciation. It was at last determined that M. F—— S——, of the embassy from Vienna, at that time *chargé d'affaires* in the absence of the Count de Mercy, should ask the Queen, as from Madame the *Gouvernante*, for a *necessaire* similar in every respect to her own. The directions to get the Archduchess's commission executed were given to me publicly. The Queen thought this stratagem sufficient for eluding all suspicion, but she deceived herself. Those who are born to thrones are, above all others, wanting in the knowledge of mankind.

In vain did I urge the manufacturer to send home the work. He required two months more for that purpose, and the moment fixed on for the departure drew near. The Queen, still too intent upon this trifle, thought that, having really ordered a *necessaire* under a pretence of presenting it to her sister, she might feign a wish to put her in possession of it earlier, and send her own, and she desired me to send it off.

I gave directions to the wardrobe-woman, whose business it was to attend to particulars of this nature, to put the *necessaire* into a condition to be packed up and carried in the Queen's name to M. de ——, who was to forward it to Brussels.

The woman in question executed her commission punctually, but on the evening of that very day, the 15th of May, 1791, she informed M. Bailly, the mayor of Paris, that preparations were making at the Queen's residence for a departure, and that the *necessaire* was already sent off under pretence of its being presented to Madame Christina.

It was necessary, likewise, to send off the whole of the diamonds belonging to the Queen. Her Majesty shut herself up with me in a closet belonging to the *entresol* looking into the garden of the Tuileries, and we packed all the diamonds, rubies and pearls she possessed in a small chest. The cases containing these ornaments being altogether of considerable bulk, had been deposited ever since the 6th of October, 1789, with the *valet de chambre* who had the care of the Queen's jewels. That faithful servant, himself guessing the use that had been made of the valuables, destroyed all the boxes, which were as usual covered with red morocco marked with the cipher and arms of France. It would have been impossible for him to hide them from the eyes of the popular inquisitors during the domiciliary visits in January, 1793, and the discovery might have formed a ground of accusation against the Queen.

I had but a few articles to place in the box, when the Queen was compelled to suspend the operation of packing it, being under the necessity of going down to cards, which began at seven precisely. She therefore desired me to leave all the diamonds upon the sofa, persuaded that, as she took the key of her closet herself and there was a sentinel under the window, no danger was to be apprehended for that night, and she reckoned upon returning very early the next day to finish the work.

The same woman who had given information of the sending away of the *necessaire* was also deputed by the Queen to take care of her more private closets. No other servant was permitted to enter them; she renewed the flowers, swept the carpets, &c. The Queen received back the key of her closets, when she had finished putting them in order, from her own hands; but this woman, desirous of doing her duty well, and having the key sometimes for a few minutes only, had probably on that account alone ordered one without the Queen's knowledge. She made a formal declaration that Her Majesty, with the assistance of Madame Campan, had packed up the whole of her jewellery some time before the departure; that she was certain of it, as she had found the diamonds and the cotton-wool which served to wrap them scattered upon the sofa in the Queen's closet in the *entresol*, and most assuredly she could only have seen these preparations in the interval between seven in the evening and seven in the morning. The Queen having met me the next day at the time appointed, the box was handed over to Leonard, Her Majesty's hairdresser.

The box remained a long time at Brussels; at length it got into the hands of Madame the Duchess d'Angoulême, being delivered to her by the Emperor on her arrival at Vienna. I will here add some particulars for which there was no proper place elsewhere. In order not to leave out any of the Queen's diamonds, I requested the first tire-woman to give me the body of the full dress, and all the assortment which served for the stomacher of the full dress on the days of State, articles which always remained at the wardrobe.

The superintendent and the *dame d'honneur* being absent, the first tire-woman required me to sign her a receipt, the terms of which she herself dictated, and which acquitted her of all responsibility for these diamonds. She had the prudence to burn this document on the crisis of the 10th of August. The Queen having determined, upon the much-to-be-lamented arrest at Varennes, not to have her diamonds brought back to France, was often very anxious about them during the year which elapsed between that period and that of the 10th of August, and dreaded above all things that such a secret should be discovered.

In consequence of a decree of the Assembly which deprived the King of the custody of the Crown diamonds, the Queen gave up those which she generally used.

She preferred the twelve brilliants called *mazarines*, from the name of the cardinal who had enriched the Treasury with them, a few rose-cut diamonds and the *sanci*. She determined to deliver, with her own hands, the box containing them to the commissioner nominated by the National Assembly, to place them with the Crown diamonds. After giving them to him, she presented him a row of fine pearls of great beauty, saying to him, "that it had been brought into France by Anne of Austria; that it was invaluable on account of its rarity; that having been appropriated by that Princess to the use of the Queens and Dauphinesses, Louis XV. had placed it in her hands on her arrival in France; but that she considered it national property." "That is a question, madam," said the commissary; "that is a matter of opinion." "Sir," resumed the Queen, "it is an opinion on which I have a right to decide, and I now set it at rest."

My father-in-law, who was drawing near his end and dying of the grief he felt for the misfortunes of his master and mistress, strongly interested and occupied the thoughts of the Queen. He had been saved from the fury of the populace in the courtyard of the Tuileries.

On the day on which the King was compelled, by an insurrection, to give up a journey to St. Cloud, Her Majesty looked upon this trusty servant as inevitably lost if, on going away, she should leave him in the apartment he occupied in the Tuileries. Prompted by her apprehensions, she ordered M. Vicq-d'Azyr, her physician, to recommend him the waters of Mont d'Or, in Auvergne, and to persuade him to set off at the latter end of May. At the moment of my going away, the Queen assured me that the grand project would be executed between the 15th and the 20th of June; that as it was not my month to be on duty, Madame Thibaut would take the journey; but that she had many directions to give me before I went. She then desired me to write to my aunt, Madame Cardon, who was by that time in possession of the clothes which I had ordered, that as soon as she should receive a letter from M. Auguié, the date of which should be accompanied with a B, an L, or an M, she was to proceed with her property to Brussels, Luxembourg or Montmédy. She desired me clearly to explain to my sister the meaning of these three letters and to leave them with her in writing, in order that at the moment of my going away she might be able to succeed me in writing to Arras. The Queen had a more delicate commission for me; it was to select from among my acquaintance a prudent person of obscure rank, but wholly devoted to the interests of the Court, who would be willing to receive a portfolio which she was to give up only to me or someone furnished with a note from the Queen. She added that she would not travel with this portfolio, but that it was of the utmost importance that my opinion of the fidelity of the person to whom it was to be entrusted should be matured and well founded. I proposed to her Madame Vallayer Coster, an amiable and a worthy artist whom I had known from my infancy, and whose sentiments were not to be doubted. She lived in the galleries of the Louvre. The choice seemed a good one. The Queen remembered that she had portioned her by giving her a place in the financial offices, and added that gratitude ought sometimes to be reckoned on. She then pointed out to me the valet belonging to her toilette whom I was to take with me to show him the residence of Madame Coster in the galleries of the Louvre, so that he might not mistake it when he should take the portfolio to her. On the evening preceding my departure, the Queen particularly recommended me to proceed to Lyons and the frontiers as soon as she should have departed. She advised me to take with me a confidential person fit to remain with M. Campan when I should leave him, and assured me she would give orders to M—— to set off as soon as she should be known to be at the frontiers, in order to protect me in going out. She condescended to add that, having a long journey to make in foreign countries, she determined to give me 300 louis. I bathed the Queen's hands with tears at the moment of this sorrowful separation, and having money at my disposal, I declined accepting of her gold. I did not dread the tiresome road I had to travel in order to rejoin her; all my apprehension was that, by treachery or miscalculation, a scheme, the practicability of which was not sufficiently clear to me, should fail. I could answer for all those who belonged to the service immediately about the Queen's person, and I was right; but her wardrobe woman gave me well-founded reason for alarm. I ventured to communicate this to the Queen; I had never taken advantage of the confidence with which I was honoured by her to do anyone an injury; but at this moment it was my duty to act in opposition to my principles. I mentioned to the Queen a number of revolutionary remarks which this woman had made to me a few days before. Her office was directly under the control of: he first *femme de chambre*, yet she had refused to obey the directions I gave her, talking insolently to me about *hierarchy overturned, equality among men*, of course, more especially among persons holding offices at Court; and this jargon of words, at that time in the mouths of all the partisans of the Revolution, was terminated by an observation which frightened me. "You know many important secrets, madam," said this woman to me; "and I have guessed quite as many. I am not a fool; I see all that is going forward here, in consequence of the bad advice given to the King and Queen; I could frustrate it all if I chose." I left this contention, in which I had been promptly silenced, pale and trembling. Unfortunately, as I began my narrative to the Queen, with particulars of the woman's refusal to obey me (and Sovereigns being all their lives importuned with complaints upon the prerogatives of places), she believed that my own dissatisfaction had much to do with the step I was taking, and she did not sufficiently fear the woman. Her office, although a very inferior one, brought her in nearly 15,000 francs yearly. Still young, tolerably handsome, with comfortable apartments in the *entresols* of the Tuileries, she saw a great deal of company, and in the evening had assemblies consisting of deputies of the revolutionary party. M. de Gouvion, major-general of the National Guard, passed almost every day with her, and it is to be presumed that she had long been subservient to the views of the party in opposition to the Court. The Queen asked her for the key of a door which led to the principal vestibule of the Tuileries, telling her she wished to have a similar one, that she might not be under the necessity of going out through the Pavilion of Flora. M. de Gouvion and M. de la Fayette would, of course, be informed of this circumstance, and persons possessing exceedingly good intelligence have assured me that, on the very night of the Queen's departure, this wretched woman had a spy with her, who saw the Royal Family set off.

As for myself, after I had executed all the Queen's orders, on the 30th of May, 1791, I set out for Auvergne. I was settled in the gloomy narrow valley of the Mont d'Or, when, about four in the afternoon of the 25th of June, I heard the beat of a drum, to call the inhabitants of the hamlet together. When it had ceased, I heard a hairdresser from Besse proclaim in the provincial dialect of Auvergne: "The King and Queen were taking flight in order to ruin France, but I come to tell you that they are stopped, and are well guarded by a hundred thousand men under arms." I still ventured to hope that he was repeating only a false report, but he went on, "The Queen, with her well-known haughtiness, lifted up the veil which covered her face, and said to the citizens who were upbraiding the King, 'Well, since you recognise your Sovereign, respect him.'" Upon hearing these expressions, which the Jacobin Club of Clermont could hardly have invented, I exclaimed, "The news is true!"

I should but ill-express the despair which overwhelmed me, and it would fill too secondary a situation in the account of so important an event. I immediately learned that a courier having come from Paris to Clermont, the attorney of the commune had sent off messengers to the chief places of the province; these again sent couriers to the districts, and the districts in like manner informed the villages and hamlets which they contained. It was through this ramification, arising out of the establishment of clubs, that the afflicting intelligence of the misfortune of my Sovereigns reached me in the wildest part of France, and in the midst of the snows by which we were environed.

On the 23rd I received a note written in a hand which I recognised as that of M. Diet, usher of the Queen's chamber, but dictated by Her Majesty. It contained these words: "I am this moment arrived. I have just got into my bath. I, and my family, exist. I have suffered much. Do not return to Paris until I desire you. Take good care of my poor Campan; soothe his sorrow. Look for happier times."

This note was, for greater safety, addressed to my father-in-law's *valet de chambre*. What were my feelings, on perceiving that, after the most distressing crisis, we were among the first objects of the kindness of that unfortunate Princess!

M. Campan having been unable to use the waters of Mont d'Or, and the first popular effervescence having subsided, I thought I might return to Clermont. The Committee of Surveillance, or that of General Safety, had resolved to arrest me there; but the Abbé Louis, formerly a parliamentary councillor, and then a member of the Constituent Assembly, was kind enough to affirm that I was in Auvergne solely for the purpose of attending my father-in-law, who was extremely ill. The precautions relative to my absence from Paris, were limited to placing us under the surveillance of the attorney of the commune, who was at the same time president of the Jacobin club; but he was also a physician of repute, and, without having any doubt that he had received secret orders relative to me, I thought it would contribute to our quiet if I selected him to attend my patient. I paid him according to the rate of payment made to the best Paris physicians, and I requested him to visit us every morning and evening. I took the precaution to subscribe to no other newspaper than the *Moniteur*. Dr. Monestier (for that was the physician's name) frequently took upon himself to read it to us. Whenever he thought proper to speak of the King and Queen in the insulting and brutal terms at that time unfortunately adopted throughout France, I used to stop him, and say coolly, "Sir, you are here in company with the servants of Louis XVI. and Marie Antoinette. Whatever may be the wrongs with which the nation believes it has to reproach them, our principles forbid our losing sight of the respect due to them from us." Notwithstanding he was an inveterate patriot, he felt the force of this remark, and even procured the revocation of a second order for our arrest, becoming responsible for us to the Committee of the Assembly and to the Jacobin Society.

The two chief women about the Dauphin, who had accompanied the Queen to Varennes, Diet, her usher, and Camot, her *garçon de toilette*; the females, on account of the journey, and the men in consequence of the denunciation of the woman belonging to the wardrobe, were sent to the prisons of the Abbaye. After my departure the *garçon de toilette*, whom I had taken to Madame Vallayer Coster's, was sent there with the portfolio she had agreed to receive. This commission could not escape the detestable spy upon the Queen. She gave information that a portfolio had been carried out on the evening of the departure, adding that the King had placed it upon the Queen's sofa; that the *garçon de toilette* wrapped it up in a napkin and took it under his arm, and that she did not know where he had carried it. The man, who was remarkable for his fidelity, underwent three examinations without making the slightest disclosure. M. Diet, a man of good family, a servant on whom the Queen placed particular reliance, likewise experienced the severest treatment. At length, after a lapse of three weeks, the Queen succeeded in obtaining the emancipation of her servants.

The Queen, about the 15th of August, had me informed by letter that I might come back to Paris without being under any apprehension of arrest there, and that she greatly desired my return. I brought my father-in-law back in a dying state, and on the day preceding that of the acceptance of the Constitutional Act, I informed the Queen that he was no more. "The loss of Lassonne and Campan," said she, as she applied her handkerchief to her streaming eyes, "has taught me how valuable such subjects are to their masters. I shall never find their equals."

I resumed my functions about the Queen on the 1st of September, 1791. I was struck with the astonishing change misfortune had wrought upon her features. Her whole head of hair had turned almost white during the transit from Varennes to Paris. She had lost the power of sleeping soundly. Wishing to have as soon as possible the consolation under her troubles which day brought to her, she would not have her shutters closed. I found all the guards, established in the most retired parts of her apartments, still in existence. A commandant of battalion usually spent the night sitting in the space between the two doors of the saloon and the bedroom. The folding doors were open on the Queen's side, and his arm-chair was placed so that he should not lose sight of her. There was even some hesitation about suffering a post-bedstead to be brought every evening near the Queen's bed for her first woman to lie upon, and it was alleged that this bedstead would prevent the commandant having his eyes directly upon that of the Queen.

The door of the room in which the Royal Family sat remained open all day, so that the guards could see them and hear what they said. The King closed it repeatedly, and it was as often immediately opened by the officer, who said to him, in an authoritative tone, "*I beg this door may not be shut;* such are my orders." One of the captains of the guard constantly passed four-and-twenty successive hours at the bottom of the dark corridor which runs behind the Queen's apartments. He had a table and two wax lights near him. This post, which was like the closest prison, was by no means sought after. Saint-Prix, an actor belonging to the Comédie Française, almost appropriated it to himself, and his conduct in it towards his unfortunate Sovereigns was always respectful and affecting. The King came to the Queen's apartments through this corridor, and the actor of the Théâtre Français often afforded the august and unfortunate couple the consolation of conversing together without any witness. To such an extent was severity carried that an officer named Collet had to get rescinded the order which enjoined him to follow the Queen to her wardrobe and to stand sentinel at the door as long as she should remain there.

The day on which I resumed my duties about the Queen she was unable to converse with me on all the lamentable events which had occurred since the time of my leaving her, having that day on guard near her an officer whom she dreaded more than all the others. She merely told me that I should have some secret services to perform for her, and that she would not create uneasiness by long conversation with me, my return being a subject of alarm. But the next day the Queen, well knowing the discretion of the officer who was to be on guard that night, had my bed placed very near hers, and having obtained the favour of having the door shut when I was in bed, she began the narrative of the journey and the unfortunate arrest at Varennes. I asked her permission to put on my gown, and, kneeling by her bedside, I remained until three o'clock in the morning listening with the liveliest and most sorrowful interest to the account I am about to repeat, and of which I have seen various details of tolerable exactness in papers of the time.

The King entrusted the Count de Fersen, who as a foreigner was exempt from national inculpations, with all the preparations for the departure. The carriage was ordered by him; the passport, in the name of Madame de Korf, was procured through his connections with that lady, who was a foreigner; and, lastly, he himself drove the Royal Family, as their coachman, as far as Bondy, where the travellers got into their berlin. Madame Brunier and Madame de Neuville, the first women of Madame and the Dauphin, there joined the principal carriage. They were in a cabriolet. Monsieur and Madame set out from the Luxembourg and took another road. They, as well as the King, were recognised by the master of the last post in France; but this man, devoting himself to the fortune of the Prince, left the French territory and drove them himself as postilion. Madame Thibaut, the Queen's first woman, reached Brussels without the slightest difficulty. Madame Gardon, from Arras, met with no hindrance, and Leonard, the Queen's hairdresser, passed through Varennes a few hours before the Royal Family. Fate had reserved all its obstacles for the unfortunate monarch.

Nothing worthy of notice occurred in the beginning of the journey. The travellers were detained a short time, about twelve leagues from Paris, by some repairs which the carriage required. The King chose to walk up one of the hills, and there two circumstances caused a delay of three hours—precisely the time when it was intended that the berlin should have been met, just before reaching Varennes, by the detachment commanded by M. Goguelat. This detachment was punctually stationed upon the spot fixed on, with orders to wait there for the arrival of a certain treasure, which it was to escort; but the peasantry of the neighbourhood, alarmed at the sight of this body of troops, came armed with staves, and asked several questions, which manifested their anxiety. M. Goguelat, fearful of causing a riot, and not finding the carriage arrive as he expected, divided his men into two companies, and unfortunately made them leave the highway in order to return to Varennes by two cross-roads.¹ The King looked out of the carriage at St. Menehould, and asked several questions concerning the road. Drouet, the postmaster, whose fatal name will long be preserved in history, struck by the forcible resemblance of Louis to the impression of his head upon the assignats, drew near the carriage, felt convinced that he recognised the Queen also, and judging that the remainder of the travellers consisted of the Royal Family and their suite, instantly mounted his horse, reached Varennes by cross-roads before the Royal fugitives, and gave the alarm.

The Queen began to feel all the agonies of terror; they were augmented by the voice of a person unknown, who, passing close to the carriage in full gallop, cried out to them, bending towards the window of their carriage, without however slackening his speed, "You are recognised!"

They arrived with beating hearts at the gates of Varennes without meeting one of the horsemen by whom they were to have been escorted into the place. They were ignorant where to find their relays; and some minutes were lost in waiting to no purpose.

---

1 Madame Campan here attributes to M. de Goguelat the steps taken by the Duke de Choiseul, the motives for which he gives in his Memoirs, p. 84.—NOTE BY THE EDITOR.

The cabriolet had preceded them, and the two ladies in attendance found the bridge already blocked up with old carts and lumber. The town-guards were all under arms. The King at last entered Varennes. M. Goguelat had arrived there with his detachment. He came up to the King and asked him *if he chose to effect a passage by force!* What an unlucky question to put to Louis XVI., who from the very beginning of the Revolution had shown, in every crisis of it, the fear he entertained of giving the least order which might cause an effusion of blood! "Would it be a brisk action?" said the King. "It is impossible that it should be otherwise, Sire," replied the aide-de-camp. Louis XVI. was unwilling to expose his family. They therefore went to the house of a grocer, mayor of Varennes. The King began to speak, and gave a summary of his intentions in departing, analogous to the declaration he had made at Paris. He spoke with warmth and affability, and endeavoured to demonstrate to the people around him that he had only put himself, by the step he had taken, into a fit situation to treat with the Assembly, and to sanction with freedom the Constitution which he would maintain, though many of its articles were incompatible with the dignity of the throne and the force by which it was necessary that the Sovereign should be surrounded. Nothing could be more affecting, added the Queen, than this moment in which the King communicated to the very humblest class of his subjects his principles, his wishes for the happiness of his people, and the motives which had determined him to depart. Whilst the King was speaking to this mayor, whose name was Sauce, the Queen, seated at the farther end of the shop, among parcels of soap and candles, endeavoured to make Madame Sauce understand that if she would prevail upon her husband to make use of his municipal authority to cover the flight of the King and his family, she would have the glory of having contributed to restore tranquillity to France. This woman was moved; she could not without streaming eyes see herself thus solicited by her Queen; but she could not be got to say anything more than, "Bless me, madam, it would be the destruction of M. Sauce. I love my King, but, by Our Lady, I love my husband too, you must know, and he would be answerable, you see." Whilst this strange and unavailing scene was passing in the shop, the people, hearing that the King was arrested, kept pouring in from all parts. M. Goguelat, making a last effort, demanded of the dragoons whether they would protect the departure of the King; they replied only by murmurs, dropping the points of their swords. Some person unknown fired a pistol at M. Goguelat; he was slightly wounded by the ball. M. Romeuf, aide-de-camp to M. de la Fayette, arrived at that moment. He had been chosen after the 6th of October, 1789, by the commander of the Parisian guard, to be in constant attendance about the Queen. She reproached him bitterly with the object of his mission. "If you wish to make your name remarkable, sir," said the Queen to him, "you have chosen strange and odious means, which will produce the most fatal consequences." This officer wished to hasten their departure. The Queen still cherishing the hope of seeing M. de Bouillé arrive with a force sufficient to extricate the King from his critical situation, prolonged her stay at

Varennes by every means in her power. The Dauphin's first woman pretended to be taken ill with a violent colic, and threw herself upon a bed in the hope of aiding the designs of her superiors; she wept and implored for assistance. The Queen understood her perfectly well, and refused to leave in such a state of suffering one who had devoted herself to follow them. But as the relief they hoped for was also apprehended by those who had arrested them, no delay in departing was allowed. The three body-guards (Valory, Dumoutier and Malden) were bound and fastened upon the seat of the carriage.

A horde of National Guards, animated with fury and the barbarous joy with which their fatal triumph inspired them, surrounded the carriage of the Royal Family.

The three commissioners sent by the Assembly to meet the King, MM. de Latour-Maubourg, Barnave and Pétion, joined them in the environs of Epernay. The two last mentioned got into the King's carriage; already the infuriated band that surrounded the illustrious victims had massacred before their eyes M. de Dampierre, a knight of St. Louis, living upon an estate in the environs of Varennes. He had hastened to pay his respects to the King; this impulse, so natural to all good Frenchmen, was punished by a cruel death. At some distance from Epernay a village priest ventured to approach the carriage, merely actuated by his desire to behold the countenance of the unfortunate monarch. He was instantly knocked down, and was about to perish in sight of the Royal Family. Shocked at these atrocious murders, Barnave darted to the window: "Are we amongst tigers?" he exclaimed. "Let that venerable old man depart unmolested. Show at this important moment the composure of a great nation worthy of winning its liberties." The old priest was saved. Madame Elizabeth, surprised and delighted with the generous emotion of Barnave, seeing him ready to throw himself out of the window, seized hold of the flap of his coat to save him from falling. Courage and humanity at that moment united the feelings of the pious daughter of the Bourbons to those of the independent plebeian who for two years had waged war upon the ancient rights of monarchy. He whose name had never been pronounced except with contempt and horror had proved himself a man of feeling; and from this time Barnave possessed an interest in the hearts of these unfortunate Princesses. They even ventured to begin to converse in a connected manner respecting the critical situation in which France and the Royal Family stood. The King, in the beginning of the discourse, notwithstanding his extreme shyness, hazarded a few remarks; but having asked what the French people would wish to attain, Pétion replied, with barbarous sincerity, "A republic, when they are so fortunate as to be ripe enough for one." From that moment the King imposed silence upon himself, which he did not once break until he reached Paris, even by monosyllables.

The deputies were invited to take some refreshment from a canteen of chicken and pastry which was in the carriage. Pétion readily accepted the offer. Madame Elizabeth poured out the wine. Pétion, doubtless in the affectation of being quite at ease, tapped his glass under the neck of the bottle to show her there was enough in it. The dignity of Barnave was offended by such gross affectation, and he would not eat anything. Being pressed by the Queen to take something, he replied, " Madam, under such solemn circumstances the deputies of the National Assembly ought to occupy the attention of Your Majesties only with their commission, and not with their wants." This line of conduct being adhered to by Barnave during the whole of the route, naturally made a favourable impression upon the minds of the Queen and Madame Elizabeth; and the Princesses had many private conversations with him at the places where the sorrowful train stopped to rest. They found him full of sense and judicious intentions, much attached to the system of a constitutional monarchy, but aware of the incalculable dangers that France would be exposed to under a republican government.

Note No. 4, Page 159.

On the Administration of the Queen's Household.

The expenses of the Queen's household were controlled by the Secretary of State, to whom the department of the King's household belonged.

The first office was that of the principal secretary for orders, in which were made out the *brevets* or titles of nomination of all the officers and ladies belonging to the establishment, and the bills known by the name of *menus* for the regulation of the expenses.

The general bill included the supplies of bread, wine, meat, wood, wax, &c., and the divers accounts comprised under this general head formed a sort of fictitious estimate of expenditure ; for instance, the bread, the wine, and the different dishes for the table were all specified, as well as the wood and charcoal, and everything else that was necessary for consumption in the household. The nature of the articles might be and was varied, but the expenditure remained the same, unless it might be in perquisites. By this means the expense of every article was so known and fixed before its consumption as not to allow of its being exceeded. Sometimes, however, articles were required, the expense of which had not been foreseen, such as some particular novelty or anything unusually rare or expensive. A separate account was kept of such things, and the cost of them was defrayed out of the perquisites.

The expenses of the stable department were provided for in the same manner by fictitious estimates which regulated the charges for liveries, equipages, and corn and hay for the horses.

For any unexpected expenses private accounts were made out, which were easily examined, as they consisted of a very few articles.

These accounts, or lists, fixed the emoluments of everyone attached to the household or connected with its supplies.

The second office, that of comptroller-general, carried into execution the orders made out from these lists, and sanctioned the use of the sum specified, and the perquisites which accrued when the expenses had not taken place.

This office was, in fact, the central point which decided and limited all the expenses, ordinary and extraordinary.

The expenses of the bed-chamber were under the regulation of the lady in superintendence, of the *dame d'honneur* and the comptroller-general of the household.

Those of the household, comprehending the kitchen and fires, were regulated by the first *maître d'hôtel*, the other *maîtres d'hôtel* and the comptroller-general.

Those of the stables by the first equerry and the comptroller-general.

By these regulations the comptroller-general became especially responsible for all that occurred.

Measures of economy were deemed advisable, and it was thought necessary to deprive the principal officers of the part assigned them in the administration of the expenses. A new office was in consequence created, under the name of commissariat-general, presided over by the comptroller-general, the minister of the King's household, and the different commissioners in the service of the King and Queen.

The Queen's household only maintained this new form two years. The original officers demanded the restoration of their ancient rights at the end of that time.

The right which the principal officers had of making out expenses which they had the power of relatively influencing for their own interests, or that of their dependents, sometimes for their old servants and always for their *protégés*, must certainly be regarded as an abuse. The principal officers had each a secretary, paid by the Queen. These secretaries had no other employment than to receive the oaths which were taken before the officers above-mentioned. The secretary of the Queen's tire-women had somewhat more to do, as that lady managed her own accounts, which she might almost be said to farm, having fixed prices for all the clothes of Her Majesty.

The different duties were fulfilled by the officers in waiting, some serving for three months together, some for six, and others in ordinary.

The Queen's council was merely nominal. The lady in superintendence and a chancellor were at its head. It sometimes met to receive accounts from the treasurer, but only as a matter of form.

The Queen had a chapel, consisting of a grand and first almoner and many others; clerks, with chaplains, preachers and attendants, serving as above stated, some quarterly and others half-yearly

The Queen had also several physicians attached to her household, to attend on her own person and likewise on those around her. These different establishments were paid from the funds of the household.

The lady in superintendence and the lady of honour presided over the bed-chamber. There were attached to it twelve honorary ladies of the bed-chamber, a *chevalier d'honneur*, gentleman in waiting and a train-bearer.

The establishment of the bed-chamber consisted of two first *femmes de chambre* and twelve others; ushers of the bed-chamber, the closet, and the ante-chamber; of *valets*, footmen and other servants of an inferior description.

It is undeniable that so many persons, the greater part of whom were unknown, must have encumbered the service rather than have been any honour to it. It may likewise be observed that the privilege of the officers to serve by three months at a time, leaving every individual at liberty to go into his province as soon as his quarter was expired, estranged him too much from the personage to whom he was attached and rendered it easy for him to magnify his own importance by inventing whatever falsehoods he might think likely to add to it. Officers in ordinary, of whom there would consequently be a sufficient number known, would have rendered the duty more agreeable and more lucrative to those who might be in the discharge of it. It is conceived that saleable places, under the name of offices, are not without inconvenience, for it is evident that through this practice many a man holds a post which would never have been assigned to him if it had not been necessary to pay for it. Even when serving by commission all who approach the King ought to be sworn, nor should this oath be regarded as a mere ceremony. Those whose offices are honourable ought to take it before their Royal master himself, and inferiors before their respective principals.

The stables are a department of the first importance, as well on account of the dignity as the expense connected with it.

The Queen's stables were governed by the first equerry; the second was an equerry *cavalcadeur*. There were twelve pages. They did not receive any salary, but their board and maintenance and education, which was a military one, were all provided for. The coachmen, postilions, &c., were under the direction of the first equerry; they wore liveries, and their expenses, like those of the bed-chamber and tables, were regulated by the lists of direction for the Queen's household, as were also the keeping and replacing of the horses, by which means the whole expenditure, or at least the greater part of it, was known beforehand, which enabled the comptroller-general to manage with ease all the regular expenses, and gave him the means of explaining more readily any which might not have been foreseen.

Many supplies were purchased by tender at the lowest price offered; as, for instance, bread, wine, meat and fish for the table, and, in general, every article of purveyorship.

It might be advisable, as a measure of economy, where there is a household comprising many separate establishments, to employ the same contractors for all of them, by which means, without adding anything to the expense of management, they might all be supplied at a much more moderate rate.

It may finally be remarked that the registers and papers of the office of comptroller-general of the Queen's household are deposited among the archives of the prefecture of the department at Versailles. They must, unavoidably, be in bad order; nevertheless, some useful information might be extracted from them.

END OF THE HISTORICAL ILLUSTRATIONS COLLECTED BY
MADAME CAMPAN

HISTORICAL ILLUSTRATIONS

AND

OFFICIAL DOCUMENTS

Note (A), Page 2.

Extract from the Memoirs of the Abbé Georgel.

THE Countess de Lamotte, who is destined to play so conspicuous a part on this stage in the drama, the lamentable scenes of which are about to be displayed, was born in Champagne, under a thatched roof and in indigent circumstances. This was either a freak of the blind goddess or the result of misfortune, for she has since proved her descent, on the side of the Counts of St. Remey, from the Royal House of Valois. D'Hozier, the genealogist, has confirmed it by his certificate. This august origin did not much ameliorate her condition. She became the wife of M. de Lamotte, a gentleman and a private gendarme. Their united resources were very limited; poverty, however, is no disgrace when it is not the result of misconduct. It was in this point of view that she presented herself before the Grand Almoner to appeal to his generosity, and at the same time to implore his good offices with the King. The Countess de Lamotte, without possessing the full splendour of beauty, was gifted with all the graces of youth, and her countenance was intelligent and attractive; she expressed herself with fluency, and the air of truth that pervaded her recitals carried persuasion along with it. It will soon be discovered that these outward attractions concealed the heart and the magic powers of a Circe.

The birth and the misfortunes of a descendant of the House of Valois excited a deep interest in the noble and compassionate breast of the Cardinal de Rohan, who would have rejoiced in placing her on a level with her ancestors, but the finances of the King did not permit him to proportion his bounty to so fair a title; he could only supply such slender support as the exigencies of the present moment demanded. This artful and insinuating woman soon imagined that the heart of her benefactor was susceptible of yet stronger impressions, which she was fully capable of inspiring in it. Gratitude and fresh wants renewed her visits and her interviews. She did not fail to remark that her presence awakened great interest in the Cardinal, who followed the impulse of his feelings. His Eminence advised her to address herself immediately to the Queen, presuming that that generous Princess would be struck by the contrast between her actual situation and her birth, and would doubtless find some means of extricating her from her painful situation. The Cardinal, in avowing that he was himself unable to procure her an interview with the Queen, in several succeeding conversations carried the excess of his confidence towards Madame de Lamotte so far as to describe to her the deep mortification he experienced in having incurred the displeasure of Her Majesty; it created, he observed, a perpetual bitterness in his soul, which poisoned his happiest moments. From this confidence arose that infernal spark which kindled into so disastrous a flame. It also gave rise to the formation of a plan of imposition, of which the annals of human credulity can furnish few parallels. The outline of the scheme was as follows: Madame de Lamotte undertook to persuade the Cardinal that she had obtained a considerable degree of intimacy with the Queen; that, influenced by the rare and excellent qualities she had discovered in the Grand Almoner, she had spoken of them so often and with so much enthusiasm to Her Majesty, that she had by degrees succeeded in removing her prejudices, and even revived in her the wish to restore her favour to the Cardinal. Her insinuations, she moreover pretended, had had so much effect that Marie Antoinette had permitted the Cardinal to address his justification to her; and, finally, had desired to have a correspondence with him in writing, which should be kept secret till the auspicious moment should arrive for the open avowal of his complete restoration to her favour. The Countess de Lamotte was to be the intermediate vehicle of this correspondence, the result of which was, undoubtedly, to place the Cardinal at the very summit of favour and influence.

Madame de Lamotte, after having increased the hopes of the Cardinal with every art and all the power of intrigue she was mistress of, at length said to him, "I am authorised by the Queen to demand of you, in writing, a justification of the faults that you are accused of." This authorisation, invented by the Countess de Lamotte and credited by the Cardinal, appeared to him the herald of an auspicious day; in a little time his apology, written by himself and couched in the fittest terms to efface the injurious impressions that so much disquieted him, was confided to Madame de Lamotte. Some days afterwards she brought an answer back to him, written on a small sheet of gilt-edged paper, in which Marie Antoinette, whose handwriting was successfully imitated, was made to say, "I have read your letter: I am rejoiced to find you not guilty. At present I am not able to grant you the audience you desire. When circumstances permit, you shall be informed of it. Remain discreet." These few words caused in the Cardinal a delirium of satisfaction, which it would be difficult to describe. Madame de Lamotte from that moment was his tutelary angel, who smoothed for him the path of happiness, and from that period she might have obtained from him whatever she could have desired.

Soon afterwards, encouraged by success, she fabricated a correspondence between the Queen and the Cardinal. The demands for money which, under different pretexts, the Queen appeared to make on the Grand Almoner in these forged letters, produced Madame de Lamotte in the whole 120,000 livres; and yet nothing could open the eyes of this credulous and immoral man to the deceit that was in this manner practised upon him.

In the meantime an unfortunate circumstance contributed to hurry the Cardinal still more unfortunately into extraordinary adventures; some monster, envious of the tranquillity of honest men, had vomited forth upon our country an enthusiastic empiric, a new apostle of the religion of Nature, who created converts in the most despotic manner, and subjected them entirely to his influence.

Some speedy cures, effected in cases that were pronounced incurable and fatal in Switzerland and Strasburg, spread the name of Cagliostro far and wide, and raised his renown to that of a truly miraculous physician. His attention towards the poor, and his contempt for the rich, imparted to his character an air of superiority and interest which excited the greatest enthusiasm. Those whom he chose to honour with his familiarity left his society in ecstasies at his transcendent qualities. The Cardinal de Rohan was at his residence at Saverne, when the Count de Cagliostro astonished Strasburg and all Switzerland with his conduct, and the extraordinary cures he had performed. Curious to behold so remarkable a personage, the Cardinal went to Strasburg; it was found necessary to use interest to be admitted to the Count. "If M. le Cardinal is sick," said he, "let him come to me, and I will cure him; if he be well, he has no business with me, nor have I with him." This reply, far from giving offence to the vanity of the Cardinal, only increased the desire he had to be acquainted with him. At length, having gained admission to the sanctuary of this new Æsculapius, he saw, as he has since declared, on the countenance of this uncommunicative man a dignity so imposing that he felt himself penetrated with religious awe, and his first words were inspired by reverence. This interview, which was very short, excited more strongly than ever the desire of a more intimate acquaintance. At length it was obtained, and the crafty empiric timed his conduct and his advances so well that at length, without seeming to desire it, he gained the entire confidence of the Cardinal, and the greatest ascendency over him. "Your soul," said he one day to the Cardinal, "is worthy of mine, and you deserve to be the confidant of all my secrets." This declaration captivated all the intellectual faculties and feelings of a man who at all times had run after the secrets of chemistry and botany.

The Baron de Planta, whom the Cardinal had employed at the time of his embassy at Vienna, also became, about the period of the history of the necklace, the most intimate confidant of his thoughts and wishes, and was one of his most accredited agents with Cagliostro and Madame de Lamotte. I remember having heard, through a certain channel, that this Baron de Planta had frequent orgies, of a very expensive nature, at the Palace of Strasburg, where, it might be said, the tokay flowed in rivers, to render the repast agreeable to Cagliostro and his pretended wife: I thought it my duty to inform the Cardinal of the circumstance. His reply was, "I know it, and I have even given him liberty to let it run to waste, if he thinks proper." This mode of expressing himself left me no doubt with respect to the enthusiasm of the Cardinal for this empiric; but I was far from believing that he had become his oracle, his guide and his compass. It was to him and to the Baron de Planta that the Cardinal revealed all that he presaged of good from his connection with Madame de Lamotte, and from the correspondence of which she was the medium.

If the Countess de Lamotte had been contented to limit herself to her first impositions, her stratagems in a little time would have been discovered, and she would have passed for an expert heroine in swindling; the credulity of the Cardinal would have furnished matter for laughter, but it would have been a mere money matter, which he who was the dupe of it would have been interested in not revealing. But when a complete absence of principle is joined to a corrupt and vitiated heart, crimes of any blackness and villainy whatsoever are only the ordinary weapons which avarice makes use of to satisfy itself. This woman, so profoundly bad, encouraged by getting 20,000 livres at the cost only of a tissue of falsehoods and a sheet of gilt-edged paper with a few letters upon it, conceived a plan the hazards and dangers of which might have checked the most determined robber. One of the Queen's jewellers had in his possession a most superb diamond necklace, worth 1,800,000 livres. Madame de Lamotte knew that the Queen, who was much pleased with it, had been unwilling, under circumstances wherein the strictest economy became an indispensable duty, to propose to the King to buy it for her. Madame de Lamotte had an opportunity of seeing this famous necklace, and Bœhmer, the jeweller, whose property it was, did not conceal from her that such an ornament being a dead article in commerce, he found it quite an encumbrance to him; that, in making the purchase of it, he had hoped to prevail on the Queen to buy it; but that Her Majesty had refused. He added that he would make a handsome present to anyone who might procure him a purchaser for it.

Madame de Lamotte had already made trial of her talents upon the credulity of His Eminence. She flattered herself that by continuing to deceive him, she might be able to appropriate both the necklace and the promised present to herself. It will be seen that she intended to persuade the Cardinal that the Queen had a great desire for this necklace; that wishing to buy it unknown to the King, and to pay for it by instalments out of her savings, she wished to give the Grand Almoner a particular proof of her goodwill, by getting him to make this bargain in her name. That for this purpose he would receive an order, written and signed by her hand, which he need not give up until the payments should be completed; that he would arrange with the jeweller to give him receipts for the amount, at different intervals, from one quarter to another, beginning from the first **payment, which could not be** made until the 30th of July, 1785; **that it** would **be essential** not to mention the Queen's name in **that** transaction, **which** was to be carried on entirely in the name of the Cardinal; **that** the secret order signed " Marie Antoinette de France " would be **quite** authority enough; and **that in giving** it **the Queen** bestowed on **His** Eminence a signal mark **of her confidence.**

Such was **the romance composed by this designing woman.** She offered **the cup of Circe to this too credulous Cardinal, and succeeded in persuading him to drink of it. Her deceptions having been hitherto so successful as to secure her from even the slightest suspicion or distrust, she boldly launched into her perilous career. The Cardinal was in Alsace. Madame de Lamotte despatched a courier through Baron de Planta, with a gilt-edged** *billet,* **in which the Queen was made to say, " The wished-for moment is not** yet **arrived, but I wish to hasten your return, on account of a** secret **negotiation which interests me personally, and** which I am unwilling **to confide to anyone except yourself. The** Countess de Lamotte **will tell you from me the meaning of this enigma."** After reading **this letter, the Cardinal longed for wings. He** arrived **most unexpectedly in a fine frost in January. His return** appeared as **extraordinary to us as his** departure **had been** precipitate. His **relations and friends little** imagined the fatal windings **of that labyrinth in which a woman,** almost unknown, had contrived **to involve the man whose eyes she** had fascinated.

The Cardinal had no sooner learnt the pretended **solution of this enigma than, delighted with** the commission **with which his Sovereign had been pleased to honour** him, he eagerly requested **to have the necessary order, so that the** necklace might be **procured with as little loss of time as possible.** The order **was not long delayed; it was dated from Trianon, and** signed **" Marie Antoinette de France." If the thickest web of** deception **had not blinded the eyes of the Cardinal, this signature** alone, so **clumsily imitated, might have shown him the snare** which awaited him. **The Queen never signed herself anything but "** Marie Antoinette **"; the words " de France" were added by the grossest** ignorance. **No remark, however, was made. Cagliostro, at that** time recently **arrived in Paris, was consulted. This Python** mounted his tripod; **the** Egyptian **invocations were made at night,** illuminated by an **immense number of wax tapers, in the Cardinal's own saloon.** The **oracle, under the inspiration of its familiar demon,** pronounced **" that the negotiation was worthy of the Prince; that** it **would be** crowned with **success; that it would raise the goodness of the** Queen **to** its height, **and bring to light that happy day which would** unfold **the** rare talents **of the Cardinal for the benefit of France** and of the **human race." I am writing facts, though it may be** imagined that **I am only relating fictions. I** should **think so myself,** were I not **certain of the statements that I** make. Be **it as it may,** the advice **of Cagliostro dissipated all the** doubts which **might** have been **inspired, and it was decided that the** Cardinal should acquit himself, **as promptly as possible, of a** commission which **was** regarded as **equally honourable and flattering.**

Everything being thus arranged, the Cardinal treated with Bœhmer and Bassange for the necklace on the conditions proposed. He did not conceal from them that it was for the Queen, and he showed them the authority under which he acted, requiring it to be kept secret from all but the Queen. The jewellers must have believed all that the Grand Almoner told and showed them, as they accepted his note, and agreed, on the 30th of January, to deliver up the necklace to him on the 1st of February, being the day of the Purification. The Countess had fixed on this day, when there was to be a grand *fête* at Versailles, as the occasion for which the Queen was anxious to have the superb ornament. The casket which contained this treasure was to be taken to Versailles that day, and carried to the house of Madame de Lamotte, whence the Queen was to be supposed to send for it. This woman, intoxicated with joy at the amazing success of her unparalleled intrigue, had chosen her own residence at Versailles as the scene of the rendering up of the necklace to a person who should come for it, commissioned in the name of the Queen to carry it to her. It was in truth a complete piece of acting. The Cardinal, to whom the time had been specified, came at dusk, on the 1st of February, to the house of Madame de Lamotte, followed by a *valet de chambre*, who carried the casket. He sent him away when he got to the door, and alone entered the place where he was to be immolated to his credulity. It was an alcoved apartment, with a closet in it, which had a glass door. The skilful actress put her spectator into this closet; the room was dimly lighted, a door opens, a voice exclaims, "From the Queen." Madame de Lamotte advances with an air of respect, takes the casket, and places it in the hands of the pretended messenger. Thus the transfer of the necklace was made. The Cardinal, a mute and hidden witness of the transaction, imagined that he knew this envoy. Madame de Lamotte told him that it was the Queen's confidential *valet de chambre* at Trianon; he wore the same garb and had much the same air. Among her different modes of deception, Madame de Lamotte had succeeded in making it appear that she had paid several visits at Trianon to the Queen, who had lavished upon her proofs of the most intimate familiarity. She often mentioned to the Cardinal the day on which she was to go, and the hour at which she was to return. His Eminence, who loved to feed his imagination on all that could nourish the idea it had taken up, often watched her setting out and coming back again. One night, when she knew that the Grand Almoner was aware of the time for her return, she got Villette, the principal agent in her schemes, to walk some way back with her, and afterwards to appear as if returning to Trianon. The Cardinal, who was in disguise, joined her, according to custom, and enquired who this person might be. She told him that it was the Queen's confidential *valet de chambre* at Trianon. At that time the necklace, so much courted, was neither bought nor delivered up; but it was thus that the prudent magician kept laying, at proper distances, the foundation stones whereon to raise and consolidate the edifice of her conjurations. This pretended *valet de chambre* was a man of the name of Villette, of Bar-sur-Aube, the friend of Madame de Lamotte and the comrade of her husband. **This woman** had initiated him into her iniquitous practices; he concurred in them, and expected to have a share in the profits that might result from them. He possessed the pernicious talent of counterfeiting the hand of the august Princess. The letters which Madame de Lamotte fabricated in the **name** of the Queen were written by him, as was also the order, signed " Marie Antoinette de France," **for** the purchase of the necklace.

The Cardinal, **having scrutinised the** features **of** the **man into whose** hands the **casket was delivered,** and imagining that he **recognised in them** those **of the pretended** *valet de chambre* at Trianon, **who had** accompanied **Madame de Lamotte one** evening **on** her way **home, had** no doubt **of the necklace being** safely conveyed to its **place of** destination.

Thus did this intriguing **woman attain her ends; and such ascendency** had she gained over **the mind of the Cardinal that, from the time** of the necklace **being given up, His Eminence incessantly** pressed the jewellers **to obtain an interview of the Queen, in** order that they might make **themselves easy respecting the purchase** he had negotiated for her. **This fact, the truth of which has been** proved beyond the possibility **of denial, by the evidence of** Bœhmer and Bassange in **court,** ought **to remove every doubt as to the sincerity of the** Cardinal, **and the** entire **persuasion he acted under that he was only** obeying the orders of the Queen. **How shall I conceal, in this** place, a fact which I would **yet** willingly **omit, but which is too** essentially connected with the consequences **of this unfortunate affair to** be passed over in silence? The **jewellers, who had often access to** the Queen on business, and were, moreover, pressed **by the Cardinal** to speak of it, took care not to leave her in ignorance **of the** negotiation and sale of the **necklace.** Notwithstanding **the writing** signed " Marie Antoinette **de France,"** which had been shown **to them;** notwithstanding the **responsibility** of the Cardinal, **who had given his** note for it, it **was** important **to** their interest **to assure** themselves that this **necklace** was **for Her Majesty, and not to** risk a thing of so **much** value on the least uncertainty.[1] **This** fact is not admitted **by MM.** Bœhmer and Bassange in **the** *proceedings;* but they **secretly** acknowledged it to one, **who** revealed it to me only on **condition that** his **name should in** no way be brought in or compromised in the affair. **The Cardinal,** in his defence, appeared never **to have any** doubt **on the subject.**[2] Bassange, being at Bâle in 1797

---

[1] Compare this passage **with the** accounts contained in the twelfth chapter **of** the Memoirs of Madame Campan.—NOTE BY THE EDITOR.

[2] In the Memoirs of Madame Campan it is shown in how obscure, doubtful, **and** unintelligible a manner the jeweller Bœhmer explained himself the first **time on** the subject of the necklace; and what was the surprise, the indignation **and the wrath** of the Queen when she was made to understand the odious nature **of the intrigue** in which her name was introduced. *The secret disclosure was made, it is said, to a person who only revealed it on condition that his name should in no way be brought in or compromised in the affair.* This disclosure, received by **an anonymous** person, can scarcely be sufficient **to** overthrow the regular and **circumstantial** details of Madame Campan. If the **Queen** only understands the

and questioned by me on this matter, did not deny it, and formally confessed that his depositions, and those of his companion in this suit, had been regulated by the direction of the Baron de Breteuil; that they had not, indeed, indiscriminately followed everything that had been desired of them, but that they were obliged to be silent on what he was not willing they should declare themselves. After such an assurance, how can we attempt to justify the Queen from a connivance little suitable either to her principles or her rank?

So shameless a manœuvre as that of Madame de Lamotte, in which the name of the Queen was introduced only to commit with still more impunity and boldness a fraud of such magnitude, ought to have shocked the delicacy and probity of this Princess. How was it that, at this moment, her indignation did not burst forth? If the Queen had only followed the first dictates of her wounded feelings, she would surely have apprised the jewellers that they had been deceived, and that they must take their precautions accordingly. Even supposing that the Queen wished to be revenged on the Cardinal and to ruin him, what had already passed, and what she had just heard, was more than sufficient to compel him to give up his place, to leave Court and to retire to his diocese. The Queen would have done an act of justice for which no one could have condemned her; the Grand Almoner would have been justly blamed for his credulity; the House of Rohan would have been grieved at his disgrace, but could not have opposed it, there would have been no shameful publicity, no criminal suit, no Bastille. Marie Antoinette, if left to her own inclinations, would surely have acted with this sincerity; but she suffered herself to be influenced by two men, who equally led her astray, though each from different motives.

[The Abbé Georgel here flatters himself that he proves the Queen to have consulted the Abbé de Vermond and the Baron de Breteuil (which is true), and that they suffered the Cardinal to fall more and more deeply into the snare, and continued him in his error, to ruin him entirely (which is false, as is proved by the Memoirs of Madame Campan). She left Versailles on the 1st of August; on the 3rd, Bœhmer went to see her at her country house. It was not until the 6th or 7th that the Queen was certainly informed of the matter, and on the 15th the Cardinal was arrested. Are any of the perfidious delays imagined by the Abbé Georgel to be formed in this rapid progress of things? This remark on our part is solely prompted by a love of truth, and not by any desire to save the Queen from the reproach of dissimulation, which, after all, does not attach to her, as Georgel only accuses the Abbé de Vermond and the Baron de Breteuil of these preconcerted delays. The *dénouement* of this scandalous business was hastened by another circumstance.]

---

former declarations of Bœhmer from a tardy and unexpected communication; if her resentment bursts out immediately on her acquaintance with it; what becomes of the supposition made by the Abbé Georgel, of a plan, conducted with coolness and deliberation, and for a considerable period, to lead the Cardinal deeper and deeper into the snare, to surprise him and to destroy him?—NOTE BY THE EDITOR.

As it wanted not more than six or seven weeks to the 30th of July, the day fixed upon for the first payment of 100,000 crowns by the Cardinal, whose presence was necessary for the payment, he was summoned in the course of the month of June. He came with the eagerness of a man who believes himself on the point of obtaining the end of his wishes. He was assured, in a little *billet*, that everything was arranged for the accomplishment of his desire, and that he would now see the effect of the Queen's promises; it was adroitly added that measures were being taken for making up the sum for the first payment; that some unforeseen events had thrown obstacles in the way of so doing, but that it was hoped, nevertheless, that no delay would occur.

The ensuing assemblies at Cagliostro's, in the meantime, were delightful; all was a joyful anticipation of the happy day when the Queen was to crown the good fortune of the Grand Almoner. Madame de Lamotte alone was in possession of a secret of a contrary nature. Saint-James, a proselyte of Cagliostro's, was admitted into those evening parties by the advice of this woman, for which she had her own reasons. She one day said to the Cardinal, "I see the Queen is greatly perplexed about this 100,000 crowns for the 30th of July. She does not write to you for fear of making you uneasy concerning it; but I have thought of a way for you to pay your court to her by setting her at ease. Write to Saint-James; 100,000 crowns will appear nothing to him when he is given to understand that it is to render the Queen a service. Profit by the enthusiasm which the attention that you and Count Cagliostro lavish upon him have inspired. The Queen will not discountenance it; speak in her name. The success of this new negotiation can only add to the interest she already takes in you.' The Cardinal thanked Madame de Lamotte for her good advice. He then thought to secure the goodwill of Saint-James by relating to him, with an air of confidence, all that had passed regarding the purchase of the necklace. He showed him the order signed "Marie Antoinette de France"; he likewise confided to him the Queen's embarrassment, and assured him that an infallible way to merit her protection would be to take upon himself the making of the first payment to the jeweller. Saint-James, like all upstarts, was more anxious for consequence than for money; he had wished to obtain the *cordon rouge* by some place or office, but he had not been able to succeed. The Cardinal promised it him, in the name of the Queen, as a recompense for the service she asked him. The financier replied, "that he looked upon himself as extremely fortunate in being able to give Her Majesty proofs of his unbounded devotion to her, and that, as soon as he should be honoured with her orders she might make herself perfectly easy with respect to the 100,000 crowns for the first payment." The Grand Almoner informed Madame de Lamotte of the favourable answer of Saint-James, and likewise gave an account of it in the first letter which he sent to the Queen through her hands. The forger who framed the answers was absent. M. de Lamotte had returned from London and had sent for him to Bar-sur-Aube, where these skilful sharpers concerted together the precautions that it was necessary to adopt in order to establish their fortunes out of the spoil of the necklace. The delay of the anxiously-expected answer from the Queen tormented the Cardinal. He communicated his uneasiness to Madame de Lamotte; he could not conceive the motive for maintaining this silence as the time for payment approached. He feared, moreover, that Saint-James might suspect him of a design to impose upon him; he added, with infinite chagrin, that what he still less comprehended was the unabating coldness of the Queen towards him outwardly, in spite of the warm and lively interest breathed for him in her letters. This last observation was a subject of daily complaint with the Cardinal after his return from Alsace. Till then Madame de Lamotte had always been able to calm, by different stratagems, these suggestions of anxiety. The diabolical genius of this woman, fruitful in expedients, undertook to put an end at once to these doubts, so perpetually renewing. She bethought her of a new method of still further abusing the Cardinal's credulity, by which she hoped to make him exert himself to the utmost to complete the first payment for the necklace, either by himself, or through M. de Saint-James. This fresh villainy required preliminaries and preparations. Meanwhile the forger Villette returned from Bar-sur-Aube, and the long-expected answer from Marie Antoinette was immediately put into the hands of the Cardinal. The Queen, it was said in the letter, would not so long have delayed her reply had she not hoped to have been able to dispense with the good offices of M. de Saint-James; that she would accept them for the first payment only, with the promise of a speedy reimbursement to him, adding, that she should wish M. de Saint-James to furnish her with an early opportunity of showing her sense of his services. Some days elapsed before the Cardinal could communicate this answer to Saint-James. In the interval, Madame de Lamotte, in concert with her husband and Villette, had arranged everything for the performance of a farce, the plan and execution of which displayed the most diabolical invention. She undertook to make the Cardinal believe that the Queen, not being able to give him the public proofs of her esteem which she could wish, would grant him an interview in the groves of Versailles between eleven and twelve o'clock, and that she could then assure him of that restoration to her favour which she was not at liberty to write. These happy tidings were effectually conveyed in a little gilt-edged note; it appointed the night and hour for meeting; never was interview more eagerly anticipated.

The Countess de Lamotte had remarked in the promenades of the Palais Royal at Paris a girl of a very fine figure, whose profile was extremely like the Queen's, and her she fixed on as principal actress in the grove. Her name was d'Oliva, and she had been made to believe that the part she undertook to perform was at the desire of the Queen, who had some plan of amusement in it. The reward offered on this occasion was not refused by a creature who made a traffic of her charms, and she undertook to act the part assigned her.

Mademoiselle d'Oliva accordingly proceeded to Versailles, conducted by M. de Lamotte, in a hired carriage, the coachman belonging to which has been examined in evidence. She was led to inspect the scene of action to which she was to be secretly conveyed by M. de Lamotte. There she was made to rehearse the part she was expected to perform. She was given to understand that she would be accosted by a tall man in a blue riding-coat, with a large flat hat, who would approach and kiss her hand with the utmost respect; and that she was to say to him, in a low tone of voice, "I have but a moment to spare; I am satisfied with your conduct, and I shall speedily raise you to the pinnacle of favour"; that she was then to present him with a small box and a rose, and immediately afterwards, at the noise of persons who should approach, to observe, still in a low voice, "Madame and Madame d'Artois are coming; we must separate." The grove and the place of entrance agreed on had been also pointed out to the Cardinal, with the assurance that he might in that place pour out without restraint his sentiments of loyal devotion, and explain his feelings in what most concerned his interests; and that, as a pledge of her good intentions towards him, the Queen would present him with a case containing her portrait, and a rose. It was well known at Versailles that the Queen was in the habit of walking in the evening with Madame and the Countess d'Artois in the grove. The appointed night arrived: the Cardinal, dressed as agreed on, repaired to the terrace of the château with the Baron de Planta; the Countess de Lamotte, in a black domino, was to come and let him know the precise time when the Queen was to enter the grove. The evening was sufficiently dark; the appointed hour glided away; Madame de Lamotte did not appear; the Cardinal became anxious; when the lady in the black domino came to meet him, saying, "I have just left the Queen—everything is unfavourable—she will not be able to give you so long an interview as she desired. Madame and the Countess d'Artois have proposed to walk with her. Hasten to the grove; she will leave her party, and, in spite of the short interval she may obtain, will give you unequivocal proofs of her protection and goodwill." The Cardinal hastened to the appointed scene, and Madame de Lamotte and the Baron de Planta retired to await his return. The scene was played as it had been arranged by Madame de Lamotte; the pretended Queen, in an evening *déshabillé*, bore a striking resemblance in figure and dress to the personage she was to represent. The Cardinal in approaching her testified emotion and respect; the false Queen, in a low voice, pronounced the words that had been dictated to her, and presented the box; in the meantime, as had been agreed, the noise as of persons approaching was made, and it became necessary to part somewhat abruptly. The Cardinal went to rejoin Madame de Lamotte and the Baron de Planta; he complained bitterly of the vexatious interruption which had shortened an interview so interesting and delightful for him. They then separated. The Cardinal appeared fully persuaded that he had spoken with the Queen, and had received the box from her hands. Madame de Lamotte congratulated herself on the success of her scheme. Mademoiselle d'Oliva, interested in keeping the part she had played secret, was conveyed back to Paris and well rewarded for her address. M. de Lamotte and M. Villette, who had counterfeited the voices and the approaching footsteps agreed on to abridge the interview, joined Madame de Lamotte, and everyone rejoiced at the successful issue. The next day a little *billet*, brought by the ordinary messenger, expressed great regret at the obstacles which had prevented a longer conversation.

Whatever the illusion might be that had so constantly blinded the Cardinal, the unimpassioned reader will scarcely believe that a Prince endowed with so much intelligence and good sense never entertained, for more than a year that this system of intrigue lasted, the slightest suspicion of the snare that was laid for him; and if it did enter his mind, why did he not put every method in force to throw a light on the behaviour and steps of his conductress? The Queen still evincing a perfect estrangement towards the Cardinal, how could he possibly reconcile this mode of treatment with the sentiments which were contained in the little *billets* he received, wherein the most unequivocal protection and the greatest interest and kindness were expressed?

This inconceivable contrast ought at least to have been the dawn of the day which should throw a light on the diabolical scheme to which he was a victim. The Cardinal acknowledges that, impelled by a boundless desire to be restored to the favour of the Queen, he always rushed with impetuosity towards the object that promised to effect his purpose, without considering the nature of the path he was made to tread. However that might be, the adventure of the grove, and the little *billet* the next morning, had given new energy to the zeal which entirely engrossed him for the interests and tranquillity of the Queen, whom he believed to be embarrassed respecting the first payment for the necklace. The return of the financier Saint-James hastened, without the Cardinal's expecting it, the *dénouement* of the intrigue which was about to involve him in endless disgrace and vexation. The Cardinal having met with this financier at Cagliostro's, did not fail to communicate to him the new orders which he imagined he had received.

[It would be needless to prolong this extract already sufficiently extended. The latter scenes and the catastrophe of this piece are well known; but we had to fulfil our promise, in page 2, to make our readers acquainted with the principal actors in this drama, who were left unnoticed by Madame Campan. We ought, nevertheless, before we finish, to make mention of one individual to whom the Cardinal, always the dupe of error, at length owed the discovery of the means which had been put in practice to fascinate his eyes as well as to deceive his judgment.]

"A certain Abbé de Juncker, a sensible and well-informed man, came," says the Abbé Georgel, "to offer his services. I felt a confidence in him because he seemed anxious for the honour and interest of the Cardinal. He it was who gave me the first idea through which the diabolical intrigue of Madame de Lamotte came to be unmasked. A monk called Father Loth had come to inform him that, urged by his conscience and by gratitude to the Grand Almoner for services he had rendered him, he was anxious to make the most important disclosures; that having lived on intimate terms with Madame de Lamotte he could no longer be silent. This man was proctor to the monks at La Place Royale, which the house of Madame de Lamotte adjoined. This woman had found means to inspire him with pity in her moments of want and distress. He often relieved her; and his kindness had at length induced her to communicate to him the particulars of her good fortune, which she attributed to the Queen and to the Cardinal. Being soon on terms of great intimacy, Father Loth saw at the house of Madame de Lamotte many things that excited his suspicions.

"A few words which her vanity and indiscretion had let fall; the boast of a considerable present from the Court jewellers, on account of her expecting to procure them a purchaser for their valuable necklace; the display of some superb diamonds, which she pretended to have had from Marie Antoinette; the communication of *billets*, which she declared to be from the Queen to the Cardinal, and from the Cardinal to the Queen; the comparison which Father Loth had taken the trouble to make between the writing of these *billets* and other writings of one M. de Villette, the friend of Madame de Lamotte, who was often shut up writing with her and her husband; the compliments which he had heard Madame de Lamotte pay a tall, beautiful woman of the name of d'Oliva, respecting the success of some part she had played in the garden of Versailles; the perplexities which had spread confusion and alarm throughout the house of this intriguing woman, in the early part of August; the declaration made in his presence that Bœhmer and Bassange would be the ruin of the Cardinal; the precipitate flight of Villette, and of M. and Madame de Lamotte, at that period— such were the details which Father Loth came to confide to me one evening between eleven and twelve, after disguising himself at the house of the Abbé de Juncker, in order that he might not be suspected, should his judicial deposition be found necessary. This monk, wishing to have the title of preacher to the King in his Order, had requested to preach the sermon of Pentecost before His Majesty The Grand Almoner had spoken to me, to examine his discourse and his delivery. I was not satisfied with it, and I gave it as my opinion that he should not preach; but I was not aware that Madame de Lamotte, who protected him, was desirous that this favour should be granted him, and that the Cardinal, yielding to the entreaties of this patroness, had procured Father Loth a well-written sermon, which he delivered with tolerable propriety.

"Amongst the particulars which I have just related, Father Loth, during the three hours' conversation I had with him, gave much important information respecting M. de Villette; and some fragments of the writings of this M. de Villette, which, he assured me, greatly resembled that of the pretended *billets* from the Queen. He assured me also that he had surprised Madame de Lamotte, the evening before her departure, burning those that she had told him were from the Queen. The monk, in speaking to me of this Mademoiselle d'Oliva, recollected the time when she was taken by M. de Lamotte to Versailles in a hired carriage; in short, he added, in such a manner as led me to suspect that he did not tell me all he knew, that he had strong reasons for believing that the Countess de

Lamotte had imposed on the credulity of the Cardinal to obtain very considerable sums from him, and even to appropriate the necklace to herself. This important communication did not yet amount to certainty; but it was like the first blush of morn, which, dissipating the thick clouds of night, announces the brightness of a fine day." ("Memoirs of the Abbé Georgel," vol. ii.)

We shall now borrow from another work the details relative to the trial:

The Cardinal was closely guarded in his apartments at Versailles. He was brought to his hotel in Paris in the afternoon, and remained there until the next day. The carriage was escorted by body-guards, and M. d'Agoult, aide-major-general, had orders not to lose sight of the prisoner, and to sleep in the same room with him.

On the evening of this transaction the Marquis de Launay, Governor of the Bastille, came to lodge His Eminence in the same prison, where several victims of ministerial despotism were groaning. The Cardinal wished to go thither on foot, under cover of the night; the favour was readily granted. On the following day, August 17th, he was sent in a carriage to the Cardinal's palace, to be present at the breaking of the seals, at which all the ministers assisted, except Marshal Ségur. M. de Rohan, looking on M. de Breteuil as his personal enemy, had required this formality; and the Baron de Breteuil had complied the more willingly as he had declared that his own sense of delicacy would not permit him to acquit himself of his ministerial duty in any manner other than publicly, and in the presence of respectable witnesses.

Doubtless, no proofs appeared of the secret crimes ascribed to the Cardinal, since nothing of that kind transpired, and no trace of it is to be found in the proceedings. The Cardinal had permission to see his friends in the hall of the Bastille. He was allowed to retain, out of all his numerous retinue, two *valets de chambre* and a secretary; this last favour showed him that he was to have the privilege of writing, at least for the purposes of his defence. He was treated in every other respect with much consideration, and his situation was rendered as tolerable as it could be in such a fortress.

This lenient treatment contributed greatly to the courage and resignation which the Cardinal almost invariably displayed.

The Abbé Georgel, grand vicar to the Grand Almoner, on whose papers seals were likewise put, testified as little uneasiness as the Cardinal. "Authority must be respected," said he; "but we may, nevertheless, enlighten it."

Madame de Lamotte, wishing to gratify at once her hatred and revenge, declared on her first examination that the Count de Cagliostro was the contriver of the fraud of the necklace; that he had persuaded the Cardinal to purchase it. She insinuated that it was taken to pieces by this Italian or Sicilian Count and his wife, and that they alone reaped the profit of it. This declaration, supported by a thousand other falsehoods, which, unfortunately, however absurd, wore but too great an appearance of probability, caused the singular personage implicated in it to be sent to the Bastille, along with the woman who resided with him. The latter remained there nearly eight months, and the pretended Count did not come out until after the suit was decided.

It is certain that Cardinal de Rohan was credulous enough to place the greatest confidence in this empirical alchemist, who had assured him that it was possible to make gold and to transmute small diamonds into large precious stones; but he only cheated the Cardinal out of large sums, under pretence of revealing to him the rarest secrets of the Rosicrucians and other madmen, who have implicitly believed, or pretended to believe, the absurd folly of the philosopher's stone, the elixir of life, &c. Thus the Cardinal saw part of his money evaporate in the smoke of crucibles, and part found its way into the pockets of the sharper, who passed himself off to him as a great alchemist.

When this person was examined by the court touching the affair of the necklace, he made his appearance before the magistrates dressed in green, embroidered with gold; his locks were curled from the top of his head, and fell in little tails down his shoulders, which gave him a most singular appearance, and completed his resemblance to a mountebank. "Who are you? Whence came you?" he was asked. "I am a noble traveller," was his reply. At these words, every countenance relaxed, and seeing this appearance of good-humour, the accused entered boldly on his defence. He interlarded his jargon with Greek, Arabic, Latin and Italian; his looks, his gestures, his vivacity, were as amusing as his speech. He withdrew, very well pleased with having made his judges laugh.

The Cardinal had sometimes permission to walk after dinner upon the platform of the towers of the Bastille, accompanied by an officer. He wore a brown great-coat with a round hat. The Court issued a decree to detain the persons of the Cardinal and the other parties. The fraud of the necklace was not the motive which determined this decree against the Cardinal de Rohan, but the forgery of the Queen's signature. It was concluded that, as soon as the true author of the forgery was discovered, all the rigour of the sentence would fall on him. On the 21st of December this decree, more frightful in imagination than really formidable, was made known to the Cardinal. He was so much affected by it that he suffered an attack of nephritic colic, to which he was subject.

The examinations were vigorously pursued. The commissioner, a councillor of Parliament,[1] repaired for this purpose to the fortress of the Bastille. On one occasion he detained the Cardinal from nine in the morning until one o'clock, and afterwards from four till midnight. It is necessary to state the etiquette observed by Prince Louis de Rohan, and that observed towards him on these days of sitting. On the appointed day he put on his State dress, his red hood, red stockings, and all the insignia of his dignity. The governor of the Bastille came to lead him from his apartment, conducted him to the door of the council chamber, left him with the magistrate and other official persons, and remained in attendance in the ante-chamber. When the judge wanted anything he

---

[1] M. Depuis de Macé.

rang. The Marquis de Launay immediately presented himself; and if a glass of water or anything else was asked for, he carried it himself to the door, where the magistrate came to meet him. After the sitting, the governor took charge of his prisoner at the very door of the council chamber, and conducted him back to his apartment.

It has been pretended that the all-powerful family of the Cardinal had so suborned the judge and the notary, that they altered the sense of the depositions and examinations, and that when they were fearful of the Cardinal involving himself in his replies, and saying something that would militate against his cause, they suddenly broke up the sitting, without even waiting for the conclusion of a sentence already begun.

The following extract, from the voluminous Memoirs of Madame de Lamotte, may be brought in support of the assertion. We quote her own words: "One day, the Cardinal and I, being confronted upon a delicate point, which neither of us had any intention to throw light upon, I said something not exactly conformable to truth. "Ah, madam," cried the Cardinal, "how can you advance what you know to be false?" "As everyone else does, sir. You know very well that neither you nor I have told a single word of truth to these gentlemen since they have begun to interrogate us." "It was not, in fact, possible," said this woman, whose testimony ought to be estimated at its proper value; "our answers were prepared for us, as well as our questions, and we were obliged to say or reply this or that, or expect to be murdered in the Bastille."

The deposition of the Countess du Barry forms an interesting anecdote in this curious affair. She came into Court in the evening of the 7th of December, where she was received with all the honours due to persons of the first quality. The notary went to hand her in, and one of the ushers carried the torch. She was conducted back again with the same respectful formalities. Her deposition turned on the following circumstances. Madame de Lamotte called one day, after the death of Louis XV., on the Countess du Barry, to offer her services as a companion.

When she declared her name and birth, Madame du Barry regarded her as unfit for the situation she came to solicit, and, thanking her, assured her that she did not wish for society, and that, moreover, she was not such a great lady herself as to take a lady of Madame de Valois' elevated rank for her companion. The latter was not quite disheartened by this polite repulse. She went again some days after; but she limited herself to begging that Madame du Barry would recommend her to some persons who might lay one of her petitions before the King. In this petition she entreated an augmentation of her pension. She had signed the words *de France* after her name. The Countess du Barry could not help showing her surprise at the sight of the signature. Madame de Lamotte replied to her remark, that as she was known to belong to the House of Valois, she always signed herself *de France*. Madame du Barry smiled at her presumption, and promised to get the petition recommended.

As long as the Countess de Lamotte saw none of her accomplices arrested, she flattered herself that the Cardinal and Cagliostro would be the victims of her fraud. But Mademoiselle d'Oliva, the principal actress in the park scene, being taken at Brussels, where she had sought refuge, began to draw aside the veil with which the Countess had hitherto covered her intrigues.

To crown her misfortunes, and insure her the punishment she deserved, Retaux de Villette suffered himself to be taken at Geneva. He was conveyed to the Bastille and confronted with the perfidious De Lamotte, who was struck as by a thunderbolt at the unexpected sight. She was now convinced that she was lost, notwithstanding her natural effrontery.

The prisoners who were detained in the Bastille on account of the necklace were transferred to the Conciergerie about midnight on the 29th of August, 1786, by an officer of the Court. The Cardinal was confined under the guard of the King's lieutenant of the Bastille, in the chambers of the chief notary. So true it is that the justice of that day had the most profound respect for birth and titles.

The examinations lasted from six in the morning until half-past four in the afternoon.

When Madame de Lamotte appeared before the assembled Grand Council she was elegantly dressed, as she had been all the time she was in prison. This audacious woman, being sent for by the judges, often repeated that "she was going to confound a great rogue." At the sight of the august assembly her confidence somewhat abandoned her; above all, when the usher said to her, in a severe tone, pointing out the stool for the accused, "Madam, seat yourself there," she started back in affright; but on the order being given a second time, she took the ill-omened seat, and in less than two minutes she recovered herself so well, and her countenance was so composed, that she appeared as if reclining in her own room upon the most elegant sofa.

She replied with firmness to all the questions of the first president. Being interrogated afterwards by the Abbé Sabathier, one of the ecclesiastical councillors whom she knew to be unfavourable to her, "That is a very insidious question," said she; "I expected you would put it to me, and I shall now reply to it." After extricating herself with sufficient address from many other questions, she made a long speech with so much presence of mind and energy that she at least astonished her judges, if she could not succeed in interesting or convincing them. As soon as she had retired, the first president ordered the stool to be removed, and sent to inform the Cardinal that the stool having been taken out of the chamber he might present himself before the Court.

The Cardinal was habited in a long violet-coloured robe (which colour is mourning for Cardinals); he wore his red hood and stockings, and was decorated with his Orders. It would seem that, whether innocent or not, his courage forsook him in the trying moment of his standing forth accused. His emotion was evident; he was extremely pale and his knees bent under him; five or six voices, probably proceeding from members gained over to his side, observed that the Cardinal appeared to be ill, and that he ought to be allowed to sit, to which d'Aligre, the first president, replied, "His Eminence the Cardinal is at liberty to sit down if he wishes it." The illustrious accused profited by this permission, and seated himself at the end of the bench where the examiners sit when they attend the grand chamber. Having soon recovered himself, he replied extremely well to the questions of the first president; afterwards, still remaining seated, he spoke with abundance of feeling for about half an hour, with emphasis and dignity, and repeated his protestations respecting the whole proceedings against him. His speech being finished, he bowed to the bench and the other magistrates. Everyone returned his salute, and those on the bench even got up, which was a peculiar mark of distinction.

Mademoiselle d'Oliva was afterwards summoned; the usher of the court came to say that as she was aware she should be obliged to be separated from her infant for some hours, she was that instant engaged in suckling it, and prayed the court to grant her a moment's delay. The voice of law was silent before that of nature, and it was agreed that she should be waited for.

Only the Cardinal and Cagliostro returned to the Bastille. M. de Rohan had in his coach the governor and an officer of the ministerial prison. The Marquis de Launay gave the order to set off, and said *à l'hôtel* instead of using the word *Bastille*.

On the 31st, the day fixed for the final decision of this singular and famous trial, after more than a year of proceedings and delays, the judges met at a quarter before six in the morning. They were sixty-two in number, but were reduced to forty-nine by the retiring of the ecclesiastical councillors on account of its being a question which involved corporal punishment.

At two o'clock the voting magistrates left off to take their dinner at a table with forty covers that the chief president had ordered to be prepared in the hall of St. Louis; but the greater part dined without sitting down, and at half-past three the court resumed its session.

At length, a little after nine in the evening, the decision of the court was made known, as follows:

1st. The instrument, which is the foundation of the suit, with the approvals and annexed signatures, are declared forgeries and falsely attributed to the Queen.

2nd. De Lamotte, being in contumacy, is condemned to the galleys for life.

3rd. Madame de Lamotte to be whipped, branded on the two shoulders with the letter V., and shut up in l'Hôpital for life

4th. Retaux de Villette banished the kingdom for life.

5th. Mademoiselle d'Oliva discharged.

6th. Cagliostro acquitted.

7th. The Cardinal acquitted of all suspicion. The injurious accusations against him contained in the memorial of Madame de Lamotte suppressed.

8th. The Cardinal is allowed to cause the judgment of the court to be printed.

The next day the court received an order for delay of execution. The Court of Versailles was much displeased with the sentence; it had hoped that the Cardinal would have been declared guilty, and the sentence passed on the Countess de Lamotte much less severe. It was likewise observed that the court had proceeded with so much severity against this female, a descendant from the House of Valois, in order to mortify, to the utmost of their power, the reigning branch of the Bourbons. The King was desirous to inspect all the writings belonging to the suit, but they only sent him copies of them.

The court, after a few days' delay, was allowed to execute its sentence with respect to the Countess de Lamotte, then in prison. She was informed one morning that her presence was required at the palace. Surprised at this intelligence (for she had for some time been refused permission to speak to anyone), she replied that she had passed a restless night, and desired to be left quiet. The gaoler replied that her counsel was waiting. "I can see him, then, to-day?" she asked, and immediately rose, slipped on a loose robe, and followed. Being brought before her judge, the clerk pronounced her sentence; immediately astonishment, fear, rage and despair pervaded her whole soul, and threw her into agitations difficult to describe. She had not strength to hear the whole of the speech addressed to her; she threw herself on the ground, and uttered the most violent shrieks. It was with the greatest difficulty that she could be removed into the palace-yard. It was scarcely six in the morning, and but few persons were present to witness the execution of her sentence.

No sooner did the Countess perceive the instruments of her punishment than she seized one of the executioners by the collar, and bit his hand in such a manner as to take a piece out; fell upon the ground, and suffered more violent convulsions than ever. It was necessary to tear off her clothes to imprint the hot iron upon her shoulders as well as they could. Her cries and imprecations redoubled; at length they took her into a coach, and conveyed her to l'Hôpital.

Madame de Lamotte found means to escape from l'Hôpital after ten months' confinement, which was effected either through her having gained over some sister of the house, or through the connivance of the Government. This last opinion may be correct, if it be true that her flight was permitted on condition that M. de Lamotte should not publish in London his account of the trial, which, it is said, he threatened to do unless his wife should be restored to him.

However that may be, a pun was made when Madame de Lamotte suddenly disappeared, which shows that no better conduct was expected of her than her life had hitherto displayed. It is said that the sister, who contrived her escape, said to her at parting: "Adieu, madam; take care you are not re-marked."—("Anecdotes of the Reign of Louis XVI.," vol. i. [We must add that the inventor of this story must have had a great rage for miserable puns to make one on such a subject.]

Note (B), Page 19.

The clergy then assembled embraced this opportunity to assert its rights. The Archbishop of Narbonne delivered a speech before the Assembly, which contained the following passages:

"My Lords and Gentlemen—No one among us is unaware of the misfortune that the Cardinal de Rohan has had, to incur the displeasure of the King. Without doubt, we have reason to fear that his guilt has been great, since His Majesty has thought proper to arrest him in a public manner, to secure his person and his papers. Of whatever nature his crime may be, we do not hesitate to say beforehand that we regard it with abhorrence. But the Cardinal de Rohan is both a Cardinal and a Grand Almoner, as well as Bishop of the Empire. This latter title, which is common to ourselves and to him, imposes on us the obligation to claim the observance of the law and regulations which prescribe that a bishop must be tried by those of his own rank. God forbid that by so doing we should pretend to render our order exempt from punishment and seduce it from the obedience due to the King!

"We profess and we teach that the power of our Kings is independent. We firmly maintain that our consecration to the service of the altar transfers to no other earthly potentate the allegiance imposed on us at our birth. It is far from our intention to claim privileges which may be incompatible with these fundamental truths; we confidently demand those which the laws, our monarchs and the nation have transmitted to us. We shall find them in the same source from which those of the peers, the nobility and the officers of Court are derived."

According to the principles contained in this harangue, the clergy composed a memorial and wrote an eloquent letter to the King, in which were the following passages:

"To a reverence for religion we owe the privileges accorded to its ministers; that of personal immunity, granted to the bishops in cases of trial, has been found conformable to the principles of the French; that every accused person should be judged by his peers. Are any alarming results expected from our exercise of this right? We are averse from establishing among the members of our body either the idea of impunity or that of independence."

Note (C), Page 24.

M. de Vergennes found himself surrounded and watched by two parties in opposition to his principles and operations, who continually endeavoured to prevent his assuming the tone necessary for the Department of Foreign Affairs. Richelieu and D'Aiguillon's party, though humbled by the fall of the latter and by the return of the Parliament, was still powerful at Court. This party disapproved of the *quietism* of M. de Vergennes, and pursued the minister with ridicule, sarcasm and the most atrocious accusations. Whatever might be the conduct of the minister, he perpetually saw before him one and frequently two parties who disapproved his measures; sometimes he was attacked on all sides, whilst throughout Europe there was not one of his treaties, nor one of his negotiations or plans, that was not opposed by some powerful interest, as generally happens in the political operations of a State so powerful as that of France.

In this situation M. de Vergennes found himself obliged to treat with every system, and to manœuvre with every party, to avoid a Continental war; and, above all—the precipice towards which almost every minister is hurried when he declares war, or suffers it to be declared—M. de Vergennes adhered tenaciously to his place. It was said *he has made a vow to die minister.* It was the principal fault in his administration. Had he possessed more decision of character, M. de Vergennes would have imitated the policy of Richelieu, and declared war upon Austria on the first insult she might indulge in, as she had ventured to do in the affairs of Cologne, Bavaria and the Scheldt. But the courage of M. de Vergennes was not equal to embarking on so stormy a sea.

Note (D), Page 27.

Ever since 1752 M. de Loménie had resolved to distinguish himself—not, however, by science, or by that piety and reserve appropriate to his profession, but by the boldness and novelty of his opinions. Philosophy was yet in its dawn when he rendered himself conspicuous by the celebrated dispute he maintained in the Sorbonne, less as a theologian than as a materialist. He rejected the innate idea or knowledge of a Divinity; he ridiculed the doctrines of a Providence; he advanced opinions favourable to the Jesuits and to the Pope's bull *Unigenitus,* and asserted that M. de Fénélon had triumphantly refuted the doctrine of Port Royal. In this manner M. de Loménie, from his earliest youth, had indulged in a mixture of materialism and Jesuitism, which at the same time procured him the support of two able and opposite parties; so that his ambition promised one time or other to be rewarded, whatever might be the success of the contests then prevalent in France between the philosophers and the Jesuits, equally inimical to Jansenism. If the Jesuits were overcome by the philosophers, the Abbé de Loménie would be found in the list of the latter; if the philosophers yielded to the Jesuits, the Abbé de Loménie had already combated the opinions of the Jansenists, and would be found to merit the attention of their adversaries; he was neither deficient in foresight nor in address. ("Memoirs of the Reign of Louis XVI.," vol. vi.)

Note (E), Page 67.

An extract from the strange proceeding of the Châtelet was forwarded to England under the idea that it would give rise to an apprehension in the mind of the Duke d'Orleans of persecutions similar to what were formerly dreaded; but, confident in his innocence, it proved the cause of his return. At last, to intimidate him, they suborned a nobleman of the Royalist or Ministerial party, at Dieppe, who had the audacity to say publicly that the Duke d'Orleans ought to be hanged.

The Prince heard of it, but did not recede, as was expected.

The day after his arrival at Paris, he presented himself before the National Assembly, where he was greeted with considerable applause. He there delivered an apology for his conduct, and was listened to with interest.

Not content with this frank and honourable proceeding, he published a paper entitled "An Exposition of the Conduct of the Duke d'Orleans in the French Revolution, drawn up by himself at London." This memoir, replete with explanation and reason, sufficed to convince the most incredulous. ("Anecdotes of the Reign of Louis XVI.")

Note (F), Page 70.

The King did not leave Versailles till one o'clock. The Queen, the Dauphin, Madame Royale, Monsieur, Madame Elizabeth and Madame de Tourzel were in His Majesty's carriage. The hundred deputies in their carriages came next. A detachment of brigands, bearing the heads of the two body-guards in triumph, formed the advanced guard, and set out two hours earlier. These cannibals stopped a moment at Sèvres, and carried their cruelty to the length of forcing an unfortunate hairdresser to dress the gory heads. The bulk of the Parisian army followed them closely. The King's carriage was preceded by the *poissardes*, who had arrived the day before from Paris, and a whole rabble of prostitutes, the vile refuse of their sex, still drunk with fury and wine. Several of them rode astride upon cannons, boasting, in the most horrible songs, all the crimes they had themselves committed, or seen others commit. Those who were nearest the King's carriage sang ballads, the allusions of which, by means of their vulgar gestures, they applied to the Queen. Waggons, full of corn and flour, which had been brought into Versailles, formed a train escorted by grenadiers, and surrounded by women and bullies, some armed with pikes, and some carrying long branches of poplar. At some distance this part of the procession had a most singular effect: it looked like a moving forest, amidst which shone pike-heads and gun-barrels. In the paroxysms of their brutal joy, the women stopped passengers, and, pointing to the King's carriage, howled in their ears, "Cheer up, friends; we shall no longer be in want of bread: we bring you the baker, the baker's wife and the little baker boy." Behind His Majesty's carriage were several of his faithful guards, some on foot and some on horseback, most of them uncovered, all unarmed, and worn out with hunger and fatigue; the dragoons, the Flanders regiment, the hundred Swiss, and the National Guards preceded, accompanied or followed the file of carriages.

I witnessed this heartrending spectacle; I saw the ominous procession. In the midst of all the tumult, clamour and singing, interrupted by frequent discharges of musketry, which the hand of a monster or a bungler might so easily render fatal, I saw the Queen preserving the most courageous tranquillity of soul, and an air of nobleness and inexpressible dignity, and my eyes were suffused with tears of admiration and grief.

Note (G), Page 83.

The termination of this year of crime and misfortune (1790) offers but one remarkable event—that of the arrest and the commencement of the trial of the unfortunate Marquis de Favras. This nobleman, whose youth was passed in storms, still preserved in his riper age the ardent imagination, the boldness and imprudence which had so often led him astray; and his loyalty, in taking place of all his other passions, had also assumed their character. The outrages of the 5th and 6th of October inspired him with the most ardent desire to attempt everything to preserve the Royal Family from the dangers that threatened them. Consequently he was actuated more by zeal than prudence in devising a plan for carrying off the King. His means of effecting it were to be an army of about thirty thousand Royalists, the enrolling and arming of which body was to be so secretly managed as not to be known till the moment of action. As an enterprise of this nature required considerable funds, in which point the Marquis de Favras was the most deficient, he tried all methods to raise them; he applied to several bankers, and communicated his plan to many of the Royalist party whom he thought most likely to afford the necessary assistance, but he found it more easy to obtain their praise than any effective co-operation.

It happened about the same time that Monsieur the King's brother, having been for several months deprived of his revenue through different operations of the Assembly, and having considerable payments to make in January, was trying to devise means to make good his engagements without applying to the public treasury. To accomplish it by a less onerous mode than that of borrowing at so critical a period, the Prince conceived the idea of giving bills for the amount of the sum required. M. de Favras, who had previously served in the Swiss guards of Monsieur, was pointed out to him by the Marquis de la Châtre, as very likely to effect the negotiation with the bankers Schaumel and Sartorius; His Royal Highness, therefore, signed an obligation for two millions, and desired his treasurer to provide for the payment.

The indiscreet expressions of the numerous confidants of the plan of M. de Favras, and the imprudence that he himself fell into, in being concerned at one and the same time with the proceedings relative to it and those which concerned the negotiation for the two millions for Monsieur, excited the attention and uneasiness of the Committee of Inquiry. M. and Madame de Favras were arrested on the 11th of December, in the night, and accused of "conspiring against the order of things established by the will of the nation and of the King; of having formed to this effect a plan for introducing armed men into the capital during the night, to put to death the three principal leaders of the administration; to attack the King's guard, carry off the Great Seal and to conduct Their Majesties towards Peronne; of endeavouring to corrupt several individuals of the National Guard, in seducing them from their duty by deceitful promises; of having conferences with several bankers for the obtaining of considerable sums, and with other persons for the diffusion of this plot throughout different provinces."

The day after the arrest of M. and Madame de Favras, the following bulletin was profusely circulated throughout the capital:

"The Marquis de Favras, of Place Royale, was arrested, with his lady, in the night of the 24th, for having laid a plan to raise thirty thousand men; to assassinate M. de la Fayette and the mayor of the city, and then to cut off our supplies of provisions. Monsieur the King's brother was at the head of this conspiracy.

(Signed) "BARRAUZ."

This public denunciation made against the King's brother, speedily aggravated as it was by the comments of the factious and the exaggerations of calumny, excited the strongest ferment in the capital, not only against that Prince, but also against the King himself, who was supposed to have an understanding with his brother. A serious catastrophe before long seemed inevitable; and undoubtedly such an event would have taken place if Monsieur, who would not have been justified in despising those dangers which threatened the Royal Family no less than himself, had not taken the only step by which the storm could be averted. That Prince went on the 26th of December to the Assembly of the Representatives of the Commune, and was received by them with all due respect and attention. "Gentlemen," said he to them, "I am induced to come among you by my desire to repel an atrocious piece of calumny. M. de Favras was apprehended yesterday by order of your Committee of Enquiry, and to-day a report is industriously spread that there is a close intimacy between him and myself. I think it due to the King, to you and to myself to inform you of the only circumstances under which I have any acquaintance with M. de Favras."

After detailing with equal exactness and perspicuity the facts attending the bond for two millions as I have given them, Monsieur added, "I have not seen M. de Favras, nor have I written to him; I have had no communication whatever with him; what else he has done is perfectly unknown to me. Yet I understood that a note signed Barrauz, thus worded (see above), has been extensively circulated in the capital. Of course, you do not expect that I shall stoop to exculpate myself from the accusation of so base a crime," &c.

This address was warmly and unanimously applauded by the Assembly and the galleries. The mayor in his reply expressed the feelings of respect and attachment entertained towards Monsieur by the Assembly, and the unbounded confidence with which his good qualities inspired them. M. de la Fayette rose after M. Bailly, and reported that he had directed the apprehension of the authors of the note, and that they were at that moment in prison. Monsieur requested they might be pardoned, but the Assembly resolved that it was necessary they should be tried and punished. The Prince likewise thought it right to inform the National Assembly of the motive which had induced him to take the step in question, he therefore sent the Assembly a copy of his speech at the Hôtel de Ville, and subjoined a note announcing that he would send them a statement of the debts he intended paying with the two millions for which he had subscribed the bond. ("History of the French Revolution," by Bertrand de Molleville, vol. ii.)

Note (H), Page 112.

The certainty of the departure of Mesdames the King's aunts made a great noise in Paris; the King could not avoid informing the Assembly of the event, and he did it in a letter, of which the following is the substance:

"Gentlemen,—Having learned that the National Assembly had referred a question arising upon a journey intended by my aunts to the committee for matters concerning the Constitution, I think it right to inform the Assembly that I was this morning apprised of their departure at ten o'clock last night. As I am persuaded they could not be deprived of the liberty which everyone possesses of going wherever he chooses, I felt that I neither ought to, nor could, offer any obstacle to their setting out, although I witness their separation from me with much regret.

(Signed)   "Louis."

Notwithstanding this letter, the two parties which divided the Assembly were in the highest state of fermentation when intelligence was received that Mesdames had been stopped by the municipality of Moret. It was at the same time announced that they had been liberated by the chasseurs of Lorraine. The heat of the debates was increased by this occurrence; it was known that individuals had preceded Mesdames, spreading among the people the reports with which the newspapers were filled by the conspirators. They were lavish of money, and scattered it by handfuls among the most brutalised men as most likely to plunge into the greatest excesses. Consequently the lives of Mesdames were threatened and were in the most imminent danger. One scoundrel, who vomited forth insults of the grossest nature against the Princesses, talked of lowering the fatal reflector and tying them up to it.

The money spread about by the persons unknown was not furnished by the Duke d'Orleans; his finances were exhausted at that time; it was English money. The Parliament granted the minister all the supplies he asked for, and dispensed with any account from him. The object and employment of these funds are at this day no longer problematical.

The Assembly soon received the following *procès-verbal* from the municipality of Moret:

"On the 20th of February, 1791, certain carriages, attended by a retinue and escorted in a manner announcing rank, appeared at Moret. The municipal officers, who had heard of the departure of Mesdames and of the uneasiness it had occasioned in Paris, stopped these carriages and would not suffer them to pass until they should have exhibited their passports. They produced two; one from the King, and countersigned Montmorin, to go to Rome; the other was not exactly a passport, but a declaration from the municipality of

Paris, acknowledging that it possessed no right to prevent these *citoyennes* from travelling in such parts of the kingdom as they should think fit.

"The municipal officers of Moret, on inspection of these two passports, between which they think they see some contradiction, are disposed to believe that, before they pay any attention to them, it is their duty to consult the National Assembly and to await the answer of that body with Mesdames; but while they are hesitating as to the course they are to pursue, certain chasseurs of the regiment of Lorraine come up with arms in their hands, and by force open the gates to Mesdames, who proceed on their way."

The reading of this *procès-verbal* was hardly ended when the ex-director, Rewbell, exhibited an extraordinary degree of surprise. How could it be imagined that the Minister for Foreign Affairs could have signed a passport, when he was well aware that their departure had been the ground for a demand of a new decree, the plan of which the committee for affairs concerning the Constitution was busied in drawing up? As everything was a scandal and a reproach in that impious age, the speaker said it was scandalous that the chasseurs of Lorraine should have so conducted themselves. "*If such acts of violence,*" said he, in conclusion, "*are permitted to remain unpunished, the belief that we have a Constitution is a strange illusion; no, there are no laws, and we live under the dominion of the sword.*"

He moved that the *procès-verbal* of the municipality of Moret should be referred to the committee of affairs concerning the Constitution and that of inquiry.

Rewbell's motion was decreed.

Being compelled to justify himself, the Minister of War declared that he had given no orders to the chasseurs of Lorraine; and that, after all, they had done nothing in the affair. The decree passed upon Rewbell's motion was supported by the Duke d'Aiguillon, and it was found, from M. de Ségur's letter, *that they were chasseurs of Hagueneau and not chasseurs of Lorraine, who had the honour of forming the escort of Mesdames at Fontainebleau and Moret.* This letter, which was signed by M. de Ségur, was inserted in the journals at his own request; that soldier prided himself upon having given the order and been obeyed. M. de Ségur in his letter, which was read only at a sitting of the 2nd of March, succeeded in convincing the Assembly of the affected ignorance of the military men who formed part of their body. "*The ancient ordinances are not abrogated,*" said the colonel of the chasseurs of Hagueneau, and not of Lorraine; "*the officer commanding did no more than conform to them, and if he did enter the town armed it was but in observance of the custom among soldiers to pay that mark of respect to cities.*"

Still, M. de Montmorin could not avoid justifying himself; he did it triumphantly by the following letter:

"M. le Président, I have just learnt that upon the reading of the *procès-verbal*, sent by the municipality of Moret, some members of the Assembly appeared astonished at my having countersigned the passport given to Mesdames by the King.

"If this circumstance requires explanation, I entreat the Assembly to reflect that the opinion of the King and his ministers upon the point is sufficiently well known. This passport would be a permission to quit the kingdom if any law forbade the passing of its limits; but no such law ever existed. Down to the present moment a passport is to be looked upon as merely an attestation of the quality of the persons who bear it.

"In this light it was impossible to refuse one to Mesdames; either their journey was to be opposed, or the inconveniences of it, among which it was impossible not to reckon their arrestation by a municipality to which they were unknown, were to be prevented.

"There were ancient laws against emigration; they had fallen into disuse, and the principles of liberty established by the decrees of the Assembly had wholly abrogated them. To refuse a passport to Mesdames, if a document of that description had been considered a real permission, would have been not only to outstrip, but actually to make law. To grant the passport when, without conferring any additional right, it might prevent disturbances could be conceived as nothing more than an act of prudence.

"These, sir, are the grounds upon which I countersigned the passports granted to Mesdames; I request you will have the kindness to communicate them to the Assembly. I shall always eagerly avail myself of all opportunities of explaining my conduct; and I shall always rely with the utmost confidence upon the justice of the Assembly."

The fate of Mesdames depended on the resolution to which the National Assembly was about to come; the two parties were ready and well prepared. The Abbé Maury, who owes the reputation of being at the head of Catholicism to real merit, was eager for the honour of being the first to speak. He eulogised the principles of good order, without which no Government can subsist, and consequently there can be neither peace nor prosperity for the people.

Several orators spoke, and all of them acknowledged that there was no law which forbade the departure of Mesdames. The discussion was so managed that the party of the faction looked upon the order of the day, the disapproval of the act of the commune of Arnay-le-Duc, as a triumph; but an obscure member, remarkable only for his gigantic form and his strength of voice, rose and roared out: "You insist that no law exists, and I maintain that a law does exist—it is the safety of the people."

General Menou put an end to the debate by one of those caustic observations which seldom fail to take effect when they are happily introduced, that is to say, when the multitude begin to be tired by the discussion. "Europe," said he "will be greatly astonished, no doubt, on hearing that the National Assembly spent four hours in deliberating upon the departure of two ladies who preferred hearing Mass at Rome rather than at Paris."

The debate was thus terminated, and the decree was conformable to the opinion of Mirabeau, who had, moreover, the honour of carrying his form of it, which was as follows:

"The National Assembly, inasmuch as there exists no law of the realm to forbid the free journeying of Mesdames the King's aunts, declares that there is no ground for questioning it, and refers the matter to the executive power." (Montigny's "Memoirs of Mesdames," vol. i.)

All particulars relating to the abode of Mesdames at Rome, Naples and, lastly, in Poland, will be found in these Memoirs.

Note (J), Page 150.

M. de Laporte, to whom I had some time previously communicated my opinion on the subject of the tribunes or galleries, told me that in the course of eight or nine months the King had been induced to spend more than 2,500,000 livres upon the tribunes alone; and that they had all along been for the Jacobins; that in truth the persons to whom the operation had been entrusted and to whom the money was delivered were violently suspected of having diverted a considerable part, and, perhaps, the whole of it, to their own purposes; but that this inconvenience was unavoidable in an expenditure of that sort, which, from the nature of it, was not susceptible of any control or check whatever; and that this consideration had determined the King to discontinue it at once.

I will not insist, as a certain fact, that the two chief undertakers of this service (Messieurs T—— and S——) did really apply the fund committed to them to their own use, although it was a matter of public notoriety that since their being entrusted with it one of them made purchases to the extent of from 1,200,000 to 1,500,000 livres, and the other to the extent of from 700,000 to 800,000 livres; but I have no hesitation in asserting and believing that they can only rebut the reproach of signal knavery by proving that they managed the operation with a want of skill and a degree of negligence almost equally culpable, for nothing was more easy than to secure the tribunes by paying them. I had made the experiment once only during my administration, but then I was completely successful. It was on the day on which I was to make in the Assembly my full reply to the denunciations which had been made against me. I was informed two days beforehand by my spies that the secret committee of the Jacobins had determined on that day to augment the number of their hirelings in the tribunes, to insure my being hooted. I immediately sent for one of the victors of the Bastille, to whom I had, before the Revolution, rendered some important services, who was entirely devoted to me, and who was a man of great weight in the Faubourg St. Antoine. Him I directed to select from among the working-men of the faubourg two hundred athletic men on whom he could rely, and to take them the next day to the Assembly, at six o'clock in the morning, in order that they might be the first there before the opening of the Chamber, and so fill the front places in the tribunes at the two ends of the Chamber; and to give them no other order than merely to applaud or hoot according to a signal which was agreed on.

This manœuvre was as successful as I could wish. My speech was repeatedly interrupted by applause, which was doubled when I ceased speaking. The Jacobins were thunderstruck at this, and could not at all understand it. I was a quarter of an hour afterwards still in the Assembly, as well as all the ministers who had made it their duty to attend me on the emergency in question; when the Abbé Fauchet rose to notice a fact which he declared to be of great importance: "I have this moment," said he, "received a letter informing me that a considerable proportion of the citizens in the tribunes have been paid to applaud the Minister of Marine."

Although this was true enough, my unaltered countenance and the reputation of the Abbé Fauchet, who was known to be an unblushing liar, turned his denunciation into ridicule, and it was considered the more misplaced, inasmuch as it was nothing unusual to hear my speeches applauded by the tribunes. True it is that I had always taken care to introduce into them some of those phrases, or rather words, which the people never failed to applaud, mechanically, when they were uttered with a certain emphasis, without troubling themselves to examine the sense in which they were used.

The Abbé Fauchet had scarcely finished making his denunciation when it was stifled by the almost general murmur which proceeded from both sides of the Chamber, and by the hootings of the tribunes pursuant to signal. This victory, gained in the tribunes over the Jacobins, cost me no more than 270 livres in assignats, because a considerable number of my champions, out of regard for the leader, would receive nothing more from him than a glass of brandy.

I gave the King all these particulars in my reply to His Majesty's later notes, and I again entreated him to permit me to make a second experiment upon the tribunes for one single week only, upon a plan which I annexed to my letter, and the expense of which did not exceed 800 livres *per diem*.

This plan consisted in filling the front rows of the two tribunes with 262 trusty fellows, whose pay was fixed at the following rates:

	Livres per diem.
1. To a leader, who alone was in the secret	50
2. To a sub-leader, chosen by the former	25
3. To ten assistants, selected by the leader and sub-leader, having no knowledge of each other, and each deputed to recruit twenty-five men and take them daily to the Assembly, 10 livres apiece; total	100
4. To two hundred and fifty men, each 50 sous a day; total	625
Total	800 livres.

The leader and sub-leader were to be placed, one in the middle of the front tribune, and the other in the same situation in the other tribune. Each of them was known only to the five assistants whom he had under his orders in the tribune in which he took his seat. The sub-leader received his directions by a signal concerted between themselves alone. They had a second signal for the purpose of passing the order to the assistants, each of whom again transmitted it to his twenty-five men by a third signal. All of them, with the exception of the leader and sub-leader, were to be engaged in the name of Pétion, for the support of the Constitution against the aristocrats and Republicans. Each assistant was to pay his own recruits, and was to receive the funds from the leader or the sub-leader, in proportion to the number of men he brought with him.

The leader was alone to correspond with a friend of a captain of the King's constitutional guard named Piquet, a man of true courage and entirely devoted to His Majesty's service. This captain was to receive from me daily the funds necessary for the expenditure of the day following, with directions for the conduct of the tribunes according to what had passed on the day preceding. He was to communicate the whole to his friend, who in his turn was to instruct the leader of the operation. By means of these various sub-divisions, this manœuvre might get wind by treachery or otherwise without any serious inconvenience resulting from it, because it cut off the possibility of all ultimate discovery and prevented inquiries from being directed to me. Nothing more was necessary than to remove any one of the persons intermediately employed. Besides, in order as far as possible to watch the fidelity of the agents of this enterprise, and in some measure to keep a check upon this expense, I had agreed with Buob, a justice of the peace, that he should daily send five of his runners, whose salary I was to pay him, into each of the tribunes to see what was going forward there, especially in the front rows; to calculate, as exactly as they could, the number of persons shouting or applauding, and give him an account accordingly. We had not neglected to apprise the assistants that this inspection was regularly made by agents of Pétion.

The King returned me this plan, after reflecting upon it for four-and-twenty hours, and authorised me to try it in the course of the following week. This was the result of it:

The first and second days our people contented themselves with silencing the tribunes; that is to say, with silencing all marks of disapprobation and applause, under pretence of hearing better, and that of itself was one great point gained.

On the third day they began slightly to applaud constitutional motions and opinions, and continued to prevent contrary motions and opinions from being heard.

On the fourth day the same line of conduct was continued, only the applause was warmer and longer persevered in. The Assembly could not make it out. Several of the members looked towards the tribunes frequently and with attention, and made themselves easy on seeing them filled with individuals whose appearance and dress were as usual.

On the fifth day the marks of applause became stronger, and they began to murmur a little against anti-constitutional motions and remarks. At this the Assembly appeared somewhat disconcerted; but one of the adjutants, on being interrogated by a deputy, replying that he was for the Constitution and for Pétion, it was supposed that the disapprobation which had been heard was the effect of some mistake.

On the sixth day the sounds of approbation and of the contrary feeling were still conducted in the same way, but with a degree of violence considerable enough to give offence to the Assembly. A motion was made against the tribunes, who repelled it by the most violent clamours, insults and threats. Some of the men employed carried their audacity so far as to raise their sticks as if to strike the deputies who were near them, and repeated over and over again that the Assembly consisted of a pack of beggars who ought to be knocked on the head. The president, being of opinion, no doubt, that it was not quite prudent to wait till the majority of those who filled the tribunes should declare themselves of that opinion, broke up the sitting.

As the members of the Assembly quitted the hall, several of the deputies accosted a considerable number of individuals coming down from the tribunes, and by dint of questions and cajolery drew from them that they were employed by Pétion. They immediately went to complain to him on the subject, under a conviction that he had been deceived in the choice of his men; that he would not approve of their conduct and would dismiss them.

Pétion, who as yet knew nothing of what had been going forward in the Assembly, swore, and certainly swore truly, that he had no hand in it, and that he had not sent anybody to the tribunes for a long time. He insisted that it was a manœuvre of his enemies, and promised to leave no stone unturned to find out its authors. I was, in fact, informed that in the evening several of his emissaries had been all over the faubourgs, and had questioned a great many working-men, but fortunately all these enquiries ended in nothing.

The letter which I addressed to the King every morning informed him of the orders I had issued for the next day with regard to the management of the tribunes; and as he had always some confidential person at the Assembly, in order that he might be accurately informed of what was going forward there, he was enabled to judge how faithfully and with what success the directions I gave were executed; and consequently His Majesty, in almost all his answers to the letters of that week, observed, "'The tribunes go on well'—'still well'—'better and better'—'admirable,'" But the scene of violence of the Saturday gave him some uneasiness.

On the following day, when I made my appearance at the levee, Their Majesties and Madame Elizabeth eyed me in the most gracious and satisfied manner. After Mass the King, as he was re-entering the room, passing close by me, said, without turning and low enough to be heard by nobody but myself, " Very well—only too rapidly—I will write to you." In fact, in the letter which the King returned to me on the same day with his answer, he observed that " the experiment had succeeded beyond his hopes, but that it would be dangerous to pursue it, especially to myself; that this resource ought to be reserved for a time of need, and that he would apprise me when that time arrived." ("Private Memoirs for the History, &c.," by Bertrand de Molleville, vol. ii.)

Note (K), Page 207.

Historical Narrative of the Transactions at the Château of the Tuileries, during the night of the 9th and 10th of August, 1792, and on the morning of the 10th.

Before my return into the Château I visited the hall of the department. I saw the Attorney-General. The authorities of the department were to remain assembled the whole night. The Attorney-General offered to pass it himself in the Château if the King thought it necessary. The King manifested a wish that it should be so. I immediately informed M. Rœderer, and that magistrate instantly proceeded to the King. It was then near midnight.

About one in the morning, the tocsin not having begun to sound until after the Mayor had quitted the King, His Majesty desired me to inform M. Pétion of it, and to communicate to him his wish that the gates of the terrace called Des Feuillans should be closed. The terrace had been declared to form a part of the area of the National Assembly. That body alone could dispose of it. Therefore, in communicating the King's wish, I pressed M. Pétion to demand what he required of the National Assembly. The Mayor could do this with the more propriety because the tocsin had sounded and the *générale* been beaten. It was certain the meeting was assembling, and that the National Assembly had recalled the Mayor to their bar full three-quarters of an hour.

M. Pétion heard the King's observations. He felt the force of them. Even before he went to the National Assembly he caused the gate which commands the riding-house yard to be shut; the Swiss received a verbal order for it in the presence of all the municipal officers and of several grenadiers who were with the Mayor. I owe this homage to truth. One grenadier suffered himself at this moment to pass the bounds of decorum. His warmth of feeling got the better of his obedience.

"Mr. Mayor," said he, "we see with the liveliest satisfaction, with a respectful gratitude, that your zeal always gets the better of the malevolence of your enemies; that you are in all places where you can usefully serve the country; but that is not enough. Why do you suffer these partial assemblages in Paris which will gradually bring on general ones? Why do you suffer yourself to be ruled by factious men who will ruin us? Why, for instance, is the Sieur Santerre always with you, always out of the reach of the law? Why is he at this moment at the Hôtel de Ville? Mr. Mayor, you are answerable for the public tranquillity, for the preservation of our property—you——"

To these words, uttered with great volubility and heard by the Mayor, he answered vaguely, "What does this mean, sir? You lose sight of respect; you forget yourself. Come, let us understand each other." Upon this, almost the whole of the National Guards surrounded the Mayor, silenced the grenadier, and forced him to withdraw; and the Mayor went to the National Assembly.

He there gave the explanations required of him, but said nothing about the terrace of the Feuillans.

The moment afterwards M. Pétion returned to the garden and proceeded to the terrace. I saw him walking there in the midst of the same group, accompanied by the same municipal officers, and by a still greater number of National Guards.

I am a witness that the *commandant de bataillon* accosted the Mayor opposite the principal gate of the castle and told him everything was quiet and that there was nothing to fear ; that the commissioners of the sections, who had met at the Faubourg St. Antoine, had separated and adjourned to Friday morning early, at the Hôtel de Ville, with the intention of coming to a final resolution; but that until that time there was no ground for apprehension.

This intelligence was too agreeable not to be seized with eagerness. The Mayor approved of it, and announced that he should soon retire. However, several persons pointed out to him that the account of the *commandant de bataillon* might be true, and still the danger might be very great.

It has been observed that the commandant came from the section of the Croix-Rouge ; that the commissioners spoken of had separated at eleven o'clock ; that since, and notwithstanding their pretended resolution, the tocsin had been sounded and the alarm-gun had been fired, that the assemblage had taken place, and that everything seemed to announce that the people would put themselves in march about five o'clock in the morning.

The Queen renewed her observations ; the King remained mute. Nobody spoke. It was reserved to me to give the last piece of advice. I had the firmness to say, " Let us go, and not deliberate ; honour commands it ; the good of the State requires it. Let us go to the National Assembly ; this step ought to have been taken long ago."

"Come," said the King, raising his right hand; " let us go; let us give this last mark of self-devotion, since it is necessary."

The Queen was persuaded ; her first anxiety was for the King, the second for her son. The King had none.

" M. Rœderer,—gentlemen," said the Queen, " you answer for the person of the King ; you answer for that of my son."

" Madam," replied M. Rœderer, " we pledge ourselves to die at your side ; that is all we can engage for." (" History of Marie Antoinette," by Montjoie.)

Note (M), Page 314.

Louis XVI. was much pleased with his first conversation with Count Maurepas, who endeavoured to interest him by relating to him sentimental anecdotes respecting the Dauphin his father, for whom Louis XVI. entertained the most profound veneration. Maurepas confirmed the King in the belief that the Duke de Choiseul had hastened the death of the late Dauphin, and always supported him in the resolution of perpetually banishing the Duke from Court, and particularly from the administration. He represented the Duke de Choiseul, both in manuscript memoirs and in his private conversations, as prodigal of the public money, and as having, for the sake of establishing for himself in France a party too powerful to be attacked, granted a multitude of unmerited pensions to the amount of twelve millions and upwards on persons who had no other claims than the protection of the House of Choiseul.

Maurepas once had a statement drawn up of the favours granted to all the Houses which bore the name of Choiseul, and demonstrated that no family in France cost one-fourth of what was absorbed by the family of this minister. Thus, as fast as the Queen pressed Louis XVI. to recall Choiseul to Court, Maurepas was labouring, on the contrary, to make him an object of detestation to the Prince. His hatred of M. de Choiseul had raised him to office, and the same sentiments preserved him his place. Hence arose the first displeasure of Marie Antoinette against M. de Maurepas. She had determined to leave no means untried for recalling to France the friend of her family and the contriver of her marriage.

The other ministers pursuing the same object as Maurepas, the latter dexterously employed the Abbé Terray to blacken the character of the Duke de Choiseul previous to his driving him from the administration of the finances. After Abbé Terray, Turgot, who entertained the same opinion of the Duke, continued to calumniate him in his private conversations and official intercourse with the King. The Chancellor Maupeou, who had wronged the Duke in part of his machinations against him, joined this party. They went so far as to assert that Marie Antoinette was daughter of the Duke de Choiseul, and to calculate the days and months of Maria Theresa's pregnancy. The period of the Duke de Choiseul's embassy to Vienna was alluded to in order to give some appearance of probability to this report, which dates alone were sufficient to refute. Vergennes found himself in hostility to the Austrian diplomacy. La Vrillière, who had executed the King's orders in exiling him to Chanteloup, after having intrigued with D'Aiguillon and Madame du Barry, did all that a man who had lost his credit and consideration could do to injure the Duke de Choiseul. In the Royal Family this was also a leading object with the King's three aunts. Thus, on whatever side Louis XVI. looked, he saw only implacable enemies to the Duke de Choiseul, with the exception of the Queen, who was enraged to find such general opposition to her early inclinations. ("Historical and Political Memoirs of the Reign of Louis XVI.," by Soulavie, vol. ii.)

Note (N), in addition to note at page 314.

M. de Vergennes, President of the Council of Finance—a place more lucrative and honourable than important in the Ministry—no sooner heard of the existence of a secret deficit, which M. de Calonne raised to the amount of one hundred millions, than he foresaw the protestations, violent discussions and resentment which would take place throughout France when the fatal moment of manifesting this State wound, in order to cure it, should arrive. He foresaw, long beforehand, the advantage which England would take of our situation. France, having surprised England in the cruel embarrassment of her colonial insurrections, had made a Sovereign people of a body of rebels. What might not England do in the interior of France when every order of the State should rise in insurrection against a deficit of one hundred millions occasioned by an extravagant Court, which the proceedings about the necklace had vilified and debased? M. Necker, in an official account, had assured the public five years before, that the receipts exceeded the expenditure by several millions, and now M. de Calonne found a deficit of one hundred millions. To what was this deficit to be attributed? To the last five years? The Court could not be thus accused without disgracing it. To the preceding period? The great reputation of M. Necker could not be thus attacked. What great advantages England might take of this dilemma!

Such were the circumstances under which it was recollected that France and England had, towards the end of 1783, engaged to negotiate a treaty. M. de Calonne and M. de Vergennes combined to render it favourable to the British nation, and our manufactures were sacrificed by their calculation. In the course of the twelve years fixed as the duration of this treaty, England was to enjoy immense advantages, and repair her own finances. This treaty, which excited universal alarm, was signed on the 20th of September, 1786, under the administration of Mr. Pitt, who had defeated Mr. Fox, then recently retired from the Ministry; and the resolution to convoke the Notables was entered into in Council, at Versailles, on the 29th of December following.

I shall not enter into the particulars of the censure which the nation passed on this treaty; it no longer exists. I shall only observe that the English merchants, to introduce a taste for their goods—their earthenware, for instance—carried their speculations to such a height as to furnish them at less than their value at long credits. We have seen the English pottery become, in the course of a month, quite the fashion at the most distinguished tables; we have all witnessed the bankruptcy of several interesting French manufactures. ("Historical Memoirs of the Reign of Louis XVI.," by Soulavie, vol. vi.)

Note (O), Page 325.

The King having purchased the Château de Rambouillet from the Duke de Penthièvre, amused himself with embellishing this mansion. I have seen a register, entirely in his own handwriting, which proves that he possessed a great variety of information on the minutiæ of various branches of knowledge. In his accounts he would not omit an article of twelve pence. The figures and letters of his handwriting, when he wished to write legibly, are small and very neat; the letters are well formed; but, in general, he wrote very badly. He was so sparing of writing-paper that he divided a sheet into eight, six or four pieces, according to the length of what he had to write. Whilst he was writing he seemed to avoid all waste of paper, and towards the close of the page he compressed the letters and made no interlineations. The last words were close to the bottom, and to the edge of the paper; he seemingly regretted being obliged to begin another page. His genius was methodical and analytical; he divided what he wrote into chapters and sections. He had extracted from the works of Nicole and Fénélon, his favourite authors, three or four hundred concise and sententious phrases: these he had classed according to the order of the subjects, and formed a second work of them, in the taste and manner of Montesquieu. To this treatise he had given the following general title: "Of Moderate Monarchy,"¹ with chapters entitled, "Of the Person of the Prince"; "Of the Authority of Bodies in the State"; "Of the Character of the Executive Functions of the Monarchy." Had he been able to carry into effect all the beautiful and grand things he had observed in Fénélon, Louis XVI. would have been an accomplished monarch, and France a powerful kingdom.

The King used to accept from his ministers the speeches which they presented to him to deliver on important occasions; but he corrected and modified them; struck out some parts, and added others; and sometimes even consulted his consort on the subject.

In these endeavours it is easy to see that he sought appropriate expressions, and with success. The phrase of the minister erased by the King was frequently unsuitable, and dictated by the minister's private feelings; but the King's was always the natural expression. One might have said, none but a King could have hit on these expressions, they were so peculiarly apposite. He himself composed, three times or oftener, his famous answers to the Parliament which he banished. But in his familiar letters he was negligent and always incorrect.

Simplicity of expression was the characteristic of the King's style; the figurative style of M. Necker did not please him; the sarcasms of Maurepas were disagreeable to him. In that multitude of speculations, which fill a paper of projects, the following remark appears in his handwriting: "That is good for nothing": in others he foresaw the future. Unfortunate Prince! he would predict in his observations that if such a calamity should happen the monarchy would be ruined; and the next day he would consent in Council to the very operation which he had condemned the day before, and which brought him nearer the brink of the precipice. ("Historical and Political Memoirs of the Reign of Louis XVI.," by Soulavie, vol. ii.)

Note (V), Page 285.

When the news of the attempt made against the King's life became publicly known, the populace evinced the greatest rage and

---

¹ De la Monarchie tempérée.

despair. They assembled under the windows of Madame de Pompadour, uttering threatening cries. She began to dread the fate of Madame de Châteauroux. Her friends every moment came in to bring her intelligence. Many only came out of curiosity to see how she behaved. She did nothing but weep and faint by turns. Dr. Quesnay saw the King five or six times a day. "There is nothing to fear," said he, "if it were any other person he might go to a ball." I told Madame that the Keeper of the Seals had had an interview with the King, from which he had returned to his own residence, followed by a crowd of people. "And that is a friend," said she, bursting into tears. The Abbé Bernis said this was not a time to form a precipitate judgment of him. Half an hour afterwards I returned into the drawing-room; the Keeper of the Seals came in. "How is Madame de Pompadour?" said he, with a cold and severe air. "As you may easily imagine," I replied; and he entered her apartment, where he remained half an hour alone with her. At length she rang; I went in, followed by the Abbé Bernis. "I must go, my dear abbé," said she. She gave orders for all her domestics to be ready to set out. To several ladies, who came to condole with her, she compared the conduct of M de Machault, the Keeper of the Seals, with that of the Duke de Richelieu at Metz. "He believes, or pretends to believe," said she, "that the priests will require me to be sent away with disgrace; but Quesnay and all the physicians say there is not the slightest danger."

Madame de Mirepoix came in, crying out, "What are all these trunks for, madam? Your servants say you are leaving us." "Alas, my dear friend, such is the will of the master; at least, so says M. de Machault." "And what is his advice?" "To set out immediately." "He wishes to be master himself," said Madame de Mirepoix, "and he is betraying you. Whoever leaves the game loses it."

M. de Marigny afterwards told me that an appearance of an intended departure would be kept up to avoid irritating the enemies of Madame; that the little Maréchal (Madame de Mirepoix) had decided the matter; and that the Keeper of the Seals would be the sufferer. Quesnay came in and, with his usual grimaces, related a fable of a fox who, being at dinner with other animals, persuaded one of them that his enemies were seeking him, and, having induced him to withdraw, devoured his share in his absence. I did not see Madame until much later, when she was going to bed. She was more calm; affairs were improving. Machault, that faithless friend, was dismissed. The King came as usual to Madame. A few days afterwards Madame paid a visit to M. d'Argenson. She returned much out of temper, and the King shortly afterwards arrived. I heard Madame sobbing. The Abbé Bernis came to me and desired me to carry her some Hoffman's drops. The King himself prepared the potion with some sugar, and presented it to her with the most gracious air. She smiled and kissed his hands. I withdrew, and the next day heard of the exile of M. d'Argenson. He was much to blame; and this was the greatest stretch of Madame's influence. The King was very much attached to M.

d'Argenson, and the war by sea and land rendered it very impolitic to discard these two ministers. ("Journal of Madame de Hausset.")

Note (W), Page 290.

Madame one day called me into her cabinet, where the King was walking up and down, with a very serious air. "You must," said she, "go and pass a few days in the avenue of St. Cloud, at a house which will be pointed out to you, where you will find a young lady ready to lie in. Like one of the goddesses of the poets, you will preside at the birth. The object of your mission is, that everything may take place according to the King's wishes, and secretly. You will be present at the christening, and give the names of the father and mother." The King began to laugh, and said, "The father is a very worthy man." Madame added, "Beloved by everybody; and adored by all who are acquainted with him." Madame went to a drawer and took out a little casket, which she opened, and produced a diamond *aigrette*, saying to the King, "I had reasons for not getting a finer one." "It is too handsome, as it is," said the King, embracing Madame; "how kind you are!" She shed tears of emotion, and placing her hand on the King's heart, said, "It is there that my wishes are centred." Tears now came into the King's eyes also; nor could I refrain from crying, though I scarcely knew why. The King then said to me, "Guimard will see you every day to advise and assist you, and at the critical moment you will send for him. But we have said nothing about the godfather and godmother. You are to announce them as if they were coming; and an instant afterwards you will pretend to receive a letter informing you that they cannot come. You will then feign not to know what to do, and Guimard will say, 'The best way is to have anybody you can get.' You will then take the servant of the house and some pauper or chair-man, and give them only twelve francs, to avoid attracting notice." "A louis," interrupted Madame, "that you may not make mischief in another way."

When the King was gone Madame said to me, "Well, what do you think of my part in this affair?" "It is that of a superior woman and an excellent friend," said I. "It is his heart that I wish to possess," answered she; "and none of these little uneducated girls will deprive me of that. I should not be so tranquil if some beautiful woman of the Court were to attempt the conquest." I asked Madame whether the young lady knew that the father of the child was the King. "I do not think so," said she, "but as he seemed to love this one, it is thought that there has been too much readiness to let her know it. Were it not for that, it was to have been insinuated to the world that the father was a Polish nobleman, related to the Queen, and that he had apartments in the Château."

After receiving some additional instructions, I went to the avenue of St. Cloud, where I found the abbess, and Guimard, a servant belonging to the Château, with a nurse and assistant, two old domestics, and a girl half housemaid, half *femme de chambre*.

The young lady was extremely pretty, and elegantly dressed, but had nothing very striking in her appearance. I supped with her and the *gouvernante*, called Madame Bertrand. I gave the lady the *aigrette*, which delighted her wonderfully. The next day I had a private conversation with her, when she asked me, "How is the Count (meaning the King)? He will be very sorry that he cannot be with me, but he has been obliged to take a long journey." I assented. "He is a very handsome man," continued she, "and loves me with all his heart; he has promised me an annuity, but I love him disinterestedly, and, if he would take me, I would go with him." She afterwards talked of her parents. "My mother," she said, "kept a large druggist's shop; and my father belonged to the six companies, and everyone knows there is nothing better than that; he was twice very near being sheriff."

Six days afterwards she was delivered of a boy, but was told, according to my instructions, that it was a girl, and, soon afterwards, that it was dead, in order that no trace of its existence might remain for a certain period, after which it was to be restored to its mother. The King gave ten or twelve thousand francs a year to each of his natural children, and they inherited from one another. Seven or eight had already died. When I returned Madame asked me many questions. "The King," said she, "is disgusted with his Princess, and I fancy he will set out for Poland in two days." "And what will become of the young lady?" said I. "She will be married to some country gentleman," she said, "and will have, perhaps, a fortune of forty thousand crowns or so, and a few diamonds." This little adventure, which thus placed me in the King's confidence, far from procuring me marks of his kindness, seemed to make him behave more coolly towards me; for he was ashamed that I should be acquainted with his low amours. He was also embarrassed about the little services which Madame rendered him. ("Journal of Madame de Hausset.")

Amongst the young ladies of very tender age, with whom the King amused himself during the influence of Madame de Pompadour or afterwards, there was also a Mademoiselle de Tiercelin, whom His Majesty ordered to take the name of Bonneval the very day she was presented to him. The King was the first who perceived this child, when not above nine years old, in the care of a nurse, in the garden of the Tuileries, one day when he went in state to his "good city of Paris," and having in the evening spoken of her beauty to Le Bel, the servant applied to M. de Sartine, who traced her out and bought her of the nurse for a few louis. She was daughter of M. de Tiercelin, a man of quality, who could not patiently endure an affront of this nature. He was, however, compelled to be silent. He was told his child was lost and that it would be best for him to submit to the sacrifice, unless he wished to lose his liberty also.

Mademoiselle de Tiercelin, now become Madame de Bonneval, was introduced under that name into the little apartments at Versailles by the King's desire. She was naturally very wild, and did not like His Majesty. "You are an ugly man," said she, throwing the jewels and diamonds, which the King had given her, out of the window. The Duke de Choiseul had the weakness to be jealous of this child and her father, who were equally harmless. He was told that the King of Prussia, being tired of Madame de Pompadour, was secretly labouring to get Mademoiselle de Tiercelin declared the King's mistress, the King certainly doted on her. The minister was assured that M. de Tiercelin was engaged in most extensive operations for effecting the object of this foreign intrigue. The father and daughter were, in consequence, separately confined in the Bastille. ("Anecdotes of the Reign of Louis XV.," by Soulavie.)

Note (X), Page 298.

The Dauphin, son of Louis XV., had for several years superintended the education of his three children, the Duke de Berri, afterwards Louis XVI., the Count de Provence and the Count d'Artois.

The deportment of the Duke de Berri was austere, severe, reserved and often rough; he had no taste for play, exhibitions or amusements. He was a youth of inviolable veracity, constantly employing himself, at first, in copying and afterwards in composing geographical maps and in filing iron. His father had shown a predilection for him, which excited the jealousy of his brothers. Madame Adelaide, who tenderly loved him, used to say, in order to encourage him and overcome his timidity: "Speak out freely, Berri; shout scold, make an uproar, like your brother d'Artois; knock down my china and break it, make some noise in the world." The young Duke de Berri only became the more silent, and could not lay aside his natural character. ("Historical and Political Memoirs of the Reign of Louis XVI.," by Soulavie, vol. ii.)

THE END

H. S. NICHOLS AND CO., PRINTERS, 3 SOHO SQUARE, LONDON, W.

www.ingramcontent.com/pod-product-compliance
Lightning Source LLC
Chambersburg PA
CBHW050849300426
44111CB00010B/1184